M000267511

PRACTICAL BUSINESS ANALYTICS

PRACTICAL BUSINESS ANALYTICS

A Proven Approach Through Successful
Personalized Learning

First Edition

William Swart and Ken MacLeod

SAN DIEGO

Bassim Hamadeh, CEO and Publisher
Alisa Munoz, Senior Project Editor
Casey Hands, Production Editor
Emely Villavicencio, Senior Graphic Designer
Greg Isales, Licensing Coordinator
Natalie Piccotti, Director of Marketing
Kassie Graves, Senior Vice President of Editorial
Jamie Giganti, Director of Academic Publishing

Copyright © 2021 by Cognella, Inc. All rights reserved. No part of this publication may be reprinted, reproduced, transmitted, or utilized in any form or by any electronic, mechanical, or other means, now known or hereafter invented, including photocopying, microfilming, and recording, or in any information retrieval system without the written permission of Cognella, Inc. For inquiries regarding permissions, translations, foreign rights, audio rights, and any other forms of reproduction, please contact the Cognella Licensing Department at rights@cognella.com.

Trademark Notice: Product or corporate names may be trademarks or registered trademarks and are used only for identification and explanation without intent to infringe.

Cover image: Copyright © 2012 iStockphoto LP/solid-istanbul.
Interior: Screenshots of Microsoft Excel: Copyright © by Microsoft.

Printed in the United States of America.

3970 Sorrento Valley Blvd., Ste. 500, San Diego, CA 92121

ACTIVE LEARNING

Throughout the text, when you see this Active Learning icon:

an interactive activity is available to complement your reading.

ACTIVE LEARNING FOR
ACADEMIC USE

If you are enrolled in a course at a higher education institution where your professor has adopted this book, find your institution in the Cognella Student Store at store.cognella.com to enroll with your cohort of classmates. This is necessary and ensures your professor receives your scores on any graded content.

If you are an educator, you will need to adopt Active Learning in order for you and your students to gain access. Please contact your Cognella Representative if you need to enroll in Active Learning.

ACTIVE LEARNING FOR
GENERAL READERS

To enroll in Active Learning for general readers, visit the Cognella Student Store at store.cognella.com. Select the option under "Cognella University."

Active Learning content for general readers is provided in a self-paced course. Grades are not reported to any professors or institutions.

TABLE OF CONTENTS

CHAPTER 7

Now That I Have Learned This Stuff ...   271

FOREWORD

You are about to be handed one of the most important tools (Business Analytics) that you can have for building your career in the business world. Like any tool, it can only be effective if you have received proper instruction in its use. The authors, obviously, put a lot of time and effort into coming up with questions that might be asked by their students. The answers to these questions are provided in concise and manageable portions, are easy to follow, logical, predictive, and linear. They also stimulate a desire in the reader to search out other resources that can be used to expand upon the knowledge contained herein. The recommended group dynamics provide the reader access to his or her classmates' insights into the subject under discussion. I only wish that this method of presenting Business Analytics had been available during my early years in the electronics industry.

Roger Tisdale

PREFACE

Q. **Were there any surprises when you started teaching?**

A. Yes. When I finished my PhD, I could not wait to apply what I learned. When I taught practitioners, however, I found that while I knew why things worked, they knew how to make them work.

Q. **What did you do about that?**

A. I decided to go into the real world to find out for myself how to apply the whys I already knew, so I got a job in the food services industry and applied Business Analytics for almost eight years.

Q. **Why did you then go back to academia?**

A. Because I wanted to teach what I had learned.

Q. **Did your experience make you a better teacher?**

A. I think so. Being able to tell the students how I had used Business Analytics tools in the real world helped them appreciate the practical nature of a class that seems pretty esoteric.

Q. **Did that change how you taught your students?**

A. Yes, I had to develop my own materials for my classes because I couldn't find a textbook that taught more than the basic math of the tools.

Q. **Did the students take well to what you were teaching?**

A. Mostly, but it bothered me that I wasn't getting through to all of them. Some students earned good grades, others earned not-so-good grades.

Q. **Well, that's pretty normal, isn't it?**

A. Yes, in academia we assume that a normal grade distribution is a sign of good teaching—you don't have quality teaching unless some of your students are failing.

Q. **When you put it that way, it sounds wrong. What did you do?**

A. I realized the focus on teaching was misplaced and that the focus should be on student learning.

Q.   **What can you do, since different students have different learning styles?**

A.   I began to adapt my material to accommodate different styles of learning: those who best learn by reading, those who learn best by watching, those who learn best by themselves, those who learn best in groups, and those who require individual attention.

Q.   **And that led you to write this textbook?**

A.   Exactly. This textbook and its Active Learning Companion help all students learn not only the hows and whys but also how to use what they learned in their place of work.

Q.   **How does this text accommodate different learning styles?**

A.   Students have the independence to choose how they want to learn the material, with the caveat that not learning it was not an option.

- The text is there for those students who learn best from written material.
- Video capture of what I would have done if I were to deliver a live lecture but giving students the freedom to watch it (or not) where and when they wanted.
- Online students can take an online quiz to demonstrate mastery any time before a due date.
- Students in face-to-face classes can come to class and take a daily quiz to demonstrate mastery.
- If students require assistance to learn the material, they can engage in interactive group learning augmented by coaching and consulting as necessary from the instructor.
- Students who complete the quiz are done, leaving me time for personal tutoring with students who still require help.

Q.   **Seems like face-to-face students have a big advantage since they can collaborate in groups.**

A.   No. Online students collaborate virtually.

Q.   **Did this improve your grades?**

A.   The results were spectacular in both face-to-face and online classes. The final averages and median grade in my undergraduate classes increased by a full letter grade. In my graduate classes, the percentage of students earning As increased from 50% to 80%.

Q.   **Are these results for face-to-face classes only?**

A.   No. We found similar results in online and face-to-face classes.

Q.   **How did students react to this process?**

A.   In all cases, student satisfaction also increased.

Q.   **You had accomplished what you wanted, so why write a textbook?**

A.   We believe that many instructors are interested in student learning, and we wanted to share our successful learning resources to encourage them to allow students to personalize their learning so as to be more successful in mastering the challenging subject matter of Business Analytics.

Q.   **What if they want to continue teaching as always?**

A.   This book will, of course, also support traditional teaching methods.

ACKNOWLEDGMENTS

This book is dedicated to our students who have motivated us to continually improve their learning experience. Their encouraging feedback and willingness to provide us with data have guided the development of this text and materials.

Special acknowledgment from William Swart

I want to say "thank you" to Ernestine Swart—my best friend, partner, lover, and wife—for the countless hours listening, reading, and counseling me on all parts of this book. I also want to thank our cat-daughters Willow and Mocha for keeping her entertained when I could not.

I also want to thank Roger Kaufman, my long-time friend and mentor, for being there whenever I needed someone with whom to brainstorm.

Special acknowledgment from Ken MacLeod

Thanks to my wife, Gerry, and sons, Greg and Tommy, for their love and patience, especially during the years they spent listening to me talk to myself while developing this dialectic approach.

Thanks also to Professor Robert Jeroslow, who told me as an undergraduate that I should pursue a PhD in Management Science. I laughed at the idea then, but he was right, as always. Thanks, too, to Professor Gary Reeves, who guided me through that PhD. They built the understanding that I try to share with my students.

A Rose by Any Other Name ...

Q. **Isn't that a weird chapter title for a book on business analytics?**

A. Maybe, but it does make a point.

Q. **Which is?**

A. The names of things do not affect what they are.

Q. **And that is relevant because ... ?**

A. When we set out to write this book, one of our hardest decisions was what the title should be.

Q. **Well, you chose *Practical Business Analytics: A Proven Approach Through Successful Personalized Learning*, which is certainly a mouthful. What was the problem?**

A. Neither of us has a degree in business analytics. That name did not exist in our day. Nevertheless, the subject matter that is currently referred to as "business analytics" has been around since the early to mid-1900s, masquerading under several names.

Q. **OK, I'll bite. What are some of the other names that are associated with business analytics?**

A. Operations (or Operational) Research, Management Science, Decision Sciences, Business Decision Modeling, and, now, Analytics.

Q. **Wow. Five different names and none of them mean anything to me. Where did they come from?**

A. From the need to survive. World War I has been called "the first mechanized war," but it was fought primarily with the same mindset that was used in the 1800s. In World War II, Germany, with its Blitzkrieg (literally, Lightning War), showed the world what could be done, and a new way of thinking about the problems of war had to be developed.

Q.   **Who developed this new way of thinking?**

A.   An interdisciplinary bunch of eminent scientists who were given the choice to either use their brains or enlist to aid in the war effort. In the early days of WWII, Britain was under siege by the Axis powers. Every citizen was mobilized to help in the war effort. Not surprisingly, most scientists who were given the choice chose the former and were assigned to multidisciplinary teams tasked with addressing urgent problems in military operations.

Q.   **What kinds of problems did they deal with?**

A.   Some problems that had never existed before:

- developing optimal search strategies for their planes to hunt submarines,
- optimizing the placement of the scarce radars along the coast to detect air raids, and
- breaking the code of the German Enigma machines,

and some problems that had always existed, but now were bigger:

- the logistics of getting food and supplies to millions of soldiers,
- planning massive deployments, such as D-Day, and
- sorting and combining the flood of information.

Because of the nature of their duties, they became known as operational researchers.

Q.   **Cool! I remember there have been some pretty good movies about them. What happened to those people after the war?**

A.   By the end of the war, Operations Research (the US term) had become its own Military Operational Specialty (MOS) whose mission was listed as:

FA49 Mission: Functional Area 49, Operations Research/Systems Analysis (ORSA), provides the Army uniquely skilled officers—problem solvers—who produce analysis and decision support products to underpin critical decisions by leaders and managers at all levels of the Department of Defense (DoD). These officers recommend potential solutions for complex strategic, operational, tactical, and business issues. ORSAs are an integral part of Title 10 roles to organize, man, train, equip, sustain, and resource transformation in the Army.

The FA49 officer "introduces quantitative and qualitative analysis to the military's decision-making processes by developing and applying probability models, statistical inference, simulations, optimizations, and economic models. The ORSA FA encompasses diverse disciplines in personnel management, doctrine and force development, training, system acquisition and resource management, as well as tactical operational and strategic planning from division through combatant command, and from MACOM through the highest levels of DoD." (DA PAM 600–3).

Q.   **Impressive! But what happened to the ones who got out of the army?**

A.   They went home and tried to get jobs, helping the new, global industries that were facing the same problems that the military had faced.

Q.   **Were there jobs for them?**

A.   Oh, yes. You wouldn't expect the old ways used to run a small Mom-and-Pop operation to work when your company now had thousands of employees.

Q.   **No, I guess not. What did they bring to the companies?**

A.   Some algebra, a lot of statistics, and most importantly, computer skills.

Q.   **Do I have to know how to program a computer?**

A.   No, but you do have to know how to work in Excel. This is not a math or programming course; it is about using those subjects for fun and profit. We will show you in detail how to use them through the use of Excel.

Q.   **Are those topics what we now call "analytics"?**

A.   Well, sort of. The most common type of analytics that we hear so much about are Data Analytics and Business Analytics—and they are not the same.

Q.   **What is the difference?**

A.   Data Analytics deals with how to sift through the volumes of data that is being generated almost every minute in the business world.

Q.   **And once the data is organized, we can use it, right?**

A.   Not necessarily. "Big data" is useless unless it is processed into understandable information.

Q.   **Is that what Business Analytics does?**

A.   Yes. Business Analytics manipulates data to give new information (the old phrase for that is "analysis and synthesis").

Q.   **Aren't "data" and "information" the same thing?**

A.   No. Data is just numbers, while information means someone has added words to the numbers to tell you what they mean.

Q.   **Once we have information, do we put it to use?**

A.   Even if the information is understandable, the question is whether it is relevant. There is lots of information out there that might not matter.

Q.   **Isn't it true that the more information you give managers, the better decisions they will make?**

A.   Well, no. More information (or data) does not lead to better decisions. Suppose you were searching on the internet for used cars. You find a website that looks helpful, but it insists on lumping all cars, new and used, into the responses you get. That is definitely more information, but it doesn't help you find a used car.

Q. **That happens all the time. Why do they do that?**

A. Marketing, mostly, hoping you will change your mind and buy a new car. Sadly, in the business world, most managers suffer from an "overabundance of irrelevant information."

Q. **Don't most decision makers know what information they need?**

A. Not necessarily. It is a very human trait to ask for as much information as possible to be sure you don't miss something, and you end up lost in a mountain of numbers you don't need.

Q. **If the decision maker really understands the problem, they wouldn't do that, would they?**

A. Good point! If a decision maker is very experienced and has a model in her or his head about how to solve the problem, then it is possible they would ask for only relevant information.

Q. **Then business analytics gives the decision maker the information they need and improves the decisions made, right?**

A. Don't be too quick. You still have to know how to use the information. For example, tell me the odds of two people in a group of 25 having the same birthday.

Q. **I don't know. It would be pretty low, wouldn't it?**

A. It is actually over 50% (you can look up the math on the internet). People can have all the information they need, but if they don't know how to use it, they will rely on their intuition, which is often wrong.

Q. **When did people first realize that we had too much information?**

A. Russell Ackoff published a paper titled "Management Misinformation Systems" (*Management Science* 14, no. 4, 147–156) in 1967, and professionals have been struggling with it ever since.

Q. **Did the operations research people contribute to this misinformation overload?**

A. No, this is what they fought against. It was already happening when they joined the business world after the war.

Q. **How did that work out, integrating military ideas into the business world?**

A. They had a hard time explaining how their military experiences could translate to the civilian sector. They spoke a very different language (computers and statistics) than was spoken in the business environment. Consequently, they made a conscious effort to differentiate themselves from the military Operations Researchers and referred to themselves as Management Scientists.

Q. **Did the change in name help their cause?**

A. The profession certainly grew, but I like to think that it is because of impressive results rather than the name change. After all, other attempts at coming up with a more descriptive name, such as Decision Sciences, Business Decision Modeling and, now, Business Analytics, hasn't done a lot.

Q.   **So, whatever you call it, you say these people can save companies money?**

A.   Yes, quite a bit of money. The discipline, which we will call Business Analytics from here on, has scored amazing successes in virtually every field of human endeavor.

Q.   **The motto of the state of Missouri is "Show Me," so what would you say to a Missourian?**

A.   I'd ask them to name an industry.

Q.   **What about the hotel industry?**

A.   Business analytics helped to increase the total annual revenues of Intercontinental Hotels by $400 million, of Marriott by $76 million, and of Carlson Rezidor by $16 million.

Q.   **How?**

A.   By doing a better job of forecasting demand, allowing the hotels to draw in customers during slow times by varying pricing. Also, modeling the behavior of the guests allowed hotels to generate revenue from non-room sources.

Q.   **Has business analytics helped hospitals?**

A.   Yes. Hospitals were able to reduce their costs by $328 million, achieve a 65% increase in patient satisfaction, decrease readmission rates by 33.9%, and improve time management by 85%.

Q.   **What about the patients?**

A.   In one example, treatments for prostate cancer reduced costs by $328 million while improving the patient recovery time by 30%.

Q.   **I suppose you can do this all day, can't you?**

A.   Easily. Since 1972, an international competition (named the Franz Edelman Award in 1983) finds the best *application* of business analytics in the world.

Q.   **Did you expect me to have heard of it?**

A.   Not really, but it is considered the World Cup of Business Analytics. It is sponsored by the Institute For Operations Research and Management Science (INFORMS), the leading international association for professionals in operations research and analytics, with over 12,500 members (www.informs.org).

Q.   **Who was Franz Edelman?**

A.   He was the founder and director of RCA's Operations Research group and for 30 years, until his death in 1982, worked to increase the visibility of the profession.

Q.   **What do they win?**

A.   Submissions report on a completed, practical application that had a significant, verifiable, and preferably quantifiable impact on the client organization. The best six are finalists, receiving the

Achievement in Operations Research and Management Science medal and are designated as Edelman Laureates. The winner also receives a $15,000 honorarium.

Q.   **I can see why I never heard of it. Why would anyone go to all that trouble for $15K?**

A.   Bragging rights, and the knowledge that you have contributed to over $292 billion in verified benefits to the world through improved efficiency, bringing better products to consumers, and even helping with peace negotiations and saving lives.

Q.   **Does anyone really care?**

A.   More than two hundred organizations have been selected as finalists since the competition began, and many more than that apply, indicating that both corporations and NPOs take this seriously.

Q.   **Have you ever submitted?**

A.   I am proud to say I was a finalist twice, in 1983 as Vice President of Operations Systems at Burger King and in 1997 when I was a consultant to Taco Bell.

Q.   **Not to make you feel old, but can you show us some recent applications?**

A.   Every year, the Franz Edelman Competition finalists represents a good mix of applications. Here is a summary of the 2020 finalists as given on the INFORMS website (www.informs.org):

Amazon.com. Amazon fulfillment centers are the bones of the company's global operations network. Order picking plays a significant role in the overall process and accounts for a large part of the building's ability to drive faster cycle times and higher throughput. Amazon's revolutionary robotics system has reduced costs by identifying ways in which Amazon can process the picking of items faster and more efficiently across multiple floors and pick stations. The technology overall has led to significant performance improvement through stowing and picking inventory to facilitate sortation of multi-item shipments, reducing robotic systems travel by 31%. This has resulted in millions in savings per Amazon Robotics fulfillment center.

Carnival Corporation & PLC. Carnival & PLC built Yield Optimization and Demand Analytics (YODA), a cutting-edge program using advanced analytics and algorithms to provide dynamic price recommendations and inventory management. The program is a global collaboration involving leaders from six brands and teams across three continents who manage prices in six currencies. Since the system deployed in late 2017, it has been used to set prices on thousands of cruise voyages. The system was built in collaboration with Revenue Analytics.

Deutsche Bahn. The largest European railway company is moving more efficiently thanks in part to a new decision support system. The system optimizes train rotations in cargo, regional, and long-distance passenger transport divisions. The changes have resulted in direct savings in addition to better planning and productivity. The productivity of the locomotives and railcars has increased up to 10% while the time savings were up to 80%.

IBM. IBM Services (Global Technology Services Unit) has developed a cutting-edge system that utilizes machine learning and advanced data analytics to identify devices, such as servers, that are at risk for an outage. The system determines contributing risk factors, e.g., outdated hardware, and prompts a fix before the problem occurs. Since 2013, executing recommended actions has reduced outages by 23%. This translates into savings of more than $1 billion every year for IBM's clients. The IBM team is also using this system to drastically reduce the number of problematic systems for clients by as much as 85%.

Ashley Smith, "2020 INFORMS Franz Edelman Award: World's Leading Operations Research and Analytics Competition Selects Finalists," Informs.org. Copyright © 2020 by INFORMS.

Intel. Efficient product feature design coupled with supply chain planning is critical to Intel's success given its scale, complexity of its products and manufacturing processes, and the highly capital-intensive nature of the semiconductor business. In response to an exponential increase in complexities, Intel developed an innovative set of capabilities using advanced analytics that span product feature design through supply chain planning with the goal of maximizing revenue while minimizing cost. This set of capabilities is fast and effective, enabling analysis of many more business scenarios in much less time than previous solutions while providing superior results including faster response to customers. Implementation of this capability over the majority of Intel's product portfolio has provided average annual benefits in increased revenue and decreased cost of $1.9 billion and $1.5 billion, respectively, with a total benefit of $21.2 billion to date while also contributing to Intel's environmental goals of reducing water usage and preventing wastewater.

Walmart. Walmart's model of offering consistently low prices depends on constantly innovating to find new ways to reduce costs. The company developed a new system using machine learning to help perfectly time markdowns to optimize sales and clear excess inventory in its stores. The technique relies on operations research and provides feedback to help avoid excess inventory ordering in the future. The technology has already helped the company save millions of dollars.

Q.   **OK, I'm impressed. Those are some major players. Who won the competition?**

A.   You can look that up for yourself. INFORMS publishes a video of all finalists' presentations, and a paper describing the application is published within a year of the competition by the *INFORMS Journal of Applied Analytics*.

Q.   **Is that true for all past competitions as well?**

A.   All finalists presentations since 2010 have been posted as videos and the papers have been published. I have listed their titles, the video links, and the citations of the associated articles in appendix A. I am sure you will find some applications that are right up your alley.

Q.   **What about earlier competitions?**

A.   Before that, most presentations were recorded on CD-ROMs and are available through INFORMS as are the associated articles. You can google if you want to see them.

Q.   **Are they worth looking at?**

A.   Yes. Good applications of business analytics carry no expiration date. When you face a problem that reminds you of this class, chances are you will find a solution in one of those presentations.

Q.   **How long do the presentations take?**

A.   About 40 minutes.

Q.   **Would I be able to understand them?**

A.   The presentations are by top management, not the business analysts, so not only will you be able to understand them, but you will also see what first-class business world presentations look like. It will be worth your time.

Q.   **I don't know. Why would I want to watch people from so many different areas talk about their problems?**

A.   It is good training. If you aspire to have a successful career, you will have experts in various areas reporting to you. You will never understand the details of what they tell you, but you should learn to focus on grasping the big idea so that you can make appropriate decisions.

Q.   **You know, that sounds a little bit like taking class—I have to trust my professors to teach me in terms that I can understand.**

A.   That is exactly what we will do in this book. Move on to the next chapter to find out how.

ACTIVE LEARNING: CHAPTER 1

2

Promises, Promises ...

Q.   **Why are you writing in a Q&A format?**

A.   Because our students like it better.

Q.   **Better than what?**

A.   Traditional textbooks.

Q.   **What did they not like about typical textbooks?**

A.   They are boring. They tell you what you must learn in wordy paragraphs in which it is hard to find what is important.

Q.   **I know what you mean! I always have to outline the paragraphs to find the important stuff. So, how are you going to tell us what we need to know?**

A.   I'm not; I'm going to answer your questions or pose questions for you to answer.

Q.   **Will that help me learn?**

A.   I am sure you have spent a considerable portion of your life sitting in classrooms and listening to lectures. Did that help you learn?

Q.   **When I stayed awake it did. Is this another way of teaching?**

A.   Lectures are called "Aristotelian" teaching, for the philosopher Aristotle, because that is how he taught his pupils back in Ancient Greece. His major rival (as a philosopher and teacher) was Socrates, and can you guess what the Socratic teaching method is?

Q.   **Questions and answers?**

A.   Very good. Being academics, we have come up with a lot of new terms to describe this old approach, such as Active Learning, or Problem-based Learning, or Flipped classes, or even an older term, Case-based teaching. While there are minor differences, they all come down to the same thing—getting the student involved in learning the material instead of having the students passively listening to lectures.

Q.   **So, for me to learn, I must ask you questions?**

A.   Yes. I will take responsibility for answering your questions as long as you take responsibility for using all the resources at your disposal to find the answers first.

Q.   **OK, well, I have this book and the accompanying materials, so I go through them and then come to you if I have any questions?**

A.   I said use *all* the materials at your disposal. Perhaps one of your most valuable resources are your classmates. Study groups have a long history, going back to Socrates, who encouraged his followers to ask and answer questions among themselves. Discussing the material with others will stimulate critical thinking and help you learn challenging concepts.

Q.   **And what will you be doing while I am trying to teach myself?**

A.   A fair question. Just as I expect you to be prepared before you come to me with questions, I have also prepared by writing this textbook and recording video lectures that you should watch before asking questions. My main job now is answering your questions.

Q.   **All you do is answer questions?**

A.   My answering your specific questions will be much more valuable to you than sitting through a live lecture where I tell you and everybody else the same thing, whether they already know it or not.

Q.   **How do I get an answer when you are not around?**

A.   If you have teammates or have a study group, text or email them first. If you are not successful in getting an answer, text or email me and I will get back to you in a timely fashion. And, if you are taking this course online, follow whatever protocols have been set up to communicate with the instructor.

Q.   **The title of this book is *Practical Business Analytics*. What makes this book "*Practical*"?**

A.   It teaches you to do. We intend for you to be able to apply what you learn in your workplace.

Q.   **That would be great, if not novel. How will you do that?**

A.   The book was inspired by the lessons learned from one of the authors who, after becoming a tenured full professor, decided that he wanted to bring real-life experiences into his classroom.

Q. **A lot of my professors talk about their consulting work. How is this more practical than that?**

A. Consultants give advice. They are not responsible for the consequences of that advice nor are they responsible for implementing recommendations in the organization This author wanted to successfully implement business analytics in a real business so that he could share his experiences with students.

Q. **You mean he left academia? Wasn't he taking a big risk?**

A. Yes, but it paid off. He had the opportunity to build a business analytics function at Burger King Corporation. As manager of Operations Research, he reported to the Director of Marketing Research and was told to "make yourself useful." He became an internal consultant, knocking on doors and convincing managers to fund projects out of their budgets with him. Can you imagine a job where your analyst's salary depended on funds that you generate?

Q. **If I was the analyst, I would be rooting for him. What made him take the risk?**

A. Realizing that no one at Burger King or, for that matter, in the restaurant industry had ever attempted to apply business analytics. He felt as though he was a kid in a candy store and that opportunities would abound.

Q. **Did they?**

A. Consider this. Beef for Burger King hamburgers was a blend of 17 different types of beef (domestic, foreign, fresh, frozen, etc.). The price of each type fluctuated weekly, and that blend had to satisfy strict requirements (at least 28% fat, no more than 50% frozen, etc.).

   What would you do?

Q. **I have no idea. How should I know?**

A. This is just one example that illustrates why giving managers more information will not necessarily improve decision-making. Burger King had access to all the above information and more. But, armed with just the information contained in chapter 5 of this book, you would have known, just as he did, how to use business analytics to reduce their annual beef costs by over $1 million.

Q. **That should have made the analyst feel better. What happened after that?**

A. That kick-started his career at Burger King. Over the next seven years, business analytics was expanded to include the first Industrial Engineering department in the restaurant industry and with IT services became the Division of Operations Systems headed by your co-author as its vice-president. The work at Burger King was recognized as one of the best applications of business analytics in the world by being a finalist for the prestigious Franz Edelman Competition conducted by the Institute of Operations Research and Management Science (INFORMS).

Q. **And, did he live ever happy afterward?**

A. Yes, but not at Burger King. He switched back to academia and incorporated what he had learned into his teaching. This book reflects what he learned, and all the material is battle tested in the real world for relevance and usability.

Q.   I can't ask more than to learn from those who have been there and done that. What else is unique in this book?

A.   The full title pretty much says it all:

Practical Business Analytics: A Proven Approach Through Successful Personalized Learning

We have already seen what makes it practical. The italicized words hopefully will answer your question.

Q.   "Proven" sounds good, but you already told me it was practical because it was based on proven results. Is this different?

A.   Yes. Business students, like all students, suffer from a level of math anxiety that makes them want to delay taking a quantitative course as long as possible. When they finally do, they usually rated them among the least favorite courses in their program. By proven we mean that we have overcome that anxiety.

Q.   How did you do that?

A.   First, we conducted research on how students learn best. We then developed materials to effectively support student learning. And then we refined our teaching methods and materials over several years. The course is regarded as above average in rigor, yet the instructors receive among the highest ratings in the end-of-semester surveys. More significantly, they have consistently been voted by graduating MBA students as having had the greatest impact on their educational experience in the program. That is our proof.

Q.   I am not sure it is proof, but it is certainly enough to make me willing to try your approach. But, what would it mean for the approach to be "Successful?"

A.   We want you to be able to perform on the job, and we would argue that the better you learn the material, the better your chances of doing so. Under this approach, our undergraduate classes final average and median grades both increased by a full letter grade. In our MBA classes, there was a shift in the average percent of As earned from 50% to 80%.

Q.   Are you saying this makes the class easier?

A.   No. Our students still rated the course as being among the most rigorous in the program. We attribute their success to them being engaged with the material.

Q.   Why do you say "Personalized Learning"?

A.   Personalized learning is the Holy Grail of education. It means that everyone can have learning customized to their individual styles and needs, and to receive guidance when they are uncertain what is best for them.

Q.   Can you really do that?

A.   We have given it our best shot, using this book with the accompanying videos and Active Learning modules to allow you to create personalization based on your learning style and the support we provide.

Q.   **What does that mean?**

A.   Every lesson starts with a simple problem that grows in scope and complexity as the lesson progresses. Mathematical and statistical concepts are seamlessly integrated and applied using Excel. The lessons in each chapter are integrated into comprehensive problems that serve as realistic comprehensive problems that are best tackled, as in the real world, through interactive face-to-face or virtual group work.

Q.   **What does that have to do with personalization?**

A.   Personalization refers to the choices you can make to learn this material. It can support you as an individual learner, as an interactive group learner, or as a traditional learner.

Q.   **Doesn't any textbook do that?**

A.   Most textbooks are written to support the traditional model of higher education, which consists of a professor lecturing—for example, explaining what is in the textbook. This textbook is about you discovering what you need to know through a simulated dialectic process.

Q.   **A what?**

A.   Dialectic is just a fancy word for our Q&A format. According to Wikipedia, a dialectic is a discussion between people holding different points of view about a subject but wishing to establish the truth through reasoned arguments. Our Q&A format mimics just such a discussion.

Q.   **So, instead of just throwing a bunch of information at me, your pretend conversation guides me toward understanding the concepts of business analytics one step at a time. What else makes this book personal?**

A.   Every lesson is covered both as a dialectic and as a video lecture. Ideally, you will read the text and watch the video lecture (in the Active Learning module), but some learners learn better one way than the other.

Q.   **Are the videos just a repeat of the text material?**

A.   No. They cover the same material but use different examples and spreadsheets.

Q.   **Then if I need to see someone doing this work, I can watch the video. If I learn better by reading, I can use these notes. If I need help, I can work with a group. Are there any exercises to let me see if I really understand the material?**

A.   Besides the videos, the Active Learning modules contain the exercises to build your understanding and quizzes to test that understanding. The exercise consists of a word problem describing a business problem that can be solved using a business analytics tool that you learned to use in the dialectic and/or video lecture. Every business analytics tool that you will learn requires you to develop an Excel spreadsheet using data provided with the problem.

Q.   **What if my Excel skills are lacking?**

A.   No worries. The Excel skills required are explained in the dialectics and demonstrated in the video lectures. By the end of the course, everyone's Excel skills will have improved.

Q.   **Won't my quiz performance be impacted as a result of my Excel skills not being up to par?**

A.   No. Your quizzes require that you be able to correctly interpret the information that is on the Excel spreadsheets. They assume that you have the correct spreadsheet.

Q.   **And, how am I going to get the correct spreadsheet?**

A.   Again, personalization. Some students prefer to study alone, some prefer to study in a group, but when it comes to developing spreadsheets—and some can become quite complex—we recommend teamwork. If you are in a flipped class, you will probably have designated teams. If you are in a traditional class, we recommend that you create an informal team with some of your classmates.

Q.   **And what will these teams do?**

A.   We recommend that each team member develop their own spreadsheet the best they can. The team should then meet and share their work and seek consensus on a correct spreadsheet. Only after a consensus has been reached, should the quiz be attempted.

Q.   **How will the team be graded?**

A.   The team will not be graded. Each team member must take their own quiz and will receive an individual grade. Remember that the questions are randomized, and each member of the team will have an individual quiz. In short, you will collaborate as a group to learn the material as individuals.

Q.   **Does this approach work?**

A.   We have already talked about this approach as being proven and successful. It encourages collaboration and discourages competition. When students compete for a grade, they focus on "beating" the competition based on what they know and, by definition, cannot go beyond that. When students collaborate as a team, the focus is on the collective. It encourages an interchange of ideas and opinions, thus creating a collective knowledge that is greater than the sum of the parts. This course covers several topics, and some students will be more adept at learning one than another. Collaboration throughout the course will encourage those that are more adept to help those who are less adept. It will also encourage those who are less adept to ask for help.

Q.   **If we all help each other to get a good grade, won't that mess up the grade distribution in the course?**

A.   Let me rephrase that. If we all help each other to learn the material, then the grade distribution will reflect what we have learned. A "high" grade distribution simply indicates that we have done a good job.

Q.   **I'll buy that. Let's get started on our learning of business analytics.**

ACTIVE LEARNING: CHAPTER 2

3

Decision Theory

OVERVIEW

Q. **What is Decision Theory?**

A. Decision theory shows us how to make the correct decision when we must choose one of several alternatives in the face of an uncertain future. It can also help us decide how much to pay for more information, if we want it, and it is available.

Q. **Isn't the correct decision obvious?**

A. Not when you realize you cannot predict the future.

Q. **Still, everyone would make the same decision, wouldn't they?**

A. The decision often depends on the personality of the decision maker. An optimist would pick a riskier alternative than a pessimist would.

Q. **So, where do we start?**

A. We'll start by showing you some decision rules that might be used by various personality types when making decisions. After that, we illustrate Expected Monetary Value (EMV), one of the more common criteria for decision-making.

Q. **I hope that's everything. Is it?**

A. We'll also talk about how to place a value on additional information to help you decide whether to buy it and then look at more complex problems, such as sequential decisions.

LESSON 3.1: **Payoff Tables and Decision Rules**

Introduction

Q.   **What does this lesson deal with?**

A.   Probably the most common situation in the business world—you have an opportunity to make money by making a decision, but how much you make depends on something that you cannot control: for example, picking the next market for your company to enter.

Q.   **What's the problem—you pick a market and get to work, right?**

A.   You might want to consider what options your competition might pick or other things that are outside of your control.

Q.   **Why do we need to study this process?**

A.   There are ways to represent these situations that can help you consider all the possibilities and thus make better decisions. Also, we will introduce terminology common to Decision Theory.

Q.   **Is there really that much to talk about?**

A.   Well there are couple of different tools to consider and a lot of different ways to look at the data. For instance, in this section we will assume that while you list out the things you don't control, you can't estimate which one is more or less likely to happen.

Learning Outcomes

When you complete this session, you will be able to:

- Explain what is meant by *uncertainty* in this lesson
- Define the following components of a decision problem:
  - Decisions
  - States-of-nature
  - Payoff Table
- Calculate, using appropriate Excel formulas and functions, the *decision* and *payoff* for each of the following decision rules:
  - Optimist (best of the best)
  - Pessimist (best of the worst)
  - Middle of the Roader (equally likely)
  - Worrier (minimize the maximum regret)
- Calculate the regret matrix

A Dialectic on Payoff Tables and Decision Rules

Q.   **Is decision-making ever easy?**

A.   Yes, if there is only one alternative.

Q.   **When is there only one alternative in a decision?**

A.   This is a situation known as Hobson's Choice, which is a story from the late 1600s in England. Hobson was an innkeeper, meaning he ran a bar, a hotel, and a horse rental agency (since they didn't have cars). The local farmers had plow horses, but plow horses are big, slow, and rather uncomfortable to ride, so if a farmer needed to travel, he would rent a horse from a nearby inn.

Q.   **How many horses did Hobson have?**

A.   Let's say Hobson had a stable of 15 horses. Of that herd, some (let's say five) were pretty good horses, while others (another five) were OK and the rest (again five) probably should have been put out of their misery.

Q.   **Why would anyone rent a horse that was almost dead?**

A.   They wouldn't, unless all the others were gone. That's what Hobson noticed. The farmers kept picking his best horses (if there were any available), then his OK horses, and the lousy horses got ridden only when none of the others were available. In essence, he was running an old-age home for horses and that was not a good way to run a business.

Q.   **What could he do?**

A.   Hobson put in a new rule. When a farmer wanted to rent a horse, the farmer would come into the bar and the two of them would settle on a price. Hobson then sent for the stable boy to bring a horse around to the front, making sure that each horse was brought out in turn. The farmer could either accept the horse given to him (remember he has already paid for it) or walk. Pretty easy decision, isn't it? Every farmer, though, had the same chance of getting a good or bad horse.

Q.   **Does that ever really happen?**

A.   Well, certainly not often. Rather than having only one alternative, most decision situations have a set of choices (decision alternatives, denoted by d_i) and you must make a choice.

Q.   **Is it ever easy to make a decision with more than one decision alternative?**

A.   Yes, if you know what is going to happen in the future.

Q.   **Given that forecasts are always wrong, how could I know what is going to happen in the future?**

A.   That is called insider trading and is illegal. Still, if you did know what was going to happen, then you would simply evaluate each alternative under that future and pick the best result.

Q.   **Assuming we are not planning to go to jail, and we have more than one alternative, what do we do?**

A.   When we must consider a number of alternatives and a number of possible futures, for each alternative we decide how each future affects the value of that alternative. We call this Decision Making under Uncertainty.

Q.   **What does that mean?**

A.   "Uncertainty" just means you have no information about the probability of each possible future. Later on, we will talk about what you do when you can estimate probabilities.

Q.   **Does working out all these estimates really help?**

A.   If nothing else, working out how each decision alternative is affected by each possible future makes sure you consider all the possibilities. It is not as bad as it sounds. You do this all the time. For instance, if you were graduating and had two job offers, you might compare the two offers in terms of how well they look based on possible changes to the economy. The problem lies in that one alternative might be better for one future but another alternative would be better for a different future, so there is no clear-cut winner.

Q.   **How do you decide which alternative is best for you?**

A.   Use a payoff table.

Q.   **How does that help?**

A.   Once you know the question you are trying to answer, the next step is to organize your data. That's all a payoff table really is, a tool for organizing what you know about each alternative.

Q.   **How do you set up a payoff table?**

A.   You list the possible choices down the left-hand side (one per row) and list the possible futures across the top (one per column). Where a row and column intersect, put the outcome of that choice for that future. This is shown in table 3.1:

TABLE 3.1 Payoff Table

	S_1	S_2	S_3	S_4
d_1	−200	450	100	75
d_2	350	75	300	−100
d_3	100	250	−100	350
d_4	125	50	100	75
d_5	100	−50	50	25

Q.   **What does all that mean?**

A.   We commonly use a *d* with a subscript to represent the decision alternatives. For a problem where you have names for the decision alternatives (maybe project titles, or investment options, or whatever), you would replace the *d*s with those names to make the table easier to understand.

Q.   **What about the *S*s?**

A.   Those are the possible futures.

Q.   **Why did you use an *S* to stand for "Future"?**

A.   This goes back to the original work on payoff tables and a peculiarity of academic writing. The original work was a dissertation on game theory back in the 1920s. In academic writing, if you present your ideas in a very straightforward manner so anyone can easily understand them, then the research will be rejected. The reasoning seems to be that if the work is easy to understand, then it can't be good research (that comment is made somewhat tongue-in-cheek, but not completely). Conversely, if a paper is hard to understand, then it must be good research. Therefore, if you want to have a better chance of having your research published, use as many confusing phrases as you can.

Q.   **Like using *S* for "Future"?**

A.   Exactly. Rather than using the term *future* (which anyone could understand), the original author made up the term *state-of-nature*, which really doesn't mean anything, so it can mean whatever he wanted it to. The first letter of state-of-nature, of course, is *S*. You need to know this because if you ever use commercial software for payoff tables, it will use an *S* to denote each possible future, and you now know how to read it.

Q.   **What do we know about the possible futures?**

A.   In this document we will focus on situations when we are *uncertain* about what state-of-nature is going to occur, which means that we do not have any idea of the relative likelihood (probability) of a state-of-nature occurring. Later on, we will look at decision-making under risk in which we can assign a probability of a state-of-nature occurring.

Q.   **Where did the numbers in the table come from?**

A.   From wherever you can get them—accounting data, the finance department, marketing research, personal calculations, outside consultants, your boss, your subordinates, or anything else you can think of.

Q.   **So, it is pretty easy to get those numbers?**

A.   Sorry, but no. Fortunately for me, this isn't a class about gathering data. That means I get to simply present the data to you and warn you that collecting good data can be the hardest part of the whole process. Then I get to drop that subject and keep moving with calculations.

Q.   **Why are some of the numbers positive and some negative?**

A.   The values (we call them payoffs) for this problem represent profits, so the negative numbers represent losses. Payoffs can be costs, however, so it is always best to check what the data represents if you didn't collect it yourself.

Q.   **Don't the negative values tell us that the data is profits?**

A.   Although negative costs would be a little unusual, they can happen, so you can't make that assumption. If you collect the data yourself, you should know what it is, but if you get from someone else it is best to ask to be sure.

Q.   How does all the data you have in the payoff table help you make a decision?

A.   By applying some rules that, as mentioned earlier, reflect different ways of making decisions.

Q.   What's the first decision rule?

A.   An optimistic one (MaxiMax).   *optimistic = MaxiMax = Best of the Best = B of B*

Q.   What does that mean?

A.   If we are optimistic, we look at only the best outcome for each alternative (without worrying about which futures we are talking about). Besides MaxiMax, this rule is also called Best of the Best, which I prefer because it tells you what to do. For each alternative, simply pick the highest profit (of course, if we were working with costs it would be the lowest cost) in that row (see table 3.2). From among those best numbers, indicate the overall best (√), and if you like, the overall worst (×).

TABLE 3.2   Payoff Table with the Best-of-the-Best Rule

	S_1	S_2	S_3	S_4	B of B
d_1	−200	450	100	75	√ 450
d_2	350	75	300	−100	350
d_3	100	250	−100	350	350
d_4	125	50	100	75	125
d_5	100	−50	50	25	× 100

Q.   What's the second decision rule?

A.   A conservative one (MaxiMin).   *Conservative = MaxiMin = Best of the Worst = B of W*

Q.   Since we chose the **highest profit** last time, do we choose the **lowest profit** this time?

A.   Very good, yes. When you are being conservative, you look at the worst that could happen. This rule is called MaxiMin, but I prefer Best of the Worst. Having found the lowest number from each row, you again mark the winner and loser in table 3.3:

TABLE 3.3   Payoff Table with the Best-of-the-Worst Rule

	S_1	S_2	S_3	S_4	B of W
d_1	−200	450	100	75	× −200
d_2	350	75	300	−100	−100
d_3	100	250	−100	350	−100
d_4	125	50	100	75	√ 50
d_5	100	−50	50	25	−50

Q.   **If each approach recommends a different alternative, then are we any better off than we were originally?**

A.   Yes, because it allows us to make decisions which align with our corporate philosophy. It can also help to predict potential conflicts within organizations.

Q.   **What do you mean?**

A.   For example, some time ago when Pillsbury still existed and before it sold its restaurant division to Diageo, a *Wall Street Journal* article reported on the different corporate philosophies between Pillsbury Corporation and its wholly owned (and most profitable) subsidiary, Burger King. It portrayed the Pillsbury philosophy as being embodied by its management team dressing in dark grey suits and driving Lincoln Continentals while Burger King management dressed in slacks and open-collar shirts and drove Jaguar convertibles. The free-wheeling, risk-taking philosophy of Burger King clashed on many occasions with the conservative philosophy of Pillsbury.

Q.   **What's the third decision rule?**

A.   Since we have looked at an optimistic criterion and conservative criterion, maybe we should look at middle of the road ("Equally Likely") criterion.

Q.   **What does "equally likely" mean?**

A.   Going back to my earlier comments on academic writing, "Equally Likely" means the same thing as "average." As I hope you know, to calculate an average (or Equally Likely score) for a row, add up the values in the row and divide by the number of states-of-nature—in this example, four. This gives you the values shown in table 3.4:

TABLE 3.4   Payoff Table with the Equally Likely Rule

	S_1	S_2	S_3	S_4	E L
d_1	−200	450	100	75	106.25
d_2	350	75	300	−100	√ 156.00
d_3	100	250	−100	350	150.00
d_4	125	50	100	75	87.50
d_5	100	−50	50	25	× 31.25

Q.   **What is the last decision rule?**

A.   Another conservative one, because the business world is basically a conservative place. This one is called MiniMax Regret.

Q.   **What?**

A.   For once I like the technical name. If you write out the name in full (Minimize Maximum Regret) and read it backward (Regret Maximum Minimize), then it tells you how to calculate the scores. The calculations are harder than for the other rules, so pay attention. Reading the name backward, the first thing we must calculate is Regret.

Q.   **How do you calculate Regret?**

A.   By using the payoffs in the payoff table. The first tricky part is that we change the way we work with the table. Up until now, for each rule we have taken our numbers from the rows (the best of each alternative's row, the worst, and the average). For MiniMax Regret (MMR), we start off looking at the columns, the states-of-nature. So, look at the S_1 column, shown in table 3.5:

TABLE 3.5   State-of-Nature 1

	S_1
d_1	−200
d_2	350
d_3	100
d_4	125
d_5	100

Q.   **What's the best payoff for this state-of-nature?**

A.   Decision alternative 2 (d2) has a payoff of 350.

Q.   **So, if you picked d_2, and S_1 occurred, you would be perfectly happy—you picked the best alternative. What if you picked d_1 and S_1 occurred?**

A.   Then you are probably kicking yourself, since d_1 has a payoff (under S_1) of −200 (let's say these are in millions of dollars, just to make it interesting), so you just lost $200 million when you could have gained $350 million. I would guess that you would regret this decision. The amount of your regret is the distance between the payoff you gained (−200) and the best payoff you could have gained (350), a distance of 350 − (−200) or 550.

Q.   **What if the data were costs, how do you calculate regret then?**

A.   Regret is a measure of distance, so it is always reported as a positive number. Thus, if you were dealing with costs, the best number would be the lowest, and your regret calculation (as shown) would give you a negative regret. Either reverse the order of the numbers in the calculation or take the absolute value of your calculation (either one will be just fine).

Q.   **Do we calculate just one regret for each column?**

A.   No. Repeat the calculation for each alternative for S_1, finding the distance of each payoff from the best payoff in the first state-of-nature. Table 3.6 shows the results.

Q.   **Is that it?**

A.   Now we get to work on the second column, State-of-Nature 2. Again, find the best payoff for the state-of-nature (this time it is 450, for d_1) and calculate the distance of each of the other payoffs from 450. Adding the second column to table 3.6, we get table 3.7.

TABLE 3.6   Regret Table for State-of-Nature 1

	S_1
d_1	550
d_2	0
d_3	250
d_4	225
d_5	250

TABLE 3.7   Regret Table for States-of-Nature 1 & 2

	S_1	S_2
d_1	550	0
d_2	0	375
d_3	250	200
d_4	225	400
d_5	250	500

Q.   **Do we do this for every state-of-nature column?**

A.   Yes, repeat for each of the last two states-of-nature and you get the complete Regret table, shown in Table 3.8.

TABLE 3.8   Regret Table

	S_1	S_2	S_3	S_4
d_1	550	0	200	275
d_2	0	375	0	450
d_3	250	200	400	0
d_4	225	400	200	275
d_5	250	500	250	325

Q.   **That's really nice, but how does it help?**

A.   This completes only the first step of the calculations for the MiniMax Regret rule. The next step (continuing to read the name of the rule backward) is to go back to looking at the rows in the Regret table and pick the maximum regret for each alternative.

Q.   **Why maximum?**

A.   We use the maximum regret because we are setting up a conservative rule, so we look at the worst case, the most we would ever regret each alternative. Put these maximum regrets in a column attached to the payoff table, as shown in table 3.9.

TABLE 3.9   Payoff Table with the MiniMax Regret Rule

	S_1	S_2	S_3	S_4	M/M R
d_1	−200	450	100	75	550
d_2	350	75	300	−100	450
d_3	100	250	−100	350	400
d_4	125	50	100	75	400
d_5	100	−50	50	25	500

Q.   **Since we have profit data, do we pick the largest regret number as the winner?**

A.   No. We continue to read the name backward and minimize the maximum regrets. This may sound odd but remember that the numbers in the M/M R column came from the Regret table. That means that they no longer represent profits, they represent units of regret. Unless you are masochistic (and if you are, don't tell me), you don't like regretting your decisions, so for the MiniMax Regret rule, the lowest number in the column is the winner and the highest number is the loser, as indicated in table 3.10. That will be true for both profit and cost data.

TABLE 3.10   Payoff Table with the MiniMax Regret Rule

	S_1	S_2	S_3	S_4	M/M R
d_1	−200	450	100	75	× 550
d_2	350	75	300	−100	450
d_3	100	250	−100	350	√ 400
d_4	125	50	100	75	√ 400
d_5	100	−50	50	25	500

Q.   **Are we finished with these decision rules yet?**

A.   For our purposes, yes. While the literature contains many more, I think that this discussion has given you enough background so that if you really wanted to, you could search for others that have been published and understand them.

Q.   **Why are there so many rules?**

A.   The most important thing to remember is that each of these rules reflects a distinct decision-making philosophy. It will help you to make recommendations that align with your company's overall decision-making philosophy.

ACTIVE LEARNING: LESSON 3.1

LESSON 3.2: Expected Monetary Value and the Value of Perfect Information

Introduction

Q. **I thought we were talking about decision-making?**

A. We are. We still have decision alternatives and your payoff is still dependent on something that you cannot control—for example, the states-of-nature.

Q. **What is different then?**

A. This time we will consider that you have some knowledge about the states-of-nature, specifically that you have an estimate of the probability that each state-of-nature will occur.

Q. **How does that help?**

A. We already looked at an average value, called the Equally Likely rule, but that rule assumed every state-of-nature had the same probability (thus, equally likely). Now we can say that one state-of-nature is more likely than another, which makes some states-of-nature less likely, since probabilities always add to 1. More precise information leads to more precise decision making.

Q. **That sounds like a weighted average. Is it?**

Expected Value = Expected Monetary Value = EMV

A. Yes, but you know we can't call it something that simple. We use the probabilities to calculate the expected payoff (based on the probabilities) associated with each decision you can make, so we call it an Expected Value. When you are dealing with money as your payoffs (that is to say, usually, in the business world), we call it an Expected Monetary Value, or EMV.

Q. **And what does "perfect information" mean?**

A. It is almost always possible to get more information, but you have to decide whether it is worth the time, effort, and price. One way to set a limit on the value of something is to consider an extreme case. Most information is not perfect (far from it, actually), but if we knew what perfect information would be worth to us, called the Expected Value of Perfect Information or EVPI, then we have an upper limit on what we would pay for it.

Expected Value of Perfect Information = EVPI

Learning Outcomes

When you complete this session, you will be able to:

- Explain what is meant by *risk* in this lesson
- Define the following:
  - Expected Monetary Value
  - Expected Value of Perfect Information
- Calculate and explain, using appropriate Excel formulas and functions, the following:
  - Expected Monetary Value (EMV)
  - The maximum EMV decision and payoff
  - The expected value of certainty (EVC)
  - The expected value of perfect information (EVPI)

A Dialectic on EMV & EVPI

Q.   **Last time, you said uncertainty means that we have no idea about the likelihood of any state-of-nature occurring. What is the term when you can estimate those probabilities?**

A.   We call that "decision-making under risk."

Q.   **How does "risk" mean we know the probabilities?**

A.   With uncertainty, we had no probability estimates for the states-of-nature. Certainty would mean you are very sure (certain) that all your data is correct (honestly, that is rare). In between those two, when you have some estimates but lack certainty, there is an element of risk in our decisions, thus the name.

Q.   **OK. Which is more common, having probabilities or saying you know nothing?**

A.   I have a hard time imagining any professional admitting that they know nothing at all, or any executive accepting such a statement without saying something to the effect of "go get me that information and don't come back until you have it!" Still, the rules for decision-making under uncertainty can be used even when you have probabilities for the states-of-nature.

Q.   **How do we estimate the probabilities?**

A.   If this were Ancient Greece, we might consult the Oracle at Delphi. Shakespeare, in the 1600s, used the incantations of the three witches in Hamlet ("Double, double, toil and trouble ... ") to foretell the future. Today, we tend to use other methods.

Q.   **Such as?**

A.   Many of the techniques involve soliciting expert opinion in one way or another. If you have enough sources, you can calculate a relative frequency. Either way, such estimates are referred to as subjective probabilities.

Q.   **Is that different from regular probabilities?**

A.   Not really, but the subjective part reminds us that if we get more information later on, that might change our probability estimates.

Q.   **Are you saying we should always wait, to get better information?**

A.   However much information you have (and you always have to pay to get more), your decision-making will still entail risk—just, hopefully, less risk.

Q.   **OK, well, once we have the probabilities, what do we do with them?**

A.   The first thing we do is add them to the table as an additional row across the bottom, matching each probability to the appropriate state-of-nature column, as shown in table 3.11.

TABLE 3.11   Payoff Table with the Expected Monetary Value Rule

	S_1	S_2	S_3	S_4	EMV 1. row EMV 2. row max
d_1	−200	450	100	75	√ 253.75
d_2	350	75	300	−100	90
d_3	100	250	−100	350	197.5
d_4	125	50	100	75	70
d_5	100	−50	50	25	−3.75
Probability	0.05	0.5	0.2	0.25	

Q.   **And how do we calculate EMV?**

A.   For each alternative (row in the table), multiply each probability by its matching payoff and then add up the results. That weighted total is the EMV.

Q.   **Is the highest EMV the winner?**

A.   For profits, yes. For costs, the lowest EMV would be the winner. In table 3.11, d_1 with an EMV of 253.75 would be the winner.

Q.   **Is that it?**

A.   No, we are just getting started.

Expected Value of Perfect Information (EVPI)

Q.   Did you say that information always costs money?

A.   Absolutely, if it is worth having (free information is worth what you pay for it). Whether you buy external marketing research or pull together an internal group or anything else, you will have to budget some money for it.

Q.   How do you convince your boss to pay for information?

A.   Perhaps the best way is to switch our mindset from "how much is it going to cost me?" to "what is it worth to me?"

Q.   How can you figure out what information is worth to you when you don't know what the information will say?

A.   To start with, we can figure out an upper bound by asking what perfect information would be worth.

Q.   Can we really get perfect information?

A.   No. We will never have information that will tell us exactly, with 100% certainty, what will happen in the future. We can, however, ask ourselves what we would do if we did know exactly what would happen, and then combine those outcomes to get a single value we call the Expected Value of Perfect Information (EVPI).

Q.   How do we do that?

A.   By remembering what I said when we first talked about decision making: if we knew what was going to happen in the future, we would just evaluate each alternative for that future, and pick the best.

Q.   But we don't know what is going to happen in the future, do we?

A.   No, but we can create (actually, already have created) a small list of possible futures.

Q.   Where do we have that?

A.   In the payoff table we set up in the first part of this lecture. I have copied it below as table 3.12:

TABLE 3.12   Payoff Table with State Probabilities

	S_1	S_2	S_3	S_4
d_1	−200	450	100	75
d_2	350	75	300	−100
d_3	100	250	−100	350
d_4	125	50	100	75
d_5	100	−50	50	25
Probability	0.05	0.5	0.2	0.25

Q.   **Do you mean S_1, S_2, S_3, and S_4?**

A.   Right. Those are the possible futures for this decision.

Q.   **How does that help? We know that S_2 is most likely to happen and S_1 is least likely, but that doesn't tell us which one will happen.**

A.   True, but we don't need the probabilities right now (we will use them a little later). What we are going to do right now is play "Let's Pretend."

Q.   **I'm sorry, what?**

A.   Let's pretend that we know S_1 is going to happen.

Q.   **Well, if we knew S_1 were going to happen, we'd choose d_2, because it has the highest payoff of 350, wouldn't we?**

A.   Yes, but we don't stop there. We do the same thing for each of the other states-of-nature.

Q.   **So, if we pretend S_2 is going to happen, we would pick d_1 with a payoff of 450, and for S_3 we would pick d_2 again, this time with a payoff of 300, and for S_4 we would pick d_3 with a payoff of 350. How does that help?**

A.   It lets us set up a smaller table showing just the winning payoffs and their probabilities (I told you we would need them), shown as the Certainty Table in table 3.13.

TABLE 3.13   Certainty Table

	S_1	S_2	S_3	S_4
Best Payoff	350	450	300	350
Probability	0.05	0.50	0.20	0.25

Q.   **What do we do with that?**

A.   Since you once again have a matched set of probabilities and payoffs, it looks like a good place to calculate an expected value, this time called the Expected Value of Certainty:

EVC (Expected Value of Certainty) = 0.05*350 + 0.5*450 + 0.2*300 + 0.25*350 = **390**

Q.   **Got it! *Perfect* information is worth 390 to me, so I would never pay any more than that for less-than-perfect information, right?**

A.   Not quite. Remember we calculated the EMV = 253.75, the expected payoff without any more information. That means you need to ask yourself how much better you did with perfect information. That is what we call the EVPI, as shown here:

EVPI (Expected Value of Perfect Information) = **EVC – max EMV**
EVPI = 390 – 253.75
EVPI = 136.25

Q.   **Are you saying I should be willing to pay 136.25 for more information?**

A.   Not at all. All it says is that you should not pay any more than 136.25 for additional information.

Q.   **That helps! So, if I had a proposal from a marketing research firm to do a study for 50, then I guess I should sign the paperwork?**

A.   No, after all, you may be paying 50 for something that is worthless. EVPI is an upper limit on what you would pay. What you do know is that you would never pay more than that for anybody's information. If you can get some data on how good the research company is, then we can calculate a more precise estimate of what you would pay. That is the next lecture, though.

ACTIVE LEARNING: LESSON 3.2

LESSON 3.3: **Decision Trees**

Introduction

Q.   **Why do we need decision trees if we already have payoff tables to help us make decisions?**

A.   A payoff table focuses very narrowly on a single decision. That is good, but sometimes you need to see how one decision affects another. When you have a sequence of decisions, a decision tree is the better tool to use.

Q.   **Why would you have a sequence of decisions?**

A.   Last time, we ended by saying that the EVPI is a rough estimate, and it was possible to find a better estimate if we knew more about the source of the information. That creates a second decision for us, though—first, whether buy the information, and then the actual decision we need to make. In general, it is not unusual for one decision to affect the outcome of another decision.

Q.   **How does a decision tree help with that?**

A.   Decision trees provide a graphical description of decisions and states-of-nature associated with decision-making. In this lesson, we will show you how to construct such a decision tree.

Learning Outcomes

- When you complete this lesson, you will be able to draw a decision tree showing the correct relationships between decisions and states-of-nature for a decision theory problem:
    - You will be able to identify the decision nodes of a decision tree (squares)
    - You will be able to identify the states-of-nature nodes of a decision tree (circles)
    - You will be able to correctly place the payoffs on a decision tree
    - You will be able to correctly place the probability of each state-of-nature, P(S), on a decision tree
- You will be able to roll back the decision tree (calculate and identify the max EMV decision and payoff).

A Dialectic on Decision Trees

Q.   **If EVPI does not help me to decide how much to pay for additional information, how do I use a decision table to figure out what I should pay for a consultant (or any other service that delivers additional information)?**

A.   You cannot use a decision table for that purpose.

Q.   **Why not?**

A.   Because decision tables, though they may have many alternatives, can deal with only one decision at a time.

Q.   **Huh?**

A.   Few decision situations are isolated from everything else. For example, if you have the opportunity to buy additional information (such as hiring a consultant), then you must first decide whether you are going to buy it. Once you make that decision, then and only then can you move on to your original decision problem. After all, the information that you buy (if you decide to buy it) may affect the choices you face in the future. Therefore, we need a tool that will let us take these relationships into account.

Q.   **What tool looks at more than one decision situation?**

A.   A decision tree.

Q.   **How do we start using a decision tree?**

A.   First you need to know the parts of a decision tree, which is a type of graph or flowchart, but it has a very limited set of symbols and is very specific as to the types of situations it can represent.

Q.   **Now I have to be an artist?**

A.   No, we will use Excel to draw the decision tree, and which will also let us perform the calculations. To draw a decision tree, we will select three shapes from the "Shapes" menu in Excel, which can be found under the insert tab as shown below in Figure 3.1.

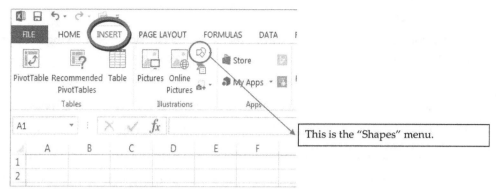

FIGURE 3.1 Location of "Shapes" menu in Excel.

Q.   Which three shapes?

A.   Very simple ones: a square, a circle (or ellipse), and an arrow. Each has a unique and very specific meaning as shown in figure 3.2.

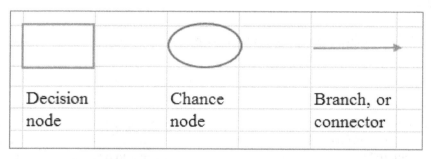

FIGURE 3.2 Symbols for a decision tree.

Q.   What do we do with these shapes?

A.   We arrange the shapes in whatever order is needed by the problem at hand, and connect the nodes by branches, representing the decision alternatives and states-of-nature. The branches also show the order in which events occur, while the rectangles and ellipses serve a purpose similar to road signs.

Q.   What is the purpose of a road sign?

A.   When you are driving down a road and see a road sign, it tells you what to expect—an exit or a rest stop, or construction, or whatever. These roads signs are very important and specific, as shown in the following story:

When my wife and I visited England, we took a ferry over to Ireland. We were late getting to the ferry, so we were about the last on, which made us the first off. As the ferry got in about midnight, this meant we had a couple hundred very tired Irish folk who wanted to get home and me in front, blocking their way. I just wanted to get out of their way, let them get past, and then find our hotel.

I drove down the ramp, came to a stop sign, and looked left and right. To the left I saw the sign shown in figure 3.3:

FIGURE 3.3 Irish road sign.

Apparently, they have a lot of experience dealing with tourists. Knowing what was coming up to the left, I very easily decided to turn right, found a parking spot, waited for everyone to pass me, and then took my wife on a tour of the slums of Dublin (she says I could get lost in an elevator).

Q.   **What important things are the squares and circles telling us?**

A.   The way you interpret the road signs is:

⇒ the next thing you see will be a set of decision alternatives

⇒ the next thing you see will be a set of states-of-nature

We need the two different symbols because the arrows are used for both decision alternatives and states-of-nature.

Q.   **Why do you use an arrow to show both the decision alternatives and the states-of-nature?**

A.   The most important thing a decision tree shows is the sequence in which things happen.

Q.   **Don't all flowcharts show sequence?**

A.   All flowcharts do, but not all diagrams. You may have seen a thing called an "influence diagram" at some point. If not, it is a collection of symbols—almost any shape will do—connected by a spider's web of arrows going all over the place, back and forth from each shape in no particular pattern or order. While somewhat the same, a decision tree has a much more defined order. A tree is read from left to right, so whatever is furthest to the left comes first, and any node to the left of another node precedes that other node.

Q.   **What's a decision tree problem look like?**

A.   Like this:

The following example is adapted from some class notes of mine, which undoubtedly means it was taken from a textbook somewhere, but I have no idea where, so consider this sufficient attribution and thanks to that nameless author.

A company is faced with a good problem: demand for their product has been growing and has now outpaced their production capacity. With further growth in demand anticipated for next year, the company must find some way to expand capacity or risk losing customers when demand cannot be met. Your boss comes to you and announces that three options are being considered: expand the existing plant, build a whole new plant from the ground up, or simply subcontract with another company. You are to analyze the situation and make a recommendation.

Your first step is to find out how much growth in demand is expected next year, so you talk to your company's sales force (and who would know the customers better than they would?). Unfortunately, you get several different answers. About 25% of the sales force is predicting high growth, another 40% is predicting moderate growth, and the last 35% is predicting low growth. Nobody thinks demand will decrease. You worked out one-year returns for each combination, as shown in table 3.14.

TABLE 3.14   First-Year Returns   *S o f N*

	High	Moderate	Low
Expand	60,000	50,000	20,000
Build	50,000	60,000	10,000
Subcontract	60,000	60,000	0

Decision (handwritten, left margin) · *PDS* (handwritten, circled)

Q.   **Isn't that a payoff table?**

A.   Yes, but any payoff table can be drawn as a decision tree (it doesn't necessarily work in reverse), and for the sake of keeping things simple, we'll start that way.

Q.   **Really? You're going to keep this simple?**

A.   Well, simpler. On the other hand, let's introduce a bit of notation that will help down the road.

Q.   **Why not just introduce it down the road?**

A.   If I do that, you will have gotten used to one way of thinking and will have to change that way of thinking. It is better to introduce the notation now.

Q.   **If you say so. What is this notation?**

A.   Some of it you already know. We use the letter *d* for a decision alternative and *s* for a state-of-nature. Then, the payoff associated with a specific decision alternative and state-of-nature would be P(d,s).

Q.   **How do you tell one payoff from another?**

A.   We use subscripts. The two tables below show an abstract table (3.15a) and a specific table (3.15b).

TABLE 3.15A   Abstract Representation of Table 3.14

Decision	State-of-Nature		
	S_1	S_2	S_3
d_1	$P(d_1,s_1)$	$P(d_1,s_2)$	$P(d_1,s_3)$
d_2	$P(d_2,s_1)$	$P(d_2,s_2)$	$P(d_2,s_3)$
d_3	$P(d_3,s_1)$	$P(d_3,s_2)$	$P(d_3,s_3)$

TABLE 3.15B   Detailed Representation of Table 3.14

Decision	Symbol	State of Nature		
		High	Moderate	Low
		S_1	S_2	S_3
Expand	d_1	$60,000	$50,000	$20,000
Build	d_2	$50,000	$60,000	$10,000
Subcontract	d_3	$60,000	$60,000	$-

Q.   **Now that you have that out of your system, what's the first step to drawing a decision tree?**

A.   Organize the information into groups of decision alternatives or states-of-nature. Usually, there will be more than one group of each type, but this is a simple problem, so we have only one of each, as shown in figure 3.4.

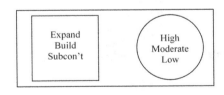

FIGURE 3.4 Groups.

I used a circle to indicate the state-of-nature group and a square to indicate the decision alternative group.

Q.   **How do you know a state-of-nature group from decision alternative group?**

A.   By looking at what you control. You (or the decision maker) control which of the decision alternatives is chosen; you do not control which of the states-of-nature occurs. In figure 3.4, the company can choose which of the expansion options they wish to implement but cannot choose what the level of growth in demand will be. Also, only the states-of-nature have probabilities associated with them.

* We Chose the [decison]
* We CanNot chose (S of N) ⟹ (SofN) only has probabilities associated with the

Q.   **What's the second step to drawing a decision tree?**

A.   Decide which of the groups comes first.

Q.   **Wouldn't we want to see what the growth in demand is before deciding whether to expand, build, or subcontract?**

A.   While that would be nice, it simply won't work. If we wait to see what demand appears, then we will not get the new capacity ready in time to meet that demand. As is usually true with decision-making, we will have to decide first and then hope for a good outcome. So, we now know what goes first, and we can draw it, as shown in figure 3.5.

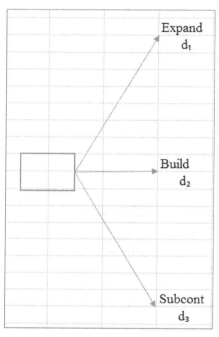

FIGURE 3.5 Decision alternatives start the tree.

Q.   **What's the third step to drawing a decision tree?**

A.   Pick any one branch (arrow) and ask, "What comes next?"

Q.   **Why only one?**

A.   I recommend a depth-first approach to drawing a tree. This means following a single set of branches further and further to the right, ignoring all the other branches until you reach the end of that path and put a payoff as the closing part. Going depth-first lets you concentrate on one small part of the tree, draw that part correctly, and then move on to another small part. When all the small parts are drawn correctly, you often find you have drawn the whole tree correctly.

Q.   **OK, so, let's start at the top and pick "Expand." Now, what?**

A.   Repeat the last step and ask, "What comes next?"

Q.   **All that's left is the states-of-nature. Do squares and circles have to alternate through the tree?**

A.   Yes, the states-of-nature come next, and, no, any order at all can be followed as long as it accurately describes the sequence in which things really must/will happen. This is such a small tree, the types of nodes had to alternate. Drawing in the states-of-nature that follow the "Expand" branch, we get figure 3.6.

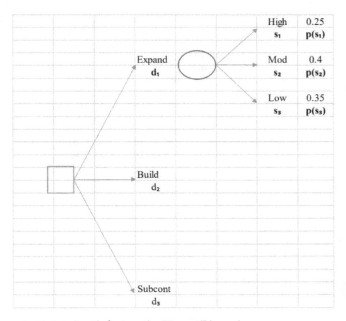

FIGURE 3.6 Depth-first on the "Expand" branch.

Q.   **Do we have to add the probabilities when we draw the state-of-nature arrows?**

A.   You don't have to do this right away when you are drawing a tree by hand, and you may find it inconvenient because it takes your mind off of the process (drawing the tree) and makes you search through the problem to find the numbers. If you have the numbers to hand though, then it can't hurt. For my part, I included them because I already know them (it's *my* example), and it is easier than drawing an extra figure just to put in the percentages.

Q.   **That circle took up a lot of room. Are we going to be able to fit the whole tree on there?**

A.   This is a common problem with drawing a tree: you never leave enough room. When drawing a tree by hand, squeeze the branches in wherever you can and then redraw the tree starting on the right (with the payoffs). The tree gets smaller as you move to the left, so there is plenty of room.

Q.   **What's the next step to drawing a decision tree?**

A.   Keep repeating the last step (pick a branch and ask, "What comes next?") until you write in the payoff at the end of a branch. When you do that, retreat to the nearest branch that is not finished, and go back to repeating that step.

Q.   **We are on the "Expand" branch, and the "High" state-of-nature, so the payoff in the table above is $60,000, right?**

A.   Right, and to save some time, I also show the payoffs for the "Moderate" and "Low" states-of-nature in figure 3.7.

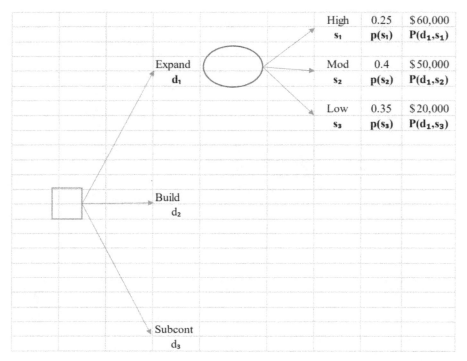

High	0.25	$60,000
s_1	$p(s_1)$	$P(d_1,s_1)$
Mod	0.4	$50,000
s_2	$p(s_2)$	$P(d_1,s_2)$
Low	0.35	$20,000
s_3	$p(s_3)$	$P(d_1,s_3)$

Expand d_1

Build d_2

Subcont d_3

FIGURE 3.7 Adding the payoffs.

Q.   **How do you draw the rest of the tree?**

A.   By repeating the pattern we have already used. We are finished with the "Expand" branch, so we do what we did before, which is to backtrack to find the nearest branch that is not complete. This is the "Build" decision alternative. We know the states-of-nature come next, so we would draw the circles and arrows, label them, and add the payoffs, as shown in figure 3.8. Notice that I shaded the recently added portion and that the only thing different is that now we are dealing with the "Build" branch (decision d_2), which changes the payoffs.

Q.   **Couldn't we just have the "Build" arrow point into the state-of-nature circle following "Expand"?**

A.   No. Ignoring for the moment that the payoffs would be different, it is still a bad idea because it is confusing to read. The rule for decision trees is that only one arrow may point into any node (as many as you need may point out).

Q.   **Are we finished yet?**

A.   Of course not. We haven't finished the "Subcontract" branch. You aren't finished drawing a decision tree until every branch ends in a payoff. Even then you aren't finished with the decision tree, only with drawing it. Figure 3.9 repeats the process for the "Subcontract" branch.

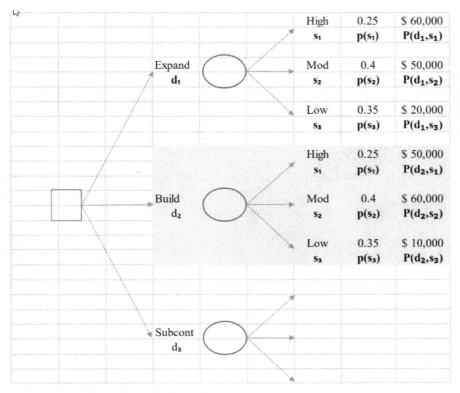

FIGURE 3.8 Finishing the "Build" branch.

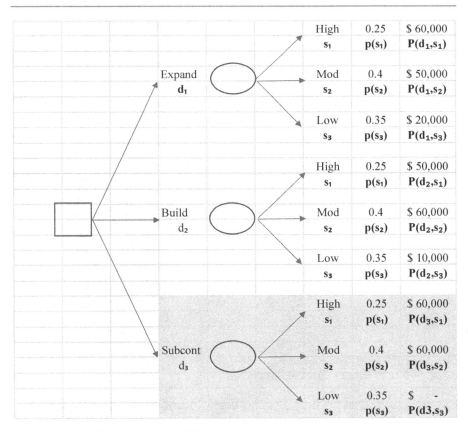

FIGURE 3.9 Finishing the drawing of the tree.

Q.   So, what's left?

A.   Calculations. We have payoffs and probabilities, so we can calculate Expected Monetary Values (EMVs) for each circle node. As we calculate the EMVs, we move backward (right to left) through the tree, placing the result in the circle that precedes the state-of-nature arrows. You know how to calculate an EMV: the sum of the probabilities times the payoffs on each branch out of the chance (circle) node. For example, for the chance node following the "Expand" decision, the EMV calculation is shown here:

$$\textbf{EMV(Expand)} = 0.25*60{,}000 + 0.4*50{,}000 + 0.35*20{,}000 = \textbf{\$42{,}000}$$

Figure 3.10 shows the results for all the nodes.

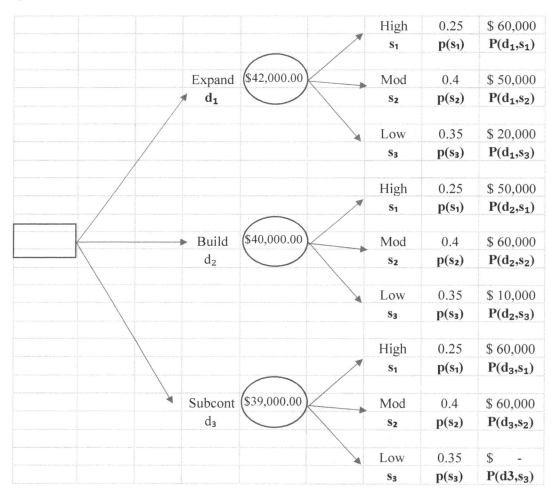

FIGURE 3.10 Decision tree with expected values.

Q.   How do you read these expected values?

A.   Follow the branches from left to right, so the decision to "Expand" has an EMV of $42,000.

Q. **Now that we have drawn it, what do we do with it?**

A. Make a decision. You should always make obvious which decision you make by bolding or high-lighting the arrow associated with the best (optimum) decision, as is shown in figure 3.11. It is customary to put the EMV that is the largest (and corresponds to the best EMV decision) in the initial decision box.

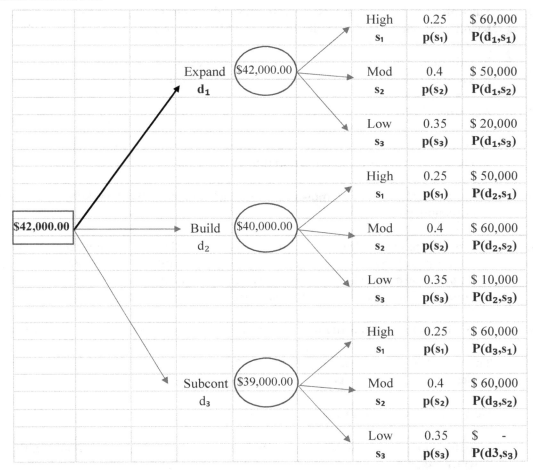

FIGURE 3.11 Finished decision tree.

Q. **That seems like a lot of work for a simple result.**

A. Of course, this is such a small tree you really wouldn't bother with it. Decision trees are most useful when you have several layers of decision alternative nodes and state-of-nature nodes to make things complicated. Before we do that, though, we need to introduce the idea of Expected Value of Sample Information (EVSI), but we'll leave that for the next lesson.

ACTIVE LEARNING: LESSON 3.3

LESSON 3.4: Expected Value of Sample Information I

Introduction

Q. **Since all we did in the last lesson was to draw a decision tree that had the same information as a payoff table, I hope that you will show me something new in this lesson.**

A. Exactly right. I had already told you before that a decision table can handle only one decision. In this lesson, I will show you how you can add additional decisions in a decision tree.

Q. **Any kind of a decision?**

A. Well, let's not lose sight of the fact that in decision theory we are talking about making a decision whose payoff depends on an uncertain future.

Q. **Yes, and that the better our knowledge of the risks associated with making a decision, the better our decision will be.**

A. Spot on! We have already mentioned that often we have little data about random events that may affect our payoffs but that we usually can secure better information about these random events through formal means such as market research, or Delphi or Analytic Hierarchy Processes to quantify unquantifiable information such as phone surveys, et cetera.

Q. **I don't know that anyone in my organization knows enough about these to be of help.**

A. That is probably true in most organizations. But there are numerous experts and consulting companies that do and will be glad to help you—for a price.

Q. **How much would it cost to hire such an expert or outfit?**

A. Actually, knowing the cost is pretty useless information (unless that cost is greater than the EVPI, in which case you would reject their services out of hand).

Q. **If you don't care about the cost, how do you decide?**

A. The key question is what the information offered by a particular firm is worth to you. That will allow you to determine whether the price is right.

Q. **Then what are we trying to decide, whether to buy the information?**

A. Exactly. If you decide that the asking price is too high, you are back to square one and you have to make the decision. If the asking price is less than what the information is worth, you must wait until you get the information you are buying before making a decision. This added decision is why we need to know about the decision trees.

Learning Outcomes

When you complete this session, you will be able to:

- Augment a simple decision tree to show the choice to purchase additional information (or not):
  - Understand and show the possible outcomes (or indicators [I]) of purchasing additional information on the decision tree
  - Understand and include the probability of obtaining a particular indicator P(I) on the decision tree
  - Include the decisions after each indicator on the decision tree
  - Include the probabilities of the states-of-nature as modified by the indicators P(S/I) as well as the corresponding payoffs on the decision tree

A Dialectic Introducing the Expected Value of Sample Information (EVSI)

Q. **What is sample information and why do we want it?**

expected Monetary value

A. The probabilities we used for the EMV were subjective, meaning that they were estimates (if we were unkind, we would say "guesses"). If your boss were to question them, it would be pretty hard to defend their accuracy. Such criticism can be dealt with by getting a second opinion from another set of experts.

Q. **You mean we can calculate what any other data would be worth to us?**

A. That would be nice, but that is more than we can do. All we can do is assess the value of the information that can be provided by a particular set of experts based on their track record in dealing with similar situations.

Q. **What do you mean by "value"?**

A. We mean an upper limit (e.g., the most) to what you should pay that particular expert to conduct the study.

Q. **How will we get such a specific answer to whether we should buy a specific expert's services?**

A. By using the Expected Value of Sample Information.

Q. **Do I really want to ask what that is?**

A. Of course you do! You simply revise the decision tree we developed in the previous lesson and then, using Bayes' rule, update our original probabilities of the states-of-nature using information provided by the experts.

Q. **I never like it when you say "simply." Why do we have to revise the decision tree?**

A. When we drew the tree, we started by making lists of the decision alternatives and the states-of-nature. We then decided which came first and then which came next for each branch.

Q. **I remember, but what has changed?**

A. We now have more groups to consider, as shown in figure 3.12.

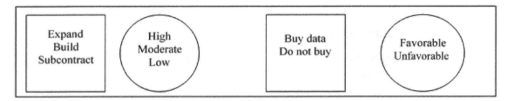

FIGURE 3.12 Decision alternative and state-of-nature groups.

The first two, of course, are the ones we had to begin with. The new decision is whether we should hire these experts (e.g., buy their data or results), and the new states-of- nature are the two possible survey results (we are assuming that these experts will tell us only whether the environment is favorable for expansion—in reality, there could be any number of outcomes).

Q. **So, as far as the decision tree is concerned, what comes first?**

A. The decision on whether to buy the market research data. We can't decide whether to expand, build, or subcontract unless we know if we will be getting more information. So, our new tree begins as shown in figure 3.13.

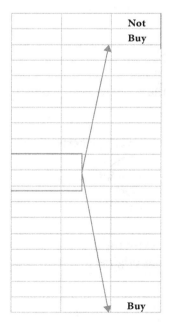

FIGURE 3.13 Start of the tree.

We now use the same technique we did before, following a depth-first approach by picking a branch and asking:

Q.   **What comes after the decision to not buy the market research data?**

A.   The tree we drew before, because we are right back where we started from. Copy the old tree, complete with payoffs and probabilities, and paste at the end of the "Not Buy" branch, in figure 3.14.

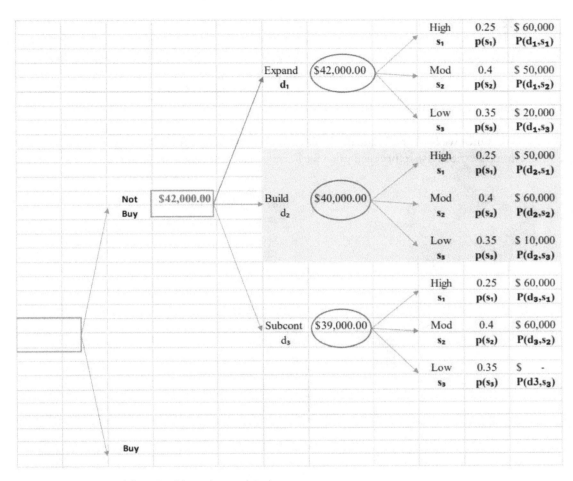

FIGURE 3.14 Tree with "Not Buy" branch completed.

Q.   **I remember! We move to the unfinished branch, "Buy," and ask, "What comes next?"**

A.   Exactly, and what comes next is reading the report to see what it says. Since this is all just planning, we have to list out each thing the report might say as a separate branch. For us, the possibilities are "Favorable," which we will represent by the symbol l_1, and "Unfavorable," which we will represent by the symbol l_2, and we will let $p(l_1)$ represent the probability that the experts will report l_1 (Favorable) and $p(l_2)$ represent the probability that the experts will report l_2 (Unfavorable).

Q.   **If I knew the probability that I would get a Favorable or an Unfavorable report, why would I need to use the experts to begin with?**

A.   We don't know those probabilities, yet, but we can figure them out by examining the track record of the expert you might hire. At this point, we are just agreeing on what we will call those probabilities. You will also see that the same calculations will give us new probabilities for the states-of-nature, which might change our decisions. Just bear with me as we include the findings of the experts in our decision tree as shown in Figure 3.15.

Q.   **This tree is going to get huge, isn't it?**

A.   Yes, so to save some room, in Figure 3.15 I have not put in the entire decision tree for the "Not Buy" branch. We know that our best (maximizes EMV) decision is to build and that our expected profit (EMV) associated with that decision is $42K. At the bottom of figure 3.15, I have shown the two possible outcomes (in this example) from the experts.

Q.   **Can't we just follow the more likely branch?**

A.   No. Once we have made the decision to pay for an expert (to follow the "Buy" branch on the tree), it makes no sense to proceed until we know what their recommendation is.

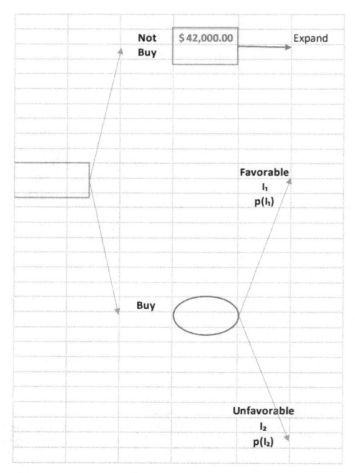

FIGURE 3.15   Including the results of expert findings in the decision tree.

Q.   **But how do I know what the results are if I haven't decided to hire the expert yet?**

A.   I am glad you picked up on that. This is all planning, to help us decide whether to hire the expert. That means we have to play "let's pretend" again, looking at each possibility as if it had happened.

Q.   **What do you mean?**

A.   Let's pretend we hired the expert and the report came back as "Favorable." We have to figure out how that affects our earlier decision. In the same way, if we pretend the report came in as "Unfavorable," we might expect that to have a very different affect.

Q.   **Wouldn't we just follow the expert's advice, and choose "Build" for a "Favorable" report and "Subcontract" for an "Unfavorable" report?**

A.   It's not that simple. You cannot accept an expert's report at face value and make a decision that you think reflects the expert's recommendation. No expert can provide you with perfect information. Furthermore, any expert's recommendation is just one more input to your decision process. Besides, if your recommendation ends up being wrong, telling your superiors that an expert told you to do it is probably not going to be of much help (and it might make them question whether they need you). We are going to do some calculations that will squeeze every bit of information out of the expert's report so we can properly incorporate that information into our decision process.

Q.   **What do you mean when you say "decision process"?**

A.   For this situation, the decision process is constructing and analyzing a decision tree for this problem.

Q.   **OK, then, how do we change the decision tree to incorporate the expert's report?**

A.   The structure of the tree doesn't change, just the data. Regardless of what the expert's recommendation is, you will still have make a choice between "Expand," "Build," or "Subcontract," and only after you make the choice will you find out whether your demand will be "High," "Moderate," or "Low." What we have to do is figure out how the information from the expert's report affects the probabilities of each state-of-nature branch.

Q.   **How do we do that?**

A.   Let me ask you: If we buy the information and it is favorable, should the probability for High Growth change?

Q.   **Yes. Wouldn't we expect the probability to go up?**

A.   Indeed! Initially we decided, on our own, that there was a 40% chance of high growth. Now, with a "Favorable" survey result, we have an outside confirmation of our guesses. This should make us more confident that high growth would occur. In the same way, we would expect moderate growth to be more likely, and low growth to be less likely. In effect, the expert's recommendation can serve to update our original subjective estimates of the probabilities of a state-of-nature occurring.

Q.   **How do we know what that update is?**

A.   In short, Bayes' rule, but to understand that, we have to introduce some notation from probability. In probability terms, we say the new probabilities of the states-of-nature are conditional on the expert's recommendation. To distinguish these conditional probabilities from our initial (subjective) probabilities of the states-of-nature, we use $p(s_i)$ for the initial (also called the *anterior* or *prior*) probability and we introduce the notation $p(s_i|I_1)$ to denote the conditional probability of a state-of-nature (s_i) occurring, given that the expert's recommendation is I_1. This is referred to as the *posterior* probability.

Q.   That's a whole lot of gibberish. Can you try to sort it out for me one more time?

A.   Sure. Let's complete the decision tree. I think that will help you to put things in perspective. In figure 3.16, I'll show how to complete the tree assuming the expert's recommendation is "Favorable" (l_1).

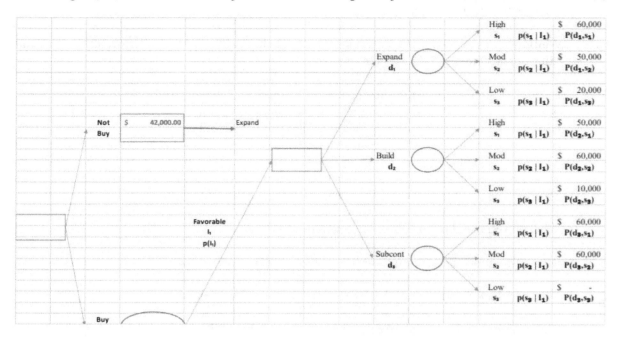

FIGURE 3.16 Partial decision tree including completion for l.

Q.   Where are all the probabilities for the states-of-nature?

A.   We don't know the numbers yet. What you should see is that where we had $p(s_i)$ in the next-to-last column for the "Not Buy" branch, we now have $p(s_i|l_1)$, showing that we expect the probabilities to change once we use the data from the expert.

Q.   But the tree doesn't look any different …

A.   It isn't. The decision we have to make is the same. We just have different data to use when making the decision, or will have, once we calculate them.

Q.   How and when will that be?

A.   We will calculate them in our next lesson. For now, take a look at figure 3.17, which shows the complete decision tree for this problem. Notice that the conditional probabilities following the "Unfavorable" report say $p(s_i|l_2)$ instead of $p(s_i|l_1)$.

Q.   That makes sense—an "Unfavorable" report would lower the probability of High demand, so the probability would be different. But how do we calculate all those different values?

A.   We use the track record of your expert in accurately predicting whether there have been favorable and unfavorable markets for expansion in situations similar to yours. We combine those accuracy probabilities with our initial probabilities to get the new values, but that is next time.

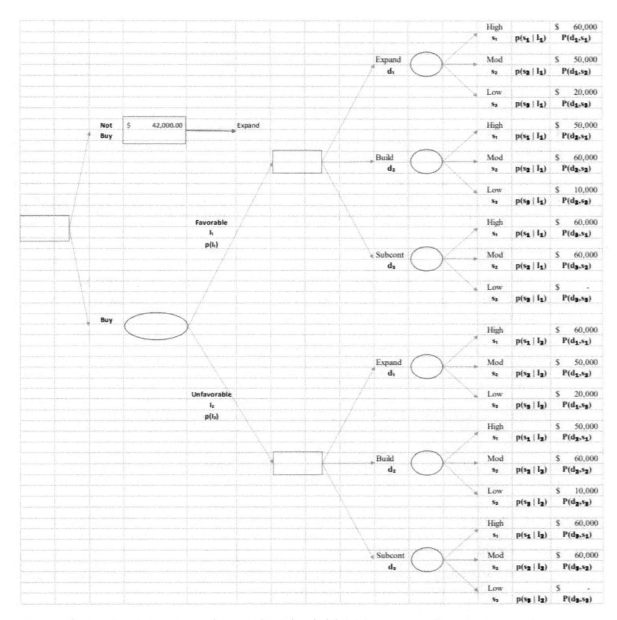

FIGURE 3.17 Complete decision tree without conditional probabilities.

ACTIVE LEARNING: LESSON 3.4

LESSON 3.5: **Bayes' Rule**

Introduction

Q.   **I thought we were going to learn to calculate new probabilities for our tree. Is that what Bayes' (whoever he was) rule does?**

A.   Yes. We know our own probability estimates for the states-of-nature. We can get information on how often an expert gave a forecast that later on matched what really happened, but what we need to know is how likely a state-of-nature is after getting an expert's opinion.

Q.   **Aren't those the same thing?**

A.   No, they are the reverse of each other. The one we can get says "the probability of the forecast given the state-of-nature" and the one we want says "the probability of the states-of-nature after getting an expert's forecast."

Q.   **Should I just ask the forecasting company how accurate they have been?**

A.   I would hardly consider them an unbiased source.

Q.   **I see what you mean. So, I should go to past customers of the company instead?**

A.   Exactly. Then, using Bayes' rule, we can use their responses to calculate what we need to know, and then use that to get a clearer picture of what a forecast from that specific forecasting company is actually worth.

Learning Outcomes

When you complete this session, you will be able to:

  Know how to update the original subjective state-of-nature probabilities P(S), referred to as anterior probabilities, when new/additional information becomes available

  Understand that new information is costly and not perfect; the quality of new information is determined by the provider's track record and given by P(I|S)

  Calculate the provider's track record, given survey data

Calculate P(S|I) given P(S) and P(I|S)

A Dialectic on Bayes' Rule

Q.   **In a previous lesson you said that we could use the "track record" of the experts (or company) to determine the value of the information they are trying to sell us. What does that mean?**

A.   Anyone can make a prediction, and a lot of people are going to try to sell you their predictions. You have to decide which one to use. About the only thing you can use is how often an expert has been right (and wrong) in the past. For our problem, if the expert has told people, in the past, that the market was going to be favorable, we can now look at what the markets actually did (since then) and see whether the expert was right (High or Moderate growth happened), or wrong (Low growth happened).

Q. **Who in the world would know something like that?**

A. No one, so you ask a lot of old clients what the expert predicted, and then ask how things turned out. Sometimes the expert would have predicted a "Favorable" market, and sometimes an "Unfavorable" market. Sometimes the market turned out to be High growth, and sometimes Moderate growth, and sometimes Low growth. Suppose we asked 20 past clients for this information and compiled the responses in Table 3.16.

TABLE 3.16 **Track Record Data**

	Favorable (I_1)	Unfavorable (I_2)
High (S_1)	14	6
Moderate (S_2)	9	6
Low (S_3)	4	16

Q. **And then you convert those numbers to probabilities?**

A. Yes, but be careful. We want to know how often the expert was right (and wrong) when each state-of-nature was occurring, so we have to work with the numbers one row at a time. That is what we mean by a "conditional" probability—we do our calculations based on some condition having happened.

Q. **What kind of condition?**

A. For our problem, the states-of-nature. Let's look just at the "High" state-of-nature. We talked to 20 former clients of the expert, 14 of them got a Favorable forecast, and 6 got an Unfavorable forecast.

Q. **How does that help us?**

A. We convert those into probabilities, 14/20 for Favorable and 6/20 for Unfavorable.

Q. **That would mean P(Favorable) = 0.7 and the P(Unfavorable) = 0.3, right?**

A. Your math is correct, but we got a problem. When we look at the Moderate, or Low states-of-nature, we are going to get different numbers for P(Favorable) and P(Unfavorable), and that is confusing. To help tell them apart, we write them as conditional probabilities, so P(Favorable GIVEN High Demand) and P(Unfavorable GIVEN High Demand).

Q. **Why do you keep putting GIVEN in all caps?**

A. Because it is important. I agree, though, that typing GIVEN over and over is inconvenient, so we use the symbol "|" to mean GIVEN. Now, if we use the label "I_1" to mean "Favorable" and the label

"l_2" to mean "Unfavorable" and go back to using Ss for the states-of-nature, we get the notation in table 3.17, which is a lot easier to write out.

TABLE 3.17   Track Record Data for the Market Research Company

		Favorable l_1	Unfavorable l_2	Sum
High	S_1	$P(l_1|s_1) = 0.7$	$P(l_2|s_1) = 0.3$	1.00
Moderate	S_2	$P(l_1|s_2) = 0.6$	$P(l_2|s_2) = 0.4$	1.00
Low	S_3	$P(l_1|s_3) = 0.2$	$P(l_2|s_3) = 0.8$	1.00

Q.   **Why do the conditional probabilities for one state-of-nature add up to one?**

A.   Think about it. There is a market out there; you are going to survey it and then make a guess about it. Whatever the market conditions really are (high, moderate, or low), you have only two choices: label it as favorable or label it as unfavorable. There is a 100% chance you will label it as one of those two. So, for each state-of-nature, the probability of one survey result (say, favorable) is simply the probability of the other survey result subtracted from one.

Q.   **Does this always work?**

A.   Sort of. This works any time you have only two survey results and you do need to be given one of the two probabilities. The general rule is that you need the accuracy probabilities for all but one survey result and you can calculate the remaining probability.

Q.   **Now that we have our conditional probabilities, what do we do with them?**

A.   Let's take a look at the decision tree we developed in the last lecture, shown again in figure 3.18 below.

Q.   **What do you expect me to see?**

A.   Tell me what is wrong with the conditional probabilities at the end of the "Favorable" branch.

Q.   **Isn't $p(s_1|l_1)$ backwards? Does it mean the same thing, or did you write it wrong?**

A.   It most definitely does not mean the same thing, and, unfortunately, I didn't write it wrong.

Q.   **Then what good are the probabilities we have? Did you make us learn that just for fun?**

A.   I don't gather data just for fun. There is a way of getting from $p(l_1|s_1)$ to a $p(s_1|l_1)$, called Bayes' rule.

Q.   **Who is Bayes?**

A.   Thomas Bayes was a nonconformist minister who lived in England during the early 1700s. Using the game of billiards as an example, he developed a method for using new information to recalculate probability estimates, now called Bayes' rule. This problem was considered one of the most difficult among those then facing mathematicians, and his solution was published in a paper entitled *Essay towards Solving a Problem in the Doctrine of Chances*. In this paper, he created the foundation for all of modern statistical inference, and he didn't even bother to publish it (a friend published the work after his death).

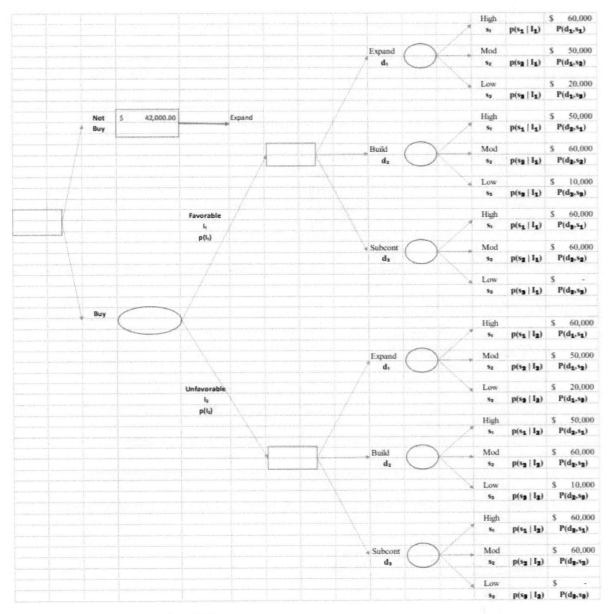

FIGURE 3.18 EVSI decision tree from EVSI I lesson.

Q.   **I always get worried when mathematicians get involved. How hard is this going to be?**

A.   I'll keep it as simple as I can, but you have to pay attention. Bayes' key finding (that we will use) comes from this statement: the conditional probability of *S* given *I* is equal to the joint probability of *S* and *I* divided by the probability of *I*, as here in symbols:

$$P(S|I) = P(S \cap I) / P(I) \qquad \text{(equation 1)}$$

Q.   **Do we know the joint probability of *S* and *I*, P(S ∩ I)?**

A.   No, but we do know (or, at least, mathematicians know)

$$P(S \cap I) = P(I|S) * P(S) \qquad \text{(equation 2)}$$

and we do know P(I|S) and P(S). Now can use equation 1 to calculate P(S|I).

Q.   **Maybe I'd follow this better with an example?**

A.   Always a good idea! Equations 1 and 2 prescribe how we can get from $p(I_1|s_i)$ to a $p(s_i|I_1)$ in three simple steps as shown in tables 3.18–3.20. Note that the table on the left gives the symbols and those on the right substitute the correct values for the symbols.

TABLE 3.18   Equation 1

		Favorable I_1	Unfavorable I_2	Sum		Favorable I_1	Unfavorable I_2	Sum	p(s)
High	S_1	$p(I_1|s_1)$	$p(I_2|s_1)$	1.00	S_1	0.7	0.3	1.00	0.25
Moderate	S_2	$p(I_1|s_2)$	$p(I_2|s_2)$	1.00	S_2	0.6	0.4	1.00	0.4
Low	S_3	$p(I_1|s_3)$	$p(I_2|s_3)$	1.00	S_3	0.2	0.8	1.00	0.35

TABLE 3.19   Equation 2

	I_1	I_2	Sum		I_1	I_2	Sum
S_1	$p(I_1 \cap s_1) = p(I_1|s_1)^* p(s_1)$	$p(I_2 \cap s_1) = p(I_2|s_1)^* p(s_1)$	$p(s_1)$	S_1	0.175	0.075	0.25
S_2	$p(I_1 \cap s_2) = p(I_1|s_2)^* p(s_2)$	$p(I_2 \cap s_2) = p(I_2|s_2)^* p(s_2)$	$p(s_2)$	S_2	0.24	0.16	0.40
S_3	$p(I_1 \cap s_3) = p(I_1|s_3)^* p(s_3)$	$p(I_2 \cap s_3) = p(I_2|s_3)^* p(s_3)$	$p(s_3)$	S_3	0.07	0.28	0.35
	$p(I_1)$ = sum of column	$p(I_2)$ = sum of column	100	p(I)	0.485	0.515	1.00

TABLE 3.20   Equation 3

	I_1	I_2		I_1	I_2
S_1	$p(s_1|I_1) = p(I_1 \cap s_1)|p(I_1)$	$p(s_1|I_2) = p(I_2 \cap s_1)|p(I_2)$	$p(s_1)$ S_1	0.361	0.1456
S_2	$p(s_2|I_1) = p(I_1 \cap s_2)|p(I_1)$	$p(s_2|I_2) = p(I_2 \cap s_2)|p(I_2)$	$p(s_2)$ S_2	0.495	0.3107
S_3	$p(s_3|I_1) = p(I_1 \cap s_3)|p(I_1)$	$p(s_3|I_2) = p(I_2 \cap s_3)|p(I_2)$	$p(s_3)$ S_3	0.144	0.5437
	1.00	1.00		1.000	1.000

Q.   **So, the numbers in table 3.20, on the right, are the ones we want?**

A.   Those are the conditional probabilities we were looking for to put in the tree, but we also picked up something else. In table 3.19, note that the p(I) are the sum of the probabilities in the column. We'll need that result as well.

Q.   **Now that we have our posterior probabilities, are we ready to analyze our decision tree?**

A.   You've got it. By the way, don't be shocked when you open a statistic book and see all the math they use to explain what looks relatively simple to us ...

ACTIVE LEARNING: LESSON 3.5

LESSON 3.6: **Expected Value of Sample Information 2**

Introduction

Q.   **Let's see, you told us we were going to learn how to decide whether an expert's information was worthwhile. In Lesson 3.3 you showed us how to set up a decision tree for calculating EVSI. Then you spent what seems like an eternity showing us how Mr. Bayes' rule could be used to update probabilities. What else could there possibly be?**

A.   Putting it all together. You've got all the pieces: you can identify decision alternatives and the random events that affect them, and you know what to do with additional information, so you are ready to define and carry out your optimal decision strategy.

Q.   **That would be nice, but what is a decision strategy?**

A.   Let's get started.

Learning Outcomes

When you complete this session, you will be able to:

- Understand the concept of sample information
  - Understand the meaning of P(S)
  - Understand the meaning of P(I)
  - Understand the meaning of P(I|S)
  - Understand the meaning of P(S|I)
- Populate a decision tree containing a decision to acquire additional information with appropriate data
- Roll back the above decision tree

- ○ Calculate the EMV at *each* chance node
- ○ Select the maximum EMV decision at each decision node
- ○ Calculate EVSI
- ▪ Calculate and discuss the efficiency of the sample information (EVSI/EVPI * 100)
- ▪ Understand the difference between a decision and a decision strategy

A Dialectic on the Expected Value of Sample Information

Q.   **OK, after we drew the tree for the Expand, Build, and Subcontract decision, we**

- ▪ **calculated EVPI to get a rough estimate of the value of new information,**
- ▪ **redrew the tree to include the decision of whether to buy the new information, and**
- ▪ **used Bayes' rule to calculate new probabilities based on the accuracy of our information.**

How do we use all that to actually decide whether to buy the extra information?

A.   First we will calculate the Expected Value of Sample Information (EVSI) and then we will figure out an overall decision strategy.

Q.   **How do we calculate the EVSI?**

A.   Using the new probabilities in the redrawn tree, calculate the expected values for each node in the tree in figure 3.19.

Q.   **Could you do a quick review of the terminology?**

A.   Sure. Starting on the left, following the Buy branch, we have the symbol I, which stands for any tool used to gather additional information. For this example:

$$I_1 = \text{the market research indicates a ``Favorable'' climate for growth}$$
$$I_2 = \text{the market research indicates an ``Unfavorable'' climate for growth}$$

Q.   **Why do we have probabilities on those?**

A.   Until we pay for the market research study, we won't know what the result is. From Bayes' rule, however, we have calculated how likely each result is, specifically:

$$P(I_1) = 0.485$$
$$P(I_2) = 0.515$$

Q.   **Then we have the same decision alternatives—Expand, Build, and Subcontract—but why did the probabilities change for the levels of demand?**

A.   Those also came from Bayes' rule. Remember, if the market research is favorable, we would expect the probability for High demand to increase, while the probability for Low demand would decrease. Table 3.21 shows all the probabilities for the states-of-nature.

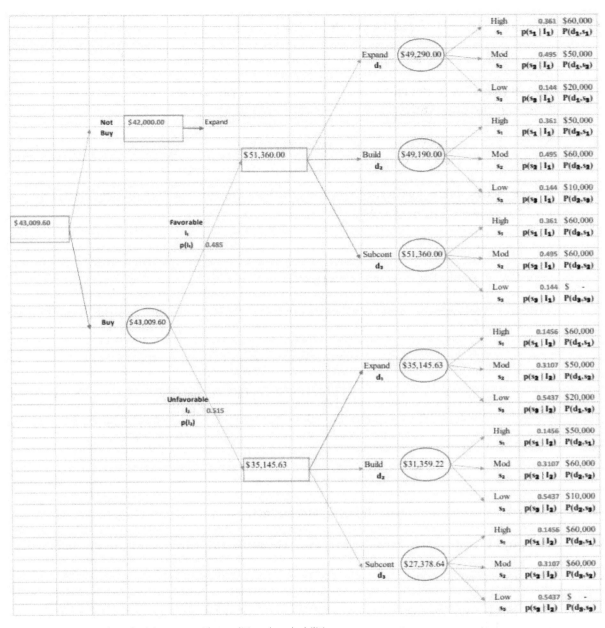

FIGURE 3.19 Complete decision tree with conditional probabilities.

TABLE 3.21 Probabilities

	Prior	Posterior Favorable Result	Posterior Unfavorable Result
High Demand	$P(S_1) = 0.25$	$P(S_1|I_1) = 0.361$	$P(S_1|I_2) = 0.1456$
Moderate Demand	$P(S_2) = 0.40$	$P(S_2|I_1) = 0.495$	$P(S_2|I_2) = 0.3107$
Low Demand	$P(S_3) = 0.35$	$P(S_3|I_1) = 0.144$	$P(S_3|I_2) = 0.5437$

Q. **And where did the numbers in the nodes (the circles and squares) come from?**

A. We used the probabilities to calculate EMVs. For each circle (ellipse), we multiplied the probabilities by the payoffs and added them up. For each square, we just picked the highest EMV.

Q.   What about those circles in the middle?

A.   Same thing. Multiply the probabilities by the EMVs in the squares.

Q.   And all that gives us the EMV in the left-most node of $43,009.60, which came from the "Buy" branch. Is that the EVSI?

A.   No. The EVSI will tell you the most you would pay for *this* market research, so you need to figure out how much better you did with the extra information.

Q.   I remember we did that with the EVPI. Well, the EMV for the "Not Buy" branch was $42,000, so the "Buy" branch is $1,009.60 higher. Is that the EVSI?

A.   Yes.

Q.   Why did you emphasize *"this"* market research?

A.   A different research company would have different reliability numbers, so they would have a different EVSI.

Q.   Does that mean we should buy the market research?

A.   Not necessarily. The tree will not make the decision for you; you have to decide what to do for yourself. To do that, you need to use the tree to map out your decision strategy.

Q.   What's a decision strategy?

A.   That's just a fancy phrase for listing out your major options and what you would do for each one.

Q.   You mean, whether to Expand, Build, or Subcontract?

A.   Before we can make that decision, we have to decide whether we will buy the market research or not.

Q.   What are our major options, then?

A.   Those that precede the Expand/Build/Subcontract decision. Looking at the tree, on the left, we see that one alternative is to "Not Buy" the information, so that is one option. If we follow the "Buy" branch, we see that it could either have a "Favorable" result or an "Unfavorable" result, so those are two more options.

Q.   What do we do next?

A.   Write out our options, like this:

Decision Strategy (Must Include All Statements)

If you do "Not Buy" the information, make the decision to expand with EMV = $42,000.

If you "Buy" the information, the EMV is $43,009.60:

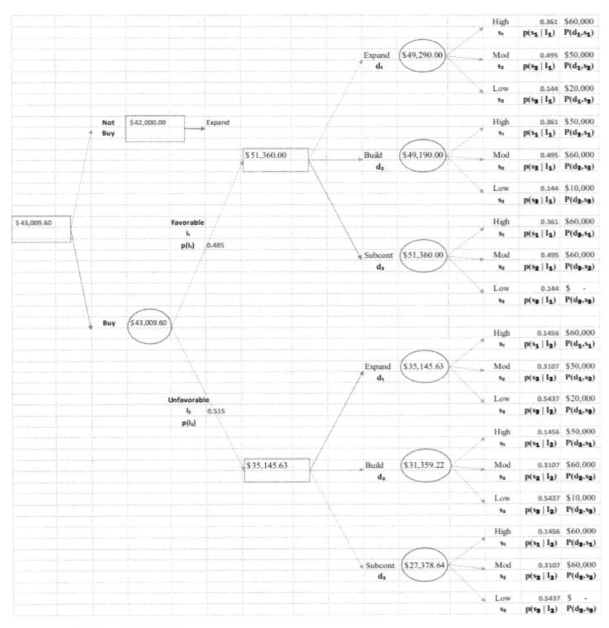

FIGURE 3.20 To Buy or Not to Buy?

a. If the market research company recommendation is "Favorable," make the decision to "Sub-contract" for an EMV of $51,360.

b. If the market research recommendation is "Unfavorable," make the decision to "Expand" for an EMV of $35,145.63.

Q. **Much better. An example always helps, but … the information that this particular company is able to provide is only worth around a thousand bucks. Maybe we should be looking for another provider?**

A. We have already learned something that will help to answer that question: the EVPI.

Q.   EVPI stands for the Expected Value of Perfect Information, and I'm not looking for perfect information, just something better. How will EVPI help?

A.   It will not help you to select another vendor, but it can help you decide whether to even look for someone with a better track record and to quickly evaluate them.

Q.   How does the EVPI do that?

A.   The original payoff table and state-of-nature probabilities, along with the EVPI calculations, are shown in table 3.22.

	High		Mod		Low	EMV	
Expand	$ 60,000.00	$		50,000.00	$ 20,000.00	$ 42,000.00	**max EMV**
Build	$ 50,000.00	$		60,000.00	$ 10,000.00	$ 40,000.00	
Subcont	$ 60,000.00	$		60,000.00	$ -	$ 39,000.00	
p(s)	$ 0.25	$		0.40	$ 0.35		

EVPI Calculations

State of Nature	Best Decision	Payoff	Probability
High	Expand, Build	60000	0.25
Mod	Build, Subcont	60000	0.4
Low	Expand	20000	0.35
Expected Value Under Certainty		EVC =	$ 46,000.00
	Expected Value of Perfect Information EVPI = EVC - max EMV =		$ 4,000.00

TABLE 3.22 EVPI Calculations.

As you can see, even perfect information can only improve your EMV by $4,000.

Q.   How do we use that?

A.   The ratio of EVSI divided by EVPI multiplied by 100 is commonly referred to as the "Efficiency of Sample Information" of the proposed vendor. In our case that would be (1009.6/4000) * 100 = 25.24%.

Q.   Obviously, the better the track record of an organization, the closer the "efficiency" of their information is going to be to 100%. However, since I am never going to get a 100%, what is reasonable?

A.   Pragmatically speaking, the highest you can get for the money you have. With EVPI, if someone opens by asking for $5,000, you know it is not worthwhile ($5,000 is greater than the EVPI of $4,000). You know that for $1,000 this market research firm can get information that is only 25.24% of as good as it can be, so it might be worth soliciting proposals from some other reputable companies and see if we can do better. After all, what do you have to lose except, of course, some time?

Q.   **How do we budget for buying information?**

A.   Unfortunately, you are going to have to pay when you get the results of the market research. That will be long before you realize any saving from making the best decision, so getting a budget to hire outside experts is always going to be a challenge ...

ACTIVE LEARNING: LESSON 3.6

LESSON 3.7: **Multistage Decision Problems**

Introduction

Q.   **Up to now, I sort of guessed whenever I had a decision to make. I have to admit, with the harder problems, I was never sure I was doing the right thing. Do all companies make decisions as systematically and logically as you showed us?**

A.   No, not all, and even those that do, not always.

Q.   **But it helps so much! We can figure out whether we have enough information to make a decision, or whether we need outside, expert advice. Why wouldn't they do that?**

A.   Pretty cool, isn't it? But not every decision (where to go to lunch?) really needs the full treatment, and sometimes there just isn't time. Still, for the major decisions, every company does its best. The advantages of this approach (we can decide whether we want to get additional information and we also can calculate how much that information is worth to us) make it a nice tool to have in our box. Decisions like this are made every day, and no other methodology that I know of helps as this one does.

Q.   **I can see how I can use this in my professional life—maybe even my personal life. Are there other business analytics tools you are going to teach me?**

A.   Of course, but we are not done with Decision Theory yet.

Q.   **What else could there possibly be?**

A.   Without getting too esoteric (best leave that to those who want to be professional business analysts), it can be useful to see how certain outcomes—meaning states-of-nature—can open the door to considering additional decisions.

Q.   **Huh?**

A.   You'll see. Let's get started.

Learning Outcomes

When you complete this session, you will be able to:

- Construct a decision tree that represents interrelated (sequential) decisions
- Roll back a multisequence decision tree
- Calculate the EMV, EVSI, decision strategy, and the efficiency of sample information for the multi-sequence decision tree

A Dialectic on Multistage Decision-Making

Q. **It is great we have a tool that handles two related decisions and that we can calculate the value of additional information.**

A. Well, the more we know, the more we realize how much we don't know.

Q. **You mean there is more to this decision theory stuff?**

A. Indeed. For example, I never limited our discussions to only two related decisions.

Q. **Now that you mention it, you never did. Incidentally, do companies really use this stuff?**

A. Go back and read the introduction to this book—I never teach anything that I have not personally used. That is why I left academia for a while, so that I could personally use these tools that I am teaching you and tell you about it. ☺

Q. **OK, so tell me how you used Decision Theory.**

A. Sure. When I was with DuPont's corporate consulting group, we worked with their marketing research group to develop a decision tree to help them decide whether they should market a new synthetic leather called Corfram. The decision tree for that situation covered all four walls of a large conference room (it was before the days of the PC).

Q. **Before the days of the PC! Wow, you really have been around for quite a while! Can you tell me more?**

A. Sorry, no. I no longer have the data and it is too long of a story. I can, however, give you an example that adds on to the EVSI problem. Consider the following scenario:

The company ships all of its production to an independent distributor who makes sure all orders are fulfilled. Although convenient, this is also costly. If the decision to build a new plant is made, and if the company actually experienced high growth in demand, then it wants to consider building its own distribution center. The final decision to build a distribution center will not be made until sometime in the future, but the size of the parcel and the site work for the new plant will have to accommodate a future distribution center.

    The company's supply chain group has done a feasibility study for the new distribution center and concluded that bringing the distribution function in-house has both risks and opportunities. Their optimistic estimate of the annual return is $20,000 with a probability of 0.3, their most likely estimate is $10,000 (0.5 probability), and their pessimistic estimate is a loss of $15,000.

Some members of the board are suspicious of the company's supply chain group estimates because they feel that internal estimates have vested interests associated with them. They would prefer that a third party conduct an independent study and recommended a firm that has a 90% track record of having their "Favorable" recommendation result in the optimistic results, a 60% chance of having their "Favorable" recommendation turn into the most likely results, and an 80% record of having the "Unfavorable" recommendation turn into pessimistic results.

Q. **I take it you literally mean we have to add this information to our previous decision tree?**

A. Exactly. Note that the decision to consider bringing in the distribution function in-house only applies if we decide to build *and* if we experience High growth, so we add the decision tree associated with this add-on only to those parts of the decision tree, as shown in figures 3.21 and 3.22, for the "Not Buy" and the "Buy" decisions, respectively. Also, while the probability stays with the "Build" branch, the payoff will be decided by the process in the boxes.

Q. **I now see what you mean by "add-on." What do we do with those little "Distribution Center Decision Process" boxes?**

A. We analyze the distribution center decision as a separate process and use the resulting max EMV as your payoffs in the original decision tree.

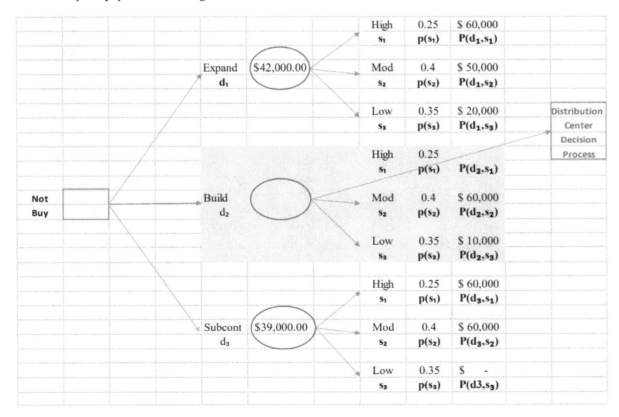

FIGURE 3.21 Adding the distribution center decision process to the "Not Buy" branch.

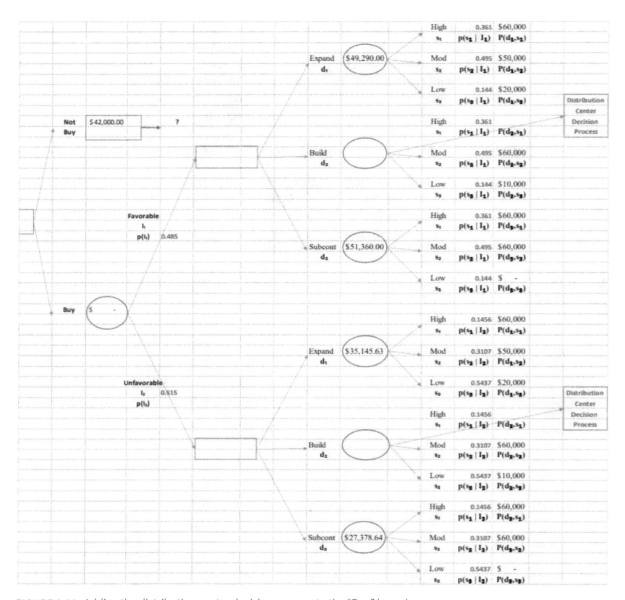

FIGURE 3.22 Adding the distribution center decision process to the "Buy" branch.

Q. Would the first node be deciding whether to buy the information from the firm the board wants to use?

A. Absolutely, and if we do use the firm, they might give a "Favorable" report or they might give an "Unfavorable" report.

Q. We also have the decision of whether to bring the distribution center in-house or not. Do we make that decision even if we don't use the firm?

A. Yes, you do, although in figure 3.23 we left that out, because this tree is getting really big.

Q.   **Then, in figure 3.23, where the square following "Do not use firm" just has the one arrow, there should really be two, like the squares following "Favorable" and "Unfavorable"?**

A.   That's right.

Q.   **And following the alternative to create the distribution center, the states-of-nature are Optimistic, Most Likely, and Pessimistic?**

A.   Yes.

Q.   **Where did all those numbers come from?**

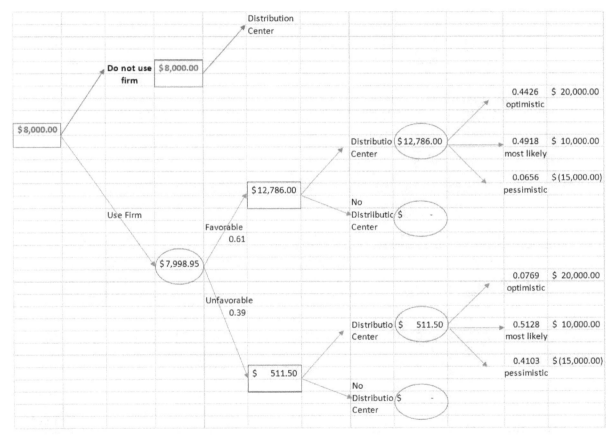

FIGURE 3.23 Distribution decision process for the "Do Not Use Firm" option.

A.   To avoid copying the tree over again, and since you know how to do the calculations, I put all the EMVs in place.

Q.   **How did you get 8,000 for the "Do Not Use" branch?**

A.   If we don't use the firm, then we have original (prior) probabilities of 0.30 for the Optimistic result of $20,000, 0.50 for the Most Likely result of $10,000, and 0.20 for the pessimistic result of –$15,000. The EMV for that is:

$$\text{EMV}_{\text{Do Not Use}} = 0.3*20,000 + 0.5*10,000 - 0.2*15,000 = 8,000$$

Q. **Got it! And if we use the firm's recommendation, that will change the probabilities for getting an optimistic, most likely, or pessimistic outcome, right?**

A. Exactly.

Q. **This is where we use Bayes' rule, setting up tables 3.23–3.25, as you did. Does this look right?**

TABLE 3.23 Equation 1

		Favorable I_1	Unfavorable I_2	Sum		Favorable I_1	Unfavorable I_2	Sum	p(s)
Optimistic	S_1	$p(I_1|s_1)$	$p(I_2|s_1)$	1.00	S_1	0.9	0.1	1.00	0.3
Most likely	S_2	$p(I_1|s_2)$	$p(I_2|s_2)$	1.00	S_2	0.6	0.4	1.00	0.5
Pessimistic	S_3	$p(I_1|s_3)$	$p(I_2|s_3)$	1.00	S_3	0.2	0.8	1.00	0.2

TABLE 3.24 Equation 2

	I_1	I_2	Sum		I_1	I_2	Sum
S_1	$p(I_1 \cap s_1) = p(I_1|s_1)^* \, p(s_1)$	$p(I_2 \cap s_1) = p(I_2|s_1)^* \, p(s_1)$	$p(s_1)$	S_1	0.27	0.03	0.30
S_2	$p(I_1 \cap s_2) = p(I_1|s_2)^* \, p(s_2)$	$p(I_2 \cap s_2) = p(I_2|s_2)^* \, p(s_2)$	$p(s_2)$	S_2	0.3	0.2	0.50
S_3	$p(I_1 \cap s_3) = p(I_1|s_3)^* \, p(s_3)$	$p(I_2 \cap s_3) = p(I_2|s_3)^* \, p(s_3)$	$p(s_3)$	S_3	0.04	0.16	0.20
	$p(I_1)$ = sum of column	**$p(I_2)$ = sum of column**	**100**	**p(I)**	**0.61**	**0.39**	**1.00**

TABLE 3.25 Equation 3

	I_1	I_2			I_1	I_2
S_1	$p(s_1|I_1) = p(I_1 \cap s_1)|p(I_1)$	$p(s_1|I_2) = p(I_2 \cap s_1)|p(I_2)$	$p(s_1)$	S_1	0.4426	0.0769
S_2	$p(s_2|I_1) = p(I_1 \cap s_2)|p(I_1)$	$p(s_2|I_2) = p(I_2 \cap s_2)|p(I_2)$	$p(s_2)$	S_2	0.4918	0.5128
S_3	$p(s_3|I_1) = p(I_1 \cap s_3)|p(I_1)$	$p(s_3|I_2) = p(I_2 \cap s_3)|p(I_2)$	$p(s_3)$	S_3	0.0656	0.4103
	1.00	1.00			**1.000**	**1.000**

A. That looks pretty good to me. Now let's go ahead and figure out what the tree is telling us.

Q. **Am I reading that right, we aren't using the outside information?**

A. The firm that the board wants to use to check up on the company's supply chain group's finding looks pretty good, but as it turns out they really add little value to what the supply chain group found, so there is no real reason to use them.

Q.   **Will the board accept that?**

A.   Good point—not all decisions are made on a strictly mathematical basis. Political realities may dictate we hire the experts, but for now, let's stay clear of political considerations and simply say that we are not going to use the firm and that the decision to bring the distribution function in-house will bring in an additional $8,000 in revenue.

Q.   **Not bad. So, we can recommend that they be brought in?**

A.   How many times have I told you to slow down? Don't forget that what we have done here is just a piece of the puzzle and that now we must integrate it with the original decision tree.

Q.   **Right! Sorry. OK, then, how does this play out with the rest of the tree?**

A.   First, we add the decision to build the Distribution Center to the "Not Buy" branch of figure 3.21, giving us figure 3.24:

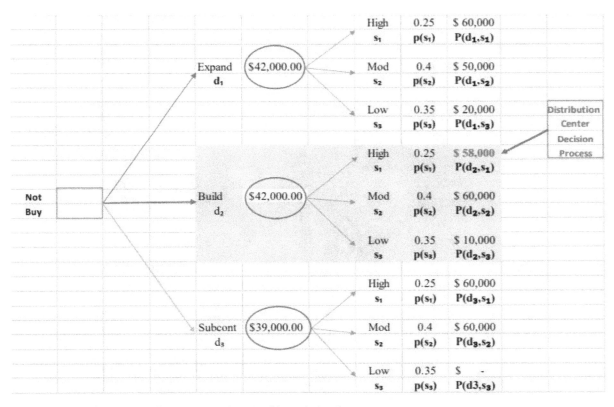

FIGURE 3.24 Multisequence decision tree—"Not Buy" branch details.

Q.   **What does that mean that "Expand" and "Build" have the same EMV?**

A.   With the additional income from bringing the distribution function in-house if the best decision is not to use the market research firm, then we can take our pick, from an EMV point of view, of whether we expand our current site or build an entirely new facility. Obviously, that may have lots of implications one way or the other.

Q.   OK. I did the "Buy" branch calculations, changing figure 3.22 to the numbers shown in figure 3.25. How do they look?

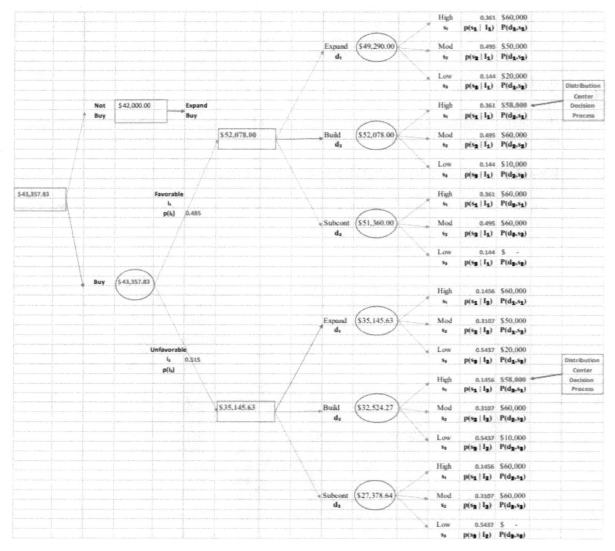

FIGURE 3.25 Multisequence decision tree—"Buy" branch details.

A.   Great job! Now we can see that bringing the distribution function in-house has changed things somewhat.

Q.   Why did the EVSI go up from $1,009.6 to $1,357.83?

A.   Buying the additional information has more value in our decision-making process now that we have the more complex problem to deal with.

Q.   When we buy the information, it changes our decisions, doesn't it?

A.   Yes, it does, which makes it even more valuable. If the information we are buying from the market research firm is "Unfavorable," then we can forget about bringing in the distribution function and just go ahead and expand our current facility. On the other hand, if the information that we are buying from the market research firm is "Favorable," then our decision should be "Build," leaving the door open to bringing in-house the distribution function.

Q.   **Holy cow! This stuff is really powerful, isn't it?**

A.   Absolutely. As I have shown you, we can string any number of consecutive interrelated decisions into this type of analysis.

Q.   **What if we can't get all the data?**

A.   One of the major benefits of a methodology such as this is that going through this type of analysis requires that you organize your facts and bring them together in some logical fashion. Going through the exercise of just building the decision tree does that for you.

Q.   **But if we do have all the data, then the tree also gives us our decision, right?**

A.   Rolling the tree back eventually guides you to a decision strategy, but always keep in mind that you are the decision maker and that you should never make a decision just because that is what the roll back of the decision tree showed as maximizing EMV. You should always make sure that you can explain the decision that you recommend, which, of course, requires that you understand the data, the assumptions, and the decision-making process.

ACTIVE LEARNING: LESSON 3.7

Comprehensive Problems are available for this chapter via Active Learning

Simulation

OVERVIEW

Q. **What is simulation?**

A. It is the art and science of constructing and using something that acts like something else, usually much more complex and/or expensive.

Q. **Why would I simulate something if I have the real thing?**

A. Because you might create havoc if you change the real thing and you don't know what you are doing.

Q. **Are you talking about something like the flight simulators used to train pilots?**

A. Exactly. It's a lot cheaper to crash a simulator than a real plane.

Q. **I can see that. But how do I relate flight simulators to business analytics?**

A. You don't. The point is that if you can get a computer to act like something as complex as an airplane, then you can get a computer to act like just about anything else. Virtually every business environment can be simulated, from fast food restaurants to hospital emergency rooms to automotive assembly lines.

Q. **Why would we ever want to simulate any of those?**

A. So that we can figure out how to make them run better. For example, did you realize that the double window drive-thrus prevalent in many fast-food restaurants came about only after simulation showed that they significantly improved customer speed of service during the peak periods?

Q. **I sure didn't. OK, where do we start?**

A. We'll talk about general simulation concepts before we get into the specifics of how to build a simulation model.

A Dialectic on General Simulation Concepts

Q.   **What's so great about simulation?**

A.   Simulation is an entirely different way of solving problems. As the great baseball player and pop philosopher Yogi Berra once said: "It's amazing what you can observe if you just look." In simulation, we try to recreate the real world as a computer representation, or model.

Q.   **Are all simulations done on computers?**

A.   Although some simulations could be done without a computer, such instances are rare.

Q.   **Why?**

A.   Simulation models are constructed so that "what-if" analyses can be easily conducted. Those analyses go faster (and more accurately) when a computer does the work.

Q.   **What is a "what-if" analysis?**

A.   A what-if analysis is the equivalent of making a physical change in the real world and then observing what happens.

Q.   **You mean, like an experiment?**

A.   Exactly like an experiment. Think of a simulation model as the equivalent of a test tube. As scientists conduct experiments in test tubes, a "simulationist" conducts experiments using a simulation model. A test tube gives the scientist a controlled setting in which to make changes. A simulation, as a representation of the real world, does the same thing.

Q.   **Can you give me some examples of what you are talking about?**

A.   Sure, let me start with a couple of examples of physical simulators. Aerospace engineers use wind tunnels to test the aerodynamic characteristics of new aircraft. Most real aircraft are too large to fit into a wind tunnel, so scientists make scale models and then the tunnel blows air over the scale model to simulate the aircraft flying. From measurements taken, inferences are made on how a real aircraft would behave under certain wind conditions. If you happen to be a NASCAR fan, you might know that virtually all teams make heavy use of wind tunnels to improve the aerodynamic characteristics of their vehicles. I have also seen models of submarines being tested in wind tunnels.

Q.   **You mean submarines that fly?**

A.   No, but the only difference between air and water is density, so scientists can extrapolate from a submarine's behavior in a wind tunnel to its behavior when it is in water.

Q.   **Flying submarines. What's next?**

A.   Well, another type of physical simulator has a "man-in-the-loop," meaning that there is a person driving or flying the simulator. These are almost always done on a computer, but the simulator is a physical box, like the game consoles many of you are semi-addicted to.

Q. OK, so I've been using simulators most of my life. Does that mean my boss is going to let me play games at work?

A. I doubt it. For the business world, we use a third type of simulator, one where, after it is designed, there is no human interacting with the simulation itself.

Q. Then how does it accomplish anything?

A. A simulation model can replicate the behavior of just about any business. Once we have a copy of how our business works, we can try new ideas for our business without actually having to take the time or spend the money to implement these ideas in the real world.

Q. But how does that help?

A. We can observe what the impact of those new ideas is going to be on our profits, cash flows, or almost any other measure of performance. And, we can see that simulated impact as far into the future as we want.

Q. Are you saying we run a computer simulation for years?

A. Not at all. A simulation can provide years of simulated results in the time it takes a computer to process the code representing the simulation model—usually only a few minutes.

Q. That sounds almost like a time machine ...

A. Exactly. A simulation model compresses time because simulation models operate according to a simulated clock. You can make the simulated clock move as fast as you can perform the associated calculations.

Q. Looking into the future sounds great, but how do you convince your boss that you have a computer that can behave like his business?

A. That gets us into an important subset of the field of simulation (as well as of software engineering) called Verification and Validation (V&V). *Verification and Validation*

Q. Cute. How long did it take to come up with two words beginning with *V*?

A. I have no idea; they aren't my words.

Q. What is "verification"?   *Verification =*

A. Verification refers to making sure that the model does what you intended it to do.

Q. Why wouldn't the simulation do what you wanted it to do?

A. You've probably heard of the term *debugging* for computer software, where a computer programmer makes sure there are no mistakes in the software that was written. If you have ever entered the wrong formula into Excel, then you know about this. Verification is the simulation term for debugging the simulation you have written.

Q.   **Then what is "validation"?**

A.   This is trickier. Validation refers to making sure that the simulation model behaves as it was intended to behave. Even after your simulation is fully verified, there is still the question of whether it is accurately mimicking the real world. That may sound the same as verification to you, but it isn't.

Q.   **How are verification and validation different?**

A.   For verification, you are looking for accidental mistakes—typos, if you will. For validation, you are looking for deliberate mistakes.

Q.   **Why would I deliberately make a mistake?**

A.   You wouldn't deliberately make a mistake, but you would deliberately type in something that you thought was right but wasn't. For example, you might tell a simulation that a machine can process 100 units an hour, which is true, but if you didn't tell the simulation that the machine has to be shut down for five minutes each hour for maintenance, then the simulation would be doing exactly what you told it to do, but the results would be wrong.

Q.   **How do you catch verification mistakes?**

A.   Compare your simulated results to the real world you are trying to simulate. If the results don't look the same, you probably have a validity error.

Q.   **Once you have a verified model, does that convince your boss the simulation works?**

A.   It might, but not always. You asked about executives accepting a simulation result. It might interest you that Burger King was the pioneer in the use of simulation in the restaurant business, going back to the late 1970s. To gain executive acceptance for the use of simulation, Burger King Operations Researchers built an actual restaurant in one of the corporate warehouses and then subjected various customer loads on the restaurant and observed key measures such as the length of the waiting lines, the average time a customer would wait in the system, and so on. They then ran their computer model subject to the same simulated customer loads and compared the results of the computer model to those obtained in the real restaurant. The results were so similar that it eliminated any doubt by executives (who watched the restaurant operating in the warehouse) as to the validity of the simulation model. Since that time, simulation models have accounted for hundreds of millions of dollars in savings for the corporation (and, of course, its franchisees). That was an extreme solution, but it worked.

Q.   **OK, I'm convinced. Just out of curiosity, how do you become a simulation expert?**

A.   There are a number of academic programs that offer master's and doctoral degrees in Modeling and Simulation. The two pioneering institutions offering simulation as a field of study are the University of Central Florida and Old Dominion University. However, because simulation is arguably the most prevalent business analytics application in both industry and the military, any aspiring executive in those areas should have a basic understanding of its concepts and that is what we try to accomplish in the rest of this chapter.

Q.   **If they have people with master's and PhDs in simulation, why do we have to bother to learn about it?**

A.   Not all simulation model development requires such expertise. There are many situations where you might be able to develop a simulation model in Excel, on your own.

Q.   **What if the situation is beyond our skills?**

A.   When the big guns have to be called in, the resulting effort usually turns into a multidisciplinary project that combines simulationists with team members who have appropriate and relevant subject matter expertise (SMEs). The simulationist provides the technical knowledge of how to build a simulation and the SME provides the knowledge specific to your company. They work together to develop a model that truly reflects the real world. You may very well be called upon as an SME in some future model building effort, and to the extent that you understand simulation, your value to the team is enhanced.

Q.   **You say that developing a simulation can turn into a major project. What is typically involved in such a project?**

A.   The stages of simulation model development usually include (but not necessarily in this order): Model Development, Data Collection, Validation and Verification, Design of the Simulation Experiment, and Optimization.

Q.   **How can you develop a model before you collect data?**

A.   Model development and data collection usual overlap. As you develop a rough model, that tells you what data you need, and as you gather data, that tells you how the model has to adapt to fit the data available.

Q.   **That doesn't sound easy …**

A.   It's not. Data collection is often the most time-consuming part of a simulation study because it requires that we have enough and the right kind of data to statistically describe all the random processes that will be included in the model.

Q.   **Why would we want a random process in our simulation?**

A.   The real world isn't the same from moment to moment. A process that takes 30 seconds one time might take 24 seconds the next time and 32 seconds the time after that. To get our simulations to include that same kind of variation, we use randomized processes, calculations that give different results each time, based on random numbers and the data we collected. A simulation model that attempts to re-create random processes observed in the real world is referred to as a "Monte Carlo" simulation (more on that in another lesson).

Q.   **If our simulation is generating random results, how does that tell us anything?**

A.   To draw inferences about the true results of a simulation, we must use statistics to describe the results. Thus, being able to define or control the margin of error when we use a simulation model is critical. Doing so is what we refer to as "designing the simulation experiment."

Q.   OK, so, we have simulation and statistics. What is "optimization"?

A.   A simulation is almost always used to compare various alternatives (the what-ifs). Selecting the best alternative is what we refer to as the optimization step of a simulation study.

Q.   **Then our team needs at least a simulationist, a statistician, and an SME (me). Simulation is definitely a multidisciplinary project. Is all this work going to be worth it?**

A.   Most definitely. Simulation can give you information that you cannot get any other way.

Q.   **Simulation sounds very hard. Are there any short cuts?**

A.   It is very hard, and every simulation is different, but there are similarities between similar applications. For example, there are special-purpose simulation languages you could use if you wanted to simulate a manufacturing process. Such a language has many short cuts and allows for the representation of complex elements common to manufacturing with just one or a few statements.

Q.   **What if we aren't in manufacturing? What about banking or other service operations, or military, or government, or ...?**

A.   There are special-purpose simulation languages for a wide variety of applications, and each will have their limitations.

Q.   **What if there isn't a language that suits our company?**

A.   Then you have to use a general language like Virtual Basic or C++. That will give you the most flexibility but at the expense of the effort it will require to build the model.

Q.   **Do all these languages do the same thing?**

A.   While each simulation is unique in details, almost all business simulations try to replicate the unpredictability of the real world. To do that, we need to learn about Monte Carlo simulations, which is what we usually mean when we say "simulation."

LESSON 4.1: Discrete Process Generators

Introduction

Q.   **I thought we were going to talk about simulation?**

A.   Monte Carlo simulation to be more precise. I take it that you are wondering about the title of this lesson. If that is the case, then let me clarify: the term *process generator* denotes a procedure to replicate random events we have observed in the real world.

Q.   **OK, but what about the qualifier "discrete?"**

A.   When you roll a die, you can only have six outcomes: a one, two, et cetera. Rolling a die is referred to as a discrete process because you can count the number of possible outcomes. On the other hand, if we wanted to agree to meet for lunch, we could have chosen any time and you would have arrived anytime close to the agreed time, depending on traffic conditions you might have encountered. In this case, your arrival time is considered a continuous process.

Q.   **I get it! You are going to teach us how to re-create something with just a few results, like the roll of a die, in a simulation, right?**

A.   You got it.

Learning Outcomes

When you complete this session, you will be able to:

- Construct a cumulative probability distribution function (cdf)
- Define and generate a random number using the Excel function rand()
- Associate a range of random numbers with a cdf
- Use Excel's VLOOKUP function to generate random events

A Dialectic on Discrete Random Processes

Q.   **OK. I am ready to get my hands dirty. How do I simulate something?**

A.   The best place to start is with the heart of any Monte Carlo simulation—modeling a random process. We will start by showing you how to simulate a discrete random process that is defined by a probability distribution.

Q.   **What do you mean by "discrete?"**

A.   A discrete random variable is one that has countable outcomes, such as the number of cars arriving at a drive-thru or the number of customers rating the service they received.

Q.   **Aren't all things countable?**

A.   No. For example, consider how long it takes to get your order at a restaurant. The exact time can be any number (within limits, of course). You cannot say it will take either 60 seconds or 61 seconds since in reality it could take 60.15 seconds and so on.

Q.   **Sounds like splitting hairs to me. Why make a big deal out of it?**

A.   Because the way we go about replicating (generating) one is totally different than the other. We replicate discrete random processes with tables, while we use formulas for continuous random processes.

Q.   **Why do you keep saying "random" process?**

A.   We will use random numbers to copy the variations that naturally happen in the real world.

Q.   **Maybe a specific example would help?**

A.   Great idea. We'll deal with discrete random processes now and with continuous random processes in another lesson.

Q.   **One step at a time is good. What is this "process" you keep talking about?**

A.   The process is just the steps we go through to simulate any discrete random generator.

Q.   **And a discrete random process is anything where we can count the outcomes, even something simple like tossing a coin?**

A.   Excellent example. Here we go:

Step 1: List all possible outcomes of the random process.

Q.   **That's easy—there are only two possible outcomes, Heads and Tails, right?**

A.   That's right. We'll refer to them as "H" for Heads and "T" for Tails. Next:

Step 2: Associate a probability with each outcome.

Q.   **Isn't it a 50/50 chance of heads or tails?**

A.   Correct, and we write that as P(H)=0.5 and P(T)=0.5.

Step 3: Define the cumulative probability for each outcome.

Q.   **I sort of remember cumulative probability distributions exist, but how do I define one?**

A.   That's just a fancy way of saying "list all the outcomes and their probabilities in a table and add up the probabilities as you go," like this:

TABLE 4.1 Cumulative Probabilities

Outcome	Probability	Cum Probability
H	0.5	0.5
T	0.5	1

Q.   **I can do that. What's next?**

A.   Step 4: Associate a random number range with each cumulative probability.

Q.   **You mentioned random numbers before, but what is a random number?**

A.   A random number really has no meaning if you think of it as a single number. Instead, a random number is always a member of a sequence of other random numbers that comes from a random number generator (RNG). The best definition is that a random number is a value between 0 and 1 (just like a probability) where you can't tell, based on the numbers you have, what number comes next.

Q. **This isn't helping. How do you know a sequence of numbers has random numbers in it?**

A. I'm not trying to be difficult, it's just that it is hard to define random numbers. Let me use an example. Look at the following sequences of numbers:

A: 1, 1, 1, 1, 1
B: 1, 2, 3, 4, 5
C: 7, 9, 5, 6, 1

Q. **A and B aren't random, but C is, right?**

A. Wrong. All three are potentially random. The question isn't whether you see a pattern in the numbers but whether you can, based on the numbers you have, predict what number comes next.

Q. **I can do that. For A, the next number would be a 1 and for B the next number would be a 6, so how can those numbers be random?**

A. You are assuming that you know the next numbers. If you are using an RNG, then the next number for A could be a 9 and the next number for B might be a 2.

Q. **How could an RNG give you five 1s in a row, or five numbers counting up?**

A. If an RNG couldn't give you five 1s in a row or five numbers counting up, then once you get the first 1, you would know something about the next number—it couldn't be a 1 or a 2. That breaks the rule that you can't predict what number comes next. Another way to put it is that each number has the same probability of coming next.

Q. **OK, well, where do we get an RNG?**

A. Back in the bad old days, we used graduate students. A graduate student would sit down with a bag containing 10 balls numbered 0 to 9. The student reaches into the bag without looking, pulls out one ball, writes down the number, puts the ball back into the bag, shakes up the bag, and pulls out another ball. A professor would have his or her graduate student repeat this until there were enough random numbers.

Q. **You're not going to ask us to do that, are you?**

A. No, now we have better ways. If you have ever watched a lottery drawing with those ping pong balls blowing around in a machine until one pops out, then you have seen an RNG in action. A simulation, though, needs millions of random numbers, so that is still too slow.

Q. **How can you generate millions of random numbers?**

A. We use computers, but there is a problem.

Q. **What problem?**

A. Computers use sophisticated algorithms to give you a string of numbers that look random, but eventually those algorithms start repeating themselves. That means they are not really random, just pseudo-random.

Q.   **What does "pseudo-random" mean?**

A.   It means that the set of numbers from the computer's RNG can pass a set of tests (which you will never need to do) that tell us the numbers are effectively, or sufficiently, random for us to use in a simulation, but since they will eventually repeat, they are not truly random.

Q.   **How many numbers can these pseudo-RNGs generate?**

A.   Billions, more than enough for us to use. Mathematicians worry about whether pseudo-random numbers are good enough (that is why they are so strange), but, as a businessperson, you simply use the best RNG you can get.

Q.   **Let's get back to this discrete random process. You said we had to "associate a random number range to each cumulative probability." How do we do that?**

A.   Random numbers have practical meaning only when they are associated with an outcome. In a lottery, a random draw only has meaning when it is associated with a lottery ticket. For our example of tossing a coin, a random number only has meaning if we can associate it with an outcome, H or T, of the flip of a coin.

Q.   **You mean I have to associate a random number either with Heads or Tails?**

A.   Yes, but every random number must be associated with one of those two outcomes, and you never associate a single random number with more than one outcome.

Q.   **Again, please?**

A.   You cannot have the same random number associated with both an H and a T. Whatever random number comes up, it must tell you either H or T was the outcome, but never both.

Q.   **So, how do you do that?**

A.   By recognizing that both a random number and a cumulative probability have values that range between zero and one. Since the cumulative probability of H is 0.5, we can associate all random numbers that have a value strictly less than 0.5 with the outcome of H. We then let all random numbers that have a value of 0.5 or greater (up to, but not including 1.0) be associated with outcome of T. Returning to our table, and Step 4, we show the lowest random number for each outcome.

TABLE 4.2   Relating Outcomes, Probabilities, and Random Numbers

Outcome	Probability	Cum Probability	Lower Random Number Range
H	0.5	0.5	0
T	0.5	1	0.5

Q.   **So, what do we do with the table now?**

A.   Start generating random numbers and using table 4.2 to associate the random numbers with the outcomes.

Q.   **What RNG are we going to use?**

A.   We can use Excel and the function =RAND(). Type that function into any cell and hit "Enter." In my case, I got 0.876143988.

Q.   **I didn't get that. What did I do wrong?**

A.   Nothing. You will get a different number because, well, you asked for a random number. The fact that a number showed up, instead of one of those annoying #ERROR messages, means you did it right.

Q.   **What do we do with the random number?**

A.   Using my random value and going to the rightmost column in table 4.2, we see that that 0.876 (I rounded) is in the second random number range (greater than 0.5). I can then look at the leftmost column and see that the corresponding outcome is T. Thus, that random number simulates one flip of the coin with the outcome that is turned up Tails.

Q.   **And we do that over and over again?**

A.   Only if you want to. A better way is to use Excel and rearrange table 4.2 so we can use the =VLOOKUP function to simulate the coin flips for us, as you can see in table 4.3.

TABLE 4.3   VLOOKUP Table

	A	B
1	Lower random number range	outcome
2	0	H
3	0.5	T

Q.   **How does the =VLOOKUP function work?**

A.   You must tell it three things: the value to look up, the table to look in, and which column from the table you want it to give you.

Q.   **What value do we want it to look up?**

A.   For us, that's easy—a random number. You can enter the =RAND function directly, like this:

$$=VLOOKUP(RAND(), ...$$

or, you could enter =RAND into some cell on the spreadsheet, let's say D10, and use a cell reference, like this:

$$=VLOOKUP(D10, ...$$

Q.   I assume the second would be A2:B3, for table 4.3, above?

A.   Very good! Since the outcome we are looking for, H or T, is in the second column of the table, our complete function would look like this:

$$=VLOOKUP(D10,\$A\$2:\$B\$3,2).$$

Q.   **Neat! Can you show me how to use it simulating coin flips?**

A.   Yes. When we develop a simulation, it is always good practice to separate data from any computations. In this case, our data is the VLOOKUP table, which we'll refer to as our random process generator, or process generator in short.

Q.   **So, we have done that. What is next?**

A.   We will develop the simulation table, which will keep track of what happens every time we flip a coin. Table 4.4 shows us the result of simulating the flip of a coin five times. Notice that we start the simulation table by listing the flips in order. The next column shows the results from using the =RAND() function, and the third column shows the results from using the VLOOKUP function. Your results will be different because RAND() will give you different random numbers than it gave me.

Q.   **Are the same steps used to generate any process?**

A.   Any process with discrete random variables. Let's summarize the steps again:

Step 1: List all possible outcomes of the random process.

Step 2: Associate a probability with each outcome.

Step 3: Define the cumulative probability for each outcome.

Step 4: Associate a random number range with each cumulative probability; this is the lower limit for the random numbers.

TABLE 4.4   Results of Simulating 5 Flips of a Coin

	A	B	C	D	E
1	**PROCESS GENERATOR**				
2					
3	Lower random number range	outcome			
4	0	H			
5	0.5	T			
6					
7	**SIMULATION TABLE**				
8					**Simulated**
9			**Coin Flip**	**RN**	**Outcome**
10			1	0.602788	T
11			2	0.280740	H
12			3	0.147070	H
13			4	0.319708	H
14			5	0.606325	T

Step 5: Rearrange for the VLOOKUP table by listing the last column of the table first (the lower limits) followed by the column containing the outcome associated value of the random variable.

Step 6: Repeat above for all other random processes associated with the problem.

Step 7: Set up for all continuous random processes (if any) as shown in the next lesson.

Step 8: Prepare the simulation table and simulate to your heart's content.

Q.   **Do we do the same thing for continuous random variables?**

A.   Well, not exactly. The above steps work for discrete distributions. When we are dealing with a continuous distribution, then we must use the inverse of the distribution instead of the =VLOOKUP function.

Q.   **I am not sure what you are talking about. Can you give us an example?**

A.   Yes, in the next lesson.

LESSON 4.2: **Continuous Process Generators**

Introduction

Q.   **How are continuous process generators different from discrete ones?**

A.   A lot of things we want to simulate have an infinite number of possible outcomes. For those situations, we need a probability generator that can give us that many outputs.

Q.   **Are any things the same?**

A.   Yes, we will use random numbers, we will match random numbers to outputs, and we will use a function in Excel to match the random numbers to the outcomes.

Q.   **Does that mean there is one simple way to handle them all?**

A.   Before we get lost in the woods, let's talk a little bit about the forest. There are about as many different random processes as there are trees in the forest, and they can be as different as different types of trees. That means we need different probability distributions to describe them.

Q.   **Why?**

A.   Because each distribution matches a particular type of random behavior.

Q.   **I thought you said random numbers represented random behavior.**

A.   Not quite. Random numbers let our simulation mimic the real world's variations, but we need a probability distribution that matches the real world to run the random numbers through.

Q.   **First, then, we must know how the real world is working, then we have to find a probability distribution that works the same way, and then we build the simulation. Is that right?**

A.   You got it. You learned to do it for discrete random processes in the last lesson. In this one, you will learn to do it for random processes that follow the normal distribution, the exponential distribution, and the uniform distribution. For each of these, we will show you how to use random numbers to generate events that follow those particular processes.

Learning Outcomes

When you complete this lesson, you will:

- Be able to use the Excel function NORNMIV to generate normally distributed random variables
- Be able to generate exponentially distributed random variables in Excel
- Be able to generate uniformly distributed random variables in Excel

A Dialectic on Generating Normally Distributed Random Variables

Q.   **I thought you said we were going to work on continuous distributions?**

A.   I did, and we are. The normal distribution is one of many continuous distributions.

Q.   **What makes it continuous?**

A.   There are an infinite (noncountable) number of simulated results.

Q.   **What does that mean?**

A.   With a discrete distribution, there is a small set of results, such as Heads or Tails (two results) for flipping a coin or 1, 2, 3, 4, 5, or 6 (six results) for rolling a die. Continuous distributions give numerical results and the numbers include decimals, so there are literally an infinite number of possible simulated results.

Q.   **Before, we assigned ranges of random numbers to each result. With an infinite number of results, how do we assign ranges?**

A.   We don't. Fortunately, there are an infinite number of random numbers, so we can do a one-to-one match of infinite random numbers to infinite outcomes.

Q.   **How can VLOOKUP handle an infinite number of outcomes?**

A.   It can't, so we'll use something else. Technically, a VLOOKUP table is the inverse of a discrete probability distribution, so what we need is the inverse of a normal (or any other continuous) distribution.

Q.   **And an inverse function is what?**

A.   The usual way of using a probability distribution is to give it an outcome and ask for the probability of that outcome. For the coin toss example, we would ask "What is the probability of getting

Heads?" and the probability distribution tells us 50%. When we invert that (do it backward), we give a probability and ask the inverse function for the outcome. That's what we did with the VLOOKUP function, using a random number as the probability, and the function told us whether that probability meant Heads or Tails.

Q. **Then we need a function that will take a random number (as a probability) and push it backward through the normal distribution and give us a number. Is there a function that will do that?**

A. Of course, but to illustrate this, look at figure 4.1, below. The bell-shaped curve is the normal distribution you all know and love, with a mean of 10 and a standard deviation of 2 (just like the probability distribution we set up for the discrete function). The dotted curve represents our cumulative probability distribution (which we had to calculate for the discrete function, but Excel will do for us now). Finally, the right-hand vertical axis is labeled "Cumulative Probability" (the equivalent of our "Lower Random Number Range").

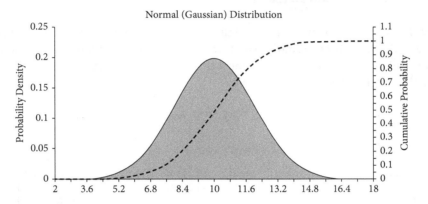

FIGURE 4.1 Example of the normal distribution with mean 10 and Std. Dev. 2.

Source: http://www.vertex42.com/ExcelArticles/mc/Normal-Distribution-Excel.html.

Q. **That's all really nice, but how does it help?**

A. With the discrete distribution, VLOOKUP took a random number, used it as a probability, matched it into the lower range, and read off the outcome. Our inverse function for the normal distribution has to take a random number, use it as a probability, find that probability on the right-hand vertical axis, and draw a horizontal line over to the cumulative probability dotted S-curve, and then read straight down to get the value off the bottom, horizontal, axis from the normal distribution.

Q. **Didn't you just say the same thing?**

A. That's my point. We are doing the same thing, but the VLOOKUP function can't handle an infinite number of outcomes. Instead, we will use the function that inverts the normal distribution, called =NORMINV.

Q. **Really clever with these names, aren't they?**

A. Maybe not, but you should be able to remember it.

Q.   **And I don't have to do any calculations to get the probabilities or cumulative distribution or anything else—just plug the numbers into the =NORMINV function in Excel and it does all the work for me?**

A.   Well, it will do all the calculations for you, but you still have to know how to interpret what it tells you.

Q.   **Let's start with using the function. What do I need to tell NORMINV?**

A.   You should remember that to use a normal distribution, you need a mean and a standard deviation. The same is true for the NORMINV function. Just as we did with the discrete distribution, you also need a random number. The format of the function is

=NORMINV(RAND(), MEAN, STD. DEV).

Q.   **OK, but could you show an example?**

A.   Sure. Let's assume the normal distribution from figure 4.1 represents waiting times for our customers. The first thing we have to do is to come up with a random number, so I chose 0.600 (that way we all get the same result). We know the mean of figure 4.1 is 10 and the standard deviation of 2, so the function would look like this:

=NORMINV(0.600, 10, 2) = 10.5067.

Conceptually, what we did is shown in figure 4.2.

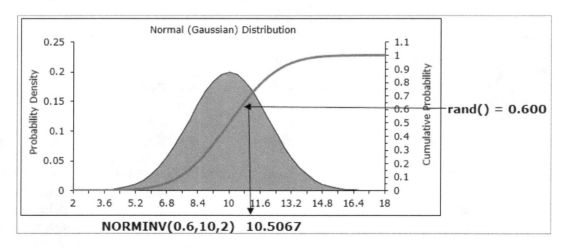

FIGURE 4.2 Example of an inverse function.

Adapted from http://www.vertex42.com/ExcelArticles/mc/Normal-Distribution-Excel.html.

Q.   **So, what does the 10.5067 tell us?**

A.   It tells us that this simulated customer will have to wait 10.5067 minutes to receive their order.

Q.   **What about the next simulated customer?**

A.   You would have a different random number and therefore a different wait time.

Q.   **How does that help my business, knowing that some random customer on some random day will wait for 10.5067 minutes to get their order?**

A.   It doesn't, but that's not what we are trying to do. We would set up a simulation in Excel and simulate lots of customers. If I simulate the establishment long enough, then a histogram of the simulated waiting times would be pretty close to a bell shape, with an average waiting time close to 10 minutes and a standard deviation close to 2.

Q.   **How do I do that in Excel?**

A.   You simply build a table and fill it in as follows (I show only five simulated customers):

TABLE 4.5   Results of Using NORMINV Function

	E	F	G
1		random	waiting
2	customer #	number	time
3	FORMULAS	=RAND()	=NORMINV(F3,10,2)
4	1	0.354565	9.253952381
5	2	0.000355	3.228368007
6	3	0.768766	11.46957915
7	4	0.386684	9.424055363
8	5	0.651999	10.78144635

I continued that simulation for 100 customers and constructed the histogram of the simulated waiting times, shown below in figure 4.3. Obviously, we did not get a perfect normal distribution, but if we included more customers in our histogram, then we would get a closer and closer approximation to the probability distribution of figure 4.1.

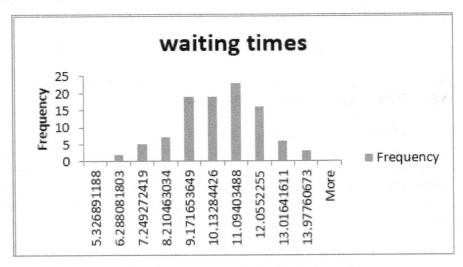

FIGURE 4.3 Probability distribution generated by the NORMINV function.

Q.   **Mmmm! So, you started with a normal distribution and you ended with a normal distribution. Seems like a great job at chasing your own tail.**

A.   Actually, simulation means mimicking or replicating something, so starting off with a normal distribution and then being able to re-create it, one customer at a time, is exactly what we mean by simulation.

Q.   **Why would I want to do this is in the business world?**

A.   We haven't done a simulation yet; all we are doing is learning how to work with a normal distribution. Think about it: besides simulating waiting times, we can also simulate other behaviors of these customers, such as what they will order from a real or proposed menu, how much they are likely to spend, how much they are going to tip, and how long they will be at their table before leaving and making it available for another customer.

Q.   **OK, that would be useful. When do we start?**

A.   First, we have to introduce the inverses of a couple more continuous distributions.

A Dialectic on Generating Exponentially Distributed Random Variables

Q.   **OK, we've covered discrete distributions and the normal distribution. What other distributions do we have to learn?**

A.   Next to the normal distributions, one of the other more applicable continuous distributions is the exponential distribution. It has been found (by yours truly as well as many others) to represent a wide variety of real-world processes.

Q.   **Why not just use the normal distribution for everything?**

A.   A lot of real-world processes do follow a normal distribution, but the normal distribution has a problem—it allows negative values.

Q.   **And the exponential distribution doesn't?**

A.   No, it doesn't, so any time you want to simulate the time interval between random events, the exponential distribution is a great one to use.

Q.   **Do we often need to simulate time intervals?**

A.   Whenever a simulation has customers arriving, you use the exponential distribution to simulate the time between one arrival and the next, such as at a drive-thru, a retail sale, or a traffic light, and even the time between the arrival of successive telephone or electronic messages. You can also use it to simulate the time between failures of equipment.

Q.   **How much is different from what we did for the normal distribution?**

A.   The process is the same as we used with the normal distribution. The only difference is that the formulas describing the exponential distribution (and thus the cumulative exponential distribution) are different.

Q.   **Do we need to know the formula for the exponential distribution or the cumulative exponential distribution?**

A.   Not really. You do need to know what the parameters are for the exponential distribution.

Q.   The **normal distribution needed the mean and standard deviation, so I assume that's what we need for the exponential distribution, right?**

A.   Not this time. The exponential distribution is defined by the average rate at which random events occur, meaning the average number of random events that occur during a unit of time. That's all we need, no standard deviation. This rate is traditionally denoted by the Greek letter lambda, λ. As with the normal distribution, what we really need is the cumulative probability distribution.

Q.   **Is it another _S_-shaped curve?**

A.   Not this time. As an example, suppose that we are using it to represent the time until the next car arrives at the drive-thru window of an establishment. Let's say that, on the average, there is one arrival per minute. This means that $\lambda = 1$. The graph of the cumulative exponential distribution is shown in figure 4.4.

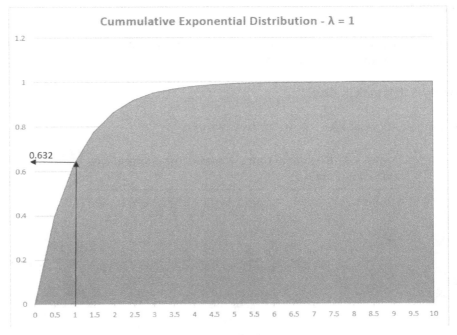

FIGURE 4.4 Cumulative distribution for $\lambda = 1$.

Q.   **How do we read that?**

A.   The horizontal line represents time (t), which is the output, and the vertical axis represents the cumulative probability that the next arrival will come on or before time t. So, if we want to know what the probability is that the next arrival will be within one minute (on the horizontal axis), then we just read it off the vertical axis, which indicates that the probability of the next car arriving within one minute is 0.632.

Q. I thought we wanted to work the other way, starting with a random number as a probability and getting an output. Do we use =EXPONINV?

A. That's right, we will use random numbers to simulate how long it will be for the customer to arrive. Unfortunately, Excel doesn't have an inverse exponential distribution.

Q. Then what do we do?

A. There is an old way of doing math called logarithms. It dealt with using the exponents of numbers to quickly multiply them. Since we are using an *exponential* distribution, it might not surprise you that the function that inverts it is called the natural log, =LN.

Q. How do we use the =LN function?

A. We take the natural log of a random number (which is between zero and one) and multiply by the negative inverse of the mean of the exponential distribution, like this:

$$t = -1/\lambda * LN(RAND()).$$

Q. I know you said that λ is the average rate of arrivals, like five per minute. Does the term $1/\lambda$ have a meaning?

A. Yes. A λ of five per minute means that $1/c$ is one-fifth of a minute, or 12.5 seconds, between arrivals. So, $1/\lambda$ is the mean time between arrivals.

Q. How does that look in Excel?

A. Table 4.6 shows what a $\lambda = 1$ distribution looks like.

TABLE 4.6 Results of Using Inverse Exponential Distribution Formula

	A	B	C	D
1	$\lambda=$	1		
2				
3		customer	random number	time till next arrival
4		FORMULAS	=RAND()	= - (1/$B$1) * LN(C$)
5		1	0.665082451	0.407844259
6		2	0.508938462	0.67542817
7		3	0.857050815	0.154258068
8		4	0.138573255	1.976356173
9		5	0.934003036	0.068275591

Q. How do we read that?

A. We put the mean arrival time in cell B1, and the =RAND() function is column C. Then using the =LN function in column D tells us the time between arrivals for each customer.

Q.   **How can you have a time between arrivals for the first customer?**

A.   Well, you can't, but we treat the first customer's time between arrivals as the time between starting the simulation (Time = 0) and the arrival of the first customer, so Customer 1 arrives at 0.40784426. Then the table tells me that Customer 2 will arrive 0.67542817 minutes after Customer 1, so Customer 2 arrives at 0.49784426 + 0.67542817, or 1.08327243.

Q.   **And Customer 3 will arrive 0.67542817 minutes after Customer 2 and so on. Is that correct?**

A.   Indeed. We will use that to simulate interarrival times in Lesson 4.3.

A Dialectic on Generating Uniformly Distributed Random Variables

Q.   **OK. I think I understand discrete and continuous process generators, so bring on some real simulation stuff!**

A.   Not so fast. You're not ready for prime time yet. Although you can handle any discrete distribution with VLOOKUP tables, specific continuous distributions are represented by specific mathematical formulas. Not everything in the world behaves according to a normal or exponential distribution, so we must develop your capability to handle some other widely applicable distributions.

Q.   **Oh, goody. What's next?**

A.   Next to the normal and exponential distribution, one of the more applicable continuous distributions is the uniform distribution. It is used when we have no information about where or when something will happen, such as the point of failure on a surface or how long a customer will have to wait. It is shaped like a rectangle, as shown in figure 4.5.

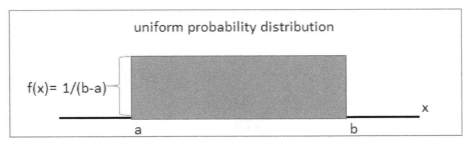

FIGURE 4.5 Uniform distribution.

Q.   **What are "a" and "b"?**

A.   The minimum and maximum values that can come out of the simulation.

Q.   **And why do you have the height as 1/(b-a)?**

A.   You should remember that the area of a rectangle is length × width, or, in this case, length × height. You also should remember that the area under a probability curve is 1. Since the length is (b – a) and the area of 1 = height * (b – a), the height is 1/(b-a).

Q.   **What does the cumulative distribution look like for a uniform distribution?**

A.   An upward sloping line between *a* and *b*, like in figure 4.6.

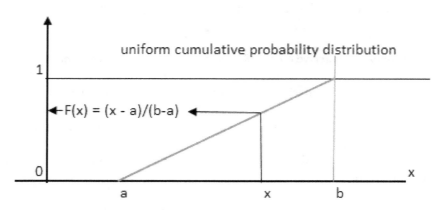

FIGURE 4.6 Uniform cumulative distribution.

To invert it, given a value, X, move up to the diagonal line and then over the left-hand axis to read the probability.

Q.   **Is the UNIFORMINV function in Excel?**

A.   Not only is there no inverse function for the uniform distribution, there isn't even another function we can use, as we did for the exponential distribution. We will have to create our own formula to invert the uniform distribution.

Q.   **And the fun keeps coming. Well, the graph was simple, so maybe the calculation is simple, too?**

A.   Actually, yes, and it is even easy to understand. All the outputs fall between the lower limit, a, and the upper limit, b, so the output is just the lower limit, a, plus a random amount of the range, b minus a, like this:

$$x = a + RAND() * (b - a).$$

Q.   **That actually makes sense. Weird. How do we do this in Excel?**

A.   Assume that the value of a security fluctuates randomly between $39.00 and $42.25 during a typical trading session. You wish to simulate the price of that stock over five trading sessions so you can test various investing strategies.

Q.   **Nice, but do stocks really follow a uniform distribution?**

A.   Maybe. We use a uniform distribution when we don't know how a value moves within a range, and there certainly are stock-investing theories that assume stock values are random. If you don't believe that, then you could use the normal, or you could observe the stock prices for any period of time you wanted, construct a histogram, and then use a VLOOKUP table. One of the benefits of simulation is that you get to decide what to do.

TABLE 4.7   Results of Using the Inverse Uniform Distribution Formula

	A	B	C	D
1		a= 39		
2		b= 42.25		
3				
4		session #	random number	price
5		FORMULAS	=rand()	=$B$1 + C5*($B$2-$B$1)
6		1	0.479910712	40.55970981
7		2	0.512229671	40.66474643
8		3	0.285298645	39.9272206
9		4	0.562286685	40.82743173
10		5	0.218390678	39.7097697

ACTIVE LEARNING: LESSON 4.2

LESSON 4.3: Building a Simulation Model

Introduction

Q.   **How do we use all those distributions to simulate something?**

A.   Think of the distributions like bricks. You need bricks, but to build a wall you also need to know how to put the bricks together. It's the same with a simulation.

Q.   **How do we get started?**

A.   You start by identifying a situation that you want to know more about.

Q.   **Right, and a simulation is copy of that situation on a computer. We use random numbers so the simulation changes, just like the real world does, but what do we do first?**

A.   You start by observing and recording, preferably in a tabular format, what is going on.

Q.   **Why?**

A.   There is no formula or recipe that you can apply to come up with a simulation model, so you have to study the situation. Simulation is much more of an art than a science. Like all arts, it requires practice, so the more successful models you build, the better you become at it.

Q.   **Practice makes perfect?**

A.   Actually, perfect practice makes perfect, so follow these lessons, view the videos, do the exercises, and ask lots of questions.

Learning Outcomes

When you complete this lesson, you will be able to:

- Construct a simulation table to organize the steps required to build a simulation model
- Employ appropriate process generators to re-create random events in the simulation table
- Develop Excel formulas to link the simulation table columns together into a simulation model
- Use Excel's VLOOKUP and NORMINV functions to generate random events

A Dialectic on Building Simulation Models

Q.   **What's the first step to building a simulation?**

A.   In the real world, having decided on what situation you want to simulate, you would observe that situation (probably taking a video of it), and then take notes of everything you need (when customers arrive, how long it takes to wait on them, how often things break—whatever seems of interest).

Q.   **Why take a video?**

A.   Two reasons: you can pause the video as you write down the data, so you don't miss anything, and in case you find you missed something (after starting the simulation) you can go back, later on, and gather that data.

Q.   **What are we going to observe?**

A.   This being a classroom, I will give you the situation and data, but I should warn you that gathering the data can be the most time-consuming (and boring) part of the whole process.

Q.   **Thank goodness for that. What's the situation?**

The Cold Slab Ice Cream Stand

The Cold Slab Ice Cream Stand has between 0 and 3 customers arriving per minute during the peak snack hours. Each number of arrivals has an equal probability of occurring. Past experience indicates that customer expenditures at the stand are normally distributed with a mean of $4.75 and a standard deviation of $0.75. The owner is interested in having us help him predict the average total revenues per minute at the stand.

Q.   **That's pretty simple, isn't it?**

A.   Even though the example is rather basic, the exact same ideas go into simulating full-scale businesses, from a Burger King restaurant to a DuPont chemical plant.

Q. I remember how to simulate a normal distribution, but why do we need to know about the arrivals?

A. The total revenues per minute depends on the number of customers that arrive (and get served) at the stand per minute.

Q. Do the customers arrive randomly?

A. Yes, we are told the number of arrivals per minute is a random variable that can assume the values of 0 arrivals, 1 arrival, 2 arrivals, or 3 arrivals. Since the probability of each is equally likely, the probability for each must be 0.25.

Q. So, with a countable number of outcomes, is that a discrete random process?

A. Exactly! And we know how to handle that. Table 4.8 is our process table where we establish the lower random number ranges for each outcome. We will rearrange that into a VLOOKUP table for the simulation (table 4.9).

TABLE 4.8 Cumulative Probabilities and Lower RN Ranges for Customer Arrivals

# customers	probability	cumulative probability	lower rn range
0	0.25	0.25	0
1	0.25	0.5	0.25
2	0.25	0.75	0.5
3	0.25	1	0.75

TABLE 4.9 Process Generator for the Number of Customer Arrivals

	A	B
1	lower rn	
2	range	# customres
3	0	0
4	0.25	1
5	0.5	2
6	0.75	3

Q. Those looks really familiar, just like the tables we built for the coin flipping. Since you told us that expenditures are normally distributed (mean of $4.57, standard deviation of $0.75), can we use the NORMINV function to simulate that?

A. Exactly! However, each (if any) customer needs their own simulated expenditures.

Q.   **That makes sense, but I how do I do that?**

A.   When putting together a simulation model, it is best to try to visualize yourself as being physically present in the situation being modeled, and then trying to record what is happening.

Q.   **Isn't the first question how many customers arrive?**

A.   Yes.

Q.   **What do I do with that?**

A.   I recommend that you set up a table in which you have the computer create the events that you would have observed had you been in the store. When making the table, it is better to record too much than not enough—and, always go step by step! Also, whenever you "see" a random event as about to occur, you need a random number and the appropriate process generator.

Q.   **Should I start with a column for arrivals?**

A.   No, small steps. The number of arrivals per minute is random, so you start with a column for a random number.

Q.   **OK, right. Then I use the random number to simulate number of arrivals, so that is the second column. What comes after that?**

A.   Each customer that arrives needs a random expenditure number …

Q.   **Then we need another random number column followed by the amount of the expenditure. Is it that easy?**

A.   No, because that is wrong. The problem tells you that EACH (caps for emphasis) customer's expenditure is random, so you have to do each customer separately.

Q.   **Right, slow down. OK, I have a random number column for the first customer, then expenditure for the first customer, and I repeat that for each customer. Wait a minute, how do I know how many customers there are?**

A.   You don't, so you have to design the simulation to adjust to the number of customers as it is randomly simulated.

Q.   **How do I do that?**

A.   For now, I'll just say, with an IF-THEN function, but really, we'll get to that later.

Q.   **What's next?**

A.   Nothing, except to add up what the client asked for—total expenditures per minute. In table 4.10 we show what the headings of such a table might look like.

TABLE 4.10   Headings for a Simulation Table for the Cold Slab Ice Cream Company

	C	D	E	F	G	H	I	J	K	L
13	(clock)	random		rn for	expenditure	rn for	expenditure	rn for	expenditure	minute totl
14	minute #	number	# of arrivals	customer 1	customer 1	customer 2	customer 2	customer 3	customer 3	revenue

Q.   Do all simulation tables look the same?

A.   In general, yes, but there is no one right table. Someone else might have additional (or fewer) columns and/or have them in a different order.

Q.   Why did you start in column C?

A.   Just so I could fit all the column headers in. The first column is always used for the simulation clock. In our simulation, we are interested in how many customers arrive each minute. That means our simulation clock will tick minute by minute, and for each minute, we will simulate the number of customers that arrive and their expenditures.

Q.   Why did you start in row 13?

A.   As a matter of good simulation practice, the problem data should always be listed separately before the simulation table is built.

Q.   Why?

A.   Data should never be used directly in the simulation functions. Instead, the cell(s) in which the data is listed should be referenced instead.

Q.   Again, why?

A.   A simulation is primarily a tool to respond to "what-if ..." questions. Many such questions revolve around "what if some of the data changed." If the data is listed outside of the simulation table, then all you do to answer the question is to change the listed value. Otherwise, it would be necessary to change the data in every table formula where it was used—something that in real simulation models would be an almost impossible task. Table 4.11 shows how we listed the data for Cold Slab. Note that cell addresses will continue to be used as we build our simulation model.

TABLE 4.11   Data Listing for Cold Slab

	A	B
1	**lower rn**	
2	**range**	**# customers**
3	0	0
4	0.25	1
5	0.5	2
6	0.75	3
7		
8	**Expenditure data**	
9	mean = $	4.75
10	Std. Dev. $	0.75

Q.   **The headings are nice, but how do we make the simulation work?**

A.   Beginning with the first minute (so we put a 1 in cell C15), we work from left to right filling in the formulas or functions we need.

Q.   **Column D says "Random Number," so I guess we would use the =RAND() function. You told us the "# of Arrivals" followed a discrete distribution, so we can use =VLOOKUP and the data in cells A1:B6. Is that right?**

A.   Very good! Table 4.12 shows the formulas as they would look in Excel:

TABLE 4.12   Start of the Simulation Table

	C	D	E
11		SIMULATING ARRIVALS	
12			
13	(clock)		
14	minute #	random number	# of arrivals
15	1	=RAND()	=VLOOKUP(D15, $A$3:$B$6, 2)

Q.   **I guess we use the =RAND function for each of the random number columns (E, G, and I) and the =NORMINV function for the expenditures. Do we then just add them up to get the total?**

A.   That would work if we were sure of getting three customers every minute, but we aren't.

Q.   **Right, you said we would use an IF-THEN function to handle that. How does that work?**

A.   Let's think about what we have. Column E tells us how many customers arrive. The possibilities are as follows:

- IF column E has a 0 in it,

    THEN expenditures for each customer column is equal to 0.

- IF column E has a 1 in it,

    THEN Customer 1 (column F) needs an expenditure value, but not 2 or 3.

- IF column E has a 2 in it,

    THEN Customers 1 and 2 (columns F and H) need an expenditure value, but not 3.

- IF column E has a 3 in it,

    THEN all Customers (columns F, H, and J) need an expenditure value.

Q.   **All that makes sense, but how do we do that in Excel?**

A.   Let's take it one column at a time. Look at that breakdown above and figure out when Customer 1 needs to calculate an expenditure.

Q. **If column E has a 1, 2, or 3 in it, but how does that help?**

A. The easy way to say that is if column E has a value greater than 0. In Excel, we write it like this:

$$=IF(E15>0,$$

Q. **How do you read that?**

A. "If the value in cell E15 is greater than 0" and the comma at the end is read as "THEN" and whatever follows the comma will only happen if E15 (the number of customers) is greater than 0.

Q. **What comes after "THEN"?**

A. You use the NORMINV function to simulate the expenditure for Customer 1, like this:

$$=IF(E15>0,NORMINV(F15,\$B\$9,\$B\$10),.$$

Q. **Does the final comma mean "THEN" again?**

A. No, this time it means "ELSE," and you put whatever should happen when E15 (the number of customers) is equal to 0.

Q. **What happens if there are no customers?**

A. The expenditures by Customer 1 is 0, so

$$=IF(E15>0,NORMINV(F15,\$B\$9,\$B\$10),0).$$

Q. **Where do we put that?**

A. In cell G15, so the spreadsheet looks like this:

TABLE 4.13 Customer 1

	C	D	E	F	G
11		SIMULATING ARRIVALS			SIMULATING EXPENDITURES
12					
13	(clock)			rn for	expenditure
14	minute #	random number	# of arrivals	customer 1	customer 1
15	1	=RAND()	=VLOOKUP(D15, \$A\$3:\$B\$6, 2)	=RAND()	=IF(E15>0, NORMINV(F15, \$B\$9, \$B\$10), 0)

Q. **When do we calculate expenditures for a second customer?**

A. According to our breakdown, when there are two or three customers, so if the value in cell E15 is greater than 1. The rest of the function is the same.

Q.   And if E15 is greater than 2, then there are three customers. Are these the formulas we would use for Customer 2 Expenditures (I15) and Customer 3 Expenditures (K15)?

$$=IF(E15>1,NORMINV(F15,\$B\$9,\$B\$10),0)$$
$$=IF(E15>2,NORMINV(F15,\$B\$9,\$B\$10),0)$$

A.   Very good! Finally, column L is the sum of the expenditures for each customer that arrived during that minute interval, so in cell L15 you put

$$=SUM(G15,I15,K15).$$

Q.   Why did you put the =RAND() function in its own column instead of inside the VLOOKUP and NORMINV functions?

A.   There is no one correct way to set up a simulation. The data should go in its own area, and if you have multiple outputs, you might want to group those as well, but as for how you arrange the simulation, you can use whatever makes sense to you.

Q.   Are we done?

A.   Not quite. We need to simulate a lot of minutes to get a feel for what is really happening.

Q.   How do we do that?

A.   Just highlight the row for Customer 1 (C15:L15) and copy down. Table 4.14 shows five customers simulated, though you would want to do a lot more.

TABLE 4.14   Completed 5-Minute Simulation of the Cold Slab Ice Cream Stand

	(clock) minute #	random number	# of arrivals	rn for customer 1	expenditure customer 1	rn for customer 2	expenditure cutomer 2	rn for customer 3	expenditure customer 3	minute totl revenue
13										
14										
15	1	0.99	3	0.60	4.94	0.81	5.42	0.66	5.06	15.42
16	2	0.15	0	0.33	0.00	0.32	0.00	0.40	0.00	0.00
17	3	0.80	3	0.39	4.53	0.91	5.78	0.80	5.38	15.69
18	4	0.49	1	0.69	5.13	0.92	0.00	0.90	0.00	5.13
19	5	0.70	2	0.61	4.97	0.95	5.98	0.95	0.00	10.95

You should try to set up your own spreadsheet (enter my random numbers rather than using the =RAND() function) to see whether you can get the same results.

Q.   Do we average the total revenue values in column K to get our answer?

A.   Yes, but that would give you only one answer. If you had a different set of random numbers, you would get a different answer.

Q.   What do we do then?

A.   That is a discussion for the next lesson.

ACTIVE LEARNING: LESSON 4.3

LESSON 4.4: Designing Simulation Experiments

Introduction

Q.   **I thought we designed the simulation last time?**

A.   We *built* the simulation last time. This time we are designing the experiment that we will run through the simulation.

Q.   **You said an experiment was changing one of the parameters. Why do we have to design that?**

A.   Before we start changing the parameters, we have to get a result we can report to our client. The problem is that every time you run a simulation model, you are likely to get a different set of results.

Q.   **But, if I get a different result each time I run the simulation, which one is right?**

A.   All of them or none of them, whichever way you prefer to think about it.

Q.   **That didn't help ...**

A.   Each run of a simulation is different because of the random numbers used. Each run is just as accurate as the next, but there is no way to show that any one run is better than any other.

Q.   **What do we do, then?**

A.   We perform an analysis of multiple runs to try to get a good estimate of what the true results are.

Q.   **I smell a load of probabilities and statistics coming my way. Am I wrong?**

A.   You are not wrong, but I will show you how to use Excel to do all the calculations.

Q.   **But I still need to be able to interpret the results, right?**

A.   Of course.

Learning Outcomes

When you complete this lesson, you will be able to:

- Use the Data Analysis Add-in for Excel to obtain the descriptive statistics for a sample of number of simulations runs

- Understand the concept of a point estimate, sampling error, and interval estimate (confidence interval) as it applies to a simulation

- Calculate the Upper Confidence Limit (UCL) and Lower Confidence Limit (LCL) to give a 95% confidence interval of a simulation statistic

- Use the sample-size formula to calculate the required sample size to obtain a specified margin of error

- Extend the simulation to the required sample size to obtain a specified margin of error and calculate the point and interval estimates for the statistic(s) of interest in a simulation output

A Dialectic on Designing Simulation Experiments

Q.   **Last time, you said that every time we run a simulation, we use different random numbers and so we get a different result. What can we do about that?**

A.   To get meaningful data out of the simulation model, you have to use it properly.

Q.   **Does "designing simulation experiments" mean figuring out which outputs to use?**

A.   No, because we are going to use all of them.

Q.   **You mean, average them all?**

A.   Yes, but it is more than that.

Q.   **We want the average revenue per minute, and we have that. What's the problem?**

A.   The problem is that when we average all the results, we end up with a single estimate, called a point estimate. A point estimate has precisely a 0% chance of being right.

Q.   **0%? Is that a typo?**

A.   Nope. There are an infinite number of possible values for the output, so picking 1 out of infinity has a probability of 1/infinity, which is zero.

Q.   **Why bother to run a simulation, then?**

A.   Instead of a point estimate, we can estimate a range of values for the output. Then we can end up with a very high probability of that range including the true value.

Q.   **Do you mean a confidence interval? How do we do that?**

A.   The key statistical concept we rely on is the Central Limit Theorem.

Q.   **I remember that! It says you can always use the normal distribution, right?**

A.   Sort of. Technically, it states that when you sample from any distribution (in our case, the simulation model), the statistical distribution of the averages of the performance measures is normal with a given sample mean and sample standard deviation—as long as we take a large enough sample.

Q.   **Ok, well then, we need a mean and a standard deviation to use the normal distribution to describe the distribution of sample means, don't we?**

A.   The sample mean is the estimate for the population mean, but we still need an estimate for the standard deviation of the distribution of sample means. By the way, we call this the "Standard Error."

Q.   **Is it hard to calculate the standard error?**

A.   Yes and no. The standard error is not a single value. It is based on the sample size we select.

Q.   **You mean the standard error changes as we change the sample size?**

A.   Exactly, and by changing the size of the standard error, we also change the width of the range that contains the true value of the mean.

Q.   **That sounds almost too good to be true. You said we have to take a large enough sample. What is a large enough sample size to give us a really small range?**

A.   We are going to do this in two steps. First, we use a large enough sample to get a good estimate of the standard deviation, then we figure out whether we need an even larger sample to get a small enough range.

Q.   **What is a "large enough" sample to get started?**

A.   Although most statistics texts indicate that a sample of size 30 is big enough, I prefer to be conservative and use a sample of size 60.

Q.   **OK ... how do I go about getting a sample of size 60?**

A.   Each line of the simulation is one estimate of the revenue per minute. For example, in table 4.15, I have copied the simulation table we built before, so we simulated five minutes, which means we have a sample of 5.

TABLE 4.15   Cold Slab Simulation

	B	C	D	E	F	G	H	I	J	K	L
12											
13		(clock)	random		rn for	expenditure	rn for	expenditure	rn for	expenditure	minute totl
14		minute #	number	# of arrivals	customer 1	customer 1	customer 2	cutomer 2	customer 3	customer 3	revenue
15		1	0.99	3	0.60	4.94	0.81	5.42	0.66	5.06	15.42
16		2	0.15	0	0.33	0.00	0.32	0.00	0.40	0.00	0.00
17		3	0.80	3	0.39	4.53	0.91	5.78	0.80	5.38	15.69
18		4	0.49	1	0.69	5.13	0.92	0.00	0.90	0.00	5.13
19		5	0.70	2	0.61	4.97	0.95	5.98	0.95	0.00	10.95

Q.   **You mean all we have to do is copy the last row of the table until you reach 60 one-minute intervals?**

A.   That's it. Of course, you have to make sure no glitches have developed.

Q.   **Why should any problems have developed?**

A.   That's the wrong way to think. Always look at the numbers and make sure they make sense, such as is the counter incrementing properly or are the random numbers changing. You must verify that your results appear to do what you intended them to do.

Q.   **OK, I've copied the simulation down for 60 replications. Now what?**

A.   Table 4.16 shows my simulation results. Of course, they are different from your results because we are using random numbers.

Q.   **Does that matter?**

A.   Not for what we are doing. When building a simulation, to verify and validate it you can "fix" the random values to stop things from changing. You do that by copying the columns with the random numbers in them and then "Paste—Special—Values" so the formula goes away and the numbers remain. Once you are satisfied the simulation is valid, you put the =RAND() functions back in and the outputs start changing again.

Q.   **When do I know I have the right outputs?**

A.   It turns out not to matter what the outputs are, just that we have enough of them.

Q.   **So, any 60 simulated output values will do?**

A.   Provided the simulation is valid, yes.

Q.   **I don't understand. How is that possible?**

A.   Table 4.17 shows the average revenue per minute for 10 different sets of 60 minutes of simulation. Each is different, and if we did that for hundreds of sets, we could create a histogram of those averages and they would show a normal curve, which we call a sampling distribution. The number we want—the average revenue per minute—is the mean of that sampling distribution (that's what the Central Limit Theorem tells us). Any one average, provided it came from a big enough sample, gives us a pretty good estimate of the true mean.

Q.   **Assuming I accept that, what do we do?**

A.   This is going to get all statistic-y, but bear with me and you will see that doing it is not as bad as reading about it. Besides telling us we are using a normal distribution, the Central Limit Theorem tells us two more things. First, the sampling distribution (from the sample means) has the same average (mean) as the distribution you are sampling from (the simulation). That is the number we are looking for.

TABLE 4.16 Simulation Results for a Sample of 60 One-Minute Intervals

	A	B	C	D	E	F	G	H	I	J
13	(clock)	random		rn for	expenditure	rn for	expenditure	rn for	expenditure	minute totl
14	minute #	number	# of arrivals	customer 1	customer 1	customer 2	customer 2	customer 3	customer 3	revenue
15	1	0.99	3	0.60	4.94	0.81	5.42	0.66	5.06	15.42
16	2	0.15	0	0.33	0.00	0.32	0.00	0.40	0.00	0.00
17	3	0.80	3	0.39	4.53	0.91	5.78	0.80	5.38	15.69
18	4	0.49	1	0.69	5.13	0.92	0.00	0.90	0.00	5.13
19	5	0.70	2	0.61	4.97	0.95	5.98	0.95	0.00	10.95
20	6	0.41	1	0.86	5.55	0.40	0.00	0.04	0.00	5.55
21	7	0.30	1	0.44	4.64	0.99	0.00	0.54	0.00	4.64
22	8	0.42	1	0.17	4.04	0.42	0.00	0.60	0.00	4.04
23	9	0.41	1	0.22	4.17	0.75	0.00	0.12	0.00	4.17
24	10	0.58	2	0.94	5.92	0.99	6.49	0.28	0.00	12.40
25	11	0.49	1	0.47	4.70	0.95	0.00	0.80	0.00	4.70
26	12	0.64	2	0.66	5.05	0.37	4.50	0.56	0.00	9.55
27	13	0.33	1	0.16	4.00	0.24	0.00	0.75	0.00	4.00
28	14	0.57	2	0.10	3.81	0.86	5.58	0.24	0.00	9.38
29	15	0.21	0	0.23	0.00	0.87	0.00	0.86	0.00	0.00
30	16	0.01	0	0.80	0.00	0.80	0.00	0.60	0.00	0.00
31	17	0.39	1	0.49	4.74	0.98	0.00	0.05	0.00	4.74
32	18	0.25	0	0.58	0.00	0.11	0.00	1.00	0.00	0.00
33	19	0.22	0	0.96	0.00	0.04	0.00	0.44	0.00	0.00
34	20	0.24	0	0.60	0.00	0.17	0.00	0.27	0.00	0.00
35	21	0.85	3	0.57	4.88	0.77	5.30	0.28	4.32	14.50
36	22	0.27	1	0.63	4.99	0.23	0.00	0.62	0.00	4.99
37	23	0.96	3	0.66	5.06	0.04	3.43	0.12	3.86	12.35
38	24	0.92	3	0.01	2.90	0.85	5.52	0.90	5.70	14.11
39	25	0.43	1	0.06	3.59	0.83	0.00	0.12	0.00	3.59
40	26	0.66	2	0.22	4.18	0.90	5.72	0.26	0.00	9.90
41	27	0.23	0	0.75	0.00	0.02	0.00	0.29	0.00	0.00
42	28	0.04	0	0.57	0.00	0.26	0.00	0.73	0.00	0.00
43	29	0.16	0	0.00	0.00	0.43	0.00	0.08	0.00	0.00
44	30	0.82	3	0.70	5.15	0.14	3.92	0.67	5.09	14.15
45	31	0.10	0	0.66	0.00	0.42	0.00	0.04	0.00	0.00
46	32	0.80	3	0.90	5.72	0.18	4.06	0.78	5.33	15.11
47	33	0.88	3	0.95	5.95	0.38	4.52	0.44	4.63	15.10
48	34	0.96	3	0.90	5.70	0.90	5.72	0.54	4.83	16.25
49	35	0.82	3	0.43	4.62	0.36	4.49	0.45	4.66	13.77
50	36	0.06	0	0.43	0.00	0.18	0.00	0.57	0.00	0.00
51	37	0.10	0	0.00	0.00	0.60	0.00	0.62	0.00	0.00
52	38	0.91	3	0.48	4.70	0.57	4.88	0.52	4.79	14.38
53	39	0.84	3	0.26	4.28	0.78	5.34	0.36	4.48	14.09
54	40	0.38	1	0.48	4.71	0.76	0.00	0.52	0.00	4.71
55	41	0.77	3	0.83	5.46	0.71	5.17	0.87	5.59	16.22
56	42	0.61	2	0.06	3.58	0.60	4.94	0.18	0.00	8.52
57	43	0.02	0	0.31	0.00	0.54	0.00	0.19	0.00	0.00
58	44	0.25	0	0.55	0.00	0.54	0.00	0.08	0.00	0.00
59	45	0.21	0	0.65	0.00	0.57	0.00	0.50	0.00	0.00
60	46	0.61	2	0.37	4.50	0.66	5.06	0.87	0.00	9.57
61	47	0.98	3	0.23	4.19	0.87	5.61	0.57	4.89	14.68
62	48	0.60	2	0.18	4.06	0.78	5.34	0.93	0.00	9.39
63	49	0.60	2	0.95	5.95	0.10	3.78	0.16	0.00	9.73
64	50	0.44	1	0.64	5.01	0.59	0.00	0.28	0.00	5.01
65	51	0.54	2	0.01	3.08	0.46	4.68	0.97	0.00	7.75
66	52	0.40	1	0.19	4.10	0.39	0.00	0.52	0.00	4.10
67	53	0.89	3	0.89	5.67	0.90	5.73	0.57	4.88	16.28
68	54	0.27	1	0.55	4.85	0.31	0.00	0.52	0.00	4.85
69	55	0.38	1	0.70	5.14	0.10	0.00	0.85	0.00	5.14
70	56	0.38	1	0.86	5.57	0.98	0.00	0.10	0.00	5.57
71	57	0.16	0	0.45	0.00	0.19	0.00	0.75	0.00	0.00
72	58	0.28	1	0.98	6.32	0.26	0.00	0.78	0.00	6.32
73	59	0.60	2	0.15	3.97	0.70	5.15	0.55	0.00	9.12
74	60	0.31	1	0.34	4.43	0.19	0.00	0.87	0.00	4.43

TABLE 4.17   Average Total Per Minute Revenues
for 10 Samples of 60 One-Minute Intervals

Sample	Sample Average
1	7.448
2	7.394
3	5.588
4	6.359
5	8.128
6	6.776
7	7.689
8	7.106
9	7.782
10	5.225

Q.   What does that tell us?

A.   That tells us it is correct to use our average of the revenue per minute as the mean of the sampling distribution, which is the mean of our confidence interval.

Q.   What do we do for the standard deviation?

A.   That's the other thing the Central Limit Theorem tells us: the standard deviation of the sample means is equal to the standard deviation of the original distribution divided by the square root of the sample size.

Q.   In English?

A.   We can calculate a standard deviation for our 60 simulations, divide that by the square root of our sample size, and get a good estimate for the standard deviation of the sampling distribution.

Q.   Do you mean that with a big enough sample, we could get the standard deviation down to zero?

A.   Theoretically, yes, but that would mean an infinitely large sample size.

Q.   This all started with choosing a sample size. Maybe it is time to actually do this instead of talking about it. Could we do an example?

A.   First pick a probability level for the confidence interval.

Q.   How about 95%?

A.   Good choice. First, we remember that 95% of all values of a normal distribution fall within 1.96 standard deviation of the mean. We already know how to calculate the standard deviation (sample standard deviation divided by the square root of n), the sample size, so we need to calculate a Lower Confidence Limit (LCL) and Upper Confidence Limit (UCL) around the mean, where

$$LCL = \bar{x} - 1.96 * S/\sqrt{n}$$
$$UCL = \bar{x} + 1.96 * S/\sqrt{n}.$$

Q. **Where did the 1.96 come from?**

A. For a normal distribution, +/– 1.96 standard deviations includes 95% of the area under a normal curve. That is a good number to remember. If you want to increase that to 99.7%, then replace the 1.96 with 3, and if you are willing to settle for a margin of error of 68%, then you can replace the 1.96 with 1. These numbers are obtained from the good ol' "Z" tables we all used in statistics.

Q. **I don't suppose there is any easy way to do this?**

A. Excel will do almost all the calculations for you.

Q. **How is that?**

A. We use the Data Analysis Add-in from Excel, but you may have to install it. To see if yours is installed, click on the DATA tab at the top of your worksheet. Look for the "Data Analysis" icon at the top right of the worksheet. If you do not see it, follow the steps shown in Figure 4.7.

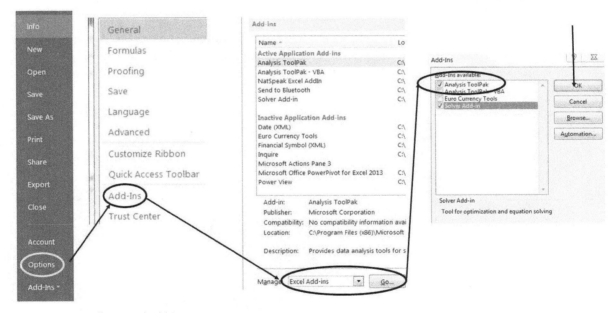

FIGURE 4.7 Installing Excel Add-ins.

1. Click on "File" to get the green bar on the left to appear

2. Click on "Options"

3. Click on "Add-ins"

4. Confirm the "Manage" box says "Excel Add-ins," then click on "Go"

5. Check the box for "Analysis ToolPak"

6. Click "OK"

Q.   That worked like a charm. So how do I go about using it?

A.   Open the DATA tab on your worksheet and double click on the Data Analysis icon.

Q.   I got a dialogue box listing a bunch of stuff I don't understand. Was that supposed to happen?

A.   Yes, it looks like the table of contents for a stats book. On that list, find "Descriptive Statistics" and double-click on it.

Q.   I got another dialogue box. How long does this go on?

A.   We're getting there. Fill out the dialogue box as shown in figure 4.8 (using the spreadsheet in table 4.17, above).

- The input range is the part of the spreadsheet you want the descriptive stats for (the per minute revenue column).

- I have included the heading "revenue" with my data (careful—you may only use one cell as your heading); check the box for "Labels in First Row."

- I have clicked on "output range," which indicates that I want my results placed starting in cell N15, and I have asked the options "Summary Statistics" and "Confidence Level for Mean."

- Click OK to get the results you see in table 4.18.

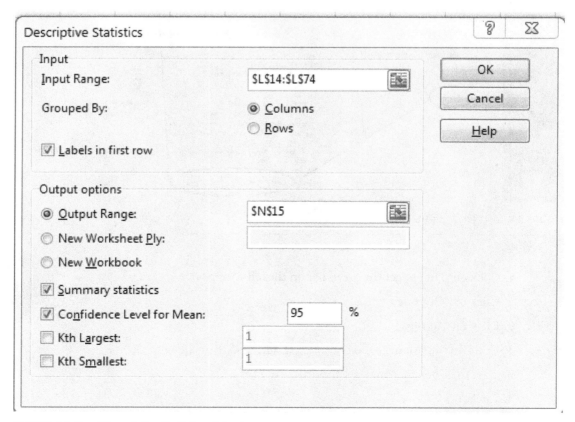

FIGURE 4.8 Excel Descriptive Statistics dialog box.

TABLE 4.18 Descriptive Statistics* from the Cold Slab Simulation

	N	O	P
15		*revenue*	
16	*statistic*	*symbol/formula*	*value*
17	Mean	$\bar{X}$	7.429789353
18	Standard Error	$S / \sqrt{n}$	0.739280094
19	Median		8.226985739
20	Mode		0
21	Standard Deviation	S	5.726438987
22	Sample Variance	S^2	32.79210347
23	Kurtosis		-1.423810686
24	Skewness		-0.001832037
25	Range		15.68990364
26	Minimum		0
27	Maximum		15.68990364
28	Sum	$\sum X$ (revenues)	445.7873612
29	Count	n	60
30	Confidence Level(95.0%)	$1.96 * S / \sqrt{n}$	1.479296052

*with some extra explanatory material from your professor

Q. Why don't I see the stuff in column O?

A. I have added the labels in row 16 and the explanations in column O.

Q. OK, well, what do I do with all that?

A. It gives you everything you need to calculate the range.

Q. I see the mean (P17), the standard deviation (P21), and n (P29), but what is the confidence level in P30?

A. That is Excel being nice to you. Since we asked for a 95% confidence level, Excel divided the standard deviation by the square root of the count and multiplied by 1.96. That is also called the Margin of Error.

Q. What do we do with the margin of error?

A. Use it to find the lower and upper control limits, like this:

$$LCL = P17 - P30 = 5.950493$$
$$UCL = P17 + P30 = 8.909085$$

Q. And then we are done?

A. Not yet. We can tell our client, Cold Slab Ice Cream Stand, that, based on the results of our simulation, we can expect the true average per minute total revenues to fall between $5.95 and $8.91 with a 95% probability.

Q. Will our client be happy with that wide a range?

A. Probably not, but remember where all this started: we can change the sample size and reduce the margin of error, thus reducing the range.

Q.   **So, we just add more rows for our simulation, but how many rows should we add?**

A.   Let's denote the margin of error by the letter e. Then, if you go to table 4.18, you see that

$$e = 1.96 * S/\sqrt{n} = \$1.48.$$

Q.   **How does that help?**

A.   We can turn that formula around: to solve for n, like this:

$$n = (1.96)^2 * S^2/e^2$$

Q.   **Still not seeing it. How does rearranging the formula help?**

A.   With a sample size (n) of 60, the margin of error was \$1.48, which gave us a range that was too wide. With this formula, you can choose the margin of error (e) that you want, and then calculate the sample size (n) you need to make that happen.

Q.   **What sample size I will need to get a \$1.00 margin of error?**

A.   Using the value in table 2 in the formula below, you'll get the result shown:

$$n = (1.96)^2 * P22 / (1)^2 = 125.97$$

Q.   **That means I have to more than double my sample size, from 60 to 125.97, right?**

A.   Exactly. You cannot, however, take a fraction of a sample, so we always round up to the nearest integer. For your example, we would take a sample of 126 one-minute intervals.

Q.   **Do I have to go back to my simulation?**

A.   Yes. Follow these steps:

- Re-open the simulation spreadsheet.
- Copy down the simulation until you get a count equal to the value of n.
- Open the Data Analysis Add-in and select Descriptive Statistics.
- Enter the data as before (mostly be sure you enter all 126 data points), and you get table 4.19. Remember that your table will not look exactly like table 4.18 because I inserted some explanatory material there that is not part of the output from Excel, but all the essential stuff will be there.

Q.   **Why isn't the margin of error in cell O47 equal to 1?**

A.   Two reasons: you rounded up, from 125.97 to 126, and ... randomness. Every time you do this, the results will be a little different.

Q.   **Do we have to re-calculate n, then?**

A.   No. Calculating the sample size only lets us control the uncertainty, not eliminate it. Rerunning the calculation for n will not make any difference; you would just be chasing your own tail.

TABLE 4.19   Descriptive Statistics for Cold Slab with n = 126

	N	O
32		*revenue*
33		
34	Mean	7.188422636
35	Standard Error	0.463714446
36	Median	6.057616621
37	Mode	0
38	Standard Deviation	5.205181748
39	Sample Variance	27.09391703
40	Kurtosis	-1.239351243
41	Skewness	0.038215943
42	Range	15.99864921
43	Minimum	0
44	Maximum	15.99864921
45	Sum	905.7412521
46	Count	126
47	Confidence Level(95.0%)	0.91774844 *Margin of error*

Q. **Using table 4.19, would we say that the per-period average total revenue for Cold Slab would be $7.19 with a margin of error $0.92, or a range of $6.27 to $8.11? Is that right?**

A. That is correct.

Q. **What is the owner asked for an estimate within $0.50?**

A. Then we would rerun the formula for a margin of error of $0.50.

Q. **Why don't we just run a very large sample size to begin with and be done with it?**

A. Because there is always a cost associated with increasing your sample size. In our case, it is just computer resources, but many real-life problems require that you go out and collect additional data, such as if we were doing marketing research or opinion polls. The sample size and margin of error concepts apply there too. The basic idea is that in running simulation, you want to be parsimonious—in other words, use just as much as you need and not more.

ACTIVE LEARNING: LESSON 4.4

LESSON 4.5: Simulating Newsboy-Type Problems

Introduction

Q.   **What's a "Newsboy" problem?**

A.   Any situation where you must buy perishable inventory without knowing how much you will sell.

Q.   **What is "perishable" inventory?**

A.   Something that goes bad or becomes obsolete quickly, so you must sell it before it becomes worthless.

Q.   **Why is that called a newsboy problem?**

A.   That is a historical term stemming from the time when newspapers were sold on street corners in most large cities. Every morning, newsboys went to the newspaper building and bought as many papers as they thought they could sell that day. If they bought too many, they lost the money they spent to buy them, but if they ran out of papers, they wished they had bought more.

Q.   **Why didn't they just buy as many papers as they thought they would sell?**

A.   They did. But the problem is that they never knew exactly how many they would sell.

Q.   **Is this a forecasting problem?**

A.   Well, it could be, but if variance is high, forecasting is unreliable. When this problem was identified, operations researchers tried to determine the number of newspapers to buy using mathematics, but that worked only if the demand for newspapers followed some specific distributions. That leaves simulation.

Q.   **Why simulation?**

A.   With simulation, we can help the newsboys regardless of the distribution of demand; so, the newsboy problem is an excellent one on which to practice your newly acquired simulation skills.

Q.   **OK, but why not give me something more useful than obsolete newsboys (or, newspersons)?**

A.   Remember that we called this lesson newsboy-type problems. There are numerous other problems that require us to make decisions about noninventoriable items.

Q.   **What do you mean by "noninventoriable item"?**

A.   That's just another word for perishable inventory (defined above). Yesterday's newspapers cannot be used to meet the demand for today's newspapers. Food trucks cannot keep food overnight and sell it the next day. Some chemical processes, once they are begun, have to be completed in a limited amount of time.

Q.   **What about fashion clothing or seasonal items, things like ski wear, seasonal foods, Halloween costumes, and the like. Are they all newsboy-type problems?**

A.   Absolutely. Even things as simple as programs for a football game or replica jerseys of star players are good for only a short time. A lot of companies face these types of problems.

Learning Outcomes

When you complete this lesson, you will be able to develop Excel formulas for:

- Number of units sold
- Number of units short
- Number of units left over

You will understand and be able to use Excel to compute:

- Goodwill cost
- Overage cost
- Revenue
- Profit

A Dialectic on Newsboy-Type Problems

Q.   **What do we do to simulate a Newsboy problem?**

A.   The same things we have done for every simulation: Model Development, Data Collection, Validation and Verification, Design of the Simulation Experiment, and Optimization.

Q.   **Don't you usually give us the data we need?**

A.   Yes, and I will this time as well. Please remember, though, that collecting this data is tedious. For this class, the real trick is to organize your data and to design the simulation table. Below is a problem that you can tackle:

   Every home football game for the last eight years at Notre Signor University (NSU) has been sold out. The revenues from ticket sales are significant, but the sale of food, beverages, and souvenirs has contributed greatly to the overall profitability of the football program. One particular souvenir is the football program for each game. The demand for programs at each game is described by the probability distribution given in table 4.20.

TABLE 4.20: Demand Distribution for NSU Football Programs

Demand	Probability
2,300	0.18
2,400	0.21
2,500	0.24
2,600	0.22
2,700	0.15

Currently, 2,500 programs are ordered for each game. Each program costs $1.00 to produce and sells for $2.00. Any programs that are not sold cost an additional $0.05 to be recycled. The university is interested in keeping track of how many additional units it could have sold if every fan that wanted a program was able to get one.

Q.   **OK, well, here goes. That demand distribution is discrete (only a few outcomes), so I will have to develop a spreadsheet with a VLOOKUP table. How is this (table 4.21)?**

TABLE 4.21   VLOOKUP and Data for NSU

	A	B	C	D	E	F
3						
4				Cum.	RN	
5		Demand	Probability	Probability	Range	
6		2,300	0.18	0.18	0	
7		2,400	0.21	0.39	0.18	
8		2,500	0.24	0.63	0.39	
9		2,600	0.22	0.85	0.63	
10		2,700	0.15	1	0.85	
11						
12	VLOOKUP TABLE					
13						
14		RN			DATA	
15		Range	Demand		Cost	$	1.00
16		0	2,300		Sell	$	2.00
17		0.18	2,400		Overage cost	$	0.05
18		0.39	2,500		Quantity odered		2500
19		0.63	2,600				
20		0.85	2,700				

A.   Excellent! Now remember that to build the simulation, it helps to visualize events unfolding as they would at NSU regarding the sales of programs. Let's close our eyes together and walk through the events.

Q.   **We are simulating selling programs at games, so we need a column for Games, right?**

A.   Right.

Q.   **The data says we order 2,500 programs for each game. Do we need a column for that?**

A.   Yes, because that is data we need at the end of the simulation.

Q.   **Well, during the game we sell programs, but we don't know how many programs we will sell. That sounds like it could be random, so we need a random number column and a column for # of Programs Sold. How am I doing so far?**

A.   Perfectly.

Q.   **I think that is all the simulation, so we calculate our outputs. The data tells us there is a cost to buy the programs, revenue from selling them, and cost to recycle unsold programs, so we need a column for each of those. Is that everything?**

A.   Not everything—you need a column to know how many short you are, and based on all that, we still need to calculate our profits.

Q.   **Bother, forgot those. OK, then, here is a spreadsheet (table 4.22). How's that look?**

TABLE 4.22   Column Headings for NSU Simulation

	B	C	D	E	F	G	H	I	J	K	L
22											
23					# Programs	# Programs	# Programs	Recycle		Program	
24	Games	Order	rn	Demand	Sold	Recycled	Short	Cost	Revenue	Cost	Profit

A.   Good Job! You're getting the hang of this. This table looks right, so let's put some formulas in each column.

Q.   **OK, here are all my formulas for row 25.**

B25 Games:	**a counter, telling how many games have been simulated**
C25 Order:	**copied from the data, =F$18**
D25 Rn:	**a random number, =RAND() or copied from a table**
E25 Demand:	**our simulated value, =VLOOKUP(D25,B$18:C$20,2)**
F25 # Programs Sold:	**the lesser of Demand or Order, =MIN(C25,E25)**
G25 # Programs Recycled:	**only if # SOLD is less than ORDER, =IF(F25<C25,C25-F25,0)**
H25 # Programs Short:	**only if # SOLD is greater than ORDER, =IF(F25>C25,F25-C25,0)**
I25 Recycle Cost:	**# RECYCLED * the recycling cost/unit, =G25*F$17**
J25 Revenue:	**# SOLD * Selling Price, =F25*F$16**
K25 Program Cost:	**ORDER * Cost/Unit, =C25*F$15**
L25 Profit:	**Revenue—Recycle Cost—Program Cost, =J25-I25-K25**

Did I do it correctly?

A.   Very nice! Your formulas should simulate the situation at Notre Signor accurately. The spreadsheet (table 4.23) shows the results for one game.

TABLE 4.23   Game 1 Simulation Results for NSU

	B	C	D	E	F	G	H	I	J	K	L
22											
23					# Programs	# Programs	# Programs	Recycle		Program	
24	Games	Order	rn	Demand	Sold	Recycled	Short	Cost	Revenue	Cost	Profit
25	1	2500	0.529664	2500	2500	0	0	$ -	$5,000.00	$2,500.00	$2,500.00

Q.   **Are we ready to run the simulation?**

A.   First, we need to know how accurate we need to be.

Q.   **Would +/- 1% be accurate enough?**

A.   Probably, but that would be up to the administration. For now, let's see what results we get.

Q.   **Do we start by calculating how big a sample we need?**

A.   No, first we need a good estimate of the mean and variance, which we get by running 60 simulations.

Q.   OK, I did that and ran the Descriptive Statistics in the Data Analysis Add-in. What do I do with all these numbers?

TABLE 4.24   Descriptive Statistics for a Sample of 60 Simulations

	Profit
Mean	2394.08
Standard Error	19.18
Median	2500.00
Mode	2500.00
Standard Deviation	148.56
Sample Variance	22069.06
Kurtosis	−0.29
Skewness	−1.05
Range	410.00
Minimum	2090.00
Maximum	2500.00
Sum	143645.00
Count	60.00
Confidence Level (95.0%)	38.38

A.   Your best estimate, at this point, of the true profits is the mean of the sample of 60 simulations, which is 2394.08 and is the first entry in table 4.24. Your best estimate of the variance is 22,069.06, shaded in table 4.24. Your margin of error is 38.38.

Q.   Didn't we just say we wanted to be +/- 1% of the mean? That would be a margin of error of 23.94, wouldn't it?

A.   Yes, so we need a larger sample.

Q.   I just went back in my notes and found the sample size formula:

$$n = 1.96^2 * \text{Variance}/e^2$$

Is that the one I must use?

A.   Yes, so go ahead.

Q.   Here is the calculation:

$$n = (1.96)^2 * 22069.06/23.94^2$$
$$n = 147.93$$

or 148 since I always have to round up any decimals to get the sample size. That means I have to run my simulation for 148 games and then run the Descriptive Statistics again. Are these results in table 4.25 right?

A.   You shouldn't ask if the numbers are right, because they are random. There is no answer key in the business world to check them against.

Q.   **What should I ask, then?**

A.   Ask whether the process you used to get the answers is correct. If you are following the correct process, you will get the right answer.

TABLE 4.25 95% Confidence Interval for Notre Signor Program Sales

Profit	
Mean	2385.03
Standard Error	12.92
Median	2500.00
Mode	2500.00
Standard Deviation	157.21
Sample Variance	24715.48
Kurtosis	−0.66
Skewness	−0.94
Range	410.00
Minimum	2090.00
Maximum	2500.00
Sum	352985.00
Count	148.00
Confidence Level (95.0%)	25.53
UCL=	$2,410.57
LCL=	$2,359.50
Point estimate =	$2,385.03

Q.   **Was my process correct?**

A.   Yes, it was.

Q.   **Then can we tell the administration that we should order between 2,360 and 2,410 programs for reach game?**

A.   That is accurate to within 1%, which for this data turns out to be a range of 50 programs.

Q.   **What if they want a smaller range, a more accurate estimate?**

A.   Then find out what they want and rerun the process to get an answer that satisfies them.

ACTIVE LEARNING: LESSON 4.5

LESSON 4.6: Simulating Inventory Policies

Introduction

Q.   **What do you mean by "inventory policy"?**

A.   With perishable inventory, the only questions was how much to order, because you would have to buy more the next period. Now we are talking about nonperishable inventory, so the problem is a little harder.

Q.   **Why is it harder?**

A.   You can carry over inventory to sell in future periods. That means you have to decide not only how many units to order but also when to order them, so an inventory policy answers those two questions.

Q.   **Is an inventory policy that much harder to simulate?**

A.   No. You have to add columns for keeping track of our inventory level as well as for when to place an order, and so on. Overall, though, simulation makes dealing with inventories a whole lot simpler than it used to be.

Q.   **Than it used to be—when?**

A.   In the BC (before computers) era. Inventories have always been a major issue, both for companies and governments (armies that run out of supplies tend to lose, which usually has undesirable consequences).

Q.   **So, how did they come up with inventory policies then?**

A.   Through mathematical procedures, which could become very hairy very quickly. And every time something different arose with respect to inventories, mathematicians and the like had to go back to work to come up with an inventory policy for that situation. Libraries abound with doctoral dissertations tackling almost any inventory quirk you can think of.

Q.   **That makes me very happy to be in the AC era. What are we doing first in developing inventory simulation models?**

A.   Let's first understand some important concepts about inventories—perhaps the most important being that you should not think of inventories as warehouses full of parts but as money that is tied up, or invested, in goods. Companies don't leave money sitting around in bank accounts, and it's the same with inventories.

Q.   **That makes sense, but do inventories tie up a lot of money?**

A.   So much that it is hard to find a business or industrial engineering curriculum that does not devote one or more courses to it. Plus, the number of books and papers that have been written on the subject is staggering.

Q.   **I'm sure they are fascinating reading but haven't Just-In-Time (JIT) manufacturing, Materials Requirements Planning (MRP), and other techniques eliminated inventories, making inventory management obsolete?**

A.   Not as much as you would think. The techniques that you mention are applicable only to dependent demand items, meaning those that are part of assemblies or subassemblies for complex products, such as doors for a car.

Q.   **And once you know how many cars will be produced, then you know how many doors will be needed. What kind of items do have inventory?**

A.   Just about any product that is not specifically made-to-order.

Q.   **So, inventory management focuses primarily on on-the-shelf products?**

A.   That is a reasonable way of thinking about it.

Q.   **Why not just forecast demand and match inventory to that?**

A.   The demand for such products is usually random. Over time, the inventory you have on hand (IOH) is depleted. Figure 4.9 shows the IOH for a hypothetical situation where the demand is random.

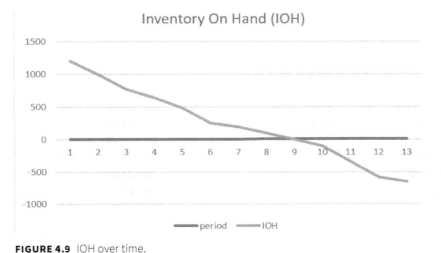

FIGURE 4.9 IOH over time.

Q.   **Why is the IOH curve going negative around period 9?**

A.   If the IOH curve goes negative, that means that we are allowing backordering and that as soon as we receive a new shipment, those backorders will be filled.

Q.   **Makes sense. So, if we do not allow backorders, then the IOH curve would stay at zero?**

A.   Indeed.

Q.   **In the introduction you said an inventory policy had to answer two questions: how much to order and when to order. How do we go about doing that?**

A.   There are two common types of inventory replenishment methods:

- Fixed order quantity with variable order interval
- Fixed order interval with variable order quantity

Q.   **Are they that different?**

A.   Fixed Order Quantity is based on two decision variables:

- The order quantity, Q
- The reorder point, P

Q.   **What's a "reorder point"?**

A.   An inventory level at which you know to place a new order for Q units.

Q.   **Who decides all this?**

A.   You do, which is why they are called "decision" variables.

Q.   **Once we know those two, what do we do?**

A.   There is one other variable, but you don't control this one, your vendor does: the lead time, L.

Q.   **Once the vendor tells us the lead time, are we ready to go?**

A.   Lead time might not be a fixed time period; it usually has some variability associated with it to give the shippers some slack and discretion.

Q.   **OK, fine. We know how much to order, when to order it, and how long it will take to show up (more or less). Why is it called a variable order interval system?**

A.   Because that is the one thing you don't know. I already said that demand was random, so you don't know how long it will take to sell off your inventory on-hand. What you do know is that when your IOH drops to the reorder point level, P, you place an order (that's why it is called a reorder point).

Q.   **Are you saying I have to sit there and watch the inventory level all the time?**

A.   Well, *you* don't have to, but someone or something does. This type of system is also referred to as a continuous review system because it requires constant monitoring of the IOH, but that is pretty much done by computer these days.

Q.   **It looks as if we know everything about this inventory system. Why do we need to simulate it?**

A.   Let me show you, in figure 4.10, what the IOH for a system like this looks like.

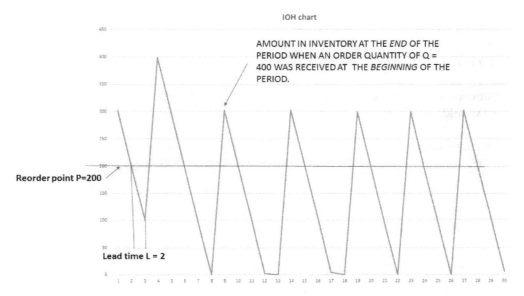

FIGURE 4.10   IOH chart for a continuous review inventory policy with Q = 400, P = 200, and L = 2.

Q.   **What were the parameters for that figure?**

A.   We assumed an inventory policy that places an order for Q = 400 units whenever the IOH gets down to 200 (P), with a lead time, L, of 2 periods and random demand; then a graph of the IOH would be as shown in figure 4.11.

Q.   **I noticed that you used the term *inventory policy*. What exactly do you mean by that?**

A.   The inventory policy consists of those items that you control. In this example, we set the values of Q and P.

Q.   **And L, the lead time?**

A.   Typically, L is determined by your supplier, sometimes in consultation with you. You could request a different shipping method if you wanted to get the order faster (or slower) or to change the cost, but it will still take time for the order to arrive.

Q. So, every time the inventory line hits 200, the reorder point, we place an order for 400 units that show up two days later. Why do some of the bottom markers flatten out?

A. Those are points in time when you ran out of stock. We are not showing negative IOH (how many units short you were), but most inventory systems do keep track of that.

Q. But how did we run out?

A. That is the problem with this type of system. Since demand is variable, sometimes your IOH doesn't last until the new order arrives.

Q. Are you saying this was a bad inventory policy?

A. Not necessarily, just that we did miss some sales.

Q. But another inventory policy might not lose sales, so, how do we determine the inventory policy we should use?

A. That depends on what you want to achieve. Most commonly, we seek to find the policy that minimizes our overall Average Total Inventory Cost (ATIC), which is given by

ATIC = average ordering costs + average shortage costs + average holding costs

Q. OK, that sounds reasonable. What do we do with that?

A. First, see if we can agree on the following statements:

- The more you order, the less frequently you have to place an order.
  - As Q gets bigger, the average ordering costs gets smaller.
- The higher you set the reorder point P, the smaller your chances of running out of stock.
  - The higher P, the lower the average shortage costs.
- The more you order, the more you will have invested in you inventory.
  - The higher Q, the higher the average holding costs.

Q. I can't argue with any of that, but how does it help?

A. To understand the situation, we make trade-offs between them.

Q. How does that work?

A. To illustrate, let's just take the average ordering cost and the average holding costs and ignore the average shortage cost for the moment.

Q. Why leave out shortage cost?

A. Because I can't show you a graph in three dimensions. I can, however, draw a picture of costs as a function of Q to help you understand.

Q.   **Understand what?**

A.   Look at figure 4.11. As you increase Q, two opposing things occur: the ordering costs decrease as the holding costs increase. The value of Q at which they intersect, Q*, is where the minimum ATIC occurs. Q* is commonly referred to as the Economic Order Quantity, or EOQ.

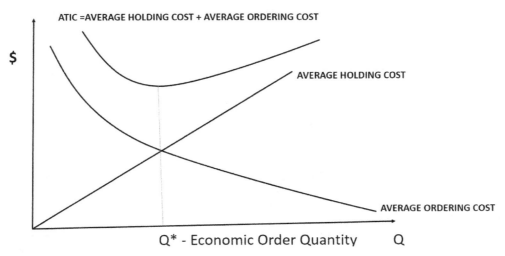

FIGURE 4.11 Conceptual representation of the EOQ.

Q.   **What would that look like in three dimensions, with shortage cost included?**

A.   If we had included the average shortage cost the minimum ATIC would occur at the bottom of bowl, so to speak, giving us values for Q and P.

Q.   **Will we be using a formula to find the EOQ?**

A.   No, those formulas don't match the real world.

Q.   **Why not?**

A.   Traditional EOQ formulas assume a constant demand and a constant lead time. Countless graduate theses and dissertations have been written about finding the EOQ when these assumptions do not hold, but, frankly, I have found them to be of little use in the real world.

Q.   **So, what do I do if I want to find the optimal inventory policy?**

A.   Simulation.

Q.   **Should have seen that coming. Wait, how about the other inventory method?**

A.   You mean fixed interval, variable order quantity models? Those are used for items that are resupplied at regular intervals—for example, vending machines. The resupply interval, I, is determined between you and the supplier, and the supplier restocks the product to a predetermined target level, T.

Q.   **You know, at this rate, you are going to run out of letters in the alphabet. What else changed?**

A.   Not much. We have two of the same costs components for the ATIC, the average holding cost and the average shortage costs, but the third component, the average ordering cost, goes away and the average resupply (or restock) cost takes its place. Look at figure 4.12 and see if the IOH graph for such a system, also called a periodic review system, makes sense to you.

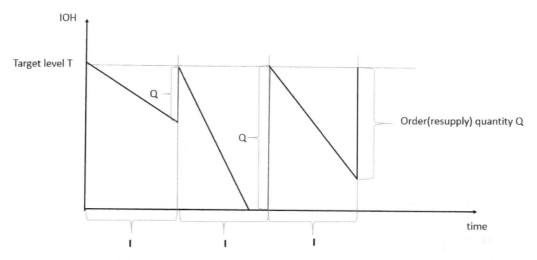

FIGURE 4.12 IOH graph for a periodic review system.

Q.   **Again, that makes sense. The value of T becomes the maximum inventory level, and we can still have stock-outs. How do we set up an inventory policy now?**

A.   The policy would consist of the target level and the resupply interval I (to the extent it can be negotiated with the vendor).

Q.   **And we would find the optimal inventory policy through simulation, right?**

A.   Indeed.

Q.   **OK. I am all conceptualized out. How about putting these concepts to practice?**

A.   In the next lesson.

LESSON 4.6.1 Simulating Fixed Order Quantity Inventory Systems

Introduction

Q. **What is a good starting point for building the simulation table for a fixed order quantity inventory system?**

A. The simulation table we built for newsboy-type problems. If you use that as the starting point, then extending the simulation is a matter of adding columns to keep track of the amount you have in inventory and when it is time to place orders and when they are received.

Q. **You make it sound rather simple—just an extension of what we already know. Is it really that simple?**

A. Yes, after you have done it a couple of times. But you will have to learn some new Excel tricks in order to build such a table for the first time.

Learning Outcomes

- When you complete this lesson, you will know how to set up the simulation table for a fixed order quantity inventory system.

A Dialectic on Simulating Fixed Order Quantity Inventory Systems

Q. **Do you have a problem for us to work on?**

A. I have a friend named Martin Fierro. He owns an Argentine-themed steak house. He is also enrolled in an on line MBA program and has tried to apply the Economic Order Quantity (EOQ) formula to manage his wine inventory. He is concerned, however, about using the results because several of the assumptions that were listed in the book do not apply to his case.

Q. **Will we use simulation to see how the EOQ model would work in practice?**

A. Yes but remember that simulation does not yield an answer to a situation directly. In this case, your friend Martin has an answer (the EOQ) that he does not trust. Simulation is ideal to see how an "answer" really would work.

Q. **What data will we need for the simulation?**

A. Here is what you need:

Martin Fierro's Tango Argentino Wine Inventory Problem

Martin Fierro, owner of Tango Argentino, an upscale Argentinian-style steak house in historic Cocoa Village, Florida, has made it a point of differentiation for his restaurant to serve Mendoza wine out of barrels, like they used to do in the small bodegas in his home country. When the last bottle of wine (the only available) is poured out of a barrel, the first few bars of Carlos Gardel's "Adios Muchachos" are played and the wait staff does a few impromptu tango steps, much to the delight of the clientele.

Martin must order his barrels of wine directly from the winery located in the province of Mendoza in Argentina. He rents space in a local cold storage facility there that charges him a flat $5.00 per barrel per month (or any portion thereof). Because he uses a proprietary blend of grapes, the winery charges him a flat fee of $2,000 whenever he places an order to cover the cost of special handling and blending that is required. He currently has 400 barrels in storage.

Getting the barrels from the winery to his restaurant requires train transport to Buenos Aires followed by container ship to a U.S. port followed by truck delivery. This process can take anywhere from one to three months (it's a toss-up how long any shipment will take). Receipts always occur at the beginning of the month.

Currently, he is using an average of 100 barrels per month, but he is equally likely to use anywhere between 98 and 102 barrels. If and when he runs out of his Mendoza wine, he substitutes a domestic equivalent, creating a goodwill loss of $100 per barrel short.

Martin is enrolled in an on line MBA program and has taken a supply chain management course. Using the EOQ formulae, he calculated that his economic order quantity should be to order 400 barrels whenever the amount that he has in cold storage gets down to 200 barrels. He is concerned, however, because his business doesn't seem to run as "cleanly" as those in the text. Consequently, he would like to see what would happen if he did use the results of the EOQ formulas.

Simulate Martin's wine inventory policy so he can see what would happen with a margin of error of +/- 10% of the true cost. In developing the simulation model, use the random numbers given in the following link:

ACTIVE LEARNING: LINK 4.6.1: RANDOM NUMBERS FOR MARTIN FIERRO

Q. **Where do we start?**

A. Let's go ahead and put the data in a spreadsheet.

Q. **OK ... here it is in table 4.26. Shall I also add the process generators?**

A. Of course. We cannot proceed without them.

Q. **Martin's demand is integer between 98 and 102. I guess that means that I should use a VLOOKUP table. So, I must have the probability of each demand occurring. Since demand can take on only 1 of 5 values, I guess that the probability for each demand is 0.2?**

A. Excellent! So, go ahead and set up the VLOOKUP table.

Q. **I put the calculations and the demand VLOOKUP table in table 4.27. Did I do the correctly?**

A. Excellent again! Now just show me the VLOOKUP table for lead time. I do not need to see the calculations. You have convinced me that you know what you are doing.

TABLE 4.26 Martin Fierro's Inventory System Data

	A	B	C	D
1	DATA			
2				
3	holding cost	$ 5.00	per barrel per month	
4	ordering cost	$2,000.00	per order	
5	goodwill cost	$ 100.00	per barrel	
6	initial inventory	400	barrels/month	
7	min demand	98	barrels/month	
8	max demand	102	barrles per month	
9	min lead time	1	month	
10	max lead time	3	months	
11				
12	INVENTORY POLICY			
13	order quantity	400	units	
14	reorder point	200	units	
15				

TABLE 4.27 Calculating the VLOOKUP for Demand

					VLOOKUP Table for demand	
		Cummulative	Lower rn		Lower rn	
Demand	Probability	Probability	range		range	demand
98	0.2	0.2	0		0	98
99	0.2	0.4	0.2		0.2	99
100	0.2	0.6	0.4		0.4	100
101	0.2	0.8	0.6		0.6	101
102	0.2	1	0.8		0.8	102

Q. OK, here they are in table 4.28. All of this was soporiferous, to say the least. Are we ready to start with building the simulation?

A. Yes, we are ready, and, yes, gathering and setting up data is tedious. While most companies keep all sorts of data, it is seldom the kind of data we need for models, which gives us no choice but to get it ourselves. Of course, if you have a university nearby, you might be able to get some interns to help out.

TABLE 4.28 VLOOKUP for Lead Times

VLOOKUP Table for lead time	
lower rn range	lead time
0	1
0.333333333	2
0.666666667	3

Q.   **Good, I'll keep that in mind. Now, let's start developing a simulation model for his inventory system. Any words of wisdom before I try my hand at it?**

A.   Yes, the key thing to remember is that we want to imagine that we are in the simulation. By that I mean imagining that you are actually seeing and recording everything that is going on with the wine inventory. As we do so, we will be generating his random events, which are sales and lead times. Everything else relating to his inventory will be calculated using appropriate Excel functions and formulas.

Q.   **Geez ... I hear you, but I have a hard time imagining something I have never seen.**

A.   Good point. In any simulation effort, the most important decision is to determine how the clock moves.

Q.   **What does that mean?**

A.   That means that we need to know when things happen that cause a change in the simulation—in our case, the inventory system. Typically, in inventory systems, we review the inventory periodically. Since our data is given in months, we can build the system by adopting the convention that we will look at our inventory monthly.

Q.   **All right, then, for inventory, it changes when inventory is received and when units are sold. Anything else?**

A.   Very good, but we also need to know what inventory calculations we need to do.

Q.   **Well, we have starting inventory; then when a shipment arrives, it gets added to inventory; and when we sell wine, we subtract it from inventory, and we get ending inventory. Anything else?**

A.   A couple of things. The variable lead time means we need to figure out when orders are received. You also forgot to mention lost sales. A good guide is to look at your data and make sure you have everything covered.

Q.   **How do we put all that into a spreadsheet?**

A.   Let's say that the clock just turned to our first month of simulated time. Table 4.29 shows the information we will calculate or generate as part of the simulation.

TABLE 4.29   Inventory Simulation Information for Martin Fierro's Establishment

	A	B	C	D	E	F	G	H	I	J	K	L
18		units	beginning			units	ending	lost	place		lead	month
19	month	received	inventory	rn	demand	sold	inventory	sales	order?	rn	time	order arr.
20	1	0	400	0.26601	99	99	301	0		0.3872211		0

Q.   **Could you explain each column?**

A.   Here goes:

- Column A: the clock, tells us what month we are in

- Column B: tells us if we have a shipment coming in at the beginning of the month

- Column C: inventory at the start of the month
- Column D: random number for demand simulation from the linked RN table
- Column E: generate demand
- Column F: minimum of demand and beginning inventory
- Column G: the difference between the beginning inventory and the units sold
- Column H: the difference between demand and units sold
- Column I: if ending inventory is less than 200, yes
- Column J: random number for lead time from the linked RN table
- Column K: generate lead time
- Column L: current month plus lead time

Note: In a real situation, we would use the RAND() function in columns D and J to generate random numbers. However, that would mean that you and I would be getting different random numbers. That would make following this lesson extremely difficult. In order to make sure that you have the same random numbers as me while developing the simulation model, I have included a link to a spreadsheet containing the random numbers that we are going use at the end of the problem statement.

Q. **All that makes sense, but how did you come up with it?**

A. A lot of experience, quite a few mistakes, and some logic. I did not sit down and write all that out the first time. I began with column C (beginning inventory), then realized I needed column B (units received) to calculate beginning inventory, and I continued from there.

Q. **So, what you said about imagining yourself in the simulation?**

A. Exactly. You imagine the system (inventory, in this case), and list what you think you will need. There is no tried and true method, so coming up with the format of a simulation is what you might think of as the "art" of simulation. Whenever you try a new simulation, just start with what you can think of at the time, and as you progress and see that you need additional information, add the appropriate new column(s).

Q. **What formulas do I need to make the simulation work?**

A. Let's do the list again:
- Column A: enter a "1"
- Column B: =IF(L20=0,0,400)
- Column C: enter "400"
- Column D: = random number from linked spreadsheet
- Column E: =VLOOKUP(D20,K$5:L$9,2)
- Column F: =MIN(E20,C20)
- Column G: =C20−F22
- Column H: =E20−F20

- Column I: =IF(G20<B$14,"YES"," ")
- Column J: = random number from the linked spreadsheet
- Column K: =IF(l20="Y",VLOOKUP(J20,N$5:O$7,2))
- Column L: =IF(l20="Y",A20+K20+1,0)

Q.   **Now that I have the columns and filled the entries for the first month, do I just copy the formulas down for the next months?**

A.   Not quite. There are still some holes in the simulation. In the first month of the simulation, we cannot look back to see if there is an order arriving. After the first month, we have to take into account whether we have an order underway before deciding to place an order and in calculating when an order placed that month would arrive at Martin's establishment.

Q.   **How do we fix that?**

A.   Let's go to the next month so you can see how to develop the "general" case, meaning a row that has the formulas that can handle all eventualities. Table 4.30 shows a five-month simulation.

TABLE 4.30   Five-Month Simulation for Martin Fierro's Establishment

	A	B	C	D	E	F	G	H	I	J	K	L
18		units	beginning			units	ending	lost	place		lead	month
19	month	received	inventory	rn	demand	sold	inventory	sales	order?	rn	time	order arr.
20	1	0	400	0.26601	99	99	301	0		0.3872211		0
21	2	0	301	0.39469	99	99	202	0		0.2745965		0
22	3	0	202	0.60546	101	101	101	0	Y	0.3237312	1	5
23	4	0	101	0.93702	102	101	0	1		0.8141445		5
24	5	400	400	0.24104	99	99	301	0		0.7457701		0

Q.   **What changed?**

A.   These are the changes from the formulas of row 20:

Column B: Check column L to see if an order is scheduled to arrive.
Column I: Place an order only if another order is not pending.
Column L: Calculate when new order is due and zero out pending order if delivered.

Q.   **How do we do that?**

A.   The formulas to develop this simulation were established in row 21 and are shown in table 4.31. They were copied (dragged down) to develop this simulation.

Q.   **Can you maybe walk me through one of them?**

A.   Sure. Let's take the formula for placing an order in column I. The first part of the first =IF statement asks whether the ending inventory (G) is at or below the reorder point $B$14.

Q.   **What happens when that is true?**

A.   If that is the case, we go to the second =IF statement, which asks whether the current month (A) is greater than the month for which the next delivery is scheduled (L).

TABLE 4.31 Formulas and Functions Used to Develop Months 2–5 of the Simulation

COLUMN	DESCRIPTION	FORMULA
A	month	enter number
B	units received	IF(L20=A21,$B$13,0
C	beginning inventory	G20+B21
D	random number for demand	from table linked to lecture notes
E	demand	VLOOKUP(D21,$H$5:$I$9,2)
F	units sold	MIN(C21,E21)
G	ending inventory	C21-F21
H	lost sales	E20-F20
I	place order?	IF(G21<=$B$14,IF(A21-L20>=0,"Y",""),")
J	random number for lead time	from table linked to lecture notes
K	lead time	IF(I21="Y",VLOOKUP(J21,$L$5:$M$7,2),"")
L	month order arrives	IF(I21="Y",A21+K21+1,IF(L20>A21,L20,0))

Q. **Why does that matter?**

A. If there is already an order coming (the next delivery is after the current month), we do not place an order. Only when the most recent order has already been delivered do we place a new order.

Q. **And the "Y" means "Yes," place an order, right?**

A. Correct, and if not, we leave the cell blank, which is what "" means to Excel.

Q. **I have to say, all this math is giving me a headache. How did you come up with all this?**

A. Remember what I said earlier—experience, and trial-and-error. You are seeing the finished product, but I didn't sit down and type in all those formulas. Just the way we are doing it, I typed in one cell and started thinking about the next cell.

Q. **How do you learn this kind of math?**

A. Actually, we are not doing any math, and I don't expect you to walk away from this able to write a simulation like this.

Q. **Then why are we doing it?**

A. I want you to see what simulation can do for you. If, at some point in your career, you decide to try a simple simulation, you know enough to do it. If you decide this is a tool you want to use a lot, then you would practice it. That's really all simulation is—practice and asking for help from people who know more.

Q. **Then, can you help me translate that last formula into English?**

A. That's a good choice of words. We are just reading symbols, translating the code into English. Just take one piece of the equation at a time and translate what the expression is doing into words.

Q.   **Do I have the key to break this code?**

A.   You do, but let's try it together. Here's the equation:

$$\text{=IF(I21="Y",A21+K21+1,IF(L20>A21,L20,0))}$$

Q.   **Well, column L determines the month the order arrives. Is the first thing to figure out whether you are placing an order?**

A.   Right, and =IF(I21="Y" does that for us.

Q.   **If we are placing an order, how long will it be until it arrives?**

A.   We already figured that out in column K, the lead time.

Q.   **Then if the answer is yes, would we add the lead time in column K to the current time in column A?**

A.   That is what comes next, A21+K21+1.

Q.   **What is the "+1" for?**

A.   The +1 takes into account that you are making this decision at the end of the month (since you are basing it on ending inventory), so this month does not count as part of the lead time.

Q.   **So, that's what happening if we are placing an order, but what if we aren't?**

A.   If you are not placing an order, then the next question is whether there is an order scheduled to arrive.

Q.   **Why? Isn't it already scheduled?**

A.   It is, but in Excel it can be hard to find something that has been scheduled, so we have to drag that along with us. Look at Month 3 in table 4.30. An order is placed that is due in Month 5. In Month 4, we had to check to see if an order had been placed that had not yet shown up (as was true), and we copied the due date, Month 5, into column L of Month 4. Then, when Month 5 rolled around, the reminder that the order was coming in was in Month 4.

Q.   **How do we do that?**

A.   The next =IF statement asks if the time the next order is scheduled to arrive (column L) is beyond this next month.

Q.   **If that is true, what do we do?**

A.   If so, we leave the time the next order is scheduled to arrive as is, but we copy it to the current month.

Q.   **What if the order is arriving next month?**

A.   If the order is arriving next month, we reset the arrival for the next order to zero, meaning there are no longer any outstanding orders.

Q.   **Is that it? Is the simulation done?**

A.   Sort of. We have the inventory simulation part of the model, but we have not set up the outputs, the inventory costs.

Q.   **Why do we need the costs? We were asked to see what would happen for this order quantity and reorder point, and we have that, don't we?**

A.   Yes, but, as a good businessperson, wouldn't you want to know whether you could lower the costs? To compare different what-ifs, we need the costs.

Q.   **What costs do we need to calculate?**

A.   We have ordering cost ($2,000 per order), a lost sale or shortage cost ($100 every time we run out of wine), and a holding cost ($5 per barrel per month).

Q.   **Do we use beginning inventory or ending inventory for the holding cost?**

A.   Good question! The standard way of handling that is to charge $5 for the average inventory held during the month. In our case, we'll define the average inventory as follows:

$$\text{average inventory} = (\text{beginning inventory} + \text{ending inventory})/2$$

Q.   **Where do we put all these calculations?**

A.   We can add a column for each kind of cost plus a column for our total inventory cost to our Excel model. Table 4.32 shows the result when we add those columns to table 4.30.

TABLE 4.32   Inventory Simulation with Costs

	A	B	C	D	E	F	G	H	I	J	K	L	M	N	O	P
18		units	beginning			units	ending	lost	place		lead	month	ordering	shortage	holding	total inv.
19	month	received	inventory	rn	demand	sold	inventory	sales	order?	rn	time	order arr.	cost	cost	cost	cost
20	1	0	400	0.266011	99	99	301	0		0.387221134		0	$ -	$ -	$ 1,752.50	$ 1,752.50
21	2	0	301	0.394686	99	99	202	0		0.274596453		0	$ -	$ -	$ 1,257.50	$ 1,257.50
22	3	0	202	0.605456	101	101	101	0	Y	0.323731173	1	5	$ 2,000.00	$ -	$ 757.50	$ 2,757.50
23	4	0	101	0.937022	102	101	0	1		0.814144517		5	$ -	$ 100.00	$ 252.50	$ 352.50
24	5	400	400	0.24104	99	99	301	0		0.745770113		0	$ -	$ -	$ 1,752.50	$ 1,752.50

Q.   **Is this where we run the simulation for 60 months to get the statistics?**

A.   Exactly. To do that, we have to "pull down" row 24 until we have a sample of 60 months and then apply descriptive statistics to column P, the total inventory cost. This yields the results shown in table 4.33.

Q.   **How did you get that table again?**

A.   We went to the Data Analysis tab under Data on top of the spreadsheet and the clicked on Descriptive Statistics. This created a dialog box, which we filled out and is shown below in figure 4.13.

TABLE 4.33 Descriptive Statistics for Running
Martin's Simulation Model 60 Months

Cost	
Mean	2680.83
Standard Error	381.45
Median	1751.25
Mode	1752.50
Standard Deviation	2954.68
Sample Variance	8730126.41
Kurtosis	1.96
Skewness	1.76
Range	9955.00
Minimum	245.00
Maximum	10200.00
Sum	160850.00
Count	60
Confidence Level (95.0%)	763.27

Q.   **Thanks! How did we do?**

A.   Going back to table 4.33, the average inventory cost per month is \$2680.83 plus or minus the confidence level, \$763.27. In other words, we are 95% certain that the true average monthly inventory cost will be between \$1917.56 and \$3444.11.

Q.   **That is almost a \$1,500 difference. Does that really help?**

A.   I can't imagine any boss being happy with that large a range. I think Martin would be happy if we give him an estimate of the average inventory cost within plus or minus 10%.

Q.   **This is where the sample size formula comes in, isn't it?**

A.   Correct. We use the formula

$$n = (1.96)2 * \sigma^2/e^2$$

and the correct value of σ^2 (sample variance) from table 4.33 together with the 10% acceptable error margin, or e = 0.1*2680.83= 268.083, to get

$$n = (1.96)^2 * (8730126.41)/(268.083)^2$$
$$n = 467 \text{ (rounded up)}.$$

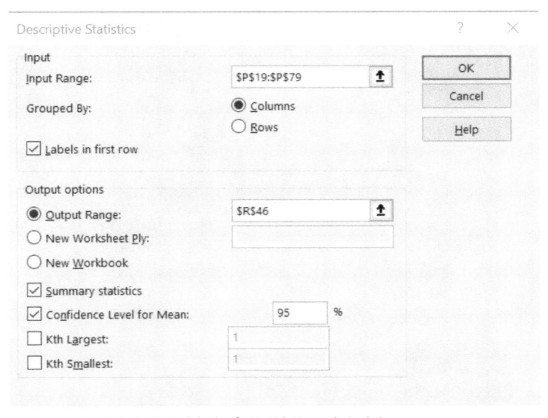

FIGURE 4.13 Descriptive Statistics dialog box for Martin's 60-month simulation.

Q.   **That means that I've got to drag that simulation down for 467 months?**

A.   Yes, and then we must get the descriptive statistics results again to get the results we want to propose. The results of doing this are shown in table 4.34.

Q.   **Looking at the last row, it looks like we did better than the stipulated margin of error of 268.083. What happened?**

A.   Statistics and randomness. The formula is a 95% confidence formula, which means we are not always going to get the exact desired results, but we should be close. It could just as easily have been a bit larger if we had a different sample of 468 months. Let's summarize the results by using the "average" function on each respective column in the 467–month simulation):

For the inventory policy:

Order Quantity: 400 units	Reorder Point: at or below 200 units
Average Ordering Cost	$445.40 per month
Average Shortage Cost	$1107.49 per month
Average Holding Cost	$989.95 per month
Average Total Inventory Cost	$2,542.84 +/- $249.55 (95% Confidence)

TABLE 4.34   Martin's Inventory Simulation Descriptive Statistics

Cost	
Mean	2542.84
Standard Error	126.99
Median	1750.00
Mode	1752.50
Standard Deviation	2744.30
Sample Variance	7531173.35
Kurtosis	2.69
Skewness	1.95
Range	9955.00
Minimum	245.00
Maximum	10200.00
Sum	1187507.50
Count	467
Confidence Level (95.0%)	249.55

Q.   **Isn't that shortage cost, $1,107.49 per month, pretty high?**

A.   Unfortunately, when you reduce the shortage cost, you wind up having to hold more units in inventory, increasing the holding cost. All these inventory costs trade off with each other, so you cannot look at changing only one of them, which is why we calculated the total average inventory cost.

Q.   **Who decides?**

A.   The boss, Martin. So, let's show him the results and then we'll know where to go next—if anywhere.

ACTIVE LEARNING: LESSON 4.6.1

LESSON 4.6.2 Optimizing Inventory Policies Using Solver

Introduction

Q. **What do you mean by "optimizing"?**

A. We built an inventory simulation last time, but no one would go through all that trouble to run the simulation one time. Building a simulation model is not an end but a means to achieve other ends, such as an optimal inventory strategy.

Q. **Huh?**

A. Remember that models are to a business analyst what test tubes are to a chemist. They are tools with which to conduct experiments.

Q. **Didn't we run an experiment to estimate Martin's total inventory cost to within +/- 10%?**

A. Yes, but now that we have a replica of his inventory system in a computer, we can run more experiments, manipulating the data and seeing the results almost instantaneously.

Q. **Why would I want to manipulate a model after all the work I put into building it??**

A. Why wouldn't you? After all that work, it would be a waste not put the simulation to use to find a better result.

Q. **How do we run an experiment?**

A. Well, we could make random changes to the data, but that would be pointless. Fortunately, Excel has some options that will help us find the best results.

Q. **Doesn't simulation already find the best results?**

A. No. Simulation only tells you the results for the numbers you type in. It doesn't tell you if there was a better result, and in a business environment, you always want to see if there are better ways to doing things, like running your inventory system.

Q. **By "running your inventory system," do you mean using different inventory policies—like using different order points and/or order quantities?**

A. Now you are getting it. With all the money that is tied up in inventories, there usually is quite an opportunity to realize savings.

Q. **So, by "optimizing" you mean finding the inventory policy that makes the total inventory cost as small as possible?**

A. Exactly.

Learning Outcomes

When you complete this lesson, you will know:

- How to install the Excel Add-in Solver
- What "Solver" means by:
  - Objective
  - Variable cells
  - Constraints
  - GRG
  - Simplex
  - Evolutionary
  - Local optimum
  - Global optimum
- How to use Solver to optimize the results of a simulation

A Dialectic on Optimizing Fixed Quantity Inventory Systems

Q. **After all the effort we put into building the simulation, were you surprised Martin didn't have time to talk about it?**

A. No, not really. He is a very busy guy, and he accepted that we knew what we were doing and that our simulation skills were superior to his.

Q. **Should we have gone in with more work done?**

A. No. He could have just as easily said, "Thank you very much" and then gotten some big-time consulting firm to do the job for him. I take it as a big compliment that he asked us to help him with his inventory.

Q. **So, how do we go about telling Martin how to manage his inventory?**

A. We are going to use Solver to help us find the best way inventory policy for him.

Q. **What is Solver?**

A. It is an Excel Add-in that must be installed. It hides out at the same place that Data Analysis does. Figure 4.14 shows the installation process.

- Click on Excel options.
- Click on Add-ins, then on Go.
- Click on the box next to Solver Add-in and then on OK and you are good to go.
- To use it, click on Data in the banner row of Excel and you will see it all the way to the right, next to Data Analysis.

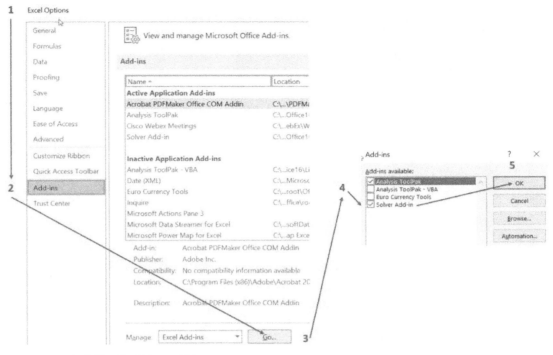

FIGURE 4.14 Installing the Solver add-in.

Q.   I have it! So, what do I do with Solver?

A.   A whole lot of things (chapter 5 is pretty much devoted to it), but for now we will concentrate on how to use Solver to find lower-cost inventory policies.

Q.   You mean optimal inventory policies, don't you?

A.   I wish. "Optimal" means the best—that is, absolutely the lowest cost. While Solver can almost always improve on our best guesses, our inventory models are just tables with lots of random numbers and bunches of calculations. Solver cannot guarantee us that for this problem.

Q.   Does Solver guarantee *the* best solution for any real problems?

A.   Yes, but we will cover that in chapter 5. For the time being, we'll settle for doing better.

Q.   OK, how do we do better?

A.   Solver needs an objective, something to maximize or minimize. For the inventory problem, that would be to minimize average total inventory cost, so in table 4.35, cell E16, we added this formula:

$$=AVERAGE(P20:P486)$$

On the spreadsheet, it shows the value $2,542.84 from the 467 samples. I have marked that, as well as the inventory policy, the order quantity (400), and reorder point (200), as shaded.

TABLE 4.35   Preparing the Simulation Table for Solver

	A	B	C	D	E	F	G	H	I	J	K	L	M	N	O	P
12	INVENTORY POLICY															
13	order quantity	400	units													
14	reorder point	200	units													
15																
16		SOLVER OBJECTIVE		total inv. cost=	$2,542.84											
17																
18		units	beginning			units	ending	lost	place		lead	month	ordering	shortage	holding	total inv.
19	month	received	inventory	rn	demand	sold	inventory	sales	order?	rn	time	order arr.	cost	cost	cost	cost

Q.   Using the simulation table as a coloring book is probably the most fun I've ever had with Excel, but why mark the inventory policy?

A.   Besides an objective, Solver needs to know what to change to improve the objective. That would be the inventory policy.

Q.   What does Solver do?

A.   Solver takes the initial policy (marked as shaded) and changes the values of the order point and the reorder level to see how the changes affect the total inventory cost.

Q.   But how does it know what to do?

A.   Solver is what we call an "algorithm," a series of rules that tell us whether changes will help (decrease cost) or hurt (increase cost).

Q.   You mean it has artificial intelligence, sort of like an Alexa or Siri, built in?

A.   That is a very good way of thinking about it. Just like Alexa or Siri, it has a bunch of rules built in. They help Solver to decide in which way to change the order quantity and the reorder point.

Q.   And the algorithm makes a change and then stops?

A.   An algorithm is a set of steps that repeat. That means that the algorithm makes one change that will improve the cost, then it makes another change that improves cost some more, and keeps repeating that until it finds the best solution it can.

Q.   So, when it can no longer improve the objective, then we reached the optimal solution?

A.   Not necessarily. For a problem like this, where Solver winds up depends on where it starts.

Q.   Are you saying if we change our starting inventory policy, then Solver will find a different best solution?

A.   Maybe. That is why, as you will see, we will always pick several different starting points. If Solver winds up with the same policy every time, then we have some assurance that we have the optimal policy. If it winds up at different places, then we'll just pick the best one and declare that the optimal solution.

Q.   Enough words. How do we use Solver to find better solutions?

A.   Click on the Solver icon in the "Data" link. Figure 4.15 shows you the Solver dialog box already filled for our inventory.

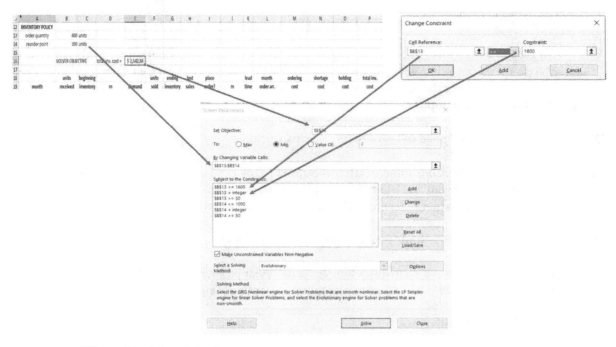

FIGURE 4.15 Filling out the Solver dialog box.

Q.   **What does "Set Objective" mean?**

A.   That is asking for the formula for the total cost, so we click on the cell F16.

Q.   **And what does "By Changing Cells" mean?**

A.   Those are numbers that Solver can control to affect the total cost, so we click on B13:B14, where we have order quantity and reorder point, our inventory policy.

Q.   **Where did the "Change Constraints" dialog box in the upper right-hand corner come from?**

A.   You get it by clicking on the "Add" button on the right side of the dialog box. What you will get will not say "Change Constraints," but the rest will be the same.

Q.   **Does that mean that we do not directly add the constraints below where it says "Subject to the Constraints"?**

A.   Exactly. You must click on "Add" and the dialog box will appear. You add the constraints one at a time. After each, you click on "Add" to indicate that another constraint is coming. When you have added all the constraints, you click on "OK" and that will be it for the constraints.

Q.   **OK. But where do the constraints come from?**

A.   Solver cannot look at all values for the order quantity and reorder point. We have to limit the options, but there are no hard and fast rules for doing so. I arbitrarily decided to keep Solver's search for the order quantity between 50 and 1,600, and between 50 and 1,000 for the reorder point.

Q.   What are those constraints that say "= Integer"?

A.   I also decided to restrict the values for both to be integer, since fractional values made no sense in Martin's problem. When you click on the pull-down menu between the "Cell Reference" and "Constraint" headings in the "Change Constraints" dialog box, you will get several options, including INT. Just select the appropriate one and move to the next constraint.

Q.   OK. What else do I need to know before I crank up Solver?

A.   There is a little check box underneath the "Subject to the Constraints" box. Unless negative values have a meaning for your situation, check it. It will make sure that you only get nonnegative answers. Also, the pull-down menu next to "Select a Solving Method" will give you three options.

Q.   I see "Simplex," "GRG," and "Evolutionary." What are they?

A.   They are three different algorithms. Simplex is for linear problems, which this is not. We will learn about that in chapter 5. The other two options are nonlinear algorithms.

Q.   So, which one should we use?

A.   We will use both. Evolutionary is the one that will probably work the best, but I usually start with GRG, just out of curiosity, and the run Evolutionary with whatever inventory policy GRG comes up with. Then, after Evolutionary gives me an answer, I do GRG one more time using the Evolutionary answer as my starting point.

Q.   Do you ever get different answers after you run Evolutionary?

A.   Yes, that is why I go through the ritual. Sometimes I get lucky.

Q.   What happens when we use GRG?

A.   Figure 4.16 is what appears when you click "Solve" after selecting GRG.

Q.   I don't see a solution. How can I decide whether I want to keep it?

A.   What you are looking for is the statement "Solver found a solution." If you don't see that, then you probably have something wrong with how you set up Solver.

Q.   But we do see that, so where is the solution?

A.   The solution appears in cells B13:B14, the ones you listed in "By Changing Cells." It only shows up when you click "OK," as is shown in table 4.36.

Q.   Did you also add that "History" box, or did Solver so that?

A.   That was me. That is not necessary, but it is handy to keep track of the solutions as we go.

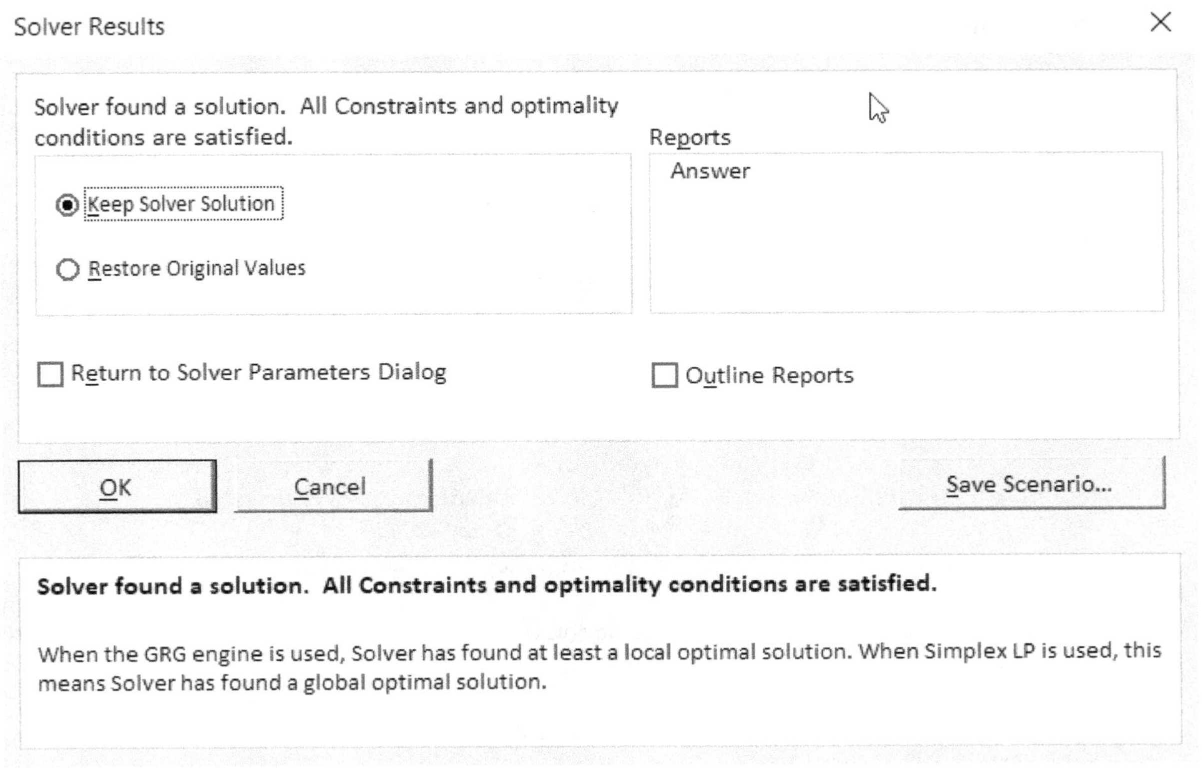

Solver Results   ✕

Solver found a solution. All Constraints and optimality
conditions are satisfied.   Reports

                                                                   Answer

  ◉ Keep Solver Solution

  ◯ Restore Original Values

  ☐ Return to Solver Parameters Dialog   ☐ Outline Reports

  | OK | Cancel | | Save Scenario... |

Solver found a solution. All Constraints and optimality conditions are satisfied.

When the GRG engine is used, Solver has found at least a local optimal solution. When Simplex LP is used, this
means Solver has found a global optimal solution.

FIGURE 4.16 Solver results dialog box.

TABLE 4.36   GRG Results

	A	B	C	D	E	F	G	H	I	J	K	L
11								Optimization Iteration History				
12	INVENTORY POLICY						Initial	GRG	Evolutionary	GRG		
13	order quantity	396	units				400	396				
14	reorder point	200	units				200	200				
15												
16		SOLVER OBJECTIVE		total inv. cost =	$2,327.38		$2,542.84	$ 2,327.38				
17												
18		units	beginning			units	ending	lost	place		lead	month
19	month	received	inventory	rn	demand	sold	inventory	sales	order?	rn	time	order arr.
20	1	0	400	0.266010904	99	99	301	0		0.3872211		0

Q.   **GRG didn't do much, did it?**

A.   It just lowered the order quantity by four, but that reduced the total inventory costs by over $200.
        Even small changes can have a pretty good cost savings.

Q.   **Now you said to run Solver using the Evolutionary algorithm, right?**

A.   Right, so click on "Data" in the top row of our spreadsheet, then click on the Solver icon to open
        the Solver box.

TABLE 4.37 Evolutionary Results

	A	B	C	D	E	F	G	H	I	J	K	L
11								Optimization Iteration History				
12	INVENTORY POLICY						Initial	GRG	Evolutionary	GRG		
13	order quantity	393 units					400	396	393			
14	reorder point	341 units					200	200	341			
15												
16		SOLVER OBJECTIVE		total inv. cost =	$2,033.58		$2,542.84	$2,327.38	$2,033.58			
17												
18		units	beginning			units	ending	lost	place		lead	month
19	month	received	inventory	rn	demand	sold	inventory	sales	order?	rn	time	order arr.
20	1	0	400	0.266010904	99	99	301	0	Y	0.3872211	2	4

Q.   Do we have to reenter everything?

A.   Nope, Solver remembers everything you did. All we have to change is replacing "GRG" with "Evolutionary" in the pull-down menu and click "Solve." Table 4.37 shows the results.

Q.   Nice! We just saved over $500 from the current policy. Shall we give Martin the good news?

A.   No. Let's make sure we are not leaving money on the table. Let's go ahead and run GRG one more time and see if we get lucky.

Q.   OK, well, I opened Solver and changed back to GRG and clicked "Solve," but nothing changed. Why not?

A.   That means table 4.37 contains the best solution we are going to find.

Q.   Now do we go see Martin to give him the good news?

A.   If you tell him we were able to reduce his total inventory costs to $2,033.58, what is the probability that you will be correct?

Q.   Right, right. We need the 95% confidence interval. Is it OK to use 467 as the sample size?

A.   Yes, that is fine.

Q.   The results are in table 4.38. As a bonus, I also calculated the components of his total inventory costs. What should I write up for Martin?

A.   I'd start with the inventory policy—an order quantity of 393 units with a reorder point of 341 units. The 95% range for costs is $1,928.18 to $2,138.98, which is within +/- 10% of the mean of $2,033.58. This is an average cost savings of $509.26.

Q.   Boy! Using Solver sure paid off for Martin's problem. Does it do as well for other types of inventory problems?

A.   Let me show you how to simulate and optimize fixed interval inventory policies, and we'll see how Solver does with them.

TABLE 4.38   Minimum Cost for Martin's Inventory Problem

Minimum Cost	
Mean	2033.58137
Standard Error	53.63701463
Median	2042.5
Mode	3712.5
Standard Deviation	1159.10569
Sample Variance	1343526.001
Kurtosis	−1.323360884
Skewness	0.352203969
Range	4635
Minimum	290
Maximum	4925
Sum	949682.5
Count	467
Confidence Level (95.0%)	105.4003659
LCL=	1928.18
UCL-	2138.98
Average ordering cost	$505.35
Average shortage cost	$114.35
Average holding cost	$1,413.88
Average total inventory cost	$2,033.58

ACTIVE LEARNING: LESSON 4.6.2

LESSON 4.6.3 Simulating and Optimizing Fixed Order Interval Inventory Systems

Introduction

Q.   **Do we still need to know the order quantity and reorder point for fixed order interval inventory systems?**

A.   Those are what we needed for a fixed order quantity system, when the amount to order was always the same, but the time between orders could vary. This time, we will place an order at regular intervals, such as once a week, and we will order enough to fill up our inventory.

Q.   **Why would we need an inventory system like that?**

A.   Many establishments receive goods on certain days of the week or month as a result of their supplier's delivery schedules. If you know that, and you know the lead time for delivery, then you know when to place your order so it shows up on time.

Q.   **Didn't you say lead times were variable?**

A.   In some situations, yes, and then we use fixed order quantity systems. When regular deliveries are already scheduled, lead times tend to be more stable, so a fixed order interval system works better.

Q.   **What did you mean by "order enough to fill up our inventory"?**

A.   Maximum inventory levels can be set by storage space, or shelf space in a display, or just by how much money you are willing to have tied up in inventory. When you know that, and the time comes to place an order, you subtract inventory on-hand from the maximum inventory level, and that is how much you order.

Q.   **Can you still run out of inventory, or have excess inventory when the new order arrives?**

A.   Yes, since demand is still variable.

Q.   **Are there any new inventory costs, other than holding, shortage, and ordering costs?**

A.   Nope, that is all we need to calculate total inventory cost.

Q.   **Are there any absolute advantages of one system over the other?**

A.   Not really. It all depends on the business situation you are dealing with.

Q.   **Is either system easier to simulate or optimize?**

A.   Again, not really. Once you know how to simulate one type of inventory system, it is no big deal to simulate another.

Learning Outcomes

When you complete this lesson, you will know how to:

- Set up a simulation table for a fixed order interval inventory system
- Use Solver to find the optimal fixed order inventory policy

A Dialectic on Simulating and Optimizing Fixed Order Interval Inventory Systems

Q. **Do you have a company that wants to use a fixed order interval system?**

A. As a matter of fact, I just got a call from Sheats Gasoline Station yesterday. They need to switch to a fixed order interval system to match their new supplier. Here is what they told me in an e-mail:

Sheats Gasoline Station Fixed Interval Inventory System
   Sheats' current price for gasoline is $3.39/gallon and the cost is $1.25 per gallon. Their daily demand is normally distributed with a mean of 3,000 gallons and standard deviation of 100 gallons. They have switched gasoline suppliers, and the new supplier is adding them to his tanker route. The tanker is scheduled to arrive at their establishment every seven days. They must place an order by the end of the day, two days before the tanker is scheduled to arrive at their establishment. The tanker is scheduled to arrive at their station prior to opening on the third day after the order is placed. The supplier charges $300 per week for adding Sheats to his route, whether an order is placed or not.
   Sheats' tanks hold 20,000 gallons. Their current inventory is 10,000 gallons and they expect a delivery of 7,000 gallons at the beginning of Day 2. They will fit into the new delivery schedule by placing their next order at the end of Day 6. It will arrive at the beginning of Day 9. They are planning to order the difference between (a) their inventory at the end of the day that an order must be placed and (b) their tank's capacity. Sheats' accounting department has adopted the policy of charging $0.02 per gallon for every gallon held in inventory at the end of each day. Whenever any shortage occurs, a flat fee of $1,000 is charged in the books. Sheats must pay for gas when the order is placed. Thus, their current inventory is paid for.
   Estimate Sheats' Total Average Profit with a +/- 10% margin of error.

Q. **That sounds just like a class assignment. Are all business world problems just like homework?**

A. The business world is more complex than homework assignments, but the complexity is about *more* rather than *different*. You will have more data, or more options, but the way we simulate it is the same. Being able to see the world as a bunch of textbook problems has been most valuable in my industry and consulting careers. It allows me to solve problems by relating the real world to what I teach or learned in the classroom.

Q. **Then let's learn something real-world. How do you set up the simulation table for a fixed order inventory system?**

A. First, take all the data listed in the statement and put it at the top of the spreadsheet, as shown in table 4.39.

Q. **Let's see what I can do on my own. Gasoline demand is normally distributed, so I would use the NORMINV function instead of a VLOOKUP table. So far, so good?**

A. You are doing great.

Q. **OK, then, since in fixed inventory systems the lead time is stable, we don't need to simulate that. That means the rest of the table is just like the fixed order quantity model we did before. Does table 4.40 look right?**

A. I'm impressed. You left out the cost calculations, but we can add them later.

TABLE 4.39   Sheats Fixed Inventory Simulation Data

	A	B	C	D
1	DATA			
2				
3	holding cost	$	0.02	per gallon per day
4	ordering cost	$	300.00	per order
5	lost sales cost	$	1,000.00	whenever a shortage occurs
6	initial inventory		10,000	gallons
7	quantity in transits		7,000	gallons
8	Initial delivery on morning of day		2	
9	Tank Capacity		20,000	gallons
10				
11	demand/day	normally distributed with mean of =	3,000	
12		std deviation=	100	
13				
14	price	$	3.39	per gallon
15	cost	$	1.25	per gallon
16				
17	INVENTORY POLICY			
18	order quantity		15,000	gallons
19	reorder interval		7	days
20	lead time		3	days
21	Place initial order at end of day		6	

TABLE 4.40   Sheats' Fixed Order Interval Inventory System Simulation

	A	B	C	D	E	F	G	H	I	J	K	L
23												
24		units	beginning			units	ending	lost	place	order	lead	day
25	time	received	inventory	rn	demand	sold	inventory	sales	order?	quantity	time	order arr.
26	1	0	10,000	0.69	3,049.59	3,049.59	6,950.41	-				0
27	2	7,000	13,950	0.73	3,061.28	3,061.28	10,889.13	-				0
28	3	0	10,889	0.16	2,900.55	2,900.55	7,988.58	-				0
29	4	0	7,989	0.65	3,038.53	3,038.53	4,950.05	-				0
30	5	0	4,950	0.01	2,767.37	2,767.37	2,182.68	-				0
31	6	0	2,183	0.71	3,055.34	2,182.68	-	872.66	Y	20,000.00	3	9
32	7	0	0	0.91	3,134.08	-	-	3,134.08				0
33	8	0	0	0.99	3,232.63	-	-	3,232.63				0
34	9	20,000	20,000	0.18	2,908.46	2,908.46	17,091.54	-				0
35	10	0	17,092	0.33	2,956.01	2,956.01	14,135.53	-				0

Q.   **I thought I should get the simulation working first. Can we go over the formulas?**

A.   Table 4.41 is a printout of the formulas from row 27, the second row of the simulation, because the first row has the data we were given (shown as shaded in table 4.40).

Q.   **Why do we have different formulas for Day 2?**

A.   Beginning inventory, in column C, takes ending inventory from the previous period (column G) and adds any order received (column B) for this period. There is no previous period for Day 1, so we just enter beginning inventory from the data.

Q.   **Is that true for all columns?**

A.   No, in column B, for instance, we used the same formula for all days.

TABLE 4.41 Formulas and Functions Used to Develop the Simulation

COLUMN	DESCRIPTION	FORMULA
A	month	enter number
B	units received	=IF(A27>$B$20,IF(A27-L24=0,J24,0), IF(A27=$B$8,$B$7,0))
C	beginning inventory	=G26+B27
D	random number for demand	from table linked to lecture notes
E	demand	=NORMINV(D27,$C$11,$C$12)
F	units sold	=MIN(C27,E27)
G	ending inventory	=C27-F27
H	lost sales	=E27-F27
I	place order	=IF(A27=$B$21,"Y", IF(MOD(A27-$B$21,$B$19)=0,"Y",""))
J	order quantity	=IF(I27="Y",$B$9-G27,"")
K	lead time	=IF(I27="Y",$B$20,"")
L	day order arrives	=IF(I27="Y",A27+$B$20,0)

Q. What does the first part in the column B formula, A27>$B$20, refer to?

A. A27 is the day counter, and B20 is the lead time, so if the day count is greater than the lead time, we need to check to see whether an order is coming in.

Q. Is that what the middle part does, IF(A27-L24=0,J24,0)?

A. Right, L24 is the next delivery date, so if the current date is equal to the next delivery date, then show the order amount, from J24.

Q. Does the last bit, IF(A27=$B$8,$B$7,0), handle the original order?

A. We only check this if the current date is less than the first possible lead time, $B$8 is the scheduled arrival of the first shipment, and $B$7 is the amount of the first shipment; so, if the current date is equal to the scheduled arrival, then show the first shipment.

Q. You make it sound simple, but how do you come up with that?

A. You have to learn how to use an IF-THEN-ELSE function in Excel, and then you have to stop and think about what you need to do in small steps. How do you know when a shipment is received? When the date is equal to the arrival date. How do you handle the first shipment? When the date is equal to the scheduled arrival date. How do you do them both? By realizing that the first shipment arrives within the lead time and checking for that. It takes practice, but you can learn to think like that.

Q. But how do you learn in the first place?

A. My very first computer programming professor, way back in the seventies (when dinosaurs roamed the earth), told me that the way you learn to become a good programmer is to "sit around the campfire and listen to old programmers talk." What he meant was that other people have probably already faced the problems you are facing, so when in doubt, ask for help. I don't have the time to cover every possible Excel function, so now you know that when you hit something in Excel that you want to do, but don't know how to do, ask.

Q.   OK, I'm asking. What is the MOD function in column I and why did you use it?

A.   I had a problem: we place an order every seven days, which sounds simple, but as the day counter gets bigger and bigger, I need a way to know if seven days have passed. I looked online and found a discussion that explained how to use the MOD function.

Q.   How does MOD do that for you?

A.   MOD calculates the remainder of a division calculation, so MOD(9,2) means the remainder of 9 divided by 2. Since 2 goes into 9 four times with 1 left over, MOD(9,2) = 1.

Q.   How does that help?

A.   Sometimes, the MOD function returns a value of zero, when one number goes evenly into another number, such as 8 divided by 2 = 4 with nothing left over, and MOD(8,2) = 0. We can use that to know when seven days have passed.

Q.   Can you walk us through the formula, one piece at a time?

A.   That is always the best way to understand a complicated function. Here is the formula for column I:

$$\text{=IF(A27=\$B\$21,"Y",IF(MOD(A27-\$B\$21,\$B\$19)=0,"Y",""))}$$
$$\text{\$B\$19 = reorder interval = 7}$$
$$\text{\$B\$20 = lead time = 3}$$
$$\text{\$B\$21 = first day to place order = 6}$$

We know the first day when we can place an order is Day 6 (that was in the problem). We also know we can place an order every seven days after that.

Q.   Then the first part, =IF(A27=$B$21,"Y", just says that if the current date is equal to the first day we can place an order, we put a "Y" to say that we will place an order. What is the second part, though?

A.   We need to place an order every seven days after Day 6, meaning Day 13 (6 +7), then Day 20 (13 + 7), et cetera. When I searched online for functions dealing with "constant interval," the first recommendation I got was =FREQUENCY, but that counts how often an interval occurs. Then I searched for functions that find numbers "divisible by 7" and got the =MOD function.

Q.   But 13 and 20 aren't divisible by 7, so how does that help?

A.   That's because we didn't start with Day 0, we started with Day 6, so 13 − 6 = 7, or 20 − 6 = 14, are divisible by 7. In words, the current date (A27) minus the first order date (B21) divided by the reorder interval (B19) will give a remainder of zero. In Excel, IF(MOD(A27-$B$21,$B$19)=0,"Y","").

Q.   Do you really think I could have figured that out on my own?

A.   Maybe not originally, but the next time you run into something like that, remember that there is a way to do it and start searching.

Q. I'm not likely to forget this class without therapy. Well, the rest of the simulation table is very much like it was for the fixed quantity simulation. How do we add the cost data?

A. Be careful—we have profit data, not cost. It is not that different though, so take a look at table 4.42.

TABLE 4.42 Simulation Table for Sheats

time	units received	beginning inventory	rn	demand	units sold	ending inventory	lost sales	place order?	order quantity	lead time	day order arr.	holding cost	ordering cost	lost sales cost	total inv cost	sales (revenues)	cost of goods sold (gas)	profit
1	0	10,000	0.69	3,049.59	3,049.59	6,950.41	-				0	139.01			139.01	10338.09	0.00	10199.08
2	7,000	13,950	0.73	3,061.28	3,061.28	10,889.13	-				0	217.78			217.78	10377.74	8750.00	1409.96
3	0	10,889	0.16	2,900.55	2,900.55	7,988.58	-				0	159.77			159.77	9832.88	0.00	9673.11
4	0	7,989	0.65	3,038.53	3,038.53	4,950.05	-				0	99.00			99.00	10300.62	0.00	10201.62
5	0	4,950	0.01	2,767.37	2,767.37	2,182.68	-				0	43.65			43.65	9381.37	0.00	9337.71
6	0	2,183	0.71	3,055.34	2,182.68	-	872.66	Y	20,000.00	3	9	0.00	300.00	1000.00	1300.00	7399.29	0.00	6099.29
7	0	0	0.91	3,134.08	-	-	3,134.08				0	0.00		1000.00	1000.00	0.00	0.00	-1000.00
8	0	0	0.99	3,232.63	-	-	3,232.63				0	0.00		1000.00	1000.00	0.00	0.00	-1000.00
9	20,000	20,000	0.18	2,908.46	2,908.46	17,091.54	-				0	341.83			341.83	9859.69	25000.00	-15482.14
10	0	17,092	0.33	2,956.01	2,956.01	14,135.53	-				0	282.71			282.71	10020.87	0.00	9738.16

Q. As you said, not that different. Shall we go show the Sheats folks our table?

A. Trust me, they don't want to see your table. All they want from you are suggestions on how to run their fixed interval inventory system and the bottom-line impact it would have.

Q. Oh, well. Let's see, this is what we still have to do:

- Run the simulation for 60 days
- Use the sample standard deviation to estimate the needed sample size to create a 10% margin of error
- Run the simulation for that sample size
- Use that data to get an estimated profit

Did I miss anything?

A. You did, but that's enough for now. Let's see what you get.

Q. Rounding up from table 4.43 (on the left), we will need a sample of 907. After running the simulation 907 times, we get the range on the left. What else do we need to do?

A. Before we get to that, what are you going to tell Sheats?

Q. Wouldn't we say this:

The expected daily profit for the fixed interval inventory policy is $4,940, with a 10% range of $4,426 to $5,455.

A. You left out something important: the policy itself. This is expected profit for a seven-day fixed order interval and a maximum inventory of 20,000 gallons.

Q. Right, but aren't they stuck with that? The tanker truck comes only once a week and their tanks have a capacity of 20,000 gallons. Should we try a lower maximum capacity?

A. Maybe, but instead we could optimize the simulation, as we did before.

TABLE 4.43   Sample Size and 10% Margin of Error for Sheats

profit			*profit*	
Mean	5080.839		Mean	4940.97
Standard Error	1007.805		Standard Error	262.36
Median	9751.814		Median	9692.03
Mode	-1000		Mode	-1000.00
Standard Deviation	7806.421		Standard Deviation	7901.46
Sample Variance	60940212		Sample Variance	62433054.26
Kurtosis	0.99498		Kurtosis	0.66
Skewness	-1.47489		Skewness	-1.40
Range	26232.65		Range	26789.07
Minimum	-15482.1		Minimum	-15888.80
Maximum	10750.51		Maximum	10900.26
Sum	304850.3		Sum	4481460.14
Count	60		Count	907
Confidence Level(95.0%)	2016.612		Confidence Level(95.0%)	514.91
			Point Estimate =	4940.97
e = 10% of Mean =	508.0839		95% Upper Confidence Limit	5455.88
N = 1.96^2 * Variance/e^2 =	906.8704	907	95% Lower Confidence Limit	4426.06

Q.   **What good would that do?**

A.   Information is always valuable, and you have a tool (the simulation) that can give you a lot of information. Remember, money speaks. If Sheats can get substantially higher profits from a different policy, then they can negotiate more (or less) frequent deliveries. And, they can always plan to increase their tank capacity (they appear to have space to add another 10,000-gallon tank).

Q.   **Should we always optimize our simulations?**

A.   What do you lose? Using a simulation to explore possibilities, in addition to evaluating existing policies, just makes sense after you put in all the work to create the model.

Q.   **Can you remind me of what I need to do to set up Solver?**

A.   Besides entering the total profit as the objective and setting up a place to change the policy (reorder interval and maximum inventory), you need to set upper and lower bounds to use the Evolutionary option. Just going by what is reasonable, the reorder interval is no less than 3 days and no more than 14. Less than 5,000 gallons could cause condensation problems, and the upper limit would be 30,000 if they add capacity. Also, I limited our search to integer values. Here is my Solver dialog box (figure 4.17).

Q.   **Did we do better?**

A.   Solver was able to increase their profits to $6,254.53, a gain of $1,313.56, as shown in table 4.44. Considering that these are average daily profits from managing their gasoline inventory alone, this is a sizable sum.

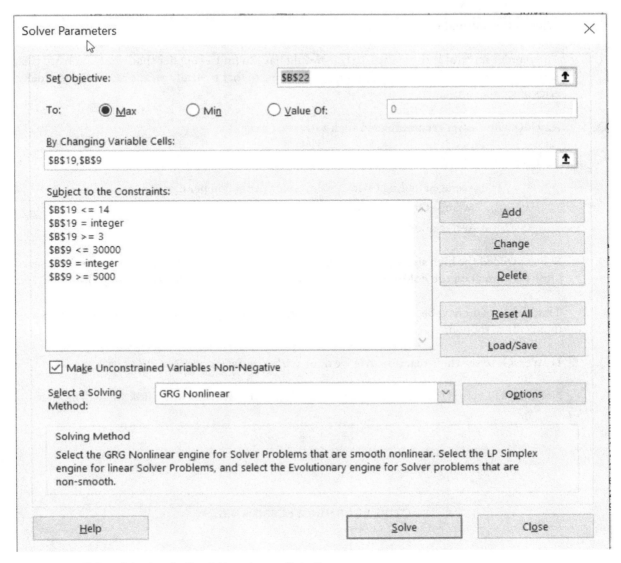

FIGURE 4.17 Solver dialog box for Sheats' inventory optimization.

TABLE 4.44 Comparison of Original and Solver Inventory Policies

	AHC	AOC	ALSC	ATIC	REVENUE	GAS COST	PROFIT
Original Policy	123.86	42.67	232.64	399.16	8461.44	3121.31	4940.97
Solver Policy	74.06	99.89	0.00	173.95	10170.03	3741.56	6254.53
Solver-Original	$ (49.80)	$ 57.22	$ (232.64)	$(225.22)	$1,708.59	$ 620.25	$1,313.56

Q. Where did those numbers come from?

A.   By averaging the 907 entries in the columns corresponding to those costs (columns M-S) in the simulation table using the original and then the optimal policy.

Q.   **What is the optimal inventory policy?**

A.   The reorder interval is three days, so they would have to find a supplier that would increase their deliveries. The maximum inventory is 15,686 gallons, so that basically means more frequent deliveries of smaller amounts.

Q.   **Any idea why Solver recommended such a drastic change?**

A.   Let's compare their inventory cost components:

Average Holding Cost	$0.02 per gallon per day
Average Ordering Cost	$300 per order
Average Lost Sales Cost	$1,000 per shortage

Q.   **Solver avoided the high shortage cost by placing more orders (increasing the order cost) but saved almost as much on the holding cost. Do you think is possible for Sheats to set up this policy?**

A.   That depends on how badly Sheats wants to make the change. Saving over $1,000 per day is a lot of incentive, though.

Q.   **I can't wait to see their reaction. Are we done with simulation now?**

A.   No, not yet. There is some pretty neat stuff coming in the next lesson. I think you will enjoy it.

ACTIVE LEARNING: LESSON 4.6.3

LESSON 4.7: Simulating Waiting Line Systems

Introduction

Q.   **What are "waiting line systems"?**

A.   Any system where the customers or products are queued up to wait for service.

Q.   **Wait a minute, what does "queued up" mean?**

A.   Another name for waiting lines is queues (at least, wherever they speak the British version of English), so "queued up" means waiting in a line. You might see this topic called Queuing Theory.

Q.   **Is there a difference between queuing systems and waiting line systems?**

A.   No difference except tradition. Much of business analytics was developed in England during World War II when it was called Operations Research, driven by the need to get the most out of the scarce resources the Brits had to fight the war.

Q.   **Why do we care about waiting lines, or queues, or whatever?**

A.   Queues are everywhere and, wherever they are, they waste somebody's time or money or both. I've never met anyone who was happy to be waiting in a line, but you do it all the time—at a drive-thru, in a doctor's waiting room, at a traffic light, or in an airplane circling over an airport. If you remember work-in-process inventory, that deals with products waiting in line to be completed.

Q.   **If there are ways of studying waiting lines, how come there are still so many of them?**

A.   Lines form whenever either the service rate (how long it takes to serve each customer) or the arrival rate (how quickly the customers are showing up), or both, are random.

Q.   **Why don't we just measure the arrival rate and make sure the service rate is the same?**

A.   Several reasons. The arrival rate is not (usually) constant. Customers tend to come in waves, or even randomly. Then, customers don't need the same service, so the service time is also random. Even if we did know when the customers would arrive, we would still have waiting lines because we cannot bring in servers when we need them to work for 30 minutes or an hour and then send them home.

Q.   **Are there any choices other than simulation?**

A.   There is a whole body of knowledge called Queuing Theory that has resulted in a host of formulas, most of them very complicated, to deal with a variety of queuing situations. However, virtually all formulas require a host of assumptions to be met, which limits their usefulness.

Q.   **So, simulation?**

A.   So much so that a number of special purpose simulation languages have been developed to facilitate simulating queuing systems, but you won't have to learn any of them in this course.

Q.   **Will simulating queuing systems be like simulating inventory?**

A.   There will be similarities, but some differences as well.

Q.   **We can still use Excel, though, right?**

A.   You know enough about Excel to simulate the simplest queuing system: one waiting line and one server. Beyond that, you would probably need a specialist in Excel programming.

Q.   **What other types of waiting line systems are out there?**

A.   Almost any combination of waiting lines and servers you can think of has been used at some point. I have borrowed figure 4.18 from one of my favorite texts to give you an idea of some common ones:

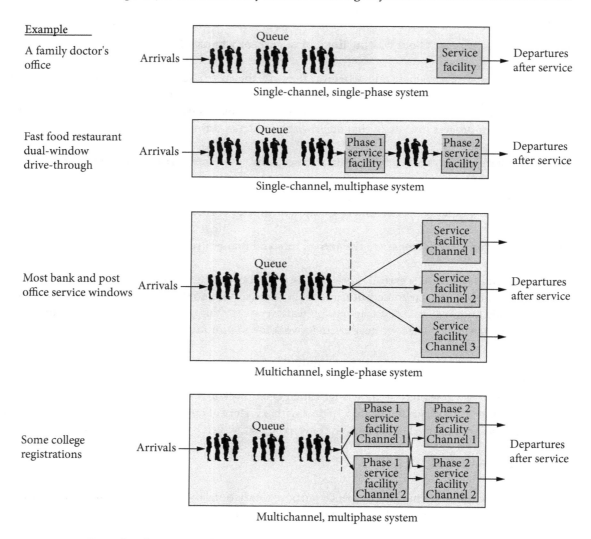

FIGURE 4.18 Examples of queuing configurations.

Adapted from Jay H. Heizer and Barry Render, Operations Management: Sustainability and Supply Chain Management. Copyright © 2013 by Pearson Education, Inc.

Q.   **So, when a fast-food place has two order stations, that would be two waiting lines, right?**

A.   Right, and when you pay at one window and pick up the order at a second window, that is two serving stations.

Q.   **I've always wondered, how do they keep all that straight?**

A.   There is a whole other queuing system inside the restaurant. Every order goes into a queue of orders that must be processed by both the kitchen staff (food prep) and drink staff, then combined to be handed to you.

Q. **Sounds complicated. Have fast-food places been using simulation for a long time?**

A. It is, and yes. Burger King pioneered the use of simulation in the restaurant industry back in the 1970s. The results were so important, Burger King was a finalist for the Best Application of Management Science (it is now called Business Analytics) in the world (and across all industries) in 1982.

Q. **Impressive. How do we start building waiting line simulations?**

A. Again, borrowing from Heizer and Render, a diagram of a car wash (a great example of a single-line, single-server system) is shown in figure 4.19.

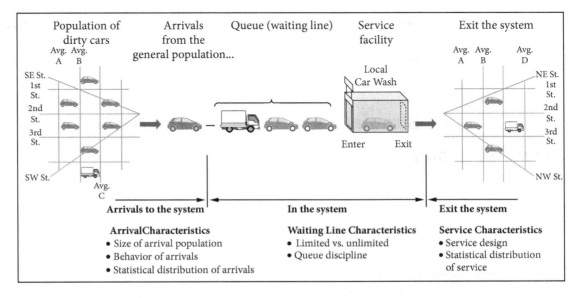

FIGURE 4.19 Components of a queuing system.

Adapted from Jay H. Heizer and Barry Render, *Operations Management: Sustainability and Supply Chain Management.* Copyright © 2013 by Pearson Education, Inc.

Q. **Are those words at the bottom all things we have to simulate?**

A. More precisely, they are all things we have to account for in the simulation. If we take them one at a time, it's not that bad.

Q. **What are all those "arrival characteristics"?**

A. Population just means, "How many customers can we expect?" Behavior means whether the customer can leave the line without being served (that is called "balking"). Since I told you before that the arrival process is random, you might expect we would need to know what kind of distribution the arrivals follow.

Q. **Why do we need characteristics of the waiting line?**

A. For this simulation, all we would need to know is how many cars can wait in line, which is what we mean by a limited queue. Other simulations might have an unlimited queue. With a limited queue, any new customers would have to balk.

Q.   **What is "queue discipline," and why don't we need to know it for a car wash?**

A.   We must know whether customers are served in order of arrival or whether they are served according to a scheduled time, as in a doctor's office. That is what we mean by queue discipline, and for this car wash, the cars stay in the order they arrive, so it is not an issue.

Q.   **You said service times are random, so we need a distribution for that, but what is "service design"?**

A.   Whatever describes the service, the number of servers, how many servers you have to see and in what order, and anything else we need to know.

Q.   **Can Excel simulate a car wash, whatever the characteristics of the individual components may be?**

A.   That depends on how clever you are with Excel. Let's see if we can find a reasonable system to simulate.

LESSON 4.7.1 Simulating Single-Line, Single-Server Queuing Systems

Introduction

Q.   **What do you mean by "reasonable"?**

A.   One that is relatively simple, yet realistic, and can be simulated by someone that is competent, albeit not necessarily a virtuoso, with Excel.

Q.   **Judging by the title of this lesson, it would be a single line, single server system?**

A.   Exactly.

Learning Outcomes

When you complete this lesson, you will know:

- The components of a queuing system
- Develop a simulation for a single-line, single-server queuing system using Excel
  - How to generate interarrival times
  - How to generate service times
  - How to build the simulation table
  - Calculate:
    - Average time in queue
    - Average time in system
    - Average server idle time
- Determine the transactional capacity of a simulation model

A Dialectic on Simulating Single-Line, Single-Server Queuing Systems

Q.   **What is a "queuing system"?**

A.   "Queue" is the British word for "line," so a "queuing system" is a "waiting line."

Q.   **Why do we want to simulate people standing still in a line?**

A.   We want to simulate how long they are standing in line.

Q.   **I've spent a lot of time standing in line, and I never enjoyed it. Why not just get rid of the lines?**

A.   That might be too expensive.

Q.   **Let me guess, we can use a simulation to find out how expensive it is, right?**

A.   Very good. Consider figure 4.20, where we show the Mountain Mudd Coffee Hut, the most basic waiting line situation: a single server system. Orders are taken at the window; the customer pays and then waits to receive the order before driving off.

FIGURE 4.20 A basic waiting line system.

Q.   **Where does the waiting line come in?**

A.   If another car arrives before the previous order is filled, then a waiting line is formed.

Q. What if another customer doesn't show up before service is completed?

A. Then the server is idle, ready to serve the next customer when they do arrive.

Q. So, if you had more servers, no one would have to wait?

A. While waiting customers create a loss of goodwill, idle servers get paid for "doing nothing." The gist of all queuing problems is to balance the cost of customer waiting time with the cost of server idle time.

Q. Are you saying that it is good to keep your customers waiting?

A. Good isn't the right word, but it might be cost effective.

Q. Do we start simulating this by looking at how many customers show up each minute?

A. That's what we did with inventory, when the only question was whether the inventory level changed from units arriving or being sold. We have a different problem here because it is not enough to know when a customer arrives.

Q. What else do we need to know?

A. We need to know when they leave, so the next customer (if there is one) can start being served.

Q. What happens in the simulation if nobody arrives or leaves during a minute?

A. That's the point—we don't want to waste time simulating minutes when nothing happens. Rather than simulating each minute, we are going to have the simulation clock jump to the next event (a customer arriving or leaving), so this is called an event-driven simulation.

Q. How do we know when the next event happens?

A. We simulate the time when the next arrival occurs, referred to as the interarrival time (also as the time between arrivals, or TBA). We also simulate the service time, and our customers leave as soon as the service is completed.

Q. How does that work in Excel?

A. We use a table that summarizes what happens at Mountain Mudd, then use that information to calculate customer waiting time and server idle time. Table 4.45 shows the columns we need.

TABLE 4.45   Time Between Arrivals and Service Time for Simulation Example

	A	B	C	D	E	F	G	H	I	J	K
9			time til								
10			next		begin				service		
11		arrival	arrival	join queue	service	time in	service	service	completed	time in	server
12	customer #	rns	(minutes)	(clock time)	(clock time)	queue	rns	time	clock time	system	idle time

Q.   **Will the columns shown in table 4.45 always work for queuing simulations?**

A.   There is no exact science to creating a simulation table, so someone else might use a different table. My experience is that table 4.45 will handle most simple waiting line simulations.

Q.   **Why did you box in columns B and C and columns G and H?**

A.   That is where you use random numbers to simulate the arrival process (columns B and C) and the service process (columns G and H). If the random process is discrete, we will use a VLOOKUP table, and if it is continuous, we will use an inverse function.

Q.   **How do we get the process generators?**

A.   We gather data by watching Mountain Mudd and noting time between arrivals and service times. We create a graph of the data we gather, and if it is bell-shaped, then we use the normal distribution, or if it looks rectangular, then the uniform distribution would fit.

Q.   **When we talked about continuous process generators, one of the examples you used to describe the time between successive arrivals was the exponential distribution. What does the data that follows an exponential distribution look like?**

A.   I collected 184 readings of the time between successive arrivals at our basic waiting line system (Mountain Mudd). Figure 4.21 shows what a graph of the 184 data points looks like.

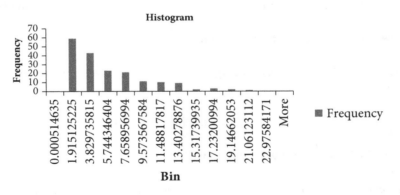

FIGURE 4.21 Histogram of time between arrivals.

Q.   **That's an exponential distribution?**

A.   Yes, most of the occurrences are to the left, the lower values, then tailing off to the right. Most of the time, the next arrival comes within 7.65 minutes (the left tail of the distribution).

Q.   **Is it enough to just eyeball the graph?**

A.   One property of the exponential distribution is that the distribution mean and standard deviation are equal. The descriptive statistics for this data are shown in table 4.46.

TABLE 4.46   Descriptive Statistics for Time Between Arrivals Data

Column 1	
Mean	5.414003
Standard Error	0.382139
Median	3.799736
Mode	#N/A
Standard Deviation	5.183583
Sample Variance	26.86954
Kurtosis	2.961421
Skewness	1.651452
Range	26.58118
Minimum	0.062807
Maximum	26.64399
Sum	996.1766
Count	184
Confidence Level (95.0%)	0.753964

With our sample of 184, we can see that the sample mean (5.414) and sample standard deviation (5.184) are pretty close together, confirming that an exponential distribution fits this data.

Q.   **How do we use this to simulate arrival times?**

A.   Remember from our coverage of process generators that the inverse of the exponential distribution is given by

$$t = -1/\lambda * LN(RAND()).$$

Q.   **I remember the formula, but what do we use for λ?**

A. $1/\lambda$ is the mean of the exponential distribution, so we use the Descriptive Statistics we ran earlier and get 5.414. To simulate how long it would be until the next arrival, you just plug in a random number.

Q.   **Are we ready to start building our queuing simulation?**

A.   We would be if we had the distribution for service times.

Q.   **You said you got those when you got the time between arrivals, didn't you?**

A.   Actually, it is pretty hard to collect two sets of data at the same time, so I had a friend who did. The histogram of the service times that were collected is shown in figure 4.22.

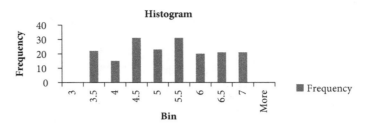

FIGURE 4.22 Histogram of service times.

Q. **That sure doesn't look like an exponential or, for that matter, a normal distribution. What does it look like to you?**

A. Well, I don't see a pattern, except all the service times are between three and seven minutes, so I am inclined to believe it is a uniform distribution.

Q. **That means any service time between 3 and 7 minutes is equally likely to occur. Do we need to know anything else about the service times?**

A. No, the graph gives us everything we need. We can use the inverse formula

$$x = a + RAND() * (b - a)$$

where "a" is the minimum value and "b" is the maximum, to simulate the service times.

Q. **OK, so, the =RAND() function will give us the random numbers and the inverse functions give us the arrival times and service times, but what else do we need to do?**

A. First, a detail: although in real simulations we want to generate random numbers using the RAND() function, for instructional purposes it is much better to generate random numbers ahead of time and use those throughout the explanation of the simulation. Table 4.47 contains a simulation of five customers arriving at Mountain Mudd. The preselected random numbers are shaded. I have also shown my process generators as data for the simulation. It is always a good practice to separate your data from the simulation table itself.

Q. **Shouldn't the clock go in the first column?**

A. That is for inventory simulations, when everything was driven by the clock. Now, everything is driven by when the customer arrives or leaves, so the first column will keep track of each customer.

Q. **Why does the simulation start with "Customer 0"?**

A. That is somewhat of a misnomer. It represents the time that the establishment opens (or when the simulation begins). All we do is determine how long it will be until the first customer arrives (column C of row 13) using the inverse of the exponential distribution and the random number in column B, 9.5934 minutes in this example.

TABLE 4.47   Simulating 5 Customers at Mountain Mudd

	A	B	C	D	E	F	G	H	I	J	K
1	DATA										
2	arrival distribution is *exponential*										
3		MTBA=	5.414 minutes								
4											
5	service time distribution is *uniform*										
6		a =	3 minutes								
7		b =	7 minutes								
8											
9			time till						service		
10			next		begin				service		
11		arrival	arrival	join queue	service	time in	service	service	completed	time in	server
12	cusomer #	rns	(minutes)	(clock time)	(clock time)	queue	rns	time	clock time	system	idle time
13	0	0.17	9.5934								
14	1	0.88	0.6921	9.5934	9.5934	0.0000	0.7	5.8	15.3934	5.8000	9.5934
15	2	0.72	1.7785	10.2855	15.3934	5.1079	0.97	6.88	22.2734	11.9879	0.0000
16	3	0.15	10.2710	12.0640	22.2734	10.2094	0.58	5.32	27.5934	15.5294	0.0000
17	4	0.32	6.1689	22.3350	27.5934	5.2584	0.49	4.96	32.5534	10.2184	0.0000
18	5		■	28.5039	32.5534	4.0495	0.29	4.16	36.7134	8.2095	0.0000
19	averages					24.6252				10.3490	1.9187

Q.   Why do you have cell C18 blacked out?

A.   Because it represents the time until the sixth customer arrives, and we are only simulating five arrivals. The rest of the row represents what happens to Customer 5.

Q.   OK. That makes sense. Can we go back to row 14, the first "real" row of the simulation and go over the entries?

A.   Sure. I have listed the formulas in row 14 for you and provided an explanation of their functions in table 4.48. Take a look at them and see if you have any questions.

Q.   In column D of table 4.48, are you saying that the formula changes for customers after Customer 1?

A.   Yes. C13 is the time after opening that the first customer arrives. C14 is the time interval between the first customer's arrival and the second customer's arrival. So, the actual clock time at which the second customer would join the queue is D13+C14.

Q.   I think I understand the formulas. Going back to table 4.47, what is row 19, "averages," all about?

A.   Those are our outputs, or measures of performance. With inventory, the outputs were the costs. For queues, the outputs are waiting times and idle times.

Q.   Why did you include time in system?

A.   Some schools of thought think that customers are most annoyed when they are in line, and once they are being served, they are happy. Another school of thought is that even if they are being served, if the service time is too long, they become (or stay) unhappy. To cover both aspects of customer satisfaction, I show both the time in queue and time in the system.

TABLE 4.48   Formulas and Explanation of Row 14 Entries of Table 4.47

Row 14 Column	Formula	Explanation
A	1	Customer number
B	0.88	Pre-selected random number. Could also use RAND().
C	=-$C$3*LN(B14)	Inverse exponential distribution. Determines time till customer 2 arrives.
D	=C13+D13	Time customer 1 joins queue.
E	=MAX(I13,D14)	Time customer 1 begins service. Cannot begin until previous customer completes service.
F	=E14-D14	Time customer 1 spent in queue before starting service.
G	0.7	Pre-selected random number. Could also use RAND().
H	=$C$6+G14*($C$7-$C$6)	Inverse uniform distribution. Determines service time for customer 1.
I	=E14+H14	Time customer 1 completes service.
J	=I14-D14	Time customer 1 was in system. Time service completed – time joined queue.
K	=MAX(E14-I13,0)	Server idle time. Idle time only incurred if prior service ended before starting service

Q.   Do we learn anything from the averages?

A.   If the server has very little idle time, customer waiting time is usually high. When the server has idle time, it usually means that customer waiting time is less. Right now (for a very small simulation), we have little idle time and more waiting time.

Q.   When calculating the averages, do we include the entries for Customer 0?

A.   No. They [Customer 0 entries] should not count since that row contains only initial conditions, which do not correspond to actual customers.

Q.   What's next?

A.   Design the simulation experiment, but that should be familiar stuff to you and does not need to be rehashed here.

Q.   Wait—before, we based the sample size on the total average revenues or costs. What measure do we use for waiting line models?

A.   You could use either average time in queue or average server time, but I would probably select an acceptable error level—say, within 5% of the true values—and run the Descriptive Statistics for both measures. Then select the largest of the two sample sizes and cover both bases.

Q.   Makes sense. Are we done yet?

A.   Not until we know how to simulate certain customer behaviors in line.

Q.   **Why would I want to do that?**

A.   We'll discuss that in the following lesson.

ACTIVE LEARNING: LESSON 4.7.1

LESSON 4.7.2 Simulating Customer Behavior in Queues

Introduction

Q.   **What do you mean by "customer behavior"?**

A.   Think about how you behave when you considering joining a line. If you have limited time and/or patience, would you join a long line?

Q.   **That depends on how long the line is and how badly I need what is at the end of the line. Is that what you are talking about?**

A.   Exactly. If you want a cup of coffee and there are five people in front of you and you are running late for an appointment, you would probably leave if the line was not moving fast enough.

Q.   **Certainly. Unfortunately, the other day a relative felt very ill and I took him to the emergency room of the local hospital, and we were there for over eight hours. I sure wanted to leave but was afraid for my relative's health, so we just hung in there. Fortunately, by the time they got to him, he already felt better, and we walked out. I get it now. We just cannot assume that a customer who joins a line will stay there forever, can we?**

A.   That is exactly the point. And, unless we can build that type of behavior into our simulation, we cannot hope to have a simulation that realistically represents the real world.

Q.   **I see that. So, how do we go about simulating that kind of behavior?**

A.   By simulating what you appeared to be doing in your two examples. It appears you first counted how many customers were in line in front of you and then you applied some sort of decision rule as to whether to stay in line. Is that correct?

Q.   **Yes. So, you are suggesting that before anything, we have to have our simulation to be able to count the number of customers in line when I get there. Next, I must be able to verbalize and quantify what my rule is for not joining the line. Is that how we are going to approach simulating customer behavior in queues?**

A.   Yes. We will first have a dialectic on counting customers, and we will follow that with a dialectic on simulating their balking behavior.

Q.   **Balking?**

A.   Yes. That just means something like "refusal behavior."

Learning Outcomes

When you complete this lesson, you will know:

- How to count the number of customers in line and in the system for the next arrival in a queuing simulation
- Remove an arrival that balks from the queuing simulation

Lesson 4.7.2.1: Counting Customers in Line

Q.   **OK, let me ask again. Why do I need to count customers?**

A.   So that you can plan the size of your waiting area, for one. If you cannot accommodate your customers, you cannot serve them, which will hurt your revenues.

Q.   **Couldn't I speed up my service times?**

A.   Speeding up service will cost money, either for new equipment or additional manpower.

Q.   **So, I can't win, can I?**

A.   You have to balance the two. You want a waiting area in which customers spend a reasonable amount of time, and you want a system where the servers won't be overworked. You can only do that if you know what the tradeoffs are, so that you can achieve that balance.

Q.   **And we get the tradeoffs from running a simulation. So, how do we go about counting customers in line in a simulation?**

A.   Let's see if we can help my friend Bill. He sells hot dogs over the counter as well as through a drive-thru. What he told me about his business is given below:

Bill's Dogs
Bill's Dogs has a drive-thru line and is concerned about the service he is delivering to his customers. He has several ideas but does not have the confidence or cash to physically test them. He has heard from one of his employees, who is a business student at a local college, that simulation is a tool that will allow him to test his ideas without spending money.

Bill has asked you to develop a simulation model of his operation. He has already had someone develop the probability distributions for service times. They are listed below. That same person had established that customer arrivals to the drive-thru were exponentially distributed with a mean time between arrivals of five minutes.

Lower rn limit	Service time (min)
0.00	1
0.30	2
0.40	3

Bill also knows that customer spending was evenly distributed between $4.00 and $6.00.

The simulation should be able to answer questions regarding the average time in line of customers, the average idle time of employees, and the total sales that Bill can expect to achieve in an hour. It should also tell him how many cars can be expected to be in line, since he is wondering whether he needs to expand his drive-thru line capacity.

Use the random numbers provided in the link below for your simulation.

ACTIVE LEARNING: LINK 4.7.2.1 RANDOM NUMBERS FOR BILL'S DOGS

Q. **Bill's has quite a cult following from the locals, and I would love to help him. How do we get started?**

A. As always, put all your data at the beginning of the spreadsheet.

Q. **Table 4.49 shows the data. How do I set up the simulation table for counting the customers in line?**

A. That requires the addition of only one column to the waiting line simulation table we used before, table 4.47. Label that column "# of customers in line" and put it between the "Join Queue" and "Begin Service" columns.

Q. **What about the other columns?**

A. Add three columns at the end, a random number for the purchase amount, revenue for that customer, and cumulative revenue. You should be able to do that.

Q. **What formula do we use to count customers?**

A. We will leave Customer 0 blank for the "# of customers in line" column and use the following formula for Customer 1, in cell E31:

$$=COUNTIF(\$J\$30:J30,">"\&D31)$$

Q. **Is this when I should sit at the feet of the master and ask what that does?**

A. No, the explanation will make more sense if you first pull the formula down and simulate the first hour of operation. The first hour of simulation ends when the last customer enters the system before 60 minutes have elapsed. That customer is allowed to complete their transaction.

TABLE 4.49 Data for Bill's Dogs Simulation

	A	B	C	D	E	F	G	H	I	J	K
1	DATA										
2		PROCESS GENERATORS									
3											
4		Service Time						Time Between Arrivals			
5											
6			service			cummulative	lower rn				
7			time (min)	probability		probability	limit		Exponential Distribution		
8			1	0.30		0.30	0.00		Mean time between arrivals (min)		5.00
9			2	0.50		0.80	0.30				
10			3	0.20		1.00	0.80				
11											
12											
13			VLOOKUP Table for service time								
14											
15					lower rn	service					
16					limit	time (min)					
17					0.00	1					
18					0.30	2					
19					0.80	3					
20											
21		EXPENDITURES									
22		Uniformly distributed									
23				a = $	4.00						
24				b = $	6.00						

Q. OK. Table 4.50 is what I got. Does the table look correct?

A. Good. The formula for cell E42 is shown at the bottom, with arrows pointing to where each of the elements in the formula are located in the table. That will make more sense to you.

TABLE 4.50 Simulation and Formula (Cell E42) for Counting Customers

	A	B	C	D	E	F	G	H	I	J	K	L	M	N	O
26			time till							service					
27			next		# of	begin				service					
28		arrival	arrival	join queue	customers	service	time in	service	service	completed	time in	server idle	rn for		cummulative
29	Customer #	rns	(minutes)	(clock time)	in line	(clock time)	queue	rns	time	(clock time)	system	time	revenues	revenues	revenues
30	0	0.17000	8.86					0.70000					0.54047		
31	1	0.88000	0.64	8.86	0	8.86	0.00	0.97000	3	11.86	3.00	8.86	0.65318	$ 5.31	$ 5.31
32	2	0.72000	1.64	9.50	1	11.86	2.36	0.58000	2	13.86	4.36	0.00	0.47370	$ 4.95	$ 10.25
33	3	0.15000	9.49	11.14	2	13.86	2.72	0.49000	2	15.86	4.72	0.00	0.61641	$ 5.23	$ 15.49
34	4	0.32000	5.70	20.63	0	20.63	0.00	0.29000	1	21.63	1.00	4.77	0.18962	$ 4.38	$ 19.87
35	5	0.13369	10.06	26.32	0	26.32	0.00	0.46208	2	28.32	2.00	4.70	0.48342	$ 4.97	$ 24.83
36	6	0.17039	8.85	36.39	0	36.39	0.00	0.00997	1	37.39	1.00	8.06	0.39765	$ 4.80	$ 29.63
37	7	0.66616	2.03	45.23	0	45.23	0.00	0.51679	2	47.23	2.00	7.85	0.51634	$ 5.03	$ 34.66
38	8	0.49280	3.54	47.26	0	47.26	0.00	0.21240	1	48.26	1.00	0.03	0.60143	$ 5.20	$ 39.86
39	9	0.76443	1.34	50.80	0	50.80	0.00	0.87831	3	53.80	3.00	2.54	0.14388	$ 4.29	$ 44.15
40	10	0.58283	2.70	52.15	1	53.80	1.66	0.52506	2	55.80	3.66	0.00	0.07953	$ 4.16	$ 48.31
41	11	0.77688	1.26	54.85	1	55.80	0.96	0.00780	1	56.80	1.96	0.00	0.98618	$ 5.97	$ 54.28
42	12	0.29733	6.06	56.11	1	56.80	0.70	0.77350	2	58.80	2.70	0.00	0.04847	$ 4.10	$ 58.38
43	13	0.64236	2.21	62.17	0	62.17	0.00	0.81279	3	65.17	3.00	3.37	0.14813	$ 4.30	$ 62.68

=COUNTIF($J$30:J41,">"&D42)

Q. No, it doesn't. What does that formula do?

A. First notice the =COUNTIF range extends from the beginning of the simulation ($J$30) to the last customer that joined the line (J41) before the current arrival. That's why we didn't put absolute references ($) for J41.

Q.   So, each time we copy the formula down, another row gets added to the range. Cute. But, what about the rest of the formula?

A.   The formula says that I want to count the number of instances ($J$30:J41) that a customer completed service after (">") the current customer arrives (D42). If they complete service after the current customer arrives, they must be in line waiting for service.

Q.   But what does the "&" symbol do?

A.   Normally, the COUNTIF function looks for a single value, whatever is in the "". The "&" tells Excel to change what it is looking for in each row, using the clock time from column D.

Q.   Then it takes only one column to count customers, that's pretty nice. What does the simulation tell us?

A.   The twelfth customer is the last one that arrives within the first hour. That gives us an estimate of $58.38 as the sales capacity of Bill's drive-thru.

Q.   And now we would estimate a sample size and all the rest?

A.   Yes. But if you wanted to estimate the sales capacity, each element of the sample would be a simulation run like we just did.

Q.   You mean I would have to do 60 repetitions of this simulation, each with different numbers, before I can calculate my sample size?

A.   Right on. Once you have the 60 reps, then you can do the descriptive stats and so on. Nothing new, just a bit tedious.

Q.   I can handle that—if I must. This dialectic turned out a whole lot simpler that I thought it would be. Is there anything else we need to know about single-server, single-queue simulations?

A.   Indeed, there is. Let's go to the next dialectic where I will show you how to consider situations in which customers arrive, take a look at the length of the line, and decide not to join it.

ACTIVE LEARNING: LESSON 4.7.2.1

Lesson 4.7.2.2: Simulating Balking

Q.   What is "balking?"

A.   It means being unwilling to do something—such as a horse not jumping a fence or a customer not joining a waiting line.

Q. **If someone doesn't want to join our line, is there anything we can do?**

A. It depends on why they are unwilling. If they just don't want our product, you're right, there is nothing we can do. If they are unwilling because the line is too long, however, then that is something we might be able to fix.

Q. **Couldn't we just make the line longer?**

A. Sometimes we can't, so the prospective customer is *unable* to join the line rather than *unwilling*. Even if we can, the customer may not be willing to wait a long time in line, so they balk.

Q. **How do we handle balking in a simulation?**

A. We will define balking as occurring whenever there are more than a certain number of customers in line. For Bill's Dogs, let's assume that if there is anyone in line, the next customer will balk and go elsewhere to eat.

Q. **Do you mean that anytime there is already someone at the drive-thru, no one will get in line?**

A. Exactly. Since we have counted the number of customers in line, anytime the number of customers in line is greater than 0, the next customer will balk.

Q. **Is that realistic?**

A. No, that would be rather extreme, but if you can handle an extreme case, you can handle anything more reasonable.

Q. **Sounds simple enough. Is it that simple to simulate a balk?**

A. Not quite. To simulate balking, we must decide what we mean by a balk, both in the real world and in the simulation.

Q. **Is there a difference?**

A. Usually, we copy what happens in the real world, but in the real world, the person sees the line and never joins it. For our simulation, the arrival actually joins the queue but immediately afterwards makes the decision to balk, so if you were watching the queue, you would see the arrival come and then leave before being served.

Q. **What is the problem with that?**

A. From a simulation standpoint, figuring out how to incorporate getting the customer out of the line in our simulation table.

Q. **How will you do that?**

A. There are two things we need to do to the Bill's Dogs simulation table: add a column to keep track of when a customer balks and add another column to serve as a counter for the number of customers in line after balking. We will then modify the formulas in some of the other columns to account for the effect of balking on some of the queue measures.

Q.   Is that as easy as you made it sound?

A.   No, it took me several tries to get it right. For Bill's Dogs, we will assume that customers are not going to wait in line to get a hot dog, which means the balk number is 0.

Q.   What does that mean in English?

A.   If there are more than zero persons in line, an arrival will simply move on to something else. Of course, we can make that number anything we wish based upon observed customer behavior.

Q.   I would wait to get one of those dogs ...

A.   Yes, but it's not you we are dealing with. Table 4.51 shows the modifications I made to the old simulation table. The headings with arrows are the columns that have been affected by the balking, including two new columns, F and Q, to keep track of which arrival balked. The formulas for row 33 are shown in table 4.52. As you can see, the simulation shows three balks during the first hour.

TABLE 4.51   Bill's Dogs with Balking When More Than Zero in Queue

	A	B	C	D	E	F	G	H	I	J	K	L	M	N	O	P	Q
25																	
26			time till														
27			next		# of	balk?	begin				service						customer
28		arrival	arrival	join queue	customer	when # >?	service	time in	service	service	completed	time in	server idle	rn for		cummulative	in line
29	Customer #	rns	(minutes)	(clock time)	in line	0	(clock time)	queue	rns	time	(clock time)	system	time	revenues	revenues	revenues	counter
30	0	0.17000	8.86														
31	1	0.88000	0.64	8.86	0		8.86	0.00	0.70000	3	11.86	3	8.86	0.54047 $	5.31	$	5.31	11.85978
32	2	0.72000	1.64	9.50	1	yes	11.86	0.00	0.97000	0	11.86	0	0.00	0.65318 $	-	$	5.31	0
33	3	0.15000	9.49	11.14	1	yes	11.86	0.00	0.58000	0	11.86	0	0.00	0.47370 $	-	$	5.31	0
34	4	0.32000	5.70	20.63	0		20.63	0.00	0.49000	1	21.63	1	8.77	0.61641 $	4.38	$	9.69	21.62707
35	5	0.13369	10.06	26.32	0		26.32	0.00	0.29000	2	28.32	2	4.70	0.18962 $	4.97	$	14.65	28.32424
36	6	0.17039	8.85	36.39	0		36.39	0.00	0.46208	1	37.39	1	8.06	0.48342 $	4.80	$	19.45	37.38544
37	7	0.66616	2.03	45.23	0		45.23	0.00	0.00997	2	47.23	2	7.85	0.39765 $	5.03	$	24.48	47.23385
38	8	0.49280	3.54	47.26	0		47.26	0.00	0.51679	1	48.26	1	0.03	0.51634 $	5.20	$	29.68	48.26499
39	9	0.76443	1.34	50.80	0		50.80	0.00	0.21240	3	53.80	3	2.54	0.60143 $	4.29	$	33.97	53.80323
40	10	0.58283	2.70	52.15	1	yes	53.80	0.00	0.87831	0	53.80	0	0.00	0.14388 $	-	$	33.97	0
41	11	0.77688	1.26	54.85	0		54.85	0.00	0.52506	1	55.85	1	1.04	0.07953 $	5.97	$	39.94	55.84566
42	12	0.29733	6.06	56.11	0		56.11	0.00	0.00780	2	58.11	2	0.26	0.98618 $	4.10	$	44.04	58.108
43	13	0.64236	2.21	62.17	0		62.17	0.00	0.77350	3	65.17	3	4.06	0.04847 $	4.30	$	48.34	65.17254
44	14	0.47977	3.67	64.39	1	yes	65.17	0.00	0.81279	0	65.17	0	0.00	0.14813 $	-	$	48.34	0

Q.   If cell D42 shows the end of the hour, why does it still show 12 customers?

A.   Because we had 12 customers, but 3 of them balked. Losing one-quarter of your customers is something you need to think about. Not only do you lose their revenue during this visit, but they are also less likely to come back in the future—a double whammy.

Q.   I can see that the first four columns in table 4.52 are identical to the Bill's Dogs simulation table. What did you do to column E?

A.   The formula for counting customers in line (column E) used to be based on how many customers had not yet completed their service when a new arrival showed up (column K). Now it is based on column Q, the "customers in line counter."

TABLE 4.52 Formulas for Queuing Simulation with Balks

COLUMN	TITLE	EXPRESSION
A	customer #	sequential number
B	arrival rns	from provided table
C	time till next arrival	=-$K$8*LN(B33)
D	join queue	=D32+C32
E	# of customers in line	=COUNTIF($Q$30:Q32,">"&D33)
F	balk? (balk number in row 29)	=IF(E33>$F$29,"yes","")
G	begin service	=IF(D33>=K32,D33,K32)
H	time in queue	=IF(F33="yes",0,G33-D33)
I	service rns	from provided table
J	service time	=IF(F33="yes",0,VLOOKUP(I33,$D$17:$E$19,2))
K	service completed	=IF(F33="yes",K32,G33+J33)
L	time in system	=IF(F33="yes",0,K33-D33)
M	server idle time	=MAX(G33-K32,0)
N	rn for revenues	from provided table
O	revenues	=IF(F33="yes",0,$D$23+N33*($D$24-$D$23))
P	cummulative revenues	=O33+P32
Q	customer in line counter	=IF(F33="yes",0,K33)

Q. **Why?**

A. If a customer balks, they leave the line. Column Q is how we show the customers have left the line.

Q. **How did you do that?**

A. Column Q is used to mark customers that balk, but what it really does is alter the service completion time, column K. If a customer is marked as balking, in column F, then we change the service completion time to 0.

Q. **How does that help?**

A. When we use the counting formula in column E, COUNTIF($Q$30:Q32,">"&D33), he will never be included in the count since any new arrival will have an arrival time >0.

Q. **Do you really expect me to figure that one out on my own?**

A. No, as I said, it took me several tries to get it right. Now that you have seen it, though, you should be able to duplicate it.

Q. **I can see that column F just flags when a customer has balked, but what about the other columns headings with arrows?**

A. Those just make sure that a "balker" is not assigned a service time (since he is gone), spends no time in the system (since he comes and goes), and spends no money (since he never got a chance to spend any).

Q.   **How come the simulation shows no time in the queue for anybody?**

A.   Because your queue number is zero. No one ever decides to join the queue.

Q.   **Silly me. Is that all there is for balking?**

A.   Well, if you have the data, you could create a probability distribution of how likely a car is to balk. That would be more realistic, since some people might wait even if there were two or three cars ahead of them, while others will balk if there is even one.

Q.   **Is there anything else I should know about simulating how customers behave in queuing systems?**

A.   There are innumerable other quirks that occur in the real world that you may wish to simulate. It all depends on what behaviors you observe within the system you want to simulate and your Excel skills. With what you have already learned and some further study and perseverance you can simulate almost anything. Good Luck!

ACTIVE LEARNING: LESSON 4.7.2.2

Comprehensive Problems are available for this chapter via Active Learning

5

Optimization

OVERVIEW

Q. What does "optimization" mean?

A. Optimization means finding the best, or optimal, solution.

Q. Don't we always want the best solution?

A. Of course, but not all models can be optimized. When we find one that can be optimized, we have hit the mother lode, so to speak. By its very meaning, an optimal solution cannot be improved upon. That virtually guarantees us that when we implement an optimal solution, it will have a positive impact on our organization.

Q. So, how do we get an optimal solution?

A. Optimization involves the use of mathematical processes, or algorithms. Also, whether a model can be optimized depends on how it is represented mathematically. That mathematics creates conditions that real world problems must satisfy, which makes the solution process even more complicated.

Q. This is starting to sound scary.

A. Don't panic. While the mathematics of optimization is formidable, you don't have to deal with it. There are apps for optimization that make optimizing transparent to the user. Once you have a model and you enter data into the app, then, voilà, the app produces the optimal solution for you.

Q. Then all I have to do is set up the model?

A. You must be able to translate your problem into a model and then you must be able to interpret the solution. But, compared to the mathematics, that is a piece of cake.

Q.   **Do many areas of business really use this?**

A.   These problems are common to many organizations in fields ranging from health care to manufacturing to sports to hospitality, to name just a few. In this chapter, we will focus on exploring business problems that have benefitted the most from optimization.

LESSON 5.1: Introduction to Constrained Optimization

Introduction

Q.   **What does this lesson deal with?**

A.   We will be introducing you to some of the most common terminology associated with optimization so that you will not look clueless when you walk into a discussion at work about approaches that might be taken to address some issues the company might be struggling with.

Q.   **Wouldn't such discussions be between business analytics experts?**

A.   Definitely not. Experts are often solutions looking for problems. To be effective, there need to be working employees such as you who are in the trenches and understand the problems. It helps everybody if you understand where they are coming from and what they are trying to do.

Q.   **I can see that. But wouldn't I be better off knowing a bit more than the terminology?**

A.   Of course. But to understand the terminology, you should also know some of the basics—that is why you will also learn about the most likely form of optimization that you are likely to come across. It is called Linear Programming, or LP for short.

Q.   **OK, but remember you said I would not have to deal with technical stuff. I will have all I can do to describe our business problems and work with the experts to set up those problems so the experts can go to town with them.**

A.   And that is what we will do in this lesson.

Learning Outcomes

When you complete this session, you will be able to:

- Define "optimization" and "Linear Programming"
- Define "variable" in linear programming
- Define "objective function" in linear programming
- Define and formulate constraints in linear programing
- Formulate a linear programming model to include variables, an objective function, and constraints

A Dialectic Introduction to Constrained Optimization

Q.   **What is constrained optimization?**

A.   An umbrella term for the set of algorithms that search for a best (optimal) solution while obeying limits (constraints) placed on the solution.

Q.   **A *set* of algorithms?**

A.   Yes. There are a lot of different algorithms, though they all work with an objective and with constraints.

Q.   **How does an algorithm know which solution is best?**

A.   You, as the user, have to tell the algorithm how to evaluate different solutions. This is what the objective does for us.

Q.   **What does the objective measure?**

A.   Generally speaking, there are two types of objectives: costs (which you want to minimize) and profits (which you want to maximize). You might have different words, but it still comes down to whether you want more of something (maximizing) or less of it (minimizing).

Q.   **What do the constraints do?**

A.   Actually, pretty much what their name implies. Constraints tell the computer what limitations exist in the real world.

Q.   **So, you tell the algorithm to "make as much money as possible and fill all orders that have been placed"?**

A.   Well, not in words. Algorithms are run on computers, and computers don't understand words. Computers understand numbers, so you have to write equations that mean the same things as the words.

Q.   **So why is there more than one algorithm?**

A.   These problems are often very complex, and how they are solved mathematically depends on the mathematical structure of the objective function and constraints.

Q.   **Mathematical structure?**

A.   Yes. For example, if the objective function and all constraints are linear, then the constrained optimization problem is referred to as linear programming. If any number of the constraints or the objective function is not linear, then we have a nonlinear programming problem, and if the variables are required to be whole numbers, then we have an integer programming problem. Within each of these broad classifications, there are many other subclassifications.

Q.   **This is not getting better. Why are we covering stuff like this in a business class?**

A.   Because an amazing number of business problems can be represented, or formulated, as mathematical problems. Thus, if we can solve the mathematical problem, then we can make that solution into a solution to the business problem, but only if the mathematical formulation is a close representation of the original problem.

Q.   **So, I have to learn a whole bunch of math?**

A.   No, not at all. You, as a subject matter expert, will be part of a team.

Q.   **Who else is on the team?**

A.   Well, at a minimum, you and a business analytics specialist.

Q.   **What do I do as a subject matter specialist?**

A.   You will be involved in formulating the business problem as a mathematical problem. That means you provide the information about the company: accounting data, corporate goals (objectives), important limitations (constraints), and any other information about your company that the business analytics expert needs.

Q.   **What does the business analytics expert do?**

A.   Turns your information into the equations and/or inequalities that represent the business situations you know about. Once you have such a model, then you run those equations through an algorithm (a computer program) for solving that kind of mathematical problem. As a matter of fact, you can solve many such problems with Excel.

Q.   **OK, that's not too bad. So, what are we going to cover now?**

A.   Linear Programming (LP). An amazing number of business models fit into this category of constrained optimization models, hence the reason for covering it first.

Q.   **How does LP work?**

A.   Let's break the words down to find out.

Q.   **Does "programming" mean giving instructions to a computer?**

A.   No, it is from an old military term that means "planning." So "linear programming" means "linear planning."

Q.   **What does "linear" mean?**

A.   "Linear" refers to the type of equations we will be using.

Q.   **What is a linear equation?**

A.   One that follows the form:

$$Y = mX + b.$$

Q.   **Is the following also a linear equation:**

$$3X + 4Y = 240?$$

A.   Yes.

Q.   **How do we know?**

A.   The exponent on the variables is 1 (zero is also allowed, but that is a trivial case). The important point is that the exponent isn't 2 or 3 or something higher, and the exponent isn't less than one, such as $\frac{1}{2}$ or $\frac{1}{3}$ or some other fraction. Also, the variables are added together, not multiplied or divided. So neither

$$3X * 4Y = 240$$

nor

$$3X/4Y = 240$$

are linear equations. The first is a quadratic equation, and the second is an asymptotic equation.

Q.   **Are all business-world relationships linear?**

A.   No, many of them are not.

Q.   **Why, then, do we use linear equations?**

A.   Mostly because they are simple (relative to nonlinear equations) to solve.

Q.   **What is the first step in the LP algorithm?**

A.   Organize the data into a set of linear expressions. This is called "formulating" because a formula is another word for an equation.

Q.   **Why do we have to set up the equations?**

A.   The computer cannot understand sentences. Another phrase to describe organizing the data is "putting it in computer-ready form."

Q.   **How do you formulate a problem?**

A.   You should have learned that in an algebra class somewhere. If you don't remember, we'll cover that in the next lesson.

A Dialectic on Formulating LP Problems

Q.   **So, where does one begin?**

A.   Converting information from a paragraph to something a computer can accept is a daily task for most businesspeople. Formulating linear programming problems is one version of this process, and if you can master it, then you will probably be able to handle most other data-conversion situations.

Q. **That's encouraging, I guess, but what is the first step?**

A. Organizing the data. It sounds trite but read the information—not once, but several times:

- The first time read it quickly. Don't take notes or start drawing relationships; simply read it. You want an overview, a feel for what the data is about.

- The second time you read the problem, go slowly and begin organizing the data.

  - Sketch out a table showing how one number relates to more than one word.

  - Add rows or columns to the table as you encounter more numbers that are similarly related.

  - If you can see more than one grouping for the data, write down all of them. Some may be irrelevant, but you don't know which ones are, so include them all at this point.

- Then take time for a third, quick read through the data to see if you missed anything.

Q. **All that just to get started?**

A. It will make more sense if you see it done, so here is an example problem.

The Glimmer Glass Company

The Glimmer Glass Company specializes in a small but very high-quality line of windows and doors. Currently, three models are produced: a window with a single pane of glass measuring 30 inches by 48 inches, a window with two 30-inch by 24-inch panes of glass, and a door with a single pane of glass measuring 3½ feet by 6 feet. Each product is framed by wood, with the windows using 1½-inch framing and the door using 3-inch framing. The amount of framing needed is determined by the perimeter of the glass. The glass comes in large pieces that are cut up as necessary and the scrap is remelted, so waste is not an issue. Assembly time for a single-pane window is 20 minutes, for a double-pane window is 30 minutes, and for a door is 50 minutes. The current inventory counts are 400,000 square inches of glass, 50,000 linear inches of 1½-inch framing, and 12,000 linear inches of 3-inch framing, with 120 labor hours available. On average, it costs Glimmer Glass $25.00 for a single-pane window, $45.00 for a double-pane window, and $70.00 for a door.

Q. **As a good student, I read through that quickly. Now what?**

A. Think about what you learned: you make three products (two types of windows and one type of door) out of glass and framing.

Q. **What do we do with all the details?**

A. Take it in small pieces and as you reread it, sketch out a table.

Q. **So, when I read that**

[c]urrently, three models are produced: a window with a single pane of glass measuring 30 inches by 48 inches, a window with two 30-inch by 24-inch panes of glass, and a door with a single pane of glass measuring 3½ feet by 6 feet,

I could write down

	Single	Double	Door
Glass			

to represent the three products and the glass used to make them. What do I do with all those numbers?

A. At this point, we aren't sure how that will fit into our table, so we'll leave it out and come back to it later. For now, continue your second read through the problem.

Q. **The next sentence,**

each product is framed by wood with the windows using 1½-inch framing and the door using 3-inch framing,

tells us something more about what we use to make the products. Does that become more rows in the table?

A. Yes. Again, just put in the words for the rows and ignore the numbers to get:

	Single	Double	Door
Glass			
1½-inch framing			
3-inch framing			

You might guess the numbers are going to go into the table, but we will worry about that later on.

Q. **Is there a way to show that the 3-inch frame is only for the doors?**

A. There is, but for now, just remember it, or make a note near your table as a reminder.

Q. **The next couple of sentences don't have any numbers or new materials. What do we do with them?**

The amount of framing needed is determined by the perimeter of the glass. The glass comes in large pieces that are cut up as necessary and the scrap is remelted, so waste is not an issue.

A. They tell us how to measure the framing requirements—we'll need that later—and give us some background information about scrap and costs. This doesn't become part of the table, but you might jot a note to yourself, or highlight it in the problem.

Q. **What is this next thing, about assembly time?**

Assembly time for a single pane window is 20 minutes, for a double pane window is 30 minutes, and for a door is 50 minutes.

A.   Time isn't exactly a material to make windows, but it is a resource. Since this deals with the products, we just add another row to our table, and then keep reading.

	Single	Double	Door
Glass			
1½-inch framing			
3-inch framing			
Assembly			

Q.   **What do we do with inventory counts?**

The current inventory counts are 400,000 square inches of glass, 50,000 linear inches of 1½-inch framing, and 12,000 linear inches of 3-inch framing, with 120 labor hours available.

A.   Interestingly, this has nothing to do with the products; it deals with glass and framing and assembly time, which are already rows in the table, so we can add a column to the right, called "Maximum," like this:

	Single	Double	Door	Maximum
Glass				
1½-inch framing				
3-inch framing				
Assembly				

Q.   **The final sentence tells us about costs. That's not a material or a resource, so what do we do with that?**

On average, it costs Glimmer Glass $25.00 for a single-pane window, $45.00 for a double-pane window, and $70.00 for a door.

A.   It gives us cost information on the three products, so we need another row.

	Single	Double	Door	Maximum
Glass				
1½-inch framing				
3-inch framing				
Assembly				
Cost				

Q.   **Is that everything?**

A.   Well, for now it is. Our table is set up and ready for data to be put into it.

Q. **Anything tricky about that?**

A. There can be, so it is usually best to put the simplest data in first, and when possible, start with the maximums. Copying from the word problem, we get:

	Single	Double	Door	Maximum
Glass				400,000 sq. in.
1½-inch framing				50,000 in.
3-inch framing				12,000 in.
Assembly				120 hours
Cost				

Q. **Is putting the units (square inches, inches, and hours) in the table important?**

A. Oh, yes. They are our first guess at the units we need to describe the data for glass (square inches), framing (inches), and assembly time (hours). I said "first guess" because we may choose to change the units later, say inches to feet or hours to minutes, for convenience sake.

Q. **Why doesn't Cost have a maximum?**

A. That's interesting, isn't it? It tells us that Cost is somehow different from the rest of the rows, which list resources or materials. When we get to writing the formulas, we will handle cost differently than the other rows. For now, it is just a handy reminder.

Q. **Can we now copy in the rest of the data?**

A. Yes and no. Yes, we must copy in the rest of the data, but, no, we don't "just" copy it in. We have to make sure the units of the data match the units of the maximums.

Q. **Why do we have to do that?**

A. Remember sitting in algebra and wondering when you would ever need any of this? This is where, so send a message to your high school teacher to apologize for not paying better attention. When we turn this table into a bunch of formulas, as I'm sure you learned in algebra class, all numbers in an equation (formula) have to have the same units.

Q. **OK, starting with glass, the maximum tells us we need "square inches" but the data gives us length and width. Do we just multiply length by width?**

A. I guess you did pay some attention, in geometry class at least. Yes, "square inches" is a measure of area, and area of a rectangle or square is calculated as length multiplied by width.

Q. **This isn't hard. For the single-pane window, 30 × 48 is 1,440 square inches; for the double-paned window, 30 × 24 is 720 square inches; and for the door, 3.5 × 6 is 21 square inches. Wait a minute, isn't that awfully small for a door?**

A. You're right, so check your data. You might notice that the door measurements are given to you in feet, not inches. Since we have to have the same units as the maximum, convert feet to inches, then calculate the area.

Q.   Missed that. OK, 3.5' × 6' becomes 42" × 72" and that becomes 3,024 square inches. Is there anything else I missed?

A.   A good question, and one you should always ask. When you reread the problem, notice that the second product is a double-paned window, which means two 30 × 24 panes, so the total square area for the double-paned window is 2 × 720 square inches, or 1,440 square inches. All of this is shown in the next table.

	Single	Double	Door	Maximum
Glass	1,440 sq. in.	1,440 sq. in.	3,024 sq. in.	400,000 sq. in.
1½-inch framing				50,000 in.
3-inch framing				12,000 in.
Assembly				120 hours
Cost				

Q.   Is the rest of this going to be as much fun?

A.   Maybe not fun, but just as detailed. There is an old saying that "the devil is in the details," and that is certainly true when formulating LP problems. You miss a detail and you get the wrong numbers, but the computer doesn't know that (computers are very gullible—they will believe whatever you tell them is true).

Q.   So, what are the details for framing?

A.   We were told the framing was measured by the perimeter of the glass (that's actually inaccurate, but I didn't want to get into the complexities of extending the measurement to account for the corners). Remembering our geometry classes, we know that the perimeter of a rectangle is twice the length plus twice the height, so a 30 × 48 pane has a 156-inch perimeter, two 30 × 24 panes have a total perimeter of 216 inches, and the 42 × 72 door has a 228-inch perimeter. The detail is that the windows use 1½-inch frame, while the door uses a 3-inch frame (that was the note you made for yourself earlier). The table now looks like this:

	Single	Double	Door	Maximum
Glass	1,440 sq. in.	1,440 sq. in.	3,024 sq. in.	400,000 sq. in.
1½-inch framing	156 in.	216 in.		50,000 in.
3-inch framing			228 in.	12,000 in.
Assembly				120 hours
Cost				

Q.   I noticed the assembly maximum is in hours, but the assembly times are in minutes, so I suppose we have to change minutes into hours?

A.   Correct in essence, but it is usually best to avoid using decimals if possible. The reason is that decimals often need to be rounded, which is less precise than a whole number. Therefore, convert the maximum from 120 hours to 7200 minutes, and then enter the rest of the data. To speed things up, I also showed the costs.

	Single	Double	Door	Maximum
Glass	1,440 sq. in.	1,440 sq. in.	3,024 sq. in.	400,000 sq. in.
1½-inch framing	156 in.	216 in.		50,000 in.
3-inch framing			228 in.	12,000 in.
Assembly	20 min.	30 min.	50 min.	7,200 minutes
Cost	$25.00	$45.00	$70.00	

Q. **Great job speeding things up. Is every formulation going to take this long?**

A. I know this has been done in incredibly boring detail, but some students have difficulty organizing data, so this is one detailed example for them to read. Once you get used to reading these problems, you can set up the tables almost as fast as you can read. Keep in mind some of the things I have pointed out, though, such as using the maximums to determine the units, or keeping track of which rows deal with which columns. This will cut down on the number of errors you make.

Q. **Isn't it convenient that all the data fit nicely into a table?**

A. This is probably the wrong time to tell you this, but that's not true for all data. Sometimes one product will be related to another product, or you will be given a limit that deals directly with a row rather than with a column. All I can say is, watch out for those complications, and make notes off to one side to describe them.

Q. **So, with the table done, are we done formulating the problem?**

A. Actually, you have only started. The table organized the data you were given in the word problem. The next step is to take the table and turn it into a set of linear equations.

Q. **Earlier, you talked about objectives and constraints. Are those the equations you mean?**

A. Yes, objectives and constraints, along with variables, are the three important parts of any formulation, but we have to talk about variables first.

Q. **Aren't variables just the letters used in algebra equations, like "X"?**

A. Yes, and no. The variables, properly called decision variables—though I usually won't bother to say that—represent the heart of the problem. A variable, however, is not a letter; it is a number.

Q. **Wait a minute, X is a number?**

A. Most numbers have precise values, but sometimes we don't know the precise value of a number. When that happens, we simply use the letter symbol to take the place of the number until we can figure out its precise value. That's exactly what we are going to do in linear programming.

Q. **We already have an awful lot of numbers. What more do we need?**

A. The numbers we already have are the inputs to the problems, parameters that describe the relationships between the products we make and the resources we use to make the products. Those numbers, though, don't tell us how to run our company.

Q.   **So, what, precisely, do we want to know in the Glimmer Glass problem?**

A.   Well, looking at the table, it would be nice to know how many windows and doors to make, and also how much glass, framing, and assembly time to use, and we really want to know what the total cost of all this is going to be. Go back to my comment that the decision variables represent the heart of the problem, and ask yourself what, out of the list, you really need to know, and what you could figure out on your own if you had a little more information.

Q.   **Wouldn't total cost be the most important number to know?**

A.   Cost is certainly an important number, maybe even the most important number, and we don't know it, but it is not a decision variable.

Q.   **So, what makes a variable a *decision* variable?**

A.   A decision variable is rather like (but not identical to) an independent variable that you used in statistics when doing regression. In regression, you had a dependent variable (usually called Y) whose value was calculated from one (or more) independent variables, usually referred to as X_i. You would look up values for the independent (X_i) variables, and using a regression equation, calculate the value for the dependent (Y) variable.

Q.   **How do we tell decision (independent) variables from other variables?**

A.   Ask yourself whether knowing the value for one variable will help you calculate the value for another variable.

Q.   **I'm thinking an example would help. Could you apply this to the Glimmer Glass problem?**

A.   Sure. You said cost was important (and I agreed), but knowing the value for cost won't tell you how many windows and doors to make.

Q.   **Would knowing how much glass and framing and time to use help?**

A.   Those are all definitely variables, but again, knowing you were going to use (to make up a number) 30,000 square inches of glass doesn't tell us what the total cost would be (except the cost for glass) nor which types of windows to put that glass in.

Q.   **It seems as if all that is left is the number of windows and doors. Is that what you are looking for?**

A.   Ask yourself whether knowing you were making (just as an example) two single-pane windows, three double-pane windows, and one door would let you calculate (using the numbers in the table) how much glass and framing and time to use, as well as the cost.

Q.   **Yes, that's not even hard. So, my variables would be as follows:**

X1 = single-pane windows
X2 = double-pane windows
X3 = doors

Is that right?

A. Yes, in essence, but, no, in detail. Definitions are important. If the definition isn't complete, then you probably don't completely understand the problem. There are very specific requirements for defining variables.

- Every variable definition will begin with "# of." You may not use "amount of ..." or "quantity of ..." or any other synonym. The purpose of this is to emphasize to you that the variables are numbers. This is an important idea.

- You must tell me what you are counting, including units if appropriate.

- Tell me why you are counting; tack a verb on the end of the definition. Using these guidelines, here are our variables for the Glimmer Glass problem:

SW = # of single-pane windows to make
DW = # of double-pane windows to make
SD = # of single-pane doors to make

You begin with "# of," you tell me what you are counting (windows or doors) and no units (pounds or inches or gallons) are needed because the windows or doors themselves are the units. Finally, you tell me what you are doing, making the products.

Q. **I thought we were supposed to be writing equations?**

A. We have finally gotten to that. Now that we know the variables and have the data in the table, we are ready to write out the constraints.

Q. **Do we start by listing the variables?**

A. You could, but it is often better to start with the constraint limits. We called them "maximums" in the table (note: it is possible to have minimums, we simply don't in this problem), so let's copy those numbers out of the table:

$\leq$ 400,000 square inches of glass
$\leq$ 50,000 inches of 1½-inch framing
$\leq$ 12,000 inches of 3-inch framing
$\leq$ 7,200 minutes of labor

Q. **Where did the "<" come from?**

A. Since these are maximum values, anything else we add to the equation must be less than the maximum (or equal to it).

Q. **Ok, so what has to be less than or equal to the maximums?**

A. Well, you use the stuff in the maximums to make windows and doors, so the amount of glass, framing, and assembly time used to make windows and doors must be less than the maximums.

Q. **But how can we calculate how much to use if we don't know how many windows and doors to make?**

A. We do have numbers for how many doors and windows to make.

Q.   **Where?**

A.   A page ago, we defined our variables as "# of _____ to make." We use the variables as the numbers, which is exactly what they were intended to do, so, let's write in the three variables the way we first defined them, so the constraints look like this:

SW	DW	SD ≤ 400,000 square inches of glass
SW	DW	SD ≤ 50,000 inches of 1½-inch framing
SW	DW	SD ≤ 12,000 inches of 3-inch framing
SW	DW	SD ≤ 7,200 minutes of labor

Q.   **Are those equations?**

A.   I've left out all the units of the variables, and I don't have any numbers with them yet, but all that's coming. For now, I want you to see that potentially every variable deals with every constraint. We've got another problem, though.

Q.   **What now?**

A.   The variables are measured as windows and doors, but the maximums have units of square inches, inches, and minutes. As already noted, equations have to have the same units everywhere.

Q.   **Didn't we take care of that when we set up the table?**

A.   We did for the table, but we haven't used that information yet. Fortunately, a set of parameters is just what we need to change the units of the variables.

Q.   **How do parameters change units?**

A.   I've copied the data table from up above:

	Single	Double	Door	Maximum
Glass	1,440 sq. in.	1,440 sq. in.	3,024 sq. in.	400,000 sq. in.
1½-inch framing	156 in.	216 in.		50,000 in.
3-inch framing			228 in.	12,000 in.
Assembly	20 min.	30 min.	50 min.	7,200 hours
Cost	$25.00	$45.00	$70.00	

Each number in the table, excluding the maximums, is measured for one unit of a product, either a single-paned window, a double-paned window, or a door. To use the assembly time as an example, the complete way to write out the parameters would be:

20 minutes per single-paned window

30 minutes per double-paned window

50 minutes per door

Q.　**How does that help?**

A.　Basic algebra. When you multiply a parameter by a variable, you also multiply the units, and the units cancel.

Q.　**Would this be a good time to ask for an example?**

A.　Probably. Working with the Assembly Time constraint (and abbreviating things), you have this:

20 $\frac{\text{Minutes}}{\text{Window}}$ * SW ~~Windows~~ = 20*SW Minutes

30 $\frac{\text{Minutes}}{\text{Window}}$ * DW ~~Windows~~ = 30*DW Minutes

50 $\frac{\text{Minutes}}{\text{Window}}$ * SD ~~Windows~~ = 50*SD Minutes

Since the maximum is 7,200 minutes, now the units are all the same.

Q.　**What would the whole equation look like?**

A.　Using all the parameters and putting "+" signs between the variables, this is what you get:

1440 SW	+	1440 DW	+	3024 SD		≤ 400,000 square inches of glass
156 SW	+	216 DW	+	0 SD		≤ 50,000 inches of 1½-inch framing
0 SW	+	0 DW	+	228 SD		≤ 12,000 inches of 3-inch framing
20 SW	+	30 DW	+	50 SD		≤ 7,200 minutes of labor

By convention, a number next to a variable is multiplied by that variable. Notice that blanks in the table translate into zeroes in the constraints. Also, by convention, we will drop all the variables that have a zero as a parameter later on.

Q.　**Great. Are we done?**

A.　Getting closer. We now have the constraints, but we still need the objective function.

Q.　**How do you set up an objective function?**

A.　There's still a set of numbers we haven't used, the costs.

Q.　**How can we use the costs if they have no maximum?**

A.　Actually, that's the whole point. The difference between a constraint and an objective is that an objective doesn't have a maximum or minimum limit.

Q.　**Why doesn't an objective have a limit?**

A.　The purpose of a constraint is to limit the values of the variables. The purpose of an objective is to try to achieve something with the variables. You don't set a limit when you are trying to accomplish something; instead, you go for as much (or as little) as you can.

Q.   How do you do that with an equation?

A.   The numbers we have with no limit are costs, so "costs" must be our objective. As good business-people, you want costs to be as low as possible, so we will minimize our objective. This gives us

$$\text{Min } Z = 25 \text{ SW} + 45 \text{ DW} + 70 \text{ SD}$$

as our objective. We created a new variable, "Z." "Z" is always reserved to refer to the objective; whether we are maximizing or minimizing is irrelevant. Combining everything we have worked out, our final formulation looks like this:

Min Z =	25 SW	+	45 DW	+	70 SD	
	1440 SW	+	1440 DW	+	3024 SD	≤ 400,000 square inches of glass
	156 SW	+	216 DW			≤ 50,000 inches of 1½-inch framing
					228 SD	≤ 12,000 inches of 3-inch framing
	20 SW	+	30 DW	+	50 SD	≤ 7,200 minutes of labor
	SW,		DW,		SD	≥ nonnegativity

Things to notice are that the variables are lined up in columns, the limits go on the right-hand side of the equation (no variables), parameters go before the variables, and there is a new constraint at the end of the formulation.

Q.   What kind of constraint is that?

A.   The new constraint is a little odd; it uses commas instead of plus signs. That last constraint simply requires that variable values, whatever they are, must never be negative (after all, you can't produce a negative amount of something). Properly done, that last constraint should be written on three different lines, one for each variable. However, the constraint is so important that the computer software has it built into the program, so you don't have to type it in (you will have to type in the other constraints). That means that while it is important enough to list every time you formulate a problem, we don't have to worry about setting it up properly, so we take a shortcut. This is the only time you are allowed to use commas in a formulation.

Q.   Now are we done?

A.   Now we are done. As noted before, I did this in a lot of excessive detail just in case any of you needed a refresher. The problem could be made more interesting by having you do more of the calculations for the parameters, such as cost sheets for the products so you have to figure out the total cost of the product, or details for number of workers and hours per worker, from which you would have to figure out the total hours available. There are also other types of variables and constraints, so in the next few sections I will give examples of how you handle more complex situations.

Q.   I am speechless. I don't even know what questions I have. If I had to start from scratch, I wouldn't have a clue how to begin.

A.   I understand how you might feel somewhat overwhelmed. But remember that this is the first time you're seeing this kind of stuff. The key to becoming comfortable with it is to try as many different formulations as you can. It has been said that 95% of all LP applications can be represented by six different types of formulations.

Q.   **I think even I can remember six different kinds of formulations.**

A.   I am sure you can remember them. The trick, however, is to recognize the right type to use when. In other words, the context of the problem can vary tremendously. You just will have to learn to separate the context from the content—and that is done through practice.

Q.   **OK ... suppose I learn how to do that with some reasonable level of proficiency. What do I do with the formulations?**

A.   In the next lesson, we will show you how to take a formulation and enter it into an Excel add-in called Solver, which will provide you with the solution to the problems.

Q.   **I can't wait ...**

ACTIVE LEARNING: LESSON 5.1

LESSON 5.2: Solving Linear Programs with Solver

Introduction

Q.   **Didn't we already solve the problem?**

A.   No, all we did was formulate the problem.

Q.   **If that didn't give us the solution, why did we bother to do all that?**

A.   Another phrase for "formulation" is "putting the problem in machine-ready form."

Q.   **What does that mean?**

A.   A spreadsheet can't read a paragraph and give you an answer. It can, however, read a set of formulas if we set them up properly. The formulation is that set of formulas, and in this section, we will go over how to feed them into a spreadsheet.

Q.   **Will that be as fascinating as all the rest of this?**

A.   Or more so.

Learning Outcomes

When you complete this session, you will be able to:

- Prepare the Solver set-up for a linear programming model

In addition, you will be able to:

- Install the Solver add-in into Excel

- Complete the Solver dialog box and obtain the optimal solution

A Dialectic on Solving Linear Programs with Solver

Q.   **You showed us, earlier, in painful detail, how to go about formulating LP problems. Do we have to go into all that detail every time?**

A.   Actually, it is a good template to follow until you get the hang of formulating LP problems, but once you have it, you can do it like the pros.

Q.   **What do the pros do?**

A.   They usually think of formulating LP problems as a three-step process:

- defining the variables,

- selecting the objective, and

- defining the constraints.

Once they go through those steps, they are ready to put the information in Solver.

Q.   **Is this where we do an example?**

A.   Yes, it is. Let's use a somewhat smaller problem:

Ken's Pottery Problem

You run a small pottery business, making ceramic bowls ($2.20 profit) and cups ($2.50 profit). Your only raw material is the clay you use. A cup uses 500 grams of clay, while a bowl uses 1¼ kilograms. It takes you 25 minutes to shape a bowl on your wheel and 45 minutes to shape a cup. A bowl must be "fired" for an hour and a cup for 48 minutes in your kiln, which can hold two items at a time. You have on hand 40 kilograms of clay and you expect to put in 30 hours at the wheel next week. The kiln must be preheated every day, so it is available only 20 hours per week. Set up your production plan for next week.

Q.   **OK, I read the problem and am ready to go. You said that the first step is to define the decision variables?**

A.   Exactly. We already made the point that the decision variables have to be independent variables in the sense that we can assign a value to them without knowing anything else or having to do any calculations to get to them.

Q.   **Right, so profit is not an independent variable because we cannot say "I want my profit to be $X" and be done with my problem. So, what should we use?**

A.   If you examine Ken's problem, what drives Ken's business is the decision of how many bowls and cups he should make. This is also sometimes referred to as deciding on his "product mix." Thus, we have:

Step 1.	Identify the decision (independent) variables - those
	things that you can make decisions about in order to achieve
	a desired objective
	X1 - # of ceramic bowls he decides to make
	X2 - # of cups he decides to make

Q.   **I see. Next, the pros select the objective. What does that mean?**

A.   Well, in the real world, you have to decide what "business" objective is most important when solving this problem. Typically, it is either to maximize (such as profit) or minimize (such as cost). Please note, however, that there are many applications that deal with objectives other than costs or profits.

Q.   **Since we are not in the real world yet, what do we do?**

A.   In Ken's case, we see that the data we are given deals with profits per item. That is a dead give-away that his business objective will be to maximize his profits. Remember, though, that we must express profit in terms of the decision variables we have defined. We know that each bowl contributes $2.20 to profits and that each cup contributes $2.50 to profits. Thus, we have:

Step 2.	Determine your objective (maximize profits or minimize costs)
	maximize Profits = 2.20 * X1 + 2.50 * X2

Q.   **That is pretty simple. So now we look for constraints. Why do we include things that keep us from making more money?**

A.   To really understand LP, you must understand how decisions and profits are impacted by constraints. We don't just include constraints for the fun of it; every constraint is there because it exists in the real world.

Q.   **So, what constraints exist in the real world?**

A.   Often, constraints reflect resources. One key concept is to realize that the decision variables are combined according to fixed recipes (in Ken's case, using clay, labor time, and kiln time) to make one unit of the decision variable (bowls and cups).

Q.   **Is this one of those "just-in-time" problems, where the company uses up all the resources?**

A.   Even in JIT manufacturing, it is very unlikely that any business will have exactly as much of each resource as they need, but it is always true that for an optimal solution, at least one of the resources will be completely used up. Conversely, it is also almost always true that some of the available resources will be left over.

Q.   **Umm, I'm not sure I got that. Can we go back to defining the constraints?**

A.   Sure. I think table 5.1 will help. It is a little different from the table we used in the "Formulating" lesson. It still has a row for each constraint, but where we had "Variables," we now have "Resources Used," and instead of "Maximums," we have "Resources Available."

TABLE 5.1   Template for Formulating Constraints for an LP Model

resources	amount of resources used	constraint type	resources available

Q.   **OK, so, a resource would be clay, right?**

A.   Right, and the point I was making is that we may, or may not, use up all the clay.

Q.   **Do we know how much clay we have?**

A.   Yes, that is given in the problem as 40 kg.

Q.   **How do we figure out how much clay is used?**

A.   Use what we know. We have variables to represent how many bowls (X_1) and cups (X_2) we will make, and we have numbers that tell us how much clay is used for each bowl and cup (1.25 kg and 0.5 kg, respectively), so putting all that together, we get table 5.2.

TABLE 5.2   Clay Resource Constraint

resources	amount of resources used	constraint type	resources available
clay (Kg)	1.25* X1 + 0.5 * X2	<=	40

Q.   **So, the table shows that whatever clay we use for bowls and cups (1.25*X1 + 0.5*X2) must be less than what we have (40 kg). That makes sense. I guess the labor constraint is put in the same way?**

A.   Exactly. However, watch out because the constraint for kiln time has a kicker in it.

Q. **Mmmm ... you mean that the kiln can accommodate two items at a time?**

A. Correct. Since this is a product-mix problem (how many products to make), not a production-scheduling problem (when to make the products), we can just change the numbers to write the constraint in terms of making one unit at a time.

Q. **How does that change the numbers?**

A. Ken can make two bowls in an hour, so we can call that one in 30 minutes, and for cups, two cups in 48 minutes becomes one in 24 minutes. He still has 20 hours (or 1,200 minutes) of kiln capacity available.

Q. **Got it! Let me go ahead and complete the table and show my work in table 5.3.**

A. Sure.

TABLE 5.3 Completed Constraints for Ken's Pottery Problem

resources	amount of resources used	constraint type	resources available
clay (Kg)	1.25* X1 + 0.5 * X2	<=	40
labor (min)	25 * X1 + 45 * X2	<=	1800
kiln time (min)	30 * X1 + 24 * X2	<=	1200
	X1>=0 X2>=0 (or X1,X2>=0)		

I am glad that you included the nonnegativity constraints as we taught you in the Formulation LP Problems learning module.

Q. **Thanks ... I am tired of looking at formulations. But how do we solve it? After all, that is what this learning module is supposed to be about.**

A. Here we go. To solve the problem, we have to get all the information in the table into Solver, but Solver cannot read equations.

Q. **What does Solver understand?**

A. Like all computers, Solver understands numbers, so we have to separate the numbers from the variables.

Q. **I'm thinking the table we have won't help, will it?**

A. It will help, but we do need to set up a different table, combining the table we used in the previous notes (Formulating LP Problems) and table 5.3, by:

1. Assigning a column to each variable.

2. Labeling the rows for the objective and constraints.

3. Inserting the coefficients where the variables (columns) match up with the objective and constraint rows.

If we follow these steps, we will get table 5.4.

TABLE 5.4   Ken's Pottery Data Preparation Table for Solver

	associate a column with each variable		row name
	X1	X2	
objective coeficients	2.2	2.5	Profit
constraint coeficients			
	1.25	0.5	clay
	25	45	labor
	30	24	kiln time

Q.   That looks like the table we used before. What about the "Resources Used" and "Resources Available"?

A.   We aren't done yet. The next thing we need is make a place for Solver to put the optimal solution, the values for X1 and X2. Once we have that, we can use all of that (the coefficients and variable values) to set up formulas in Excel that Solver can use. Table 5.5 shows the final result.

TABLE 5.5   Data Set-Up Table for Solver

I	J	K	L	M	N	O	P	Q
47			associate a column		row	Excel	constraint	resources
48			with each variable		name	equation	type	available
49			X1	X2				
50	variable value		0	0				
51								
52	objective coeficients		2.2	2.5	Profit	0		
53								
54	constraint coeficients							
55			1.25	0.5	clay	0	<=	40
56			25	45	labor	0	<=	1800
57			30	24	kiln time	0	<=	1200

Q.   That was quite a transformation. Based on the labels, L50:M50 are the variable values, and I recognize Q55:Q57 as the constraint limits, but why are some cells shaded, and what is in column O?

A.   The shaded cells are the ones Solver needs. Before I get to column O, note that I put in zeros for the values of X1 and X2. We need some sort of number there, and since we haven't produced anything yet, X1 = 0 and X2 = 0 makes sense.

Q.   **OK, fine, but what about column O?**

A.   That is the objective and "Resources Used" calculation for the current values of X_1 and X_2. The easiest Excel formula to use to do that is our old friend SUMPRODUCT. Here are the formulas that go in the corresponding cells:

CELL	FORMULA
CELL O52	=SUMPRODUCT($L$50:$M$50,L52:M52)
CELL O55	=SUMPRODUCT($L$50:$M$50,L55:M55)
CELL O56	=SUMPRODUCT($L$50:$M$50,L56:M56)
CELL O57	=SUMPRODUCT($L$50:$M$50,L57:M57)

Q.   **OK, I get it. What next?**

A.   Next, we install and open Solver.

Q.   **Where is Solver?**

A.   It is an add-in, just like Data Analysis. Figure 5.1 shows where to find it on the tool bar.

FIGURE 5.1 Finding the Solver add-in on the tool bar.

Q.   **Gotcha. Now, do I just click it to get going?**

A.   Yes, let's do that and we'll get what is shown on Figure 5.2.

Q.   **OK. What do I do with all that?**

A.   First, you must get used to Solver's terminology. The "Set Objective" is the cell where the objective function value is calculated, O52. Underneath, you must check whether you are maximizing (profit) or minimizing (cost).

Q.   **What does "Value Of" mean?**

A.   You can ask Solver to find values of X_1 and X_2 that yield a specific profit (e.g., if you put a zero there, you will get break-even values for X_1 and X_2).

Q.   **Ok, so what is "By Changing Cells"?**

A.   That is where Solver will put the optimal values for the variables. Since we have (0, 0) there, those values will change (hence the title).

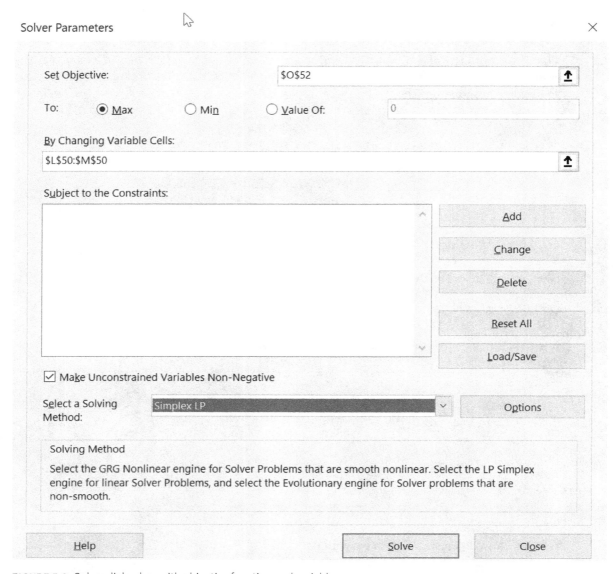

FIGURE 5.2 Solver dialog box with objective function and variables.

Q.   And the big box in the middle is for the constraints?

A.   Right, but we do not type them in the blank area of the box. Instead, we will enter them one by one. To do this, we click on the "Add" button to the right, which yields figure 5.3.

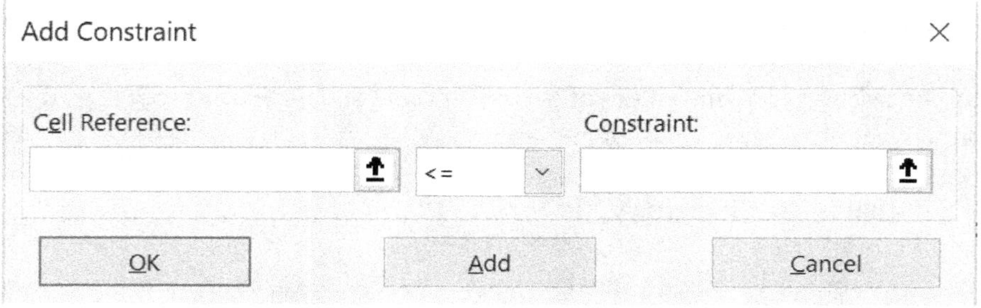

FIGURE 5.3 Constraint input dialog box.

Q.   **What does "Cell Reference" mean?**

A.   Allow me to point out, first, that the box looks very much like our table: on the left is an area for the "Resources Used" and on the right an area for "Resources Available." Of course, in Solver terms, "Resources Used" becomes "Cell Reference," and "Resources Available" becomes "Constraint."

Q.   **That actually made sense. Above, we set up a formula in column O for "Resources Used," so would that go under "Cell Reference"?**

A.   Yes, and the in the "Constraint" box you click on the amount of the resource available. You must also check the drop-down list in the middle to make sure you have the inequality ($\leq$, =, or $\geq$) correct.

Q.   **Do I click "Add" or "OK"?**

A.   Click "Add" if you have another constraint to enter, and "OK" when you have entered all the constraints (except the nonnegativity constraints).

Q.   **What do we do with the nonnegativity constraints?**

A.   There is a checkbox under the "Constraints" box labeled "Make Unconstrained Variables Non-Negative." Check it, and that takes care of it.

Q.   **Anything else?**

A.   Next, to "Select a Solving Method," use the drop-down list to choose "Simplex LP."

Q.   **Now are we done?**

A.   Yes. Figure 5.4 shows what you should have.

Q.   **So how do we get the solution?**

A.   Click on the "Solve" button to start the algorithm. When you do, the first thing you will see is the dialog box, shown in figure 5.5 titled "Solver Results." Solver indicates that it has found an optimal solution (always look for this message).

Q.   **Won't Solver always find a solution?**

A.   Not always—especially if you made a data input error. Worse, if your model contains no solution that satisfies all constraints, Solver does give a solution, but that solution will not be optimal (which almost always means you formulated an incorrect model).

Q.   **But if Solver finds an optimal solution, then we are done, right?**

A.   Well, no. Just because the model solved does not mean that your model correctly represents the business problem that you set out to solve. There is no sure-fire way to find out if your model is correct. The best you can do is analyze the answers and put them through a "sanity check" to see if they make sense. Regardless, table 5.6 shows our solution in the spreadsheet.

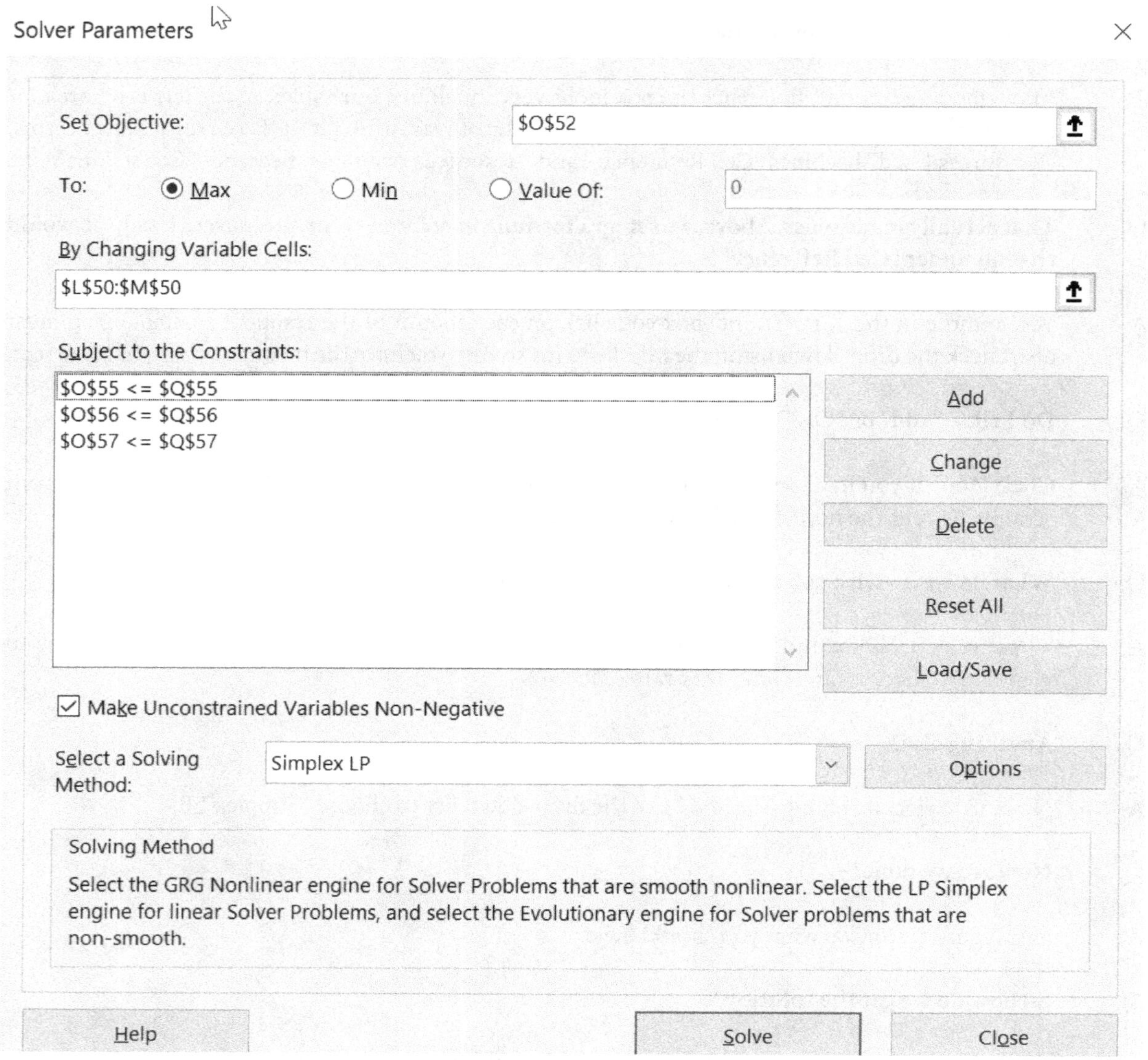

Solver Parameters   ✕

Se**t** Objective: $O$52   ⬆

To: ● Max   ○ Mi**n**   ○ **V**alue Of: 0

By Changing Variable Cells:

$L$50:$M$50   ⬆

Su**b**ject to the Constraints:

$O$55 <= $Q$55		**A**dd
$O$56 <= $Q$56		**C**hange
$O$57 <= $Q$57		**D**elete
		Reset All
		Load/Save

☑ Ma**k**e Unconstrained Variables Non-Negative

S**e**lect a Solving Method: Simplex LP   ⌄   **O**ptions

Solving Method

Select the GRG Nonlinear engine for Solver Problems that are smooth nonlinear. Select the LP Simplex engine for linear Solver Problems, and select the Evolutionary engine for Solver problems that are non-smooth.

Help   **S**olve   Cl**o**se

FIGURE 5.4 Solver dialog box.

Q.   **Finally, some numbers ... but what do they mean?**

A.   They give you what you wanted at the start, the optimal variable values, and based on those, the optimal (highest) total profit and the amount of each resource to use.

Q.   **So, the variable values are in cells L50:M50, and the total profit is in O52. Why do we need to know the amount of resources used in cells O55:O57?**

A.   That gives you information that can be useful in planning your business, such as what resources are used up or whether you had idle kiln time.

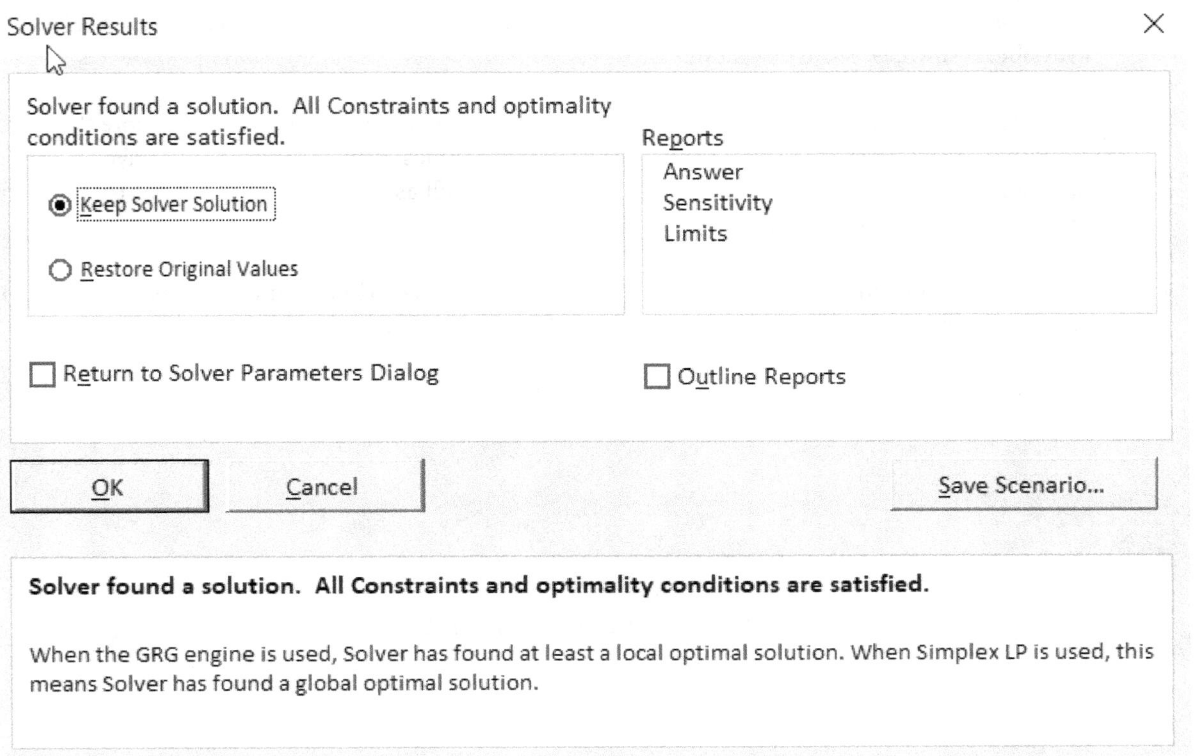

Solver Results   ✕

Solver found a solution. All Constraints and optimality
conditions are satisfied.
                                                            Reports
                                                              Answer
  ⦿ Keep Solver Solution   Sensitivity
                                                              Limits
  ◯ Restore Original Values

  ☐ Return to Solver Parameters Dialog   ☐ Outline Reports

  OK   Cancel   Save Scenario...

Solver found a solution. All Constraints and optimality conditions are satisfied.

When the GRG engine is used, Solver has found at least a local optimal solution. When Simplex LP is used, this
means Solver has found a global optimal solution.

FIGURE 5.5 Solver results.

TABLE 5.6 Solver Output

	J	K	L	M	N	O	P	Q
47			associate a column			Excel	constraint	resource
48			with each variable		name	equation	type	available
49			X1	X2				
50	variable value		14.4	32				
51								
52	objective coefficients		2.2	2.5	profit	111.68		
53								
54	constraint coefficients							
55			1.25	0.5	clay	34	<=	40
56			25	45	labor	1800	<=	1800
57			30	24	kiln time	1200	<=	1200

Q.   **What does this solution show?**

A.   Cell O55 indicates that you only used 34 kg out of the 40 kg of available clay, while cells O56 and
O57 tell you that you have used every bit of labor and kiln time that was available. So, you have a
little bit of clay leftover (you probably need to place an order for next week), and the kiln was used
to capacity, so you weren't wasting any of that.

Q. **OK ... earlier you told us that this was in fact the maximum profit that anyone could get with the available resources. So, are we done?**

A. First, let me point out that this maximum profit is guaranteed. However, there can be more than one combination of values for X_1 and X_2 that yield the same values. If that is the case, we have alternate optimum solutions. Excel can tell us what these are, as well as a lot more if we ask for the Answer and Sensitivity reports in the Solver Results output box.

Q. **I think I am burned out and need some time to absorb all of this. Can we deal with the other stuff some other time?**

A. Good idea. It's time for a break.

ACTIVE LEARNING: LESSON 5.2

LESSON 5.3: Conducting a Sensitivity Analysis

Introduction

Q. **We already have the solution. What else do we need?**

A. Solver provides more than the optimal solution to a linear program; it also provides a wealth of additional information to help the decision-maker gain confidence in the solution.

Q. **Why wouldn't we be confident that our optimal solution is right?**

A. The accuracy of the data is always suspect.

Q. **Why don't we get better data to start with?**

A. More accurate data may be too expensive to obtain.

Q. **More expensive than wrong data?**

A. The more accurate data may not be needed. In this lesson, we will learn how sensitive the optimal solution is to changes in the data for the objective function coefficients as well as the constraint limits. Knowing whether the solution changes as the data changes tells us whether more accurate data is required.

Q.   **Once we are confident in our data, then are we done?**

A.   You can also use the Sensitivity Report to answer a host of "what-if" questions that can arise during the implementation phase of a linear programming model.

Learning Outcomes

When you complete this session, you should be able to:

- Interpret Solver's Answer Report
- Interpret Solver's Sensitivity Report
  - From the "Variable Cells" output, you will be able to:
    - Interpret Reduced Costs
    - Interpret the "Allowable Increase"
    - Interpret the "Allowable Decrease"
    - Explain what happens to the optimal solution when a change in the objective function coefficient is within the allowable range
    - Explain what to do when a change in the objective function coefficient is outside the allowable range
  - From the "Constraints" output, you will be able to:
    - Explain the "Shadow Price"
    - Explain the Allowable Increase
    - Explain the Allowable Decrease
    - Explain what happens to the optimal solution when a change in the constraint right-hand side (RHS) is within the allowable range

A Dialectic Explaining Solver's Answer Report

Q.   **Since we already have the answer, why do we need Solver's Answer Report?**

A.   First, let's see how you get them. I have copied figure 5.5 (from the previous lesson) below. On the right-hand side, there is a list of reports you can get. You need the "Answer" and "Sensitivity" reports. Then, click "OK."

Q.   **What should have happened?**

A.   You should see the following two new work sheets on the bottom of your workbook:

| Answer Report 1 | Sensitivity Report 1 | **Model** |

Click on the Answer Report 1 tab, and you will see the three tables shown in table 5.7.

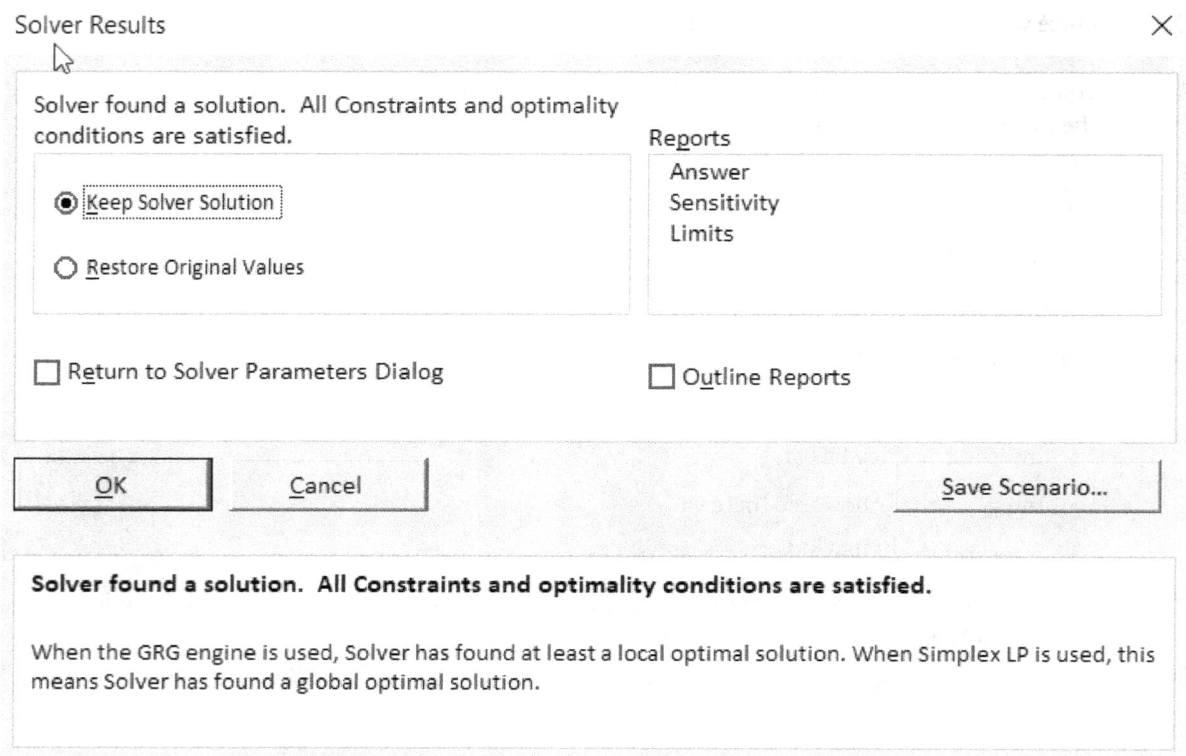

Solver Results   ✕

Solver found a solution. All Constraints and optimality
conditions are satisfied.

Reports

◉ Keep Solver Solution

Answer
Sensitivity
Limits

○ Restore Original Values

☐ Return to Solver Parameters Dialog   ☐ Outline Reports

OK   Cancel   Save Scenario...

Solver found a solution. All Constraints and optimality conditions are satisfied.

When the GRG engine is used, Solver has found at least a local optimal solution. When Simplex LP is used, this means Solver has found a global optimal solution.

FIGURE 5.6 Solver results.

Q. **How do these tables relate to our problem solution?**

A.   Once again, you have to translate from Solver's words to simple English. For instance, the first table is referred to as Objective Cell, meaning the objective function. Solver decided to call it "profit equation" instead of just "profit" and gives you the original value as well as the optimal value.

Q. **I already knew all that from table 5.7. How come it is giving it to me again?**

A.   Simply because it wants to. Actually, in table 5.7, Solver summarizes a lot of information in one place. So, it is just good housekeeping.

Q. **OK ... now what about the next table labeled "Variable Cells"?**

A.   Exactly that, all the information about your variables: the Excel cell it is in, the label you gave it, the original value, the optimal value, and what kind of variable it is (continuous or integer). Again, all the information is in one place, and you can use it to check whether you entered anything incorrectly (we didn't).

TABLE 5.7 Answer Report 1 Worksheet Contents

14	Objective Cell (Max)					
15	**Cell**	**Name**	**Original Value**	**Final Value**		
16	$O$52	profit equation	0	111.68		
17						
18						
19	Variable Cells					
20	**Cell**	**Name**	**Original Value**	**Final Value**	**Integer**	
21	$L$50	variable value X1	0	14.4	Contin	
22	$M$50	variable value X2	0	32	Contin	
23						
24						
25	Constraints					
26	**Cell**	**Name**	**Cell Value**	**Formula**	**Status**	**Slack**
27	$O$55	clay equation	34	$O$55<=$Q$55	Not Binding	6
28	$O$56	labor equation	1800	$O$56<=$Q$56	Binding	0
29	$O$57	kiln time equation	1200	$O$57<=$Q$57	Binding	0

Q. **Still old stuff, isn't it?**

A. Yes, but we are about to see some new stuff. Take a look at the table labeled "Constraints." All the first part is what you already know—the Excel location, the names that you had assigned, and the actual values (no original values this time). Then comes something new.

Q. **Why do we need to see the equations?**

A. Error checking. If you are getting a bad answer, this report can help you spot whether you clicked on the wrong cells when setting up the constraints.

Q. **What is this "Status" thing?**

A. The status column simply tells you whether that constraint's resources are all used up, in which case it is called a "binding" constraint. If you have some resources left over, as in the case with clay, the constraint is called "Not Binding."

Q. **I get it. Now, what is the next column all about?**

A. It tells you how much of each resource is left over. This is also referred to as the "slack" of the constraint.

Q. **So, any constraint that has zero slack is a binding constraint?**

A. Exactly. Be aware that you should decide whether a constraint is binding by whether it has a slack of zero. Do not believe Excel's status column—it sometimes lies.

Q. **Great ... all I need is something else to confuse me. This stuff is bad enough by itself!**

A. I understand. Still, Solver gives you the ability to find optimal solutions to complex problems, so overall it is worth it. As a parting gift, I summarized how to read the Answer Report in table 5.8.

TABLE 5.8   Summary Interpretations from the Answer Report

Objective Cell (Max)

Cell	Name	Original Value	Final Value	
$O$52	profit equation	0	111.68	This is the maximum profit that Ken can get with the available resources

Variable Cells

Cell	Name	Original Value	Final Value	Integer	
$L$50	variable value X1	0	14.4	Contin	This is the number of bowls (X1) that Ken must make to get his maximum profit
$M$50	variable value X2	0	32	Contin	This is the number of cups that Ken must make to get his max profit

Constraints

Cell	Name	amt of the resource used Cell Value	Formula	Status	Slack	
$O$55	clay equation	34	$O$55<=$Q$55	Not Binding	6	This is the amount of clay that Ken will have left over after he makes 14.4 bowls and 32 cups
$O$56	labor equation	1800	$O$56<=$Q$56	Binding	0	This is the amount of labor that Ken will have left over after he makes 14.4 bowls and 32 cups
$O$57	kiln time equation	1200	$O$57<=$Q$57	Binding	0	This is the amount of Kiln time lefte over after he makes 14.4 bowls and 32 cups

ACTIVE LEARNING: LESSON 5.3.1

A Dialectic Explaining Solver's Sensitivity Report

Q.   **Is this another report telling us what we already know?**

A.   Yes and no. Some of it is repetitious, but a lot of it is new—and very useful.

Q.   **I clicked on the Sensitivity Report 1 tab in the workbook, so what is new and useful?**

A.   You should see table 5.9. Notice there are two parts: the top one for Variables, X1 and X2, and the bottom one for Constraints, Clay, Labor, and Kiln Time. The first few columns, Cell, Name, and Final Value, are things you already knew.

Q.   **The next column is called either Reduced Cost or Shadow Price. What are those?**

A.   Actually, they are similar. Both tell you the change in the objective (increase in total profit) if you make more of a variable or have more of a resource.

Q.   **Why are the reduced costs both zero?**

A.   You are already making as much as you can of each variable, so there is no further profit to be gained.

Q.   **So why is the shadow price zero for Clay?**

A.   Suppose your friendly clay salesman walks in and offers you a great deal on the purchase of more clay. Would you consider purchasing some more clay?

TABLE 5.9   Solver's Sensitivity Report

6	Variable Cells						
7			Final	Reduced	Objective	Allowable	Allowable
8	Cell	Name	Value	Cost	Coefficient	Increase	Decrease
9	$L$50	variable value X1	14.4	0	2.2	0.925	0.811111111
10	$M$50	variable value X2	32	0	2.5	1.46	0.74
11							
12	Constraints						
13			Final	Shadow	Constraint	Allowable	Allowable
14	Cell	Name	Value	Price	R.H. Side	Increase	Decrease
15	$O$55	clay equation	34	0	40	1E+30	6
16	$O$56	labor equation	1800	0.0296	1800	450	300
17	$O$57	kiln time equation	1200	0.048666667	1200	102.8571429	240

Q.   **Is this some sort of trick question? Why would I pass up a good deal?**

A.   Because you do not need any more! The Final Value is 34, the Constraint RH Side is 40, which means you already have 6 kg lying around that you cannot use (we called that "slack" in an earlier lecture).

Q.   **That makes sense, but what does that have to do with the shadow price?**

A.   Since you don't need more clay, there would be no increase in the total profit. The Shadow Price shows that.

Q.   **OK, so do the other two show that we could make more profit?**

A.   Not a lot of profit, but, yes. If you worked for one extra minute, you would gain 2.96 cents in total profit. In the same way, running the kiln for an extra minute would gain an extra 4.8667 cents of profit.

Q.   **Why do Labor and Kiln make us more profit, but not Clay?**

A.   It is a question of what you need. When a resource is scarce (when the slack is zero), then it has economical value. If you knew what this economic value is (to you), then you could make a decision as to whether to get some more.

Q.   **And you would make that decision based on cost of that resource?**

A.   Precisely. If the cost is less than (or equal to) the increase in profit (reduced cost or shadow price), then you would consider getting it. Otherwise you would not.

Q.   **So, if I work more and run the kiln more, I could increase profit 2.96 + 4.867 = 7.827?**

A.   Unfortunately, it doesn't work that way. You can change only one resource (or variable) at a time.

Q.   **Why can you change only one resource at a time?**

A.   The simple answer is because one will be clearly better than the other. For example, if you could get the resource for free, why would you bother to get labor if you get more profit from kiln? The less simple answer is that if you change two numbers in the problem (more kiln time and more labor) then the values of the Shadow Price change, so you will likely get some increase, but usually not as much as you thought.

Q.   **Oh, well. Moving on, what is this Allowable Increase and Allowable Decrease all about?**

A.   Good question. Let's start with clay. We do know we don't need more clay, so no matter how much clay was delivered to us, we wouldn't change the solution.

Q.   **That makes sense, but why does the spreadsheet say the Allowable Increase for clay is 1E+30?**

A.   In Excel, this is simply the largest number the computer can conceive. Practically, you should think of it as being equivalent to ∞. So, when you see 1E+30, it means no matter how much more clay you get, the solution won't change.

Q.   **Good to know. The Allowable Decrease, though, is 6. Does that mean we can lose up to 6 kg?**

A.   Exactly. The amount of clay we can get rid of before it starts impacting our profit is given in the Allowable Decrease column. In our case, it says that if you get rid of more than 6 units (the amount we didn't use, you may remember), it will start impacting your optimal profit.

Q.   **I see. By how much would the seventh kilogram of clay that I get rid of decrease my profit?**

A.   I don't know.

Q.   **??**

A.   There are limits to the information we can extract from the Solver output. If we wanted that information, we would go back and rerun Solver with the quantity available of clay being 33 kgs.

Q.   **Couldn't we do this with just about everything we are talking about?**

A.   Sure. But that would give you a whole lot of different answer sheets to keep track of and consume a fair amount of time. You might as well learn to use the tables and resort to additional runs when you must.

Q.   **Makes sense to me. Let's go back and talk a bit about labor and kiln time.**

A.   Sure. Using similar reasoning we know that the shadow price of labor will remain at $0.0296 if you do not decrease the amount of labor by more than the allowable decrease of 300 or if you do not increase the amount of labor by more than the allowable increase of 450.

Q.   **Got it. So, the shadow price for kiln time remains at $0.048666667 if we do not increase the amount of kiln time by more than the allowable increase of 102.8571429 or as long as you do not decrease the amount of kiln time by more than the allowable decrease of 240.**

A.   Exactly right. Let me see if I can summarize in table 5.10 what we have just said about the "Constraints" table.

TABLE 5.10 Summary Interpretation from the Constraints Table of the Sensitivity Report

12	Constraints							
13			Final	Shadow	Constraint	Allowable	Allowable	
14	Cell	Name	Value	Price	R.H. Side	Increase	Decrease	the shadow price is valid as long as your resources stay in the region
15	$O$55	clay equation	34	0	40	1E+30	6	40-6 AND 40 + 1E+30
16	$O$56	labor equation	1800	0.0296	1800	450	300	1800 - 300 AND 1800 + 450
17	$O$57	kiln time equation	1200	0.048666667	1200	102.8571429	240	1200 - 240 AND 1200 + 102.8571429
18								
19		we would pay $0 for an additional unit of clay						
20		we would pay up to $0.0296 for an additional unit of labor						
21		we would pay up to $0.048666667 for an additional unit of kiln						

Q. That will be a great reference. Now, I notice there is one more table in the Sensitivity Report that we have not dealt with yet.

A. Correct. It is shown in table 5.11 and is referred to as the variable cells report.

TABLE 5.11 The Adjustable Cells Table from the Sensitivity Report

6	Variable Cells						
7			Final	Reduced	Objective	Allowable	Allowable
8	Cell	Name	Value	Cost	Coefficient	Increase	Decrease
9	$L$50	variable value X1	14.4	0	2.2	0.925	0.811111111
10	$M$50	variable value X2	32	0	2.5	1.46	0.74

Q. What does it do?

A. It deals with the variables, specifically their objective coefficients, rather than the constraints and their limits.

Q. So, I get an allowable increase and decrease for the profit of bowls (X1) and cups (X2)?

A. Exactly. Prices can change for any number of reasons (new competition, cost of resources, annual sales, etc.) or simply because the data we used to estimate the profit per unit has a margin of error to it.

Q. I've said this before, but is it time for an example?

A. Sure. Suppose a new pottery opened up down the street from you that specializes in making bowls. To match their prices, you had to cut the price (and therefore, the profit) of your bowls to $2.00, a decrease of $0.20. Look at table 5.10.

Q. OK, well, Bowls is X1 and profit went down, so the Allowable Decrease for Bowls is 0.81111. Our decrease was only 0.20, so 0.20 is less than the Allowable Decrease, so we are all right. Won't we make less profit, though?

A. Very good! Yes, the number of bowls we make won't change as long as the change (increase or decrease) stays between the Allowable Increase and the Allowable Decrease, but the Total Profit (profit per unit times the # of units) will change.

Q.   **What if the cost of clay increased, hurting both Bowls and Cups?**

A.   Then just like before, we would have to rerun the problem. The allowable changes are only accurate when only one parameter is changing.

Q.   **Do you think you could summarize this for me as you did for the other tables?**

A.   Check out table 5.12.

TABLE 5.12   Summary Interpretation of the Adjustable Cells Table from the Sensitivity Report

			Final	Reduced	Objective	Allowable	Allowable	the solution X1=14.4 and X2=32 is optimal as long as the profit
6	Variable Cells							
7/8	Cell	Name	Value	Cost	Coefficient	Increase	Decrease	per unit is in the following range
9	$L$50	variable value X1	14.4	0	2.2	0.925	0.811111111	(2.2 - 0.811111111) AND (2.2 + 0.925)
10	$M$50	variable value X2	32	0	2.5	1.46	0.74	(2.5 - 0.74) AND (2.5+1.46)

Q.   **Thanks! You told us about the Reduced Cost earlier, but what if you had a variable that had a reduced cost other than zero?**

A.   Suppose, for example, that Ken had another product that he could make, such as vases, and that Solver decided not to make any (a variable that has a value of zero in the optimal solution is referred to as a non-basic variable). Let's assume then that the reduced cost for that non-basic variable is $2.00. This represents by how much the profitability (objective function coefficient) has to increase before it becomes profitable to make vases. Thus, if Ken wants to make vases, he has to find a way to get $2.00 more in profits per vase (maybe by considering a price increase?).

Q.   **Wow! That is a pretty handy piece of information to have in a business environment.**

A.   Indeed, it is. And that is why you are learning this material.

ACTIVE LEARNING: LESSON 5.3.2

LESSON 5.4: Introduction to Flow Networks

Introduction

Q.   **What is a "flow network"?**

A.   A set of linear programming problems that have a special mathematical structure that allows them to be solved easily.

Q. **What does that matter, if the algorithm does all the work for us?**

A. It mattered years ago, when computer speeds and memory were not up to today's capabilities. It matters now because there is a large group of problems that share this structure, so it is worth covering.

Q. **How did all this start?**

A. Early business analytics applications (or management science/operations research, as it was called at the time) dealt with operational issues in the military, since they originated during WWII. One of the most challenging tasks facing the military during those days was how to keep rapidly advancing (or retreating) forces supplied with essential goods (as Napoleon said, an army marches on its stomach). For example, the war in the Pacific was fought on multiple distant islands that had to be supplied from centers in the United States. Determining what goods should be sent from which supply center to which depots was an ongoing problem, one that had to be resolved with each changing report from the front.

Q. **Do all flow problems deal with logistics?**

A. The efficiency of the transportation problems prompted operations researchers to try to find similar mathematical structures in other linear programming models, ones which may not have had anything to do with logistics, but the name "transportation problem" stuck. Today, an amazing number of different applications fall into the category of transportation problems, which is why we devote this lesson to them.

Learning Outcomes

When you complete this session, you will be able to:

- Represent a transportation problem as a network problem
  - Understand the meaning of nodes and arcs
    - Understand that arcs represent variables in linear programming
    - Understand that nodes represent constraints in linear programming
- Set up a transportation problem for Solver
  - For the variables
    - Define arcs by their origin (from) and destination (to)
    - Name arcs so they can be identified in the Solver output
    - Assign the initial values to the variables
  - For the objective
    - Add the objective coefficients column
    - Use SUMPRODUCT to define the objective function
  - For the constraints
    - List the nodes as constraints
    - Determine the actual flow in/out by using the SUMIF function

- Add the correct type of constraint (depending on total available/total demand)
- Add the rhs column
  - Fill out the Solver dialog box and run Solver

A Dialectic on Transportation-Type Problems

Q.   **So, where will the transportation algorithm take us?**

A.   Cute. I suppose you could use the algorithm to plan a holiday, but I wouldn't recommend it. As I said in the introduction, transportation problems arose out of the critical need to get supplies that were needed, in the right quantities, to the right place, at the right time. All of that was complicated just a bit by the on-going war.

Q.   **Sounds like a major logistics nightmare to me. How did they do it?**

A.   Well, I'm not going to have you memorize the algorithm, if that is what you are worried about, (although it is an extremely interesting story). What we will do is to show how such problems can be solved routinely and effectively today.

Q.   **Why? I am not particularly interested in logistics.**

A.   You probably should be, for there are very few jobs that are not affected by logistics, but regardless, this algorithm has been applied to a surprising number of business problems that don't involve moving supplies around.

Q.   **OK. Surprise me.**

A.   I'll do my best. Let's begin by going back to the future and start with the problem described below:

A BK Transportation Problem

The BK Corporation is a major user of ground beef. The ground beef is prepared at three packing plants in Denver, Dallas, and Chicago and then shipped by truck to four distribution centers located in Miami, Philadelphia, Los Angeles, and New Orleans. As a result of the increasing cost of diesel fuel, management has initiated a study to manage the rising shipping costs to the extent possible.

For the next month, purchase orders have been placed with each packing plant, and demand at each distribution center has been forecast and shipping costs per truck load have been estimated. With this information, as given below, BK wants to determine the minimum total cost for shipping from the packing houses to the distribution centers.

		relative shipping cost ($/truck load)				
			warehouse			
		Miami	Philadelphia	Los Angeles	New Orleans	ordered (truck loads)
	Denver	2,064	1,748	1,017	1,299	75
	Dallas	1,308	1,468	1,238	506	125
packing plant	Chicago	1,381	759	2,015	927	100
	Demand (truck loads)	80	65	70	85	

Q.   **Not burgers again! Can't you come up with something else?**

A.   If you are sick and tired of burgers, pretend that you are reading an ordinary textbook and think of this as XYZ Corporation shipping widgets—or whatever else catches your fancy. The point is that this problem is just an illustration, and what you can learn from it can fit many different applications. So, for the time being, quit acting like a vegan and focus on the substance of the problem and not the context.

Q.   **Not quite as dramatic as a war, is it?**

A.   No, but very important to the company. The first thing to realize is that this is a linear programming problem.

Q.   **So, it has variables, constraints, and an objective?**

A.   Exactly—I'm glad you remember that.

Q.   **You said variables are the most important thing, so here there should be three—how much to ship from each plant, right?**

A.   Partially. Each plant needs to know how much to ship out, but they also need to know where to ship it.

Q.   **So, we also need to know how much to ship to each distribution center?**

A.   Even that won't cover it. We have to know how much to ship from each of the three processing plants to each of the four distribution centers, so there are 12 variables.

Q.   **That's a lot. Are there just as many constraints?**

A.   No, that's fairly simple, one constraint for each processing plant (so you don't exceed supply) and one constraint for each distribution center (so you meet its demand).

Q.   **That doesn't sound too bad. Is it always that simple?**

A.   For a transportation problem, it is always that simple, but not, usually, that small. Most companies have many more shipping points (call them plants or warehouses or suppliers or whatever) and many more reception points (distribution centers or outlets or retail locations or whatever). Luckily, we can think of a transportation problem as a network flow problem.

Q.   **What do you mean by a "network flow problem"?**

A.   That's always a problem: do I show a confusing diagram first, and then label it, or do I give the label first, and then show what I mean? This time, figure 5.7 shows a network representation of the BK problem.

Q.   **What makes it a network?**

A.   Tying the circles (called nodes) together with arrows in a generally left-to-right pattern (though one-directional flow is not a requirement).

Q.   **What are the circles for?**

A.   Each node corresponds to a plant or a distribution center.

Q.   **So, what do the arrows do?**

A.   Each arrow represents whether that plant can ship to that warehouse (if a plant cannot ship to a warehouse, we would just not show the arrow). Each arrow has a cost associated with it, which I have not shown on the network because it would clutter up the diagram.

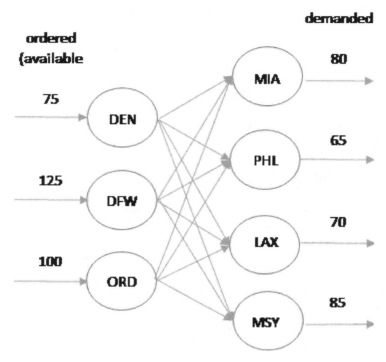

FIGURE 5.7 Network representation of the BK transportation problem.

Q.   **How does this help with LP?**

A.   From a linear programming perspective, each arrow corresponds to a variable and each node to a constraint. For the plants, the constraints would make sure that you don't ship out any more than you have available. For the warehouses, the constraints would make sure that what flows in from all plants satisfies the demand.

Q.   **Is it supposed to look like a pile of spaghetti and meatballs?**

A.   It is supposed to look like a map. Imagine the nodes spread out on a map of the United States, and it would probably be a little clearer.

Q.   **OK, call it a map. What do we do with it?**

A.   I am going to use it to explain how to go directly to the Solver set-up for the linear program that corresponds to this transportation problem. In other words, I am going to skip the entire model formulation step.

Q.   **Gotta love that! I was getting sick and tired of messing with all those subscripts ...**

A.   I thought you might (I get tired of messing with all those subscripts myself). In developing the Solver set-up, we will follow the exact same sequence of steps we did when doing it for a linear programming (algebraic) model.

Q.   **Wasn't the first step to define the variables?**

A.   Very good! You also have to assign them an initial value. In table 5.13, I defined the variables (one per arrow) in columns I, J, and K. Column I shows the node an arrow starts from and column J shows the node an arrow ends at. To read Solver's Answer and Sensitivity reports more easily, I gave each arrow (variable) a name in column K. Then, as usual, I have assigned (in column L) an initial value of zero to each of the variables.

TABLE 5.13 Setting Up the Solver Run—Part I

N19			fx	=SUMPRODUCT(L6:L17,N6:N17)			
	I	J	K	L	M	N	O
1							
2		VARIABLES				OBJECTIVE	
3							
4				initial			
5	from	to	name	value		obj coeff	
6	DEN	MIA	DENMIA	0	$	2,064	
7	DEN	PHL	DENPHL	0	$	1,748	
8	DEN	LAX	DENLAX	0	$	1,017	
9	DEN	MSY	DENMSY	0	$	1,299	
10	DFW	MIA	DFWMIA	0	$	1,308	
11	DFW	PHL	DFWPHL	0	$	1,469	
12	DFW	LAX	DFWLAX	0	$	1,238	
13	DFW	MSY	DFWMSY	0	$	506	
14	ORD	MIA	ORDMIA	0	$	1,381	
15	ORD	PHL	ORDPHL	0	$	759	
16	ORD	LAX	ORDLAX	0	$	2,015	
17	ORD	MSY	ORDMSY	0	$	927	
18							
19					TOTLCOST $	-	

Q.   **What are the numbers in column N?**

A.   Those are the shipping costs from the problem statement (a couple of pages back), which will be our objective (minimize costs). As before, I calculated the objective function value using the

SUMPRODUCT function (in cell N19), multiplying each variable value (in column L) by the matching cost per unit (in column N). You can see that formula at the top of the sheet.

Q.   **This doesn't look much better than all the subscripts ...**

A.   Well, just remember that if you did this the old way you would have to develop the model and, on top of that, set up the spreadsheet. And don't forget that it is not necessary to draw the network diagram—we did that just to help you visualize what we are doing in the Solver set-up process above.

Q.   **I guess if you put it that way, this is shorter. Wasn't the next part entering the constraint coefficients and right-hand-side info? How do we do that?**

A.   Table 5.14 shows us that. Remember that the arrows became the variables and the nodes had the constraints. Each plant node has a supply constraint to make sure it does not ship out more than is available and each distribution center node has a demand constraint to make sure its demand is filled.

TABLE 5.14   Setting Up the Solver Run—Part II

SUM	▾	:	✕	✓	*fx*	=SUMIF($I$6:$I$17,Q6,$L$6:$L$17)								
	H	I	J	K	L	M	N	O	P	Q	R	S	T	U
1														
2			VARIABLES				OBJECTIVE				CONSTRAINTS			
3														
4					initial									
5		from	to	name	value		obj coeff		name	node	actual in/out	const type	rhs	
6		DEN	MIA	DENMIA	0		$ 2,064			DEN	$L$6:$L$17)	=	75	
7		DEN	PHL	DENPHL	0		$ 1,748			DFW	0	=	125	
8		DEN	LAX	DENLAX	0		$ 1,017			ORD	0	=	100	
9		DEN	MSY	DENMSY	0		$ 1,299			MIA	0	=	80	
10		DFW	MIA	DFWMIA	0		$ 1,308			PHL	0	=	65	
11		DFW	PHL	DFWPHL	0		$ 1,469			LAX	0	=	70	
12		DFW	LAX	DFWLAX	0		$ 1,238			MSY	0	=	85	
13		DFW	MSY	DFWMSY	0		$ 506							
14		ORD	MIA	ORDMIA	0		$ 1,381							
15		ORD	PHL	ORDPHL	0		$ 759							
16		ORD	LAX	ORDLAX	0		$ 2,015							
17		ORD	MSY	ORDMSY	0		$ 927							
18														
19						TOTLCOST	$ -							

Q.   **Are the supply constraints "≤" and the demand constraints "≥"?**

A.   They can be, but if we add all the orders at the plants and all the demands at the distribution centers, we get the same amount, so each constraint can be of type "=."

Q.   **What if they hadn't added up to the same amount?**

A.   We have a trick for that, but we don't need it now. Notice I used the node names in column Q, so Solver will use the node names in the output files.

Q.   **What do you mean by "actual in/out?"**

A.   Just that. The problem told us how much each plant has to ship out and how much each center wants to ship in. Those are the constraint limits in column T, labeled "RHS." In column R, we have to add up how much was actually shipped out of each plant or into each center. We compare the actual to the limits to make sure we obey all the constraints.

Q.   **What is the =SUMIF function you used?**

A.   A very powerful function that adds up certain cells only if they meet some criterion. You should become familiar with it because it has many applications besides the handy dandy one here.

Q.   **OK, so how does it work?**

A.   You should click on the link that appears when you type in the function name and opening parenthesis to get a video and full explanation. In our application above, the function looks at all the entries in the "from" column (I) and compares each to the entry in cell Q6, which is "DEN." For all entries in column I that are "DEN," the corresponding entries in column L ("initial value") are summed.

Q.   **That is really cool! So that is how it works for the plants. I guess that for the warehouses I have to look at the entries in the "to" column (J), but the rest is the same?**

A.   Exactly. All you have to do is replace the I by a J in the SUMIF function and you are all set to go.

Q.   **Great. So, where am I going next?**

A.   To Solver. You are done with the set-up. Let me show you in figure 5.8 what the Solver dialog box looks like when filled out.

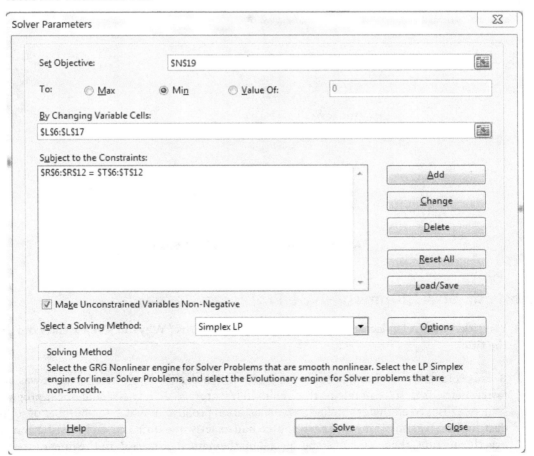

FIGURE 5.8 The Solver dialog box for the BK transportation problem.

Q.   That looks so simple! I guess you just entered your constraints by entering all left sides in column R and then the entries in the RHS column T?

A.   Yes. And that only worked because all my constraint types where the same. Table 5.15 shows what the output looks like. I am going to let you look at the Answer and Sensitivity reports on your own—they contain the exact same information as that for any other LP.

Q.   You have got me curious now. What other kind of network problems are there?

A.   We'll talk about that some other time after you have digested this.

TABLE 5.15   The Solver Solution for the BK Transportation Problem

	I	J	K	L	M	N	O	P	Q	R	S	T
1												
2		VARIABLES				OBJECTIVE				CONSTRAINTS		
3												
4				initial								
5	from	to	name	value		obj coeff		name	node	actual in/out	const type	rhs
6	DEN	MIA	DENMIA	5		$ 2,064			DEN	75	=	75
7	DEN	PHL	DENPHL	0		$ 1,748			DFW	125	=	125
8	DEN	LAX	DENLAX	70		$ 1,017			ORD	100	=	100
9	DEN	MSY	DENMSY	0		$ 1,299			MIA	80	=	80
10	DFW	MIA	DFWMIA	40		$ 1,308			PHL	65	=	65
11	DFW	PHL	DFWPHL	0		$ 1,469			LAX	70	=	70
12	DFW	LAX	DFWLAX	0		$ 1,238			MSY	85	=	85
13	DFW	MSY	DFWMSY	85		$ 506						
14	ORD	MIA	ORDMIA	35		$ 1,381						
15	ORD	PHL	ORDPHL	65		$ 759						
16	ORD	LAX	ORDLAX	0		$ 2,015						
17	ORD	MSY	ORDMSY	0		$ 927						
18												
19					TOTLCOST	$ 274,510						

ACTIVE LEARNING: LESSON 5.4.1

A Dialectic on Assignment-Type Problems

Q.   You titled this "A Dialectic on Assignment-Type Problems." Why did you use the word "Type" in the title?

A.   Because old habits tend to hang on, I suppose. Back in the old days when the quest was on to find faster methods to solve problems that required less storage than traditional linear programming, someone discovered that if you had a transportation problem in which the number of sources and destinations was the same and each source had exactly one unit and each destination required exactly one unit, then you had some special mathematical properties in the linear programming model that would allow you to solve the problem even more efficiently than the transportation problem. These problems became known as "assignment problems."

Q.   **That seems to be a strange set of requirements for a transportation problem. Was this made up so some PhD student could do a dissertation and perhaps get a theoretical paper published?**

A.   Probably, but the problem was given a sense of reality by putting it into an assignment context. If you think of the sources as being jobs and the destination as being machines, where each machine could do some jobs faster than others, then the problem became one of assigning jobs to machines. Similarly, if you were a swimming coach and you had four swimmers for a medley relay team (where each swimmer swam a different stroke), then the problem would be to assign swimmers to strokes to minimize the total time to finish the race.

Q.   **Interesting applications. But, do I have to know anything special to deal with such problems if and when?**

A.   Nope. You already know all it takes to solve such problems. Just treat them like good ole transportation problems and the answers will be yours.

Q.   **Easy for you to say ...**

A.   And for you to do. Just go ahead and give Exercise 5.4.2 a try.

Q.   **Off into unchartered waters I go. You'll hear from me when I get in trouble.**

A.   Have no fear.

ACTIVE LEARNING: LESSON 5.4.2

LESSON 5.5: Integer and Combinatorial Optimization

Introduction

Q.   **What do "integer" and "combinatorial" mean?**

A.   Pretty much the same thing—combinatorial optimization is a subset of integer programming.

Q.   **Why list both of them, then?**

A.   Integer programming requires that all variables have integer (whole number) values rather than the decimal solutions that are common in linear programming. Combinatorial optimization further restricts the integer value to be either zero or one. This allows for modeling a variety of combinatorial problems of great practical significance, such as scheduling and capital budgeting.

Q.   **What's wrong with decimals?**

A.   For many problems, decimal values do not make sense. For example, how do you make a fraction of a cup or ring (or any other product, for that matter)? The initial response is to just round off the answers. Unfortunately, for large problems, rounding of many variables may result in a number of constraints being violated, and this can invalidate the Solver solution. To overcome this problem, Solver gives us the option to specify which variables must be integer. It will then generate the optimal solution that also satisfies the integer requirements for the specified variables.

Learning Outcomes

When you complete this session, you will be able to:

- Develop integer programming models
- Develop binary programming models with
  - Precedence constraints
  - Either/or constraints
  - Conditional constraints
- Set up the Solver parameter box for integer and binary programs
- Interpret the Solver solution to integer and binary programming problems

A Dialectic on Integer Optimization

Q.   **Up to now, we've been OK with variables having fractions as values. What changed your mind?**

A.   Now that you have mastered the fundamentals of linear programming, I think you are ready to go beyond that.

Q.   **Is it that complicated?**

A.   As a matter of fact, the modeling process is identical to what you used for LP. Once you have a LP model and you decide that you want integer answers, it only takes a few keystrokes in Solver.

Q.   **Will I need to know how to do this?**

A.   It is good to have more than one tool in your box, so, yes, you should know how to do this in case you need it someday. Besides, it is simple.

Q.   **If it is that simple, go ahead and show.**

A.   OK. Let's go back to Ken's Pottery problem that we used to develop your modeling skills in Lesson 5.2. The solver solution was given in table 5.6. Here it is:

TABLE 5.16

	J	K	L	M	N	O	P	Q
47			associate a column			Excel	constraint	resource
48			with each variable		name	equation	type	available
49			**X1**	**X2**				
50	variable value		14.4	32				
51								
52	objective coefficients		2.2	2.5	profit	111.68		
53								
54	constraint coefficients							
55			1.25	0.5	clay	34	<=	40
56			25	45	labor	1800	<=	1800
57			30	24	kiln time	1200	<=	1200

Q.   **Right, and you said I could just round the numbers. Can't we still do that?**

A.   Now that we know about integer optimization, the first thing that you should remember is to never round the answer to an LP and assume that it is the optimum integer solution.

Q.   **So, what's wrong with rounding?**

A.   Real-life LP problems often have hundreds, if not thousands, of variables and constraints. When you round the variables, there is a good chance that you will violate some of the constraints (which is not a good thing). Even if none of the constraints are violated, while the rounded solution could be the optimal integer solution, there is no guarantee (and the odds are against it).

Q.   **OK, I get it. Never round off the LP solution. So, what do I do?**

A.   You can go back to your Solver dialog box and click on the "Add" button to add the integer constraints. In other words:

1. Click on the variables that you want to be integer.

2. Go to the drop-down cell, and instead of an inequality, select "int," and you will get the dialog box, shown in figure 5.9.

FIGURE 5.9 Specifying That a Variable Should Be Integer.

3. Just as before, click on "OK" and get the Solver parameter dialog box, shown in figure 5.10.

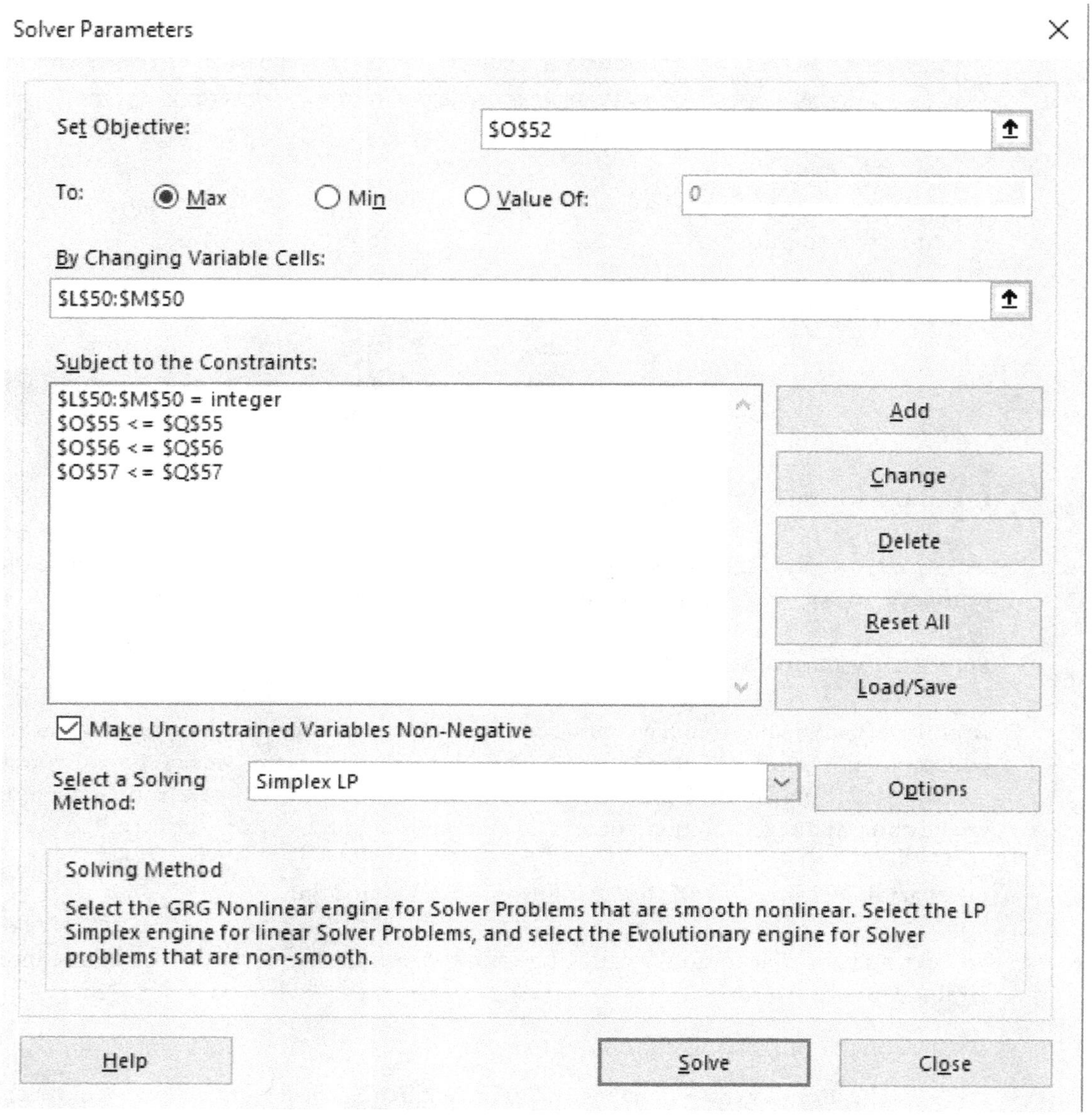

Solver Parameters   ✕

Se̱t Objective: $O$52   ⬆

To: ⦿ M̲ax   ◯ Mi̲n   ◯ V̲alue Of: 0

B̲y Changing Variable Cells:

$L$50:$M$50   ⬆

S̲ubject to the Constraints:

$L$50:$M$50 = integer $O$55 <= $Q$55 $O$56 <= $Q$56 $O$57 <= $Q$57	Add
	C̲hange
	D̲elete
	R̲eset All
	Load/Save

☑ Ma̱ke Unconstrained Variables Non-Negative

Se̱lect a Solving Method: Simplex LP   ⌄   Op̲tions

Solving Method

Select the GRG Nonlinear engine for Solver Problems that are smooth nonlinear. Select the LP Simplex engine for linear Solver Problems, and select the Evolutionary engine for Solver problems that are non-smooth.

He̱lp   S̲olve   Cl̲ose

FIGURE 5.10 Solver parameters for integer version of Ken's Pottery.

4. Again, as before, click on "S̲olve" to obtain the optimal (integer) solution to the problem.

You must still verify that you indeed got the optimal solution by examining the Solver Results box that Solver produces and is shown together with the new solution in figure 5.11.

Q.   Isn't that the same solution we got when we rounded down?

A.   Well, yes, but with a really small problem like this, that isn't surprising. In more complex problems (hundreds of variables) it would be very unlikely. The benefit is that now you *know* the integer solution is optimal.

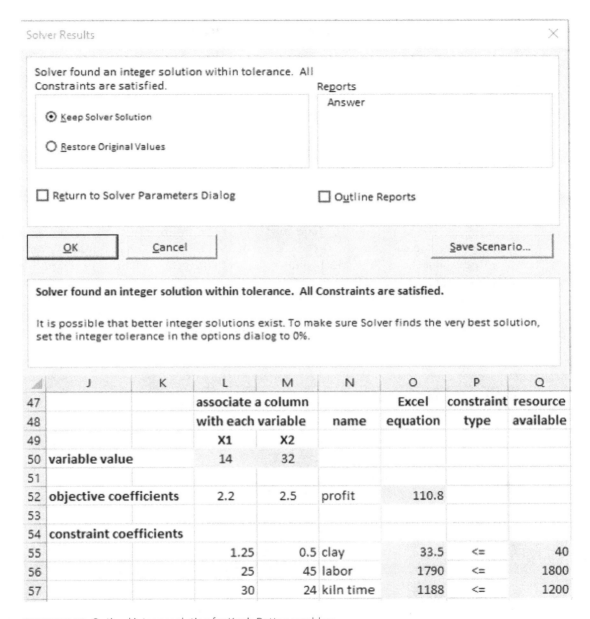

FIGURE 5.11 Optimal integer solution for Ken's Pottery problem.

Q. **The maximum profit has dropped from $111.68 to $110.80. Do we always make less profit when we do an integer solution?**

A. No, but you will never make more by requiring integer answers. If it just so happens that the LP solution has integer answers without the integer restrictions, then the objective function value will be the same.

Q. **I would guess that an LP problem giving all variables with integer values is rather unlikely, right?**

A. Au contraire! All assignment and transportation problems that we discussed in Lesson 4 have LP solutions that are integer. And those are not the only ones. What determines whether an LP has an integer optimal solution is the mathematical structure of its constraints.

Q. **Augh! What does "mathematical structure" even mean, anyway?**

A. Do you really want to know?

Q. **Not if I don't need to.**

A. Fair enough. Simply put, Solver does what it does based on some pretty complex mathematics. I spent most of my PhD program learning all that mathematics, since that is what my professors knew and hence that is what they taught me.

Q. **So now you are going to teach it to us?**

A. No. In my first job as a professor, I happened to have the entire operations research group from a local Fortune 500 company in my class. They all used LP, but, much to my consternation, they had no idea about the mathematics behind it. Rather to their consternation, I knew nothing about how to use the commercial LP codes that they used every day. I learned something: you can use LP without knowing the math behind it, so you are safe.

Q. **Thank goodness for that operations research group. Are we finished?**

A. Yes.

Q. **Hip, Hip, HOORAH!**

ACTIVE LEARNING: LESSON 5.5.1

A Dialectic Introduction to Combinatorial Optimization

Q. **What are combinatorial problems?**

A. When the variables can only assume two values (1 or 0), they are referred to as a binary variable.

Q. **Why would we do that?**

A. If we were trying to make a yes/no (go/no go, on/off) decision, then 1 = yes and 0 = no.

Q. **Why would we need to do that?**

A. In a linear program, that would mean that the solution can give us the best choices to optimize the objective function, which opens many applications of interest.

Q. **Where does "combinatorial" come in?**

A. From the word *combinations*.

Q.   **Combinations of what?**

A.   Of decisions. Suppose you must choose from a number of projects to fund. You keep funding projects until you run out of money. Then $X_1 = 1$ means you fund Project 1, $X_2 = 1$ means you fund Project 2, et cetera.

Q.   **Where do combinations come into it?**

A.   Think of two projects, so you have X_1 and X_2, each of which can be a 1 or a 0. Now, think of putting the values of X_1 and X_2 into a pair like this: (X_1, X_2). The following table shows all the combinations of 1s and 0s that you could have:

TABLE 5.17   Funding Options for Two Projects (X1, X2)

Combination	Result
(0,0)	Fund neither project
(1,0)	Fund only Project 1
(0,1)	Fund only Project 2
(1,1)	Fund both projects

So, two projects give you four decisions to make. Every time you add another project to consider, the total number of combinations you must consider increases exponentially.

Q.   **Exponentially?**

A.   Like an exponent. One binary variable can give you two different alternatives for an answer (0 or 1). If you have two variables, combined they can give you four alternatives for an answer (shown above). Table 5.18 shows how quickly the number of combinations (alternatives) grows.

TABLE 5.18   Exponential Growth of a Binary Variable

# of Variables	# of Alternatives	Exponents
1	2	2^1
2	4	2^2
3	8	2^3
.	.	.
.	.	.
.	.	.
10	1,204	2^{10}

As you can see, one variable gives you 2^1 alternatives, two variables give you 2^2 alternatives ($2^2 = 4$), and three variables give you 2^3, or 8, alternatives. In general, if you have n variables, there will be 2^n alternatives for an answer.

Q.   So, what?

A.   So, in the business world, you have lots of options to consider. Just 20 options, requiring 20 variables, would be 2^{20} = 1,048,576 alternatives to consider. Because the number of alternatives for an answer involves having to look at so many different combinations, we refer to LP problems that have binary problems as "combinatorial optimization."

Q.   OK, that's a lot of alternatives. Will Solver find the best one for us?

A.   Indeed, it will. Do you think you are ready to tackle one?

Q.   Bring it on—I did pretty good with modeling LPs.

A.   Yes, you did. Let's see what you can do with the following problem.

Margaritaville

"Parrothead" Buffet, premier of the Conch Republic, located off the Florida Keys, promotes tourism to the Republic with the motto "Changes in Latitudes, Changes in Attitudes." Land Sharks, as the tourists are referred to by the locals, embrace the motto with gusto, and almost anything that is peaceful goes. Margaritaville, the capital of the Conch Republic, has established an international reputation for their medium-rare cheeseburgers served with mustard and an onion slice and for all their clocks being fixed at 5:00 p.m.

Having "imported" tourists from all over the world that were looking for their lost shaker of salt, Parrothead has decided that there is great opportunity for exporting the Margaritaville experience to regions and countries that have identified tourism as an engine for economic development. The Margaritaville portfolio consist of the following investment options: (a) planning, (b) infrastructure development, (c) beach resort, (d) marina, (e) hotel, (f) casino, and (g) vacation club (time share).

Parrothead insists that he will not export a Margaritaville experience until a detailed site development plan has been created. If one does not exist, his site development team is available to take on the task (for a fee). Also, he will not develop the Margaritaville project until a region's infrastructure has been brought up to minimal touristic standards. That include appropriate access via air, land, or sea, appropriate utilities such as electricity and water, and a trained workforce (if an appropriate work force is unavailable, Parrothead's training department can undertake the training).

Parrothead's policies for the development of the Margaritaville experience include the following:

A. Planning and infrastructure development must be completed before any investment decision will be implemented.

B. Marinas can only be developed at sites that have a beach resort or a vacation club.

C. Casinos can only be included in properties that have a beach resort or hotel.

D. A site can only have a beach resort or a hotel, not both. It does not have to have either.

Parrothead and representatives from the Ministry of Tourism of the Republic of Slobovia had reached agreement on the establishment of a Margaritaville experience in that country. They had spent the last year developing benefit and cost measures for the various investment options for the establishment of a Margaritaville in Slobovia. These are shown in the table. The two sides are interested in determining how to obtain maximum benefit for the 500 monetary units the Slobovian government has available to allocate to their Margaritaville development.

	Planning X1	Infrastructure X2	Beach Resort X3	Marina X4	Hotel X5	Casino X6	Vacation Club X7
BENEFITS (touristic attractiveness)	0	924	200	20	200	50	75
COSTS (monetary units)	25	300	140	20	50	28	60

Q. **Maybe I was a little optimistic. Where do I begin?**

A. As always, the first step is to figure out what the decision variables are.

Q. **Don't we want to know how to obtain the maximum benefit with the 500 monetary units available?**

A. Yes, but that is the objective, not the actual decision.

Q. **Do we want to decide whether to build a beach resort, marina, hotel, casino, or vacation club?**

A. That's it, but don't forget you also have to decide whether to do the planning and the infrastructure.

Q. **Didn't you say that was required?**

A. Only if you decided to do any of the other things. There is no sense in planning and doing the infrastructure unless you are going to do some of the other things as well.

Q. **OK. You indicated that a binary variable could represent a yes or no decision. Can I say that, for example, $X_1 = 1$ means to do the planning and $X_1 = 0$ means to not do it?**

A. Now you are on the right track! You must do that for each of the other six alternatives as well.

Q. **What next?**

A. Now you must write the objective and the budget constraint.

Q. **Sure. That would be just as we did with LP, isn't it?**

A. Yes. Let's go ahead and start our Solver set-up. Table 5.19 shows that this is exactly as we did in Lesson 3.

TABLE 5.19 Start of Solver Set-Up for Margaritaville

	A	B	C	D	E	F	G	H	I	J	K
1				Beach				Vacation	Excel	constraint	resources
2		Planning	Infrastructure	Resort	Marina	Hotel	Casino	Club	equation	type	available
3		X1	X2	X3	X4	X5	X6	X7			
4	variable value	0	0	0	0	0	0	0			
5	objective coefficient	0	924	200	20	200	50	75	0		
6											
7	constraint coefficients										
8	cost	25	300	140	20	50	28	60	0	<=	500

Q.   **Can I go ahead and run Solver now?**

A.   Sure, but you will only get garbage.

Q.   **I thought you said that it looked good?**

A.   It did and does. But didn't you forget to include Parrothead's policies (A–D)?

Q.   **I saw those, but did not think they went into the model ...**

A.   If you don't put them in, the algorithm won't know about them and might not adhere to them.

Q.   **Hadn't thought about that. So how do you put them into the model?**

A.   Let's take them one at a time.

Policy A states that planning and infrastructure must be completed before you do any of the fun stuff.

Q.   **Is that as simple as it sounds?**

A.   Obviously (I think), planning must be completed before you do the required infrastructure upgrades. If you decide to do the infrastructure upgrades, then that must precede any further work.

Q.   **Yes, but how do I get that into the model?**

A.   Let's look at the requirement that planning must precede infrastructure and the possible variable values.

TABLE 5.20

X1, X2	Meaning	Policy A
0, 0	No Planning, No Infrastructure	Good
0, 1	No Planning, Infrastructure	Violated
1, 0	Planning, No Infrastructure	Good
1, 1	Planning, Infrastructure	Good

Looking at the table, we only have a problem if there is no Planning ($X_1 = 0$) but we build the infrastructure ($X_2 = 1$), when $X_1 < X_2$. This then implies that

$$X_1 \geq X_2, \text{ or}$$
$$X_1 - X_2 \geq 0$$

Q.   **I would not have thought to do that. Since the infrastructure precedes any of the other possible projects, we would also need:**

$X_2 - X_3 \geq 0$ (Infrastructure precedes beach resort)

$X_2 - X_4 \geq 0$ (Infrastructure precedes marina)

$X_2 - X_5 \geq 0$ (Infrastructure precedes hotel)

X2 – X6 ≥ 0 (Infrastructure precedes casino)

X2 – X7 ≥ 0 (Infrastructure precedes vacation club)

How does that look?

A.   Great! Now give policy B a try.

Q.   **Let's see.**

Policy B: A marina can only be included if there is a beach resort or vacation club.

Marina is X4, beach resort is X3, and vacation club is X7. No beach resort (X3 = 0) and no vacation club (X7 = 0) means no marina (X4 = 0). On the other hand, beach resort (X3 = 1) or vacation club (X7 = 1) or both, then you can build the marina (X4 = 1), but you don't have to. So, that translates to

$$X4 \le X3 + X7, \text{ or}$$
$$X3 + X7 – X4 \ge 0.$$

How am I doing?

A.   I am impressed. Looks like you are getting the hang of it. Keep going.

Q.   **OK.**

Policy C: A casino can only be an option if we also have a beach resort or hotel.

Well, that is basically the same as policy B, except for different variables (casino is X6, beach resort is X3, and hotel is X5), so

$$X6 \le X3 + X5, \text{ or}$$
$$X3 + X5 – X6 \le 0.$$

While I am at it,

Policy D: A site cannot have both a hotel and a beach resort, but it can have neither.

In this case, if there is a beach resort (X3 = 1), then there is no hotel (X5 = 0). Conversely, if X5 = 1, then X3 = 0. They can't both be 1, so

$$X3 + X5 \le 1.$$

How does that look, Boss?

A.   Pretty darn good. Go ahead and enter those constraints in the Solver set-up page.

Q.   **Wait a minute. What constraints do we need to enter to make sure that our variables are binary?**

A.   Glad you asked. We do not have to put any constraints for that in the Solver set-up page. We can take care of that when we fill in the Solver parameter box.

Q.   **OK. Is this right for the Solver set-up page (table 5.21)?**

A.   Looks great. Let's go ahead and enter the information in the Solver parameter dialog box.

TABLE 5.21   Solver Set-Up Page for Margaritaville

	A	B	C	D	E	F	G	H	I	J	K
1				Beach				Vacation	Excel	constraint	resources
2		Planning	Infrastructure	Resort	Marina	Hotel	Casino	Club	equation	type	available
3		X1	X2	X3	X4	X5	X6	X7			
4	variable value	0	0	0	0	0	0	0			
5	objective coefficient	0	924	200	20	200	50	75	0		
6											
7	constraint coefficients										
8	cost	25	300	140	20	50	28	60	0	<=	500
9	a.	1	-1						0	>=	0
10			1	-1					0	>=	0
11			1		-1				0	>=	0
12			1			-1			0	>=	0
13			1				-1		0	>=	0
14			1					-1	0	>=	0
15	b.			1	-1			1	0	>=	0
16	c.			1		1	-1		0	>=	0
17	d.			1		1			0	<=	1

Q.   Done. Please check it out in figure 5.12 & 5.13.

A.   Good job! I see that in figure 5.13 you are specifying how to make the variables to be binary. Go on and click the Solver button.

Q.   I just clicked the "Solver" button on the Solver parameter box. What do the results in table 5.22 tell us?

A.   Thank you. I have shaded the cells of interest.

Q.   What could we afford to do?

A.   The 500 monetary units allowed for a full deployment of the Margaritaville offerings. The hotel was selected over the beach resort, but everything else was selected.

Q.   OK, and we got a benefit of 1,269 while spending only 483 monetary units. Is that right?

A.   Exactly. We did use most of our budget, but the return was pretty good.

Q.   What about the Answer and Sensitivity reports?

A.   We don't need them. The Answer Report contains no more information than I just presented, and combinatorial optimization, as we have discussed it here, is integer programming, which does not provide a sensitivity analysis.

Q.   So how can I find out what happens if the costs or benefits change?

A.   Any question about changes to the data (constraints or objective function values) can be answered by direct manipulation of the model.

Q.   There are two things bugging me about this application. One is, what are "monetary units"?

A.   Each "unit" represents the equivalent of a million Margarita dollars (or whatever their currency is). What is the other thing that is bugging you?

Solver Parameters   ✕

Se_t Objective: $I$5   ⬆

To: ⦿ _Max   ○ Mi_n   ○ _Value Of: 0

_By Changing Variable Cells:

$B$4:$H$4   ⬆

_Subject to the Constraints:

$I$9:$I$16 >= $I$9:$I$16 $B$4:$H$4 = binary $I$17 <= $K$17 $I$8 <= $K$8	**A**dd **C**hange **D**elete **R**eset All **L**oad/Save

☑ Ma_ke Unconstrained Variables Non-Negative

Se_lect a Solving   Simplex LP   ⌄   O_ptions
Method:

Solving Method

Select the GRG Nonlinear engine for Solver Problems that are smooth nonlinear. Select the LP
Simplex engine for linear Solver Problems, and select the Evolutionary engine for Solver problems
that are non-smooth.

_Help	_Solve	Cl_ose

FIGURE 5.12 Solver parameter dialog box for Margaritaville.

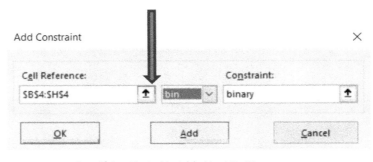

FIGURE 5.13 Specifying That a Variable Must Be Binary.

TABLE 5.22   Optimal Tourism Investment Decisions for Margaritaville

			Beach				Vacation	Excel	constraint	resources
	Planning	Infrastructure	Resort	Marina	Hotel	Casino	Club	equation	type	available
	X1	X2	X3	X4	X5	X6	X7			
variable value	1	1	0	1	1	1	1			
objective coefficient	0	924	200	20	200	50	75	1269		
constraint coefficients										
cost	25	300	140	20	50	28	60	483	<=	500
a.	1	-1						0	>=	0
		1	-1					1	>=	0
		1		-1				0	>=	0
		1			-1			0	>=	0
		1				-1		0	>=	0
		1					-1	0	>=	0
b.			1	-1			1	0	>=	0
c.			1		1	-1		0	>=	0
d.			1		1			1	<=	1

Q.   **The meaning of the objective function coefficients. I see that they are referred to as "benefits." But then it says, "Touristic Attractiveness."**

A.   The objective of tourism development is to create economic impact. To objectively estimate the impact in dollars and cents (or whatever currency) for projects that do not yet exist is impossible, however. Touristic attractiveness is a surrogate for earnings.

Q.   **How does it work?**

A.   The rationale is that the more attractive a destination, the more its economic impact will be. You can learn more about this in Gearing, Swart, and Var, "Determining the Optimal Investment Policy for the Tourism Sector of a Developing Country," *Management Science* 20, no. 4 (1973): 487–498.

ACTIVE LEARNING: LESSON 5.5.2

Comprehensive Problems are available for this chapter via Active Learning

Predicting and Forecasting with Regression

OVERVIEW

Q. **Impressive title. Is there a difference between prediction and forecasting?**

A. Indeed, there is. Prediction is estimating the outcomes for data, any data, such as regional sales data being used to predict sales for a new region. Forecasting is prediction when the data includes measurements that have been taken over time, usually called time series data, such as sales for one region over the last 10 quarters being used to forecast sales for next quarter.

Q. **So, where does regression fit in?**

A. Regression is the tool we use to look for relationships between variables, so it can be used for both predicting and forecasting.

Q. **We see whether one variable causes change in another variable, right?**

A. Very wrong. Regression will never tell you one variable caused a change in another variable. All regression can do is tell you how closely the variables changed together.

Q. **Is regression used for other things besides predicting and forecasting?**

A. You can use regression any time you need to know whether variables are significantly related. For example, regression shows that smoking is a significant factor in patients who have been diagnosed with lung cancer. The purpose is not to predict who is going to get lung cancer but in building a case that will induce smokers to quit.

Q. **After all the effort I put into forgetting statistics, would it be possible to get a refresher before we go much further?**

A. OK. Regression is a statistical technique that finds the best possible mathematical relationship between one or more (called independent, or predictor) variables and another (called the dependent or forecast) variable. The relationship is referred to as a regression model.

Q.   **I thought regression was the opposite of progression, so moving backward rather than moving forward. How does that have anything to do with forecasting?**

A.   The term "regression modeling" is actually a mistake. The first paper dealing with these calculations found the relationship between the heights of three generations of families, so grandparents, parents, and grandchildren (once fully grown). The study found little relationship between the heights of grandparents and parents, or parents and grandchildren, but found a strong relationship between grandparents and grandchildren. The author wrote that "the heights of the grandchildren regressed back to the heights of the grandparents." People picked up on the word "regressed" and called it "regression" analysis, even though it has little to do with moving backward.

Q.   **Are the calculations really simple and easy to understand?**

A.   Well, that depends on what stage of life you are at. If you are in school, then you will probably find that your professor may hold the philosophy that unless you understand the theory, you will become a menace to society when turned loose with the knowledge to apply it.

Q.   **I have been told that by more than one of my professors. Isn't it true?**

A.   For this topic, no. The cartoon in figure 6.1 illustrates why:

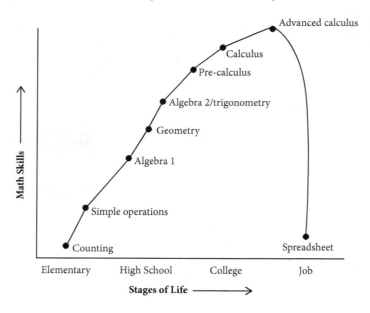

FIGURE 6.1 Life cycle of mathematical rigor.

Source: Adapted from http://pearlsofrawnerdism.com/life-and-maths/.

Q.   **Do you mean that I can use a spreadsheet to do all the regression calculations?**

A.   Yes, with a caveat. Excel has regression calculations built into it, but that capability is limited. Data analytics pros use other far more powerful (and expensive) software.

Q. "Limited" describes my current level, so let's go with Excel.

A. Not so fast—first we have to do a bunch of boring definitions.

Q. Why do we always have to do definitions that we don't remember anyway?

A. When you get your degree and wind up on a team that does this kind of work, then the definitions will become important. Definitions make sure that everybody is talking about the same thing. Unless you have precise definitions, especially when working with numbers, nobody can understand anyone else. So, definitions.

Q. What definitions do we need to know?

A. Well, did you know there are two types of statistics?

Q. No, I thought one would be enough. What is the first type?

A. Descriptive statistics is defined as summarizing, organizing, and presenting information about a set of data. These would be means, median, and standard deviation—all the things we used earlier in the class.

Q. What is the second type of statistics?

A. Inferential statistics is defined as determining whether observations made with samples can be generalized to the population from which the samples were selected.

Q. What kind of data do we use?

A. You shouldn't have asked. Data can be from a survey or can be meta-data. Each of those can be observational or experimental data.

Q. What is the difference between survey data and meta-data?

A. This is one of those times when I think people are just making life difficult. Survey data means you gathered the data yourself. Meta-data (doesn't that sound impressive?) just means someone else gathered the data.

Q. Is observational versus experimental just as simple?

A. No, this one is a little more subtle. Observational data is what it sounds like—you sit back and observe with no interaction with what is going on. Experimental data means you do something that the subject has to react to, and you watch the reaction.

Q. Which is better?

A. Neither, or more exactly, it depends on what you need. The problem with observational data is the subject might not do what you want to observe. You can waste a lot of time and get nothing useful. The problem with experimental data is that by interacting you might change the result, so you never know whether the data is correct. By setting up the situation, though, you are sure of collecting the data you want.

Q.   So, however we choose to collect the data, who do we collect it from?

A.   Good question. Your choices are to collect data from everybody that might be involved (called the "population") or just from some of the people involved (called a "sample").

Q.   Let me guess—collecting from everybody is harder.

A.   Obviously. Making sure you have covered all possibilities is difficult at best, often impossible. That is why we usually are happy with a sample.

Q.   Are there any problems with using a sample?

A.   A huge one: do you have the right sample? Remember in simulation when we had one set of random numbers giving us one set of outputs? Then I changed the random numbers and got different outputs. Well, that happens with samples—every sample can have different means and standard deviations and all that other descriptive statistics stuff.

Q.   So, what do we do?

A.   Make the sample big, so even if you don't sample everybody, you get enough to get a good picture of what is going on.

Q.   That does not sound like you. You made us go through hoops in the Designing Simulation Experiments lesson to learn how to calculate the sample size necessary to get a specified margin of error. Can't we do that here?

A.   Actually, no. In simulation we dealt with only one variable. When learning about inventories, we used average total inventory cost. When learning about queuing, we dealt with average time in queue and so on. In regression we are dealing with one dependent variable and a number of independent, or predictor, variables. Thus, the question becomes how to combine all the variables to get a desired margin of error.

Q.   And how do we do that?

A.   We don't. Hence my earlier answer of getting the sample as big as you can. The literature offers various guidelines ranging from n > 10 + 8*(# of independent variables) to n > 104 + (# of independent variables). But these are just rules of thumb. And, often, we just can't get as much data as suggested by the rules of thumb.

Q.   Sounds sort of like "full speed ahead and darn the torpedoes."

A.   Exactly. However, we will learn to evaluate the results to determine their statistical significance.

Q.   OK, I get it. What other definitions do we need?

A.   Actually, that's pretty much it.

LESSON 6.1: **Building the Regression Model**

Introduction

Q.   **What does a "regression model" do for us?**

A.   In simple terms, a regression model explains the relationship of one variable to one or more other variables.

Q.   **How does it "explain" such relationships?**

A.   Through a formula that expresses one variable as a mathematical result based on the others. For this to work, though, you first must assume the type of relationship between the variables.

Q.   **What do you mean by "type of relationship"?**

A.   The type of mathematical formula that you wish to get. The most common assumption is that the relationship between the variables is linear. However, depending on the statistical software that is being used, one can chose from a variety of relationships including quadratic, exponential, lognormal, et cetera.

Q.   **Can we start by assuming a linear relationship?**

A.   Yes. With that assumption, you are saying that the relationship between the one variable Y, also called the dependent variable, and another group of variables, $\{X_1, X_2, X_3, ...\}$, also called the independent variables, can be expressed by this formula:

$$Y = \beta_0 + \beta_1 X_1 + \beta_2 X_2 + \beta_3 X_3 + ... + \varepsilon$$

Q.   **What are those βs?**

A.   They are the Greek letter Beta. What they are, are numbers, and those numbers are what the regression calculations will give us, so they are called "regression coefficients." Once you know that values for all the βs and all the Xs, you use the equation to calculate (predict) the value for Y. Since the value for Y depends on the values of the Xs, Y is called the dependent variable (the Xs are independent variables).

Q.   **Where do the Xs come from?**

A.   From your head, so to speak. They represent the variables that you or your associates think can explain the value of Y.

Q.   **Can I use anything I want?**

A.   The only stipulation is that you must know the values of X before you can explain (or predict) the value of Y.

Q.   **Is there a limit to how many Xs you can have?**

A.   Theoretically, no, but practically, yes. The more variables you have, the more data you will have to collect to predict Y. Since there is no such thing as perfect data, the more data you collect, the more risk you have of accumulating errors in your prediction.

Q.   **Is that what the ε is all about?**

A.   Precisely. It is a reminder that any prediction has an inherent margin of error associated with it. The regression procedure yields the values of the βs that make the error ε as small as possible.

Learning Outcomes

When you complete this session, you will:

- Understand what dependent and independent variables are
- Understand what a regression model is
- Know what regression coefficients are
- Know how to use Excel's Regression function in the Data Analysis add-in
  - Identify the Input <u>Y</u> Range
  - Identify the Input <u>X</u> Range
  - Know the meaning of Residuals
- Know how to interpret Excel's Regression output:
  - The SUMMARY OUTPUT
    - You will be able to interpret Adjusted R Square
    - You will be able to interpret the Standard Error
  - The ANOVA
    - You will be able to interpret *F* and *SIGNIFICANCE F*
    - You will be able to interpret the *Coefficients* and *P-values*
  - The RESIDUAL OUTPUT
    - You will be able to interpret the *Residuals*
    - You will know how to calculate the *Predicted Y*

A Dialectic on Building Regression Models

Q.   **Can we do an example?**

A.   Sure. I just came back from the Conch Republic where I helped their premier establish the relationship between Parrothead consumer confidence and Margaritaville GDP and unemployment rate. Here is a description of what I worked on:

The Conch Republic

It is 2013. "Parrothead" Buffet, premier of the Conch Republic located off the Florida Keys, promotes tourism to the Republic with the motto "Changes in Latitudes, Changes in Attitudes." Land Sharks, as the tourists are referred to by the locals, embrace the motto with gusto and almost anything that is peaceful goes.

Parrothead relies on the almost unquenchable thirst of tourists for beer, which they chase with Margaritas while consuming the famous local cheeseburgers, to provide revenues used to finance the affairs of the Republic. However, he is also dedicated to keeping Margaritaville great and his constituents happy and prosperous. To that end, he wants to be able to forecast the consumer confidence of his "parrotheads," as his constituents affectionately refer to themselves. He suspects that parrothead consumer confidence is related to Margaritaville GDP and unemployment rate.

Use the last 15 years of actual data to perform a linear regression to quantify consumer confidence as a function of GDP and unemployment rate.

Year	Consumer Confidence	GDP	Unemployment Rate
1	102	7	7.4
2	100	3.6	7.1
3	95	3.1	7.9
4	103	2.9	7.1
5	115	3.8	5.4
6	117	3.4	5.2
7	92	1.7	5.6
8	69	−0.2	7.8
9	62	3.3	7.5
10	66	2.4	7.9
11	91	4	7.1
12	100	2.7	5.6
13	105	3.7	5.4
14	125	4.5	4.9
15	138	4.3	4.5

Q.   **That helps. We use Consumer Confidence as our Y variable, GDP and Unemployment Rate as our two X variables, and we use regression to come up with values for β_0, β_1, and β_2, right?**

A.   Very good.

Q.   **Could you show me how to use regression?**

A.   Absolutely. First, put the Margaritaville data in a spreadsheet (Figure 6.3, below):

1. Put the dependent variable (Y) data in column C, also labeled as Consumer Confidence

2. Put the first independent variable (X_1) in column D, also labeled as GDP

3. Put the second independent variable (X_2) in column E, also labeled as Unemployment Rate

Since we have already used the Excel's Data Analysis Add-in, I'll just say you click on Analysis and then click on Regression, as shown in Figure 6.2.

Data Analysis   ?   X

Analysis Tools   OK

Histogram   Cancel
Moving Average
Random Number Generation
Rank and Percentile   Help
Regression
Sampling
t-Test: Paired Two Sample for Means
t-Test: Two-Sample Assuming Equal Variances
t-Test: Two-Sample Assuming Unequal Variances
z-Test: Two Sample for Means

FIGURE 6.2 Regression link in the Data Analysis dialog box.

Q.   **What happens then?**

A.   You get the dialogue box as shown in Figure 6.3.

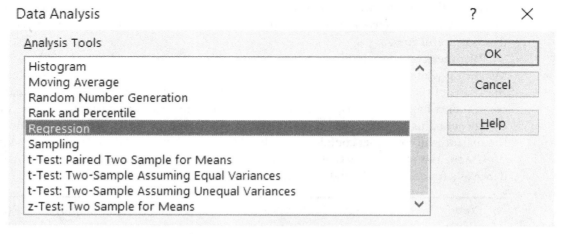

	A	B	C	D	E	F
1			Consumer		Unemployment	
2			Confidence	GDP	Rate	
3		Year	Y	X_1	X_2	
4		1	102	7	7.4	
5		2	100	3.6	7.1	
6		3	95	3.1	7.9	
7		4	103	2.9	7.1	
8		5	115	3.8	5.4	
9		6	117	3.4	5.2	
10		7	92	1.7	5.6	
11		8	69	-0.2	7.8	
12		9	62	3.3	7.5	
13		10	66	2.4	7.9	
14		11	91	4	7.1	
15		12	100	2.7	5.6	
16		13	105	3.7	5.4	
17		14	125	4.5	4.9	
18		15	138	4.3	4.5	

FIGURE 6.3 Filling out the Regression dialog box.

Q.   **How did you fill that in?**

A. We are trying to forecast Consumer Confidence, whose values are found in Column C, so for the Input $\underline{Y}$ Range, highlight C3:C18.

Q. **OK, but we have two X variables but only one Input X Range. What do we do?**

A. We enter all the independent variables, X_1 and X_2, at once, so we highlight D3:E18 for the Input $\underline{X}$ Range.

Q. **Why did we include the labels in Row 3?**

A. That makes the outputs easier to read, but we have to check the "Labels" box so the calculations don't try to use those values.

Q. **Anything else we have to do?**

A. We want the regression results to appear in a new worksheet, so we clicked on the "New Worksheet Ply" for the output option and entered the name REGRESSION. Finally, we checked the box "Residuals" to indicate that we wish to see the difference between the predicted and actual values of Consumer Confidence for each year of data.

Q. **Is that all there is to running a regression?**

A. That's it, just like when we ran Solver. All that's left to do is to click "OK" to get our regression results. The new tab "REGRESSION" will appear with all the output we need: the SUMMARY OUTPUT, the ANOVA, and the RESIDUAL OUTPUT.

Q. **What do they mean?**

A. Let's look at the SUMMARY OUTPUT first. It is given in table 6.1. The information contained in that table reveals the accuracy with which the independent variables explain the variance in the dependent variable.

TABLE 6.1   SUMMARY OUTPUT of a Regression

	A	B
1	SUMMARY OUTPUT	
2		
3	*Regression Statistics*	
4	Multiple R	0.872277395
5	R Square	0.760867854
6	Adjusted R Square	0.721012497
7	Standard Error	11.22716398
8	Observations	15

Q. **Huh?**

A.   The values for the dependent variable (the Y-variable) are all over the place. Regression matches them up with the values of the X-variables and then sees how far they are from a straight line. The closer the Y-variables are to a straight line, the higher the R-Square value. Since we have more than one X-variable, we must adjust the R-Square value to account for that, so we use Adjusted R-Square.

Q.   **What is the range for Adjusted R-Square?**

A.   The adjusted R-Square is a score between zero and one. The closer the value is to 1, the closer the predicted values are to the actual values. Given that all data contains random error, it is practically impossible to get a value of one.

Q.   **If you can't get a one, what is a good value?**

A.   If you are looking for a threshold, so any number above the threshold is "good," there isn't one. It would be nice if there were, but that is not how R-Square works. R-Square tells you how "much" of the value of the Y-values is explained by the X-variables. Whatever we have is not explained by the X variables we attribute to randomness (error) in data.

Q.   **But if you had to pick a number, what would you pick?**

A.   If I had to pick a number, then I would say that most experts across many fields would be happy with an Adjusted R-Square above 0.6.

Q.   **And any time the Adjusted R-Square is less than 0.6, we should not use the regression model?**

A.   No, that's not how it works. Sometimes, your data just has a lot of randomness in it, so the regression model, even with an Adjusted R-Square less than 0.6, may be as good as you are going to get, so you would use it.

Q.   **Is there anything you can do when there is a lot of random error in your data?**

A.   Two things. First, exercise due diligence in determining whether there may be other potential explanatory, or independent, variables, meaning brainstorming with associates to think of other, additional independent variables.

Q.   **Suppose we have done that, and we still have a low Adjusted R-Square. Do we have to give up on regression?**

A.   You wouldn't give up on regression. First, you report the Adjusted R-Square when you present your results, and then you use your results to create a range for your forecast, just as we did in Simulation.

Q.   **How do we calculate a range?**

A.   When we can't explain the variation in Y-values, we say the error (the over- or underprediction) is random. In other words, we assume our regression model is correct, but the rest of the variance in the Y-values cannot be forecast. If you recall, our regression model had an error term, ε, included in the right-hand term of our regression model. That is the random error, defined as having a normal distribution with a mean of zero and a standard deviation given by the Standard Error given in cell B7 of Table 6.1 (above).

Q.   **So, any prediction I made with the regression equation will be within plus or minus two standard errors of the true value?**

A.   Right, as long as you qualify that by saying "with a probability of 95%."

Q.   **Fine, I can do that, but don't I need a regression equation first?**

A.   Yes, and you can find that in the section labeled ANOVA, which is shown in table 6.2. I have shaded the items that require attention.

TABLE 6.2   **ANOVA Output from Regression**

	A	B	C	D	E	F	G
9							
10	ANOVA						
11		df	SS	MS	F	Significance F	
12	Regression	2	4812.742801	2406.371	19.09073	0.000186994	
13	Residual	12	1512.590532	126.0492			
14	Total	14	6325.333333				
15							
16		Coefficients	Standard Error	t Stat	P-value	Lower 95%	Upper 95%
17	Intercept	β_0 = 163.54370	18.96528608	8.623319	1.73E-06	122.2218974	204.8655146
18	X_1	β_1 = 4.9408093	1.988908544	2.484181	0.028737	0.60734991	9.274268814
19	X_2	β_2 = -12.66788(	2.521192535	-5.02456	0.000297	-18.16109274	-7.174679453
20							
21	Prediction Equation Y = 163.543706 + 4.9408809362 X_1 - 12.66788609 X_2						

Q.   **What does ANOVA mean?**

A.   It is an acronym for ANalysis Of VAriance—a statistical tool that in regression is used to determine the influence that the independent variables have on the dependent variable. Stated another way, it is a test that tells us whether we are better off by using the regression equation to predict the dependent variable than simply using random numbers.

Q.   **That seems to be a no brainer. Am I missing something?**

A.   It is not a no brainer if you think of the purpose of regression as being to predict. The question is whether your regression equation will do a better job predicting than a random guess. That seems like a low threshold, but if you can't pass that test, then your regression is really bad and shouldn't be used.

Q.   **How do I know whether I have passed that test?**

A.   By looking at the *Significance F* value in cell F12. A low value (close to zero) means that the predicted values are due to the regression equation, while a high value (close to one) indicates that the predictions appear to be random guesses.

Q.   **So, table 6.2 tells us that the results of our regression will help us in predicting the value of Consumer Confidence because the *Significance F* value is so small (0.00018699)?**

A.   You got the idea.

Q.   **But where do we get the regression equation?**

A.   That's the second table of the ANOVA results. You can see the word "Intercept" in cell A17, which corresponds to the β_0 term of our regression model, while A18 and A19 contain the names of the independent variables, X_1 and X_2. Column B, under the label *Coefficients*, contains the values for the coefficients in the regression model (I have manually inserted their labels (β_0, β_1, and β_2). Thus, the prediction equation that the regression calculated is given by:

$$\text{Prediction Equation: } Y = 163.543706 + 4.9408809362\, X_1 - 12.66788609\, X_2$$

Q.   **Wow! Just like magic. You have the numbers in column E of the second table, labeled *P-value*, shaded. Why?**

A.   They tell which parts of the regression equation we should use.

Q.   **How does it do that?**

A.   For each coefficient, β_0, β_1, and β_2, we ask whether it is better to use a value of zero (meaning that part of the equation should be ignored) or the coefficient we calculated. Another way to say that is to ask, "What the probability is that our regression coefficients are not due to randomness, but due to the relationship between our variables?" The *P-value* gives us the probability that the regression coefficient value is not due to randomness, but due to the relationship between our variables.

Q.   **So, what is a low enough *P-value* for us not to ascribe it to randomness?**

A.   Usually we use the threshold value of $p < 0.05$ to conclude that the value is not due to randomness.

Q.   **I understand. One last question—how did regression determine the value of the βs?**

A.   The regression process selects the values of the βs to minimize the sum of the square residuals. That is the reason regression is sometimes referred to as the method of least squares. But your question provides an excellent lead-in to the RESIDUAL OUTPUT of our regression, which is shown in table 6.3.

TABLE 6.3   RESIDUAL OUTPUT of the Regression

RESIDUAL OUTPUT

Observation	Predicted Y	Residuals
1	104.3870144	-2.387014404
2	91.3886284	8.611371599
3	78.78391484	16.21608516
4	87.93006185	15.06993815
5	113.9121966	1.087803365
6	114.4694501	2.530549891
7	101.0029198	-9.002919756
8	63.74603256	5.253967441
9	84.83923115	-22.83923115
10	75.32534829	-9.325348291
11	93.36495215	-2.364952146
12	105.9437291	-5.943729118
13	113.4181157	-8.418115698
14	123.7047062	1.295293765
15	127.7836988	10.2163012

Q.   **OK. So, what exactly is a residual?**

A.   It is the difference between an actual value for the dependent variable Y (Consumer Confidence) and the value predicted by the regression equation. For example, let's take the year 1 data from figure 6.3:

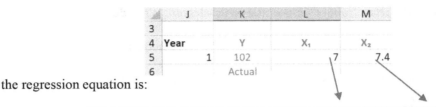

the regression equation is:

Predicted Y = 163.543706 + 4.940880962*L5 -12.66788609*M5

Predicted Y =   104.3875157

and the residual is calculated as follows:

Residual =   Actual - Predicted Y
Residual =   102 -104.3875157
Residual =   -2.387014404

Q.   **So, it is the error. It is just by how much your prediction missed the actual value, isn't it?**

A.   Exactly. And what regression does is to make the sum of all the squared errors as small as possible.

Q.   **Why not just make the sum as small as possible?**

A.   Because then large positive errors could cancel out large negative errors and wind up with a zero number in spite of there being both positive and negative misses.

Q.   **Makes sense. So, am I ready to start using my regression model to predict Consumer Confidence?**

A.   While everything that we have done so far is necessary and is standard procedure for any regression study, it is not sufficient. By that I mean that we should verify that our model and all of its components are statistically significant. We'll see how to do that in the next lesson.

ACTIVE LEARNING: LESSON 6.1

LESSON 6.2: **Developing a Robust Regression Model**

Introduction

Q.   **You used the term "robust" in the title of this lesson. What does it mean?**

A.   That simply means that every term in the regression model is statistically significant.

Q.   **By "statistically significant," I gather that you mean that they make real contributions to the prediction that is unlikely to be caused by randomness?**

A.   Exactly. There are five statistical tests that we will conduct after we obtain the regression equation. Only when a model passes all five tests will it be deemed fit to be used for making predictions.

Q.   **Sounds like there is a gauntlet of statistics ahead of us. Let's get started.**

Learning Outcomes

When you complete this session, you will be able to:

- Test a regression output to determine its statistical validity:
  - *Test 1*: Determine if the adjusted R-Square indicates whether enough of the variability in the data can be explained by the regression equation (adjusted R-Square >0.6)
  - *Test 2*: Determine if at least one of your independent variables has predictive power over the dependent variable
  - *Test 3*: Determine if your independent variables are indeed independent of each other (no multicollinearity)
  - *Test 4*: Determine if your regression coefficients are significantly different from 0
  - *Test 5*: Determine if the distribution of residuals appears to be bell-shaped
  - Graph the actual and predicted values of the dependent variable on a line graph
- Use the robust model to develop a forecast or prediction:
  - Develop a point estimate forecast of the dependent variable
  - Develop an interval estimate forecast of the dependent variable

A Dialectic on Building Robust Regression Models

Q.   **What tests do we need to perform on the Consumer Confidence forecast?**

A.   Actually, we are going to look at another aspect of the Margaritaville economy—manufacturing. Parrothead wants to diversify the Margaritaville economy to something besides tourism.

Q. **What can you manufacture on a tropical island, other than hangovers?**

A. While Margaritaville's endless miles of white sand beaches attract large flocks of tourists, silica sand is the principal ingredient in the manufacture of plate glass, which is primarily used in automobiles and construction. Current sources for silica sand are Australia and South East Asia, but Parrothead reasons that Margaritaville's proximity to the United States could provide a competitive advantage for the establishment of a plate glass manufacturing facility on its shores.

Q. **What does he want us to do, forecast erosion of sand?**

A. No, he has asked for our help in forecasting the total U.S. demand for plate glass for the next five years. He can use that to figure out what share of that market he might be able to capture with Margaritaville glass.

Q. **What can we use to forecast plate glass demand?**

A. If we can establish the relationship between plate glass demand, automobile production, and building contracts awarded, that might give us a good forecast.

Q. **Where do we get that kind of information?**

A. You can get almost anything online, but you have to be sure you use a site that has good data, such as a government or industry source. I got permission to use numbers from a textbook (*Forecasting Methods for Management*, Makridakis and Wheelwright, 1990) and have put them in a spreadsheet since I know we will be doing a regression.

TABLE 6.4 Plate Glass Sales, Automobile Production, and Building Contracts Issued Data

TIME	Plate Glass Sales (millions)	Automobile Production (millions)	Building Contracts Awarded (millions)
1	280.00	3.909	9.43
2	281.50	5.119	10.36
3	337.40	6.666	14.50
4	404.20	5.338	15.75
5	402.10	4.321	16.78
6	452.00	6.117	17.44
7	431.70	5.559	19.77
8	582.30	7.920	23.76
9	596.60	5.816	31.61
10	620.80	6.113	32.17
11	513.60	4.258	35.09
12	606.90	5.591	36.52
13	513.60	4.258	35.09
14	606.90	5.591	36.42
15	629.00	6.675	36.58
16	602.70	5.543	37.14
17	656.70	6.933	41.30
18	778.50	7.638	45.62
19	877.60	7.752	47.38

Q. Then Y represents Plate Glass Sales, X_1 is Automobile Production, and X_2 is Building Contracts Awarded. That would make our model

$$Y = \beta_0 + \beta_1 X_1 + \beta_2 X_2 + \varepsilon.$$

What are the regression results?

A. Following the process outlined before, but without the RESIDUAL OUTPUT, I got table 6.5:

TABLE 6.5 Annotated SUMMARY OUTPUT and ANOVA Regression Results

	A	B	C	D	E	F	G
1	SUMMARY OUTPUT						
2							
3	*Regression Statistics*						
4	Multiple R	0.972135					
5	R Square	0.9450464					
6	Adjusted R Square	0.9381772	**TEST 1:** Is adjusted R Square >0.6?				
7	Standard Error	39.322718					
8	Observations	19					
9							
10	ANOVA				**TEST 2:** Is *F* >5?		
11		*df*	*SS*	*MS*	*F*	*Significance F*	
12	Regression	2	425464.9935	212732	137.577	8.31707E-11	
13	Residual	16	24740.41811	1546.28			
14	Total	18	450205.4116				
15	**TEST 3:** Is there multi-colinearity?						
16		*Coefficients*	*Standard Error*	*t Stat*	*P-value*	*Lower 95%*	*Upper 95%*
17	Intercept	3.3205708	46.03518657	0.07213	0.94339	-94.2696652	100.911
18	Automobile Production (millions)	39.323772	8.557787713	4.59509	0.0003	21.18207271	57.4655
19	Building Contracts Awarded (millions	10.579259	0.856515909	12.3515	1.4E-09	8.763526209	12.395
20				**TEST 4:** Are all ABS(*t Stat*) > 2.0?			

Q. What are the gray highlights?

A. I indicated where the information to conduct each test was in the regression output.

Q. Didn't we already talk about the Adjusted R-Square?

A. Yes, but I wanted to include it again in this set of tests.

Q. If I recall correctly, we look at the Adjusted R-Square because we have more than one independent variable, and a widely accepted value is a Percentage of Variance Explained greater than 0.6, so with a value of 0.9381 we should be pretty sure we pass this test. Did I get all of that right?

A. Correct. Our two variables account for a large majority of the randomness in plate glass sales, so we are pretty happy.

Q.   **Is there any scientific basis for the 60% threshold?**

A.   Unfortunately, none at all. Keep in mind that most real-world data don't give results as good as you get in these classroom examples. You should try to find out what is considered acceptable for your discipline or talk to senior colleagues to find out what your company has used in the past.

Q.   **What do we do if the Adjusted R-Square is less than 0.6?**

A.   If it is less, we should attempt to find additional independent variables to explain the dependent variable. If we cannot, then we proceed assuming the percentage that is not explained is due to error in the data (the ε in our model equation).

Q.   **I thought we talked about the *Significant F* value. Why did you highlight the *F* value instead?**

A.   What I said was that the *Significance F* value indicated the probability that the relationship of the independent variables to the dependent variable was not strictly random. There is a direct relationship between the *F* value and the *Significant F* value. An *F* value of 5 indicates a *Significant F* value < 0.05. This value for *F* is also somewhat arbitrary, but its relationship to the *Significance F* gives it a little more credence.

Q.   **Do the first two tests always agree with each other?**

A.   Usually, but not always. When they disagree, you have to try to figure out why.

Q.   **Then from Tests 1 and 2 we can be reasonable sure there is a relationship between the independent and dependent variables, and it is reasonably strong. What does Test 3 tell us and what does the term "multicollinearity" mean?**

A.   Literally, multicollinearity refers to more than one line located in the same place. Remember that regression is trying to find the best straight line to fit the variables we are using. Multicollinearity checks to see whether the variables, considered one at a time, give you the same (collinear) regression line. If so, then one or more of the variables is redundant.

Q.   **What do you mean "redundant"?**

A.   Redundant variables (also called "correlated") tell you the same thing instead of adding new information. That means you don't need both variables in your regression equation.

Q.   **How does that work?**

A.   Suppose you are testing a regression equation $Y = X_1 + X_2$ and suppose that $X_1 = 5 + X_2$. Then, I could use $Y = 5 + X_2 + X_2$, simplified to $Y = 5 + 2X_2$ instead.

Q.   **Are all correlated variables related, mathematically?**

A.   No, sometimes they simply have the same relationship to the dependent variable you are trying to forecast. The result is the same, though.

Q. **What does it matter if I keep two correlated variables in the regression?**

A. It matters because all variables have error associated with it. If you keep two correlated variables in the regression, you are duplicating the error.

Q. **How do we determine whether the independent variables are correlated?**

A. By running the "Correlation" option under Data Analysis. On your data sheet, click on Data Analysis and select "Correlation." You will get the dialogue box shown in figure 6.4.

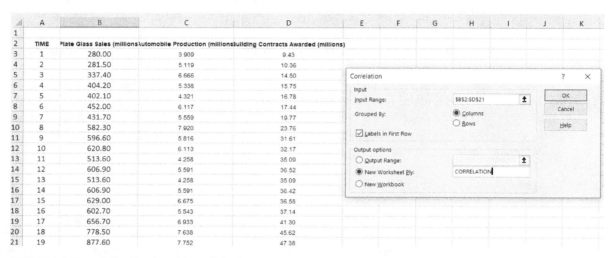

FIGURE 6.4 Completing the Correlation dialog box.

Q. **Do I enter just the independent variables as the "Input Range"?**

A. No, you need to enter both the dependent and independent variables. Be sure to include the column labels and check the Labels in First Row box. Click on New Spreadsheet Ply and enter the name for the spreadsheet—CORRELATION, then click OK to get your Correlation output, which is shown in table 6.6.

TABLE 6.6 Correlation Output

	A	B	C	D
1		Plate Glass Sales (millions)	Automobile Production (millions)	Building Contracts Awarded (millions)
2	Plate Glass Sales (millions)	1		
3	Automobile Production (millions)	0.648895117	1	
4	Building Contracts Awarded (millions)	0.934090679	0.435102335	1

Q. **What do these numbers tell us?**

A. The correlation coefficients "measure" the extent to which one variable explains the other—very much like the Adjusted R Square value. The correlation coefficients range between -1 to $+1$, since the variables could move together (increase or decrease) in a positive correlation or one could increase while the other decreases for a negative correlation.

Q.   **Why do you have the first row and the first column shaded?**

A.   To remind myself that the first row and the first column are associated with the *dependent* variable. Anything not shaded is associated with the *independent* variables.

Q.   **Then the correlation coefficient between Automobile Production and Building Contracts is 0.435102335. What does that mean?**

A.   You need to decide how much correlation you can allow. For our purposes, we will adopt the convention (arbitrary) that when the correlation coefficient between two independent variables is greater than 0.7, multicollinearity exists.

Q.   **You said that was arbitrary. Could you use other threshold values?**

A.   Of course. Again, you have to find out what level of correlation your company or discipline finds unacceptable.

Q.   **What do you do if the correlation coefficient is too close to +1 or −1?**

A.   To remove multicollinearity, one of the two correlated variables must be removed from the data set.

Q.   **You mean *totally* removed? How do you do that?**

A.   To remove the variable, take its column in your data sheet and remove it to a place where you will no longer include it with the Input X Range.

Q.   **How do you decide which of the two should be removed?**

A.   Look at the column in the correlation matrix which corresponds to the *dependent* variable showing the correlation between the dependent variable and the two independent variables. Since we want to predict the value of the dependent variable, we would keep the independent variable with the highest correlation with the dependent variable.

Q.   **I see. But in this case, the conclusion was that there is no multicollinearity, so we pass the test?**

A.   Correct. And once we conclude that there is no multicollinearity, there will never be.

Q.   **Then on to Test 4. What are we testing this time?**

A.   Whether the values shown for the βs are significantly different from 0.

Q.   **Why do we test whether they are different than zero?**

A.   If the value were zero, then 0*X is zero, which means the independent variable X had nothing to do with the dependent variable, Y. If they are not significantly different than zero, then we may as well call them zero and remove the corresponding variable from our data set.

Q.   So, what is the test?

A.   We test the null hypothesis that the value of β was drawn from a normal population that had a mean value of zero.

Q.   How does that help?

A.   If the value of β is more than 1.96 standard deviations from zero, then we would be 95% sure that the value was not zero.

Q.   But why did you highlight the *t Stat*?

A.   In regression, many times we do not have a big enough sample to justify assuming a normal distribution. A guy named William Gosset, who worked for the Guinness Brewing Company, came up with a distribution that did the same as the normal distribution, except it worked for small samples. With small samples, we use the t-tables instead of Z-tables.

Q.   I wonder how many beers he had under his belt when he did that? I do not recall reading about the Gosset t distribution in my stats class.

A.   You won't. Guinness did not allow their employees to use their own name when publishing so Gosset wrote under the alias of Student. You will see reference to Student's t distribution in most stats books.

Q.   OK, well then, provided the *t Stat* is greater than 1.96, we conclude the parameter β is not zero. Anything else?

A.   Actually, we use 2 instead of 1.96, because it is a little more conservative and, honestly, easier to remember. Also, the *t Stat* can be negative, so it has to be greater than +2 or less than –2.

Q.   What if the *t Stat* is between –2 and 2?

A.   Any time you see a value that, in absolute value, is less than 2 (that's another way to say it), its corresponding variable must be removed from the data set.

Q.   After removing the variable values, do we have to rerun the regression?

A.   Exactly. You have a new regression problem and it should be treated as such.

Q.   Looking at table 6.5, the *t Stats* for β_1 (Auto Production) is 4.595 and for β_2 (Building Contracts) is 12.351, both of which are well above 2, but the *t Stat* for β_0, the Intercept, is only 0.07213, so we assume β_0 is equal to zero. What do we do now, since there is no variable to remove?

A.   We still rerun the regression, but we do it differently than we would for any other coefficient. Go back to the data sheet, click on Data Analysis and select Regression, which brings up the previous regression dialog box (all the data should still be there). We have to check the box "Constant is Zero," as shown in figure 6.5. Also, change the name of the output sheet to "no int." The result, shown in table 10, will appear.

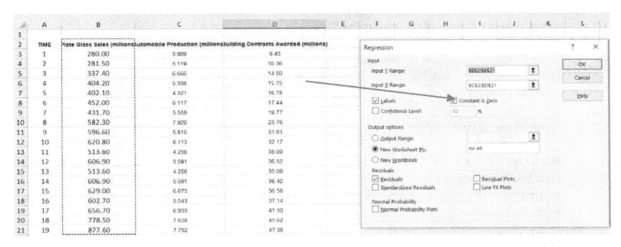

FIGURE 6.5 Removing the Intercept from the Regression.

Q.   Do I have to repeat all the earlier tests?

A.   Yes, you do.

Q.   OK, then the Adjusted R-Square is still greater than 0.6 and the *F* value is still above 5, indicating that both Test 1 and Test 2 are a pass. Since Test 3 passed last time, and once passed will always pass, there is no need to rerun the Correlation. When I look at column D for Test 4, I see that all ABS(*t Stat*) are >2.0, so TEST 4 also appears to be OK. Are we ready to move on to Test 5?

A.   Good job! Yes, just one more test to pass.

TABLE 6.7 Regression with No Intercept

	A	B	C	D	E	F
1	SUMMARY OUTPUT					
2						
3	*Regression Statistics*					
4	Multiple R	0.9979				
5	R Square	0.995804				
6	Adjusted R Square	0.936734				
7	Standard Error	38.15484				
8	Observations	19				
9						
10	ANOVA					
11		*df*	*SS*	*MS*	*F*	*Significance F*
12	Regression	2	5873473.307	2936736.653	2017.278	5.92711E-20
13	Residual	17	24748.46323	1455.791955		
14	Total	19	5898221.77			
15						
16		*Coefficients*	*Standard Error*	*t Stat*	*P-value*	*Lower 95%*
17	Intercept	0	#N/A	#N/A	#N/A	#N/A
18	Automobile Production (millions)	39.85213	4.293612364	9.281724902	4.56E-08	30.79339855
19	Building Contracts Awarded (millions)	10.58287	0.829658399	12.75569297	3.93E-10	8.832441598

Q.   What is Test 5 supposed to accomplish?

A.   In our discussion so far, we have alluded several times to the assumption that the error term, ε, in our regression model is normally distributed with a mean of zero. Test 5 is intended to verify that assumption.

Q.   How do we do that?

A.   We have to build a special graph, called a histogram, from the Residual Outputs. You may recall that the residuals are the errors—the difference between the actual data values and the values predicted by the regression model. We want to see whether the histogram looks anything like a normal distribution.

Q.   How do we do that?

A.   Follow these steps:

1. Go to the RESIDUAL OUTPUT.

2. Click on Data Analysis and then open the histogram option.

3. Fill out the histogram dialog box as shown in figure 6.6.

  a. Check the Labels box to indicate that the heading is included with the data.

  b. The Input Range contains the residuals, including the column heading.

  c. Click the output Range button to see the histogram next to your data.

  d. Click on the specific cell where you want the output placed—cell E25 in this case.

  e. Click on the Chart Output box.

  f. Click on OK to create histogram.

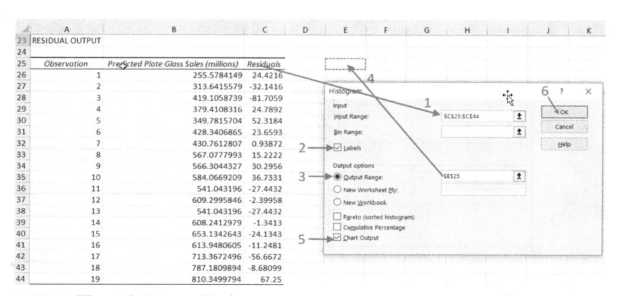

FIGURE 6.6 Filling out the Histogram dialog box.

Q.   **What about the <u>B</u>in Range entry? Did you mean for that to be left blank?**

A.   Yes. You can fill it in if you want to specify the sizes and number of class intervals you want in the histogram, but if you leave it blank, they will be selected automatically, which is fine for what we are doing.

Q.   **Anything else?**

A.   Just click on the OK button. You'll see the histogram data appear starting in your specified cell E25. However, Excel likes to play hide and seek with the histogram chart, so you'll have to scroll around until you find it. When you do, just drag it close to the data output. Table 6.8 shows what it looks like when you are done.

TABLE 6.8   Histogram Output for the Residuals of the Regression

	A	B	C	D	E	F	G	H	I
23	RESIDUAL OUTPUT								
24									
25	*Observation*	*Plate Glass Sales*	*Residuals*		*Bin*	*Frequency*			
26	1	255.5784149	24.42158505		-81.7059	1			
27	2	313.6415579	-32.14155786		-44.4669	1			
28	3	419.1058739	-81.70587386		-7.22793	6			
29	4	379.4108316	24.78916842		30.011	7			
30	5	349.7815704	52.31842956		More	4			
31	6	428.3406865	23.65931348						
32	7	430.7612807	0.938719346						
33	8	567.0777993	15.22220068				Histogram		
34	9	566.3044327	30.29556734						
35	10	584.0669209	36.73307911						
36	11	541.043196	-27.44319599						
37	12	609.2995846	-2.399584647						
38	13	541.043196	-27.44319599						
39	14	608.2412979	-1.341297866						
40	15	653.1342643	-24.13426433						
41	16	613.9480605	-11.24806051						
42	17	713.3672496	-56.66724964						
43	18	787.1809894	-8.680989396						
44	19	810.3499794	67.25002057						

Q.   **How do we verify that the distribution of residuals was normal with a mean of zero?**

A.   First, look at the graph. All we need to see to believe the distribution is normal is that the graph is unimodal.

Q.   **What does "unimodal" mean?**

A.   That is the statistical way of saying "only one hump."

Q.   **Our histogram has only one hump, so that takes care of that. What about having a mean of zero?**

A.   We use the Histogram Data for that. It shows we have eight negative residuals and seven positives. That's close enough to an even spread to say the mean is equal to zero. Hence, I'll declare that Test 5 is passed.

Q.   Whoa! That is quick and dirty. What if our bosses want something a little more precise?

A.   Robert Woolsey, a well-known character in operations research, wrote a book titled *Operations Research: A Quick & Dirty Manual*, so quick-and-dirty is not always bad. (Google it sometime.) But, getting back to your question, if you don't want to go the Q & D way, then you go back to the basics.

Q.   What do you mean by "the basics"?

A.   Check the descriptive statistics for the residuals, in table 6.9.

TABLE 6.9   Descriptive Statistics for the Residuals

Residuals	
Mean	0.12752
Standard Error	8.50665
Median	−1.3413
Mode	−27.4432
Standard Deviation	37.0796
Sample Variance	1374.9
Kurtosis	0.09212
Skewness	−0.31215
Range	148.956
Minimum	−81.7059
Maximum	67.25
Sum	2.42281
Count	19
Confidence Level (95.0%)	17.8718

Q.   What do we look for?

A.   The mean and the confidence interval. The mean is 0.12752, so if the 95% confidence interval around the mean, +/− 17.8718, includes zero, then we can conclude that the mean is statistically equal to zero. Thus, the statistics confirm the Q & D.

Q.   I cannot even imagine having to do this for a problem with many variables. Isn't there a better way?

A.   Yes, it is called stepwise multiple regression and it performs these steps for you. However, Excel's Data Analysis add-in does not have it, so we are showing you how to do it manually.

Q.   Lucky me! Are we done with all these tests yet?

A.   Yes, but let me show you how to construct a graph of actual values versus predicted values. Such a graph is worth a million words in describing how good your results are and in instilling confidence for using the model for forecasting.

Q.   **Do we have to solve our equation for all the past data?**

A.   No, Excel did that for us in the Residual Outputs. Copy and paste the *Predicted Plate Glass Sales*, column C from the RESIDUAL OUTPUT onto a new worksheet. Next to that, copy and paste the actual Plate Glass Sales from our data sheet. Highlight both columns, and then insert a line chart next to our data. It is shown in figure 6.7.

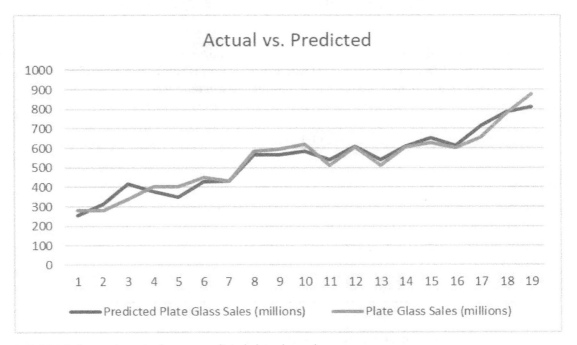

FIGURE 6.7 Comparing actual versus predicted plate glass sales.

Q.   **I agree the model did a good job for the past data, and that makes me think it will do a good job predicting the next five years of plate glass sales, but how do we get those predictions?**

A.   By using the regression values of the βs from cells B17–B19 in table 6.7 (copied into table 6.10, below) in the regression equation:

$$Y = \beta_0 + \beta_1 X_1 + \beta_2 X_2$$

TABLE 6.10   Regression Coefficients of the Robust Model

	Coefficients
Intercept	$\beta_0 = 0$
$X_1 =$ Automobile Production (millions)	$\beta_1 = 39.852128$
$X_2 =$ Building Contracts Awarded (millio	$\beta_2 = 10.582867$

This gives us the prediction equation

$$Y_t = 39.852128 * X_{1t} + 10.582867 * X_{2t}.$$

Q.   **What is that t subscript by the Y and Xs?**

A.   That is to indicate that to predict Plate Glass Sales in a particular year, t, we need to have the automobile production and the building contracts awarded for the same year.

Q.   **That makes no sense. If we are forecasting Plate Glass Sales for the next five years, we would need forecast values for Automobile Production and Building Contracts Awarded. Where are we going to get those?**

A.   You can probably google them. The government and/or industry groups collect data and make estimates so they can have an idea of where the economy is going. Also, most libraries have research librarians who can help. That is where I got the data in table 6.11.

TABLE 6.11   Prediction Data

Year	Y	X_1	X_2
20	?	6.4	48.51
21	?	7.9	51.23
22	?	8.4	57.47
23	?	8.6	61.03
24	?	8.9	66.24

Q.   **Shall I just plug it into the prediction equation?**

A.   That would give you a prediction, but without a confidence interval, you would be pretty sure your prediction was wrong.

Q.   **To get a confidence interval, I need the sample standard deviation. Where do I get that?**

A.   Excel calls the sample standard deviation "Standard Error," and you can find it for this problem in cell B7 of table 6.7. To make everything easy, I have set up the spreadsheet in table 6.12.

- Copy and paste the standard error to the new spreadsheet (cell B2)
- Copy and paste the regression coefficients (cells B2:C7)
- Copy and paste the Auto Production and Building Contracts values into D6:H7
- Create the forecast formula (as shown) for Row 8 to give the predictions for each year
- Create formulas (as shown) in rows 9 and 10 for the Upper and Lower Control Limits

Q.   **Why did you put a 1 in the first cell for each year?**

A.   Just to make the =SUMPRODUCT function work. It gives you something to multiply the Intercept by.

TABLE 6.12 Worksheet for Prediction Calculations

◢	A	B	C	D	E	F	G	H
1						YEAR		
2	Standard Error	38.15484183						
3								
4		✛	*Coefficients*	20	21	22	23	24
5		Intercept	0	1	1	1	1	1
6		X_1 = Automobile Production	39.85213	6.4	7.9	8.4	8.6	8.9
7		X_2 = Building Contracts Awarded)	10.58287	48.51	51.23	57.47	61.03	66.24
8			Predicted Y	768.43	856.99	942.96	988.60	1055.69
9			UCL	843.21	931.78	1017.74	1063.38	1130.48
10			LCL	693.65	782.21	868.17	913.82	980.91
11		=SUMPRODUCT($C$5:$C$7,D5:D7)						
12		=D8+1.96*$B$2						
13		=D8-1.96*$B$2						

Q. Then, for year 20, Plate Glass Sales are predicted to be between 693.65 and 843.21 with a probability of 95%. Are we done with regression yet?

A. No. Let's move on to the next lesson where you will learn how to handle qualitative variables when making predictions.

ACTIVE LEARNING: LESSON 6.2

LESSON 6.3: **Regression with Qualitative Variables**

Introduction

Q. **What are qualitative variables?**

A. Variables that do not have numbers associated with them.

Q. **If they have no numbers associated, why do we need them to make predictions?**

A. Because qualitative factors can have a huge impact on the price of certain items. If you ever looked at diamonds, for example, you know that *carat* is a measure of weight, but not all one-carat diamonds are priced the same. Color and clarity also affect the price of a diamond, but neither one is a number. Both clarity and color are subjectively determined by gemologists who classify them into groups, with the clearest diamond being in the highest group and so on. To predict the price of a diamond, you will need to take into account those two qualitative variables.

Q.   **Would another example be pricing a house, where location is important?**

A.   Yes, and there are many, many other applications in which it is necessary to use qualitative variables.

Learning Outcomes

When you complete this session, you should be able to:

- Differentiate between a quantitative and qualitative variable
- Transform a qualitative variable into an equivalent set of quantitative variables:
  - Determine the number of levels of the qualitative variables
  - Specify a "base case"
  - Define the appropriate number of "dummy" variables (one less than the number of levels) of the qualitative variable
  - Replace each qualitative variable in the regression by the appropriate number of dummy variables
- Use standard multiple regression methods to develop the robust regression equation and correctly use it to forecast

A Dialectic on Quantifying Qualitative Variables

Q.   **I thought you said qualitative variables didn't have numbers. Why are we "quantifying" them?**

A.   If we transform the qualitative variables into quantitative variables, then we can do the regression exactly like you did in the previous lesson.

Q.   **Are there any other types of variables we will need to learn about?**

A.   All you need to worry about are the qualitative variables, but you should be aware that qualitative variables are sometimes called categorical variables, indicator variables, and more. Regardless of the name, we will handle them the same way.

Q.   **How do we transform the qualitative variables into quantitative variables? Do you have an example?**

A.   Sure. A while back I was working on the problem described below:

Training Effectiveness

TRADOC, the U.S. Army Training and Doctrine Command, is considering changing certain training modules for National Guard members from traditional face-to-face to a web-based online format or a social media platform. The objective is to determine the feasibility of freeing up classroom time for more hands-on training activities.

The course selected to try the concept is an Abrams Tank engine diagnostics module. Individuals in the class have taken an electromechanical aptitude test. Ten Guard members have been selected at random for each training format. At the end of the training period, everyone completed an end-of-module exam. The aptitude test scores and the training method, as well as the end of course exam scores, are given in table 6.13. Do these results support one delivery method over another?

Q. Then our dependent variables would be the end-of-module score, and the independent variables would be the quantitative aptitude test score and the qualitative training delivery method. How do we turn a training delivery method into a number?

A. We designate one level of the qualitative variable, say, Traditional, as the base case and create dummy variables, cleverly called "Online" and "Social Media," for the other levels.

TABLE 6.13 Training Effectiveness Problem Data with Qualitative Variable

Guard Member	Delivery Method	Aptitude Test Score	End-of-Module Exam Score
1	Traditional	94	14
2	Traditional	96	19
3	Traditional	98	17
4	Traditional	100	38
5	Traditional	102	40
6	Traditional	105	26
7	Traditional	109	41
8	Traditional	110	28
9	Traditional	111	36
10	Traditional	130	66
11	Online	80	38
12	Online	84	34
13	Online	90	43
14	Online	97	43
15	Online	97	61
16	Online	112	63
17	Online	115	94
18	Online	118	74
19	Online	120	76
20	Online	120	79
21	Social Media	92	55
22	Social Media	96	53
23	Social Media	99	55
24	Social Media	101	52
25	Social Media	102	35
26	Social Media	104	46
27	Social Media	107	57
28	Social Media	110	55
29	Social Media	111	42
30	Social Media	118	81

Q.   I don't know how you can come up with variable names that quickly, but what's a dummy variable?

A.   A dummy variable has a value of 1 or 0. For those soldiers that used online training, the dummy variable Online will have a value of 1. For all the rest of the soldiers, the variable Online will have a value of 0.

Q.   OK, and Social Media would be 1 for 10 of the soldiers and 0 for the rest, but what about the base case, Traditional?

A.   We don't need a dummy variable for Traditional, because it simply has a zero for both of the dummy variables. I have set up table 6.14 to show the new variables.

Q.   Why don't you just add another column for Traditional and place a 1 in it when the delivery method is traditional?

A.   Because of multicollinearity. A third dummy variable would be redundant, not giving the regression any new information.

Q.   What happens if I add a column for Traditional anyway?

A.   The regression will not run. You will get an error message.

Q.   Since all the variables are now quantitative, are we ready to run the regression?

A.   Yes.

Q.   Done. The initial regression output is in table 6.15. Do we need to do the five tests for a robust model?

A.   Yes, so run through them with me:

   ▪ *Test 1:* Adjusted R-Square is 0.760972, which is greater than 0.6

   ▪ *Test 2:* F is 31.77489, much greater than 5

   ▪ *Test 3:* Not shown, so you will have to trust me on this one, but none of the entries for the independent variables is above 0.7 or below −0.7

   ▪ *Test 4:* All the *t Stats* are above +2 or below −2

   ▪ *Test 5:* Not shown, but the histogram of the residuals is unimodal and by my "eyeball" estimation looked normal

   Y = End-of-Module Exam Score
   X_1 = Online
   X_2 = Social Media
   X_3 = Aptitude Test Score

The regression model then becomes

$$Y = -86.27 + 30.37672 * X_1 + 22.28867 * X_2 + 1.125782 * X_3.$$

TABLE 6.14   Training Effectiveness Data with Dummy Variables

Guard Member	End-of-Module Exam Score	Online	Social Media	Aptitude Test Score
1	14	0	0	94
2	19	0	0	96
3	17	0	0	98
4	38	0	0	100
5	40	0	0	102
6	26	0	0	105
7	41	0	0	109
8	28	0	0	110
9	36	0	0	111
10	66	0	0	130
11	38	1	0	80
12	34	1	0	84
13	43	1	0	90
14	43	1	0	97
15	61	1	0	97
16	63	1	0	112
17	94	1	0	115
18	74	1	0	118
19	76	1	0	120
20	79	1	0	120
21	55	0	1	92
22	53	0	1	96
23	55	0	1	99
24	52	0	1	101
25	35	0	1	102
26	46	0	1	104
27	57	0	1	107
28	55	0	1	110
29	42	0	1	111
30	81	0	1	118

TABLE 6.15   Training Effectiveness Regression Results

	A	B	C	D	E	F	G
1	SUMMARY OUTPUT						
2							
3	*Regression Statistics*						
4	Multiple R	0.886397					
5	R Square	0.785699					
6	Adjusted R Square	0.760972	Test 1 is OK				
7	Standard Error	9.634874					
8	Observations	30					
9							
10	ANOVA				Test 2 is OK		
11		*df*	*SS*	*MS*	*F*	*Significance F*	
12	Regression	3	8849.065789	2949.689	31.77489	7.52936E-09	
13	Residual	26	2413.600878	92.8308			
14	Total	29	11262.66667				
15							
16		*Coefficients*	*Standard Error*	*t Stat*	*P-value*	*Lower 95%*	*Upper 95%*
17	Intercept	-86.27	17.03405322	-5.06456	2.83E-05	-121.2839511	-51.25595538
18	On-line	30.37672	4.322996617	7.026774	1.84E-07	21.49067259	39.26276621
19	Social media	22.28867	4.315430473	5.164878	2.18E-05	13.41817794	31.1591667
20	Aptitude test score	1.125782	0.15885642	7.086787	1.59E-07	0.7992475	1.452315595
21				Test 4 is OK			

Q.   Nice, but what are we going to predict with this?

A.   Nothing. We were not asked to predict any scores. Rather, we were asked whether any training delivery method was better than any other.

Q.   Yes, but how do we figure that out?

A.   Use the regression model, but set it up three times: once for any soldier using the traditional delivery, Y_T; once for any soldier using the online delivery, Y_O; and once for any soldier using the social media delivery, Y_S.

Q.   Won't the equations be the same?

A.   Yes, but the os and 1s for the dummy variables will show you something interesting.

Q.   Well, for the traditional delivery, the equation would be

$$Y_T = -86.27 + 30.37672 * X_1 + 22.28867 * X_2 + 1.125782 * X_3,$$

except X_1 and X_2 would both be equal to 0, so that leaves

$$Y_T = -86.27 + 1.125782 * X_3.$$

Is that right?

A.   Perfect. Now, what would the equation be for any soldier using online delivery?

Q. **Then X_1 would be 1 and X_2 would be 0, so we would get**

$$Y_O = -86.27 + 30.37672 * X_1 + 1.125782 * X_3,$$

but what does that tell us?

A. Subtract Y_T from Y_O and what do you get?

Q. **Oh, boy, algebra. Let's see, $Y_O - Y_T$ would be**

$$Y_O - Y_T = (-86.27 + 30.37672 * X_1 + 1.125782 * X_3) - (-86.27 + 1.125782 * X_3)$$

or

$$Y_O - Y_T = 30.37672 * X_1.$$

Everything went away but the X_1. What just happened?

A. Rearrange it like this:

$$Y_O = Y_T + 30.37672 * X_1$$

and you can see that using the online delivery method is expected to add 30.37672 points to the soldiers score on the end-of-module exam.

Q. **Nice. How did the social media delivery do?**

A. Subtracting the equations for Y_S from Y_T, we get

$$Y_S - Y_T = (-86.27 + 22.28867 * X_2 + 1.125782 * X_3) - (-86.27 + 1.125782 * X_3)$$

or

$$Y_S = Y_T + 22.28867 * X_2$$

so delivery via social media did 22.28867 points better than traditional delivery, but not as well as online delivery.

Q. **Is this reliable?**

A. Those statements were based on a robust model in which all the results you identified are statistically significant, so based on the results of these 30 soldiers, yes, it is reliable.

ACTIVE LEARNING: LESSON 6.3

LESSON 6.4: **Forecasting with Trend and Seasonality**

Introduction

Q. **Seasonality makes me think of fall, spring, summer, and winter. Is that what we are talking about?**

A. Yes, and more. Any event that is predictable and recurring can be designated as a "seasonal" event. For example, when forecasting retail sales, we must include Black Friday as a seasonal event or our demand forecast for that period will be way off. Many businesses, such as car rentals or restaurants, have regular patterns that occur within a week, while cash flow of utilities have a pattern within each month. If you sell hunting and/or fishing equipment, then you must designate the start of the hunting or fishing season as a seasonal event. And, if you have sports bar, then you must include the major sporting events as a seasonal factor.

Q. **Seasonality is much broader than I originally thought. How about trend?**

A. Think of that as the long-term growth or decline in business. That is simply another factor we have to consider if we want to create good forecasts.

Learning Outcomes

When you complete this session, you should be able to:

- Define and recognize a "time series"
- Understand the concept of trend and seasonality
- Define a regression model for a time series that includes trend and seasonality
- Obtain a robust regression model for data that exhibits trend and seasonal behavior
- Use the robust model to forecast

A Dialectic on Trend and Seasonality

Q. **Will we be using regression to forecast with trend and seasonality?**

A. Yes. We will be treating the seasonal events with qualitative variables. Trend is dealt with as a quantitative variable.

Q. **Should we always include trend and seasonality in our forecast?**

A. Whenever you have data that is related to time, we suggest that you add a trend and seasonal component to your model and let the regression decide if any or all are significant.

Q.   **That makes sense. How are trend and seasonality added to a forecast?**

A.   As a matter of fact, I just came back from a meeting with Parrothead and he wants us to help him forecast beer sales in the Conch Republic. Below is a summary of what I got out of the meeting:

Conch Republic Beer Sales

It is 2013. "Parrothead" Buffet, premier of the Conch Republic located off the Florida Keys, promotes tourism to the Republic with the motto "Changes in Latitudes, Changes in Attitudes." Land Sharks, as the tourists are referred to by the locals, embrace the motto with gusto and almost anything that is peaceful goes.

Parrothead relies on the almost unquenchable thirst of tourists for beer, which they chase with Margaritas while consuming the famous local cheeseburgers, to provide revenues from which to finance the affairs of the Republic. At this point, he is contemplating a major expansion to the port of Margaritaville to accommodate sailors from around the world coming to look for their "lost shaker of salt." He needs to know what the beer sales will be for year six (Q1 through Q4) to see whether the taxes derived from the sale of beer can finance the planned expansion of the port.

The quarterly beer sales in the Conch Republic are listed below. You have been engaged to provide Parrothead and his cabinet (referred to as the Coral Reefers) with the required forecast of beer sales.

Year	QTR 1	QTR 2	QTR 3	QTR 4
1	5,260,102	6,513,290	6,042,439	5,263,439
2	4,938,744	6,566,901	6,211,027	5,802,052
3	5,037,033	6,867,742	6,470,857	5,474,194
4	5,471,073	7,239,436	6,853,986	6,001,214
5	6,281,184	7,771,753	7,624,108	7,617,259

Note: The base case for the qualitative variable QUARTER is Q4

Q.   **What do we do with this data?**

A.   First, we have to rearrange it so all the Sales are in a single column, so we show the Year in column B, the Quarter in column C, and the Sales in column D.

TABLE 6.16   **Regression Set-Up for Beer Sales Forecasting in the Conch Republic**

	A	B	C	D	E	F	G	H	I	J	K	L	M	N
2		Year	Quarter	Sales	Time	Q1	Q2	Q3						
3		1	Q1	5,260,102	1	1	0	0						
4		1	Q2	6,513,290	2	0	1	0						
5		1	Q3	6,042,439	3	0	0	1						
6		1	Q4	5,263,439	4	0	0	0						
7		2	Q1	4,938,744	5	1	0	0						
8		2	Q2	6,566,901	6	0	1	0						
9		2	Q3	6,211,027	7	0	0	1						
10		2	Q4	5,802,052	8	0	0	0						
11		3	Q1	5,037,033	9	1	0	0						
12		3	Q2	6,867,742	10	0	1	0						
13		3	Q3	6,470,857	11	0	0	1						
14		3	Q4	5,474,194	12	0	0	0						
15		4	Q1	5,471,073	13	1	0	0						
16		4	Q2	7,239,436	14	0	1	0						
17		4	Q3	6,853,986	15	0	0	1						
18		4	Q4	6,001,214	16	0	0	0						
19		5	Q1	6,281,184	17	1	0	0						
20		5	Q2	7,771,753	18	0	1	0						
21		5	Q3	7,624,108	19	0	0	1						
22		5	Q4	7,617,259	20	0	0	0						

Regression dialog box (overlaid on columns I–N):

Regression   ?   ×

Input
Input Y Range: $D$2:$D$22
Input X Range: $E$2:$H$22

☑ Labels   ☐ Constant is Zero
☐ Confidence Level: 95   %

Output options
○ Output Range:
◉ New Worksheet Ply: REGRESSION
○ New Workbook

Residuals
☑ Residuals   ☐ Residual Plots
☐ Standardized Residuals   ☐ Line Fit Plots

Normal Probability
☐ Normal Probability Plots

OK   Cancel   Help

Q. What is the "Time" data in Column E?

A. That simply counts your data consecutively, starting at one, and going through 20. We will use that to ask the regression to let us know if, as time increases, there is a corresponding significant increase or decrease in beer sales.

Q. And that takes care of trend. Columns F, G, and H must be for the Seasonality, but shouldn't there be another column, for Q4?

A. You have forgotten about showing all 0s as the base case. Look at any Q4 row and you will see that is what I did.

Q. Right, so Q1, Q2, and Q3 are the dummy variables for the qualitative seasons, showing a 1 whenever the dummy variable matches up with the Quarter. Is that everything?

A. Yes. I have filled in the regression dialog box in table 6.16. I performed all five tests, and the only problem was with Test 4, which indicated that Q1 had to be removed from the regression. The final regression results with the robust model are shown in table 6.17.

TABLE 6.17 Robust Regression Model for the Conch Republic Beer Sales

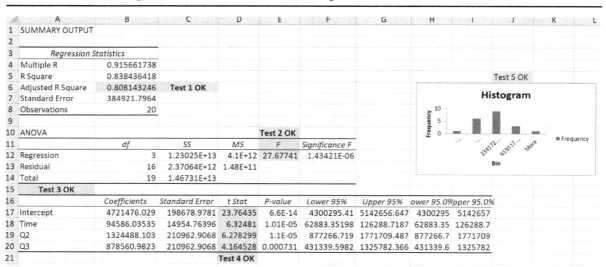

Q. If I am reading this right, the regression model would be

$$Y = 4{,}721{,}476.029 + 94{,}586.03535*Time + 1{,}324{,}488.103*Q2 + 878{,}560.9823*Q3,$$

but what does that tell us?

A. Think of the regression model as consisting of two parts: the trend line (in brackets, below) and the seasonal effect:

$$Y = [4{,}721{,}476.029 + 94{,}586.03535*Time] + [1{,}324{,}488.103*Q2 + 878{,}560.9823*Q3]$$

Trend Line   Seasonal Effects

Q.   **Sorry, but how does that help?**

A.   The trend line tells us that average sales have been increasing 94,586.03535 each quarter. The seasonal effect tells us that Quarter 2 has sales 1,324,488.103 higher than the trend line, and Quarter 3 has sales 878,560.9823 higher than the trend line.

Q.   **Why do we add both Quarters 2 and 3 to the forecast?**

A.   We don't. For each quarter, only one of the dummy variables will have a value of 1, so only one of the adjustments will be added.

Q.   **What about Quarters 1 and 4?**

A.   There is no adjustment for those quarters—their average sales are right on the trend line. Table 6.18 shows the forecast for our data while figure 6.8 shows this information graphically.

TABLE 6.18 Trend Line, Seasonal Factor, and
Forecast for Conch Republic Beer Sales

Time	Sales	Trend line	Seasonal factor	Fcast
1	5,260,102	4816062	0	4816062
2	6,513,290	4910648	1324488.103	6235136
3	6,042,439	5005234	878560.9823	5883795
4	5,263,439	5099820	0	5099820
5	4,938,744	5194406	0	5194406
6	6,566,901	5288992	1324488.103	6613480
7	6,211,027	5383578	878560.9823	6262139
8	5,802,052	5478164	0	5478164
9	5,037,033	5572750	0	5572750
10	6,867,742	5667336	1324488.103	6991824
11	6,470,857	5761922	878560.9823	6640483
12	5,474,194	5856508	0	5856508
13	5,471,073	5951094	0	5951094
14	7,239,436	6045681	1324488.103	7370169
15	6,853,986	6140267	878560.9823	7018828
16	6,001,214	6234853	0	6234853
17	6,281,184	6329439	0	6329439
18	7,771,753	6424025	1324488.103	7748513
19	7,624,108	6518611	878560.9823	7397172
20	7,617,259	6613197	0	6613197

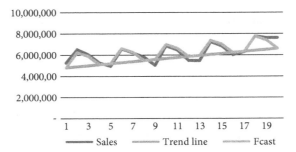

FIGURE 6.8 Actual versus forecasted beer sales in the
Conch Republic.

Q. Nice! Are we done?

A. No. We still need to use the equation to forecast a full year of beer sales.

Q. OK, well, using the same format we used before (table 6.12) to build table 6.19:

- Copy the Standard Error from cell B7 in table 6.17 into table 6.19
- Copy the entries cells of cell A17:B20 in table 6.17 into table 6.19
- Add a column for every quarter for which I want to forecast beer sales
- Put a 1 in the intercept row
- Our data ended in time period 20, so my forecasts must be for time periods 21, 22, 23, and 24, so put those numbers in the Time row
- Put a 1 at the intersection of a row and column containing a Q2 and then a Q3
- Calculate the Forecasted beer sales by taking the SUMPRODUCT of column C and each of the Quarters in turn
- Finally, calculate the Upper and Lower Confidence Limits by adding and subtracting 1.96 times the Standard Error

Did I miss anything?

TABLE 6.19   Forecasted Beer Sales for the Conch Republic

	A	B	C	D	E	F	G
1							
2	Standard Error	384921.7964					
3					QUARTER		
4							
5			Coefficients	Q1	Q2	Q3	Q4
6		Intercept	4721476.029	1	1	1	1
7		Time	94586.03535	21	22	23	24
8		Q2	1324488.103	0	1	0	0
9		Q3	878560.9823	0	0	1	0
10			Forecasted Sales	$ 6,707,782.77	$ 8,126,856.91	$ 7,775,515.82	$ 6,991,540.88
11			UCL	$ 7,462,229.49	$ 8,881,303.63	$ 8,529,962.55	$ 7,745,987.60
12			LCL	$ 5,953,336.05	$ 7,372,410.19	$ 7,021,069.10	$ 6,237,094.16

A. Bravo! I think you are ready for prime time.

ACTIVE LEARNING: LESSON 6.4

Comprehensive Problems are available for this chapter via Active Learning

Now That I Have Learned This Stuff ...

Q. **Whew! We just covered A LOT of material. Who knew Excel could do all that?**

A. Excel is a powerful tool.

Q. **Sometimes, though, it felt that we were forcing it. Is Excel the best way to do the things we did?**

A. No, but I cannot visualize a business that does not have Excel, so you will be able to apply what you have learned no matter where you wind up.

Q. **Is Excel all we need or is there specialized Business Analytics software?**

A. Any organization that has an established Business Analytics function will have special purpose software.

Q. **Why didn't we use that software?**

A. License fees for special purpose software can be prohibitive.

Q. **What do you mean by special purpose software?**

A. Software that is specifically designed to:

- handle linear programs with thousands of variables and constraints (Excel will only handle a few hundred)

- simulate complex queuing problems—you recall the gyrations we had to go through to just simulate a single server, single line system

- handle tens of thousands of data points and obtain a robust model without having to do all the robustness tests manually

- automate the construction and analysis of complex decision trees

- forecast time series using advanced techniques that go way beyond multiple regression with trend and seasonality

- assist in the development of optimal or near optimal vehicle routes

Q.   **Where can I learn more about such software?**

A.   Appendix B contains links to the biannual software survey published by INFORMS. It gives you a snapshot of the commercial software products available to do all we did this semester and much more. Just remember, you won't need that software until you have a project that requires it.

Getting Started

Q.   **Now that I have learned this material, do you think I'll get an assignment to use it?**

A.   Not unless you are hired by a Business Analytics department, or something similar.

Q.   **Why not?**

A.   You will have a job to do, and you will be expected to do it as it has always been done by your predecessors. Unless those people understood business analytics, you will be waiting a long time for such an assignment.

Q.   **You showed us how the Edelman contestants were doing amazing things. How is it possible that people don't know about business analytics?**

A.   Business analytics isn't like total quality management; rather than changing an entire company, it solves specific problems. Unless you are involved with that area, you probably will not be aware of what is going on there.

Q.   **If I wanted to, how would I get started with Business Analytics?**

A.   By identifying a problem, or process that YOU think can be improved with some of the tools you have learned.

Q.   **Any suggestions?**

A.   An excellent way of developing some ideas is to google for applications of business analytics, operations research, or management science in your industry.

Q.   **And, once I found one, should I go to my boss and ask for permission to work on that problem?**

A.   I usually worked on my ideas on my own time, before going to my boss.

Q.   **Since I am working to help my company, why can't I do the work on company time?**

A.   You already have a full-time job, so your boss might not think you playing with ideas is helping the company. Also, the price of failure is high and can be career limiting. You want to make sure that what you are proposing will work. Once I had some concrete indications of success, I could go to my boss with a better chance of getting my idea accepted.

Getting a Champion

Q. **Once I have taken the idea as far as I can on my own, what do I ask my boss for?**

A. It is likely that your idea will have to go to a higher authority, particularly if it requires a budget. So, you are seeking your boss's endorsement and support for taking the idea up the organization.

Q. **What if my boss doesn't like my idea?**

A. Then, if you are committed to the project, you must take a risk—either jump over your boss to someone further up the command hierarchy or present your idea to someone outside your department.

Q. **Why is that a risk?**

A. Leapfrogging the chain of command is usually not gratefully accepted. Going to someone outside of your chain of command is usually not appreciated by your boss either. If you think your idea is good enough to risk your job, then go for it. Just make sure your resume is up to date and you are marketable. Regardless, test the waters before you do either.

Q. **What do you mean by "test the waters?"**

A. Have someone you trust and who has the ear of the individual you are seeking to champion your cause up the organization broach the subject to him or her.

Q. **And let them take the credit?**

A. That is why you have to trust them. Anyway, it is unlikely they will be able to explain your idea, so they will arrange for you to have a one-on-one discussion about your idea or project.

Q. **That sounds like politics to me—backroom deals, et cetera. Does that really happen?**

A. You bet! When you have an idea, you do what you have to do to get it noticed. Otherwise, all you will have is a long, but less rewarding, career.

Q. **Are the risks worth it?**

A. The higher the risks you take, the higher the rewards, but the more likely that you will be changing jobs (no good deed goes unpunished). The real trick is to change jobs when you want to, not after you are fired.

Q. **You reached pretty high levels in both industry and academia. Is that how you got there?**

A. Let's just say I got there and leave it at that.

Communicating Business Analytics to the Leadership Team

Q. **OK. Moving on, let's say that I have found a champion—either my boss or a potential future boss—to move my idea up the chain of command. What happens next?**

A. Unless your idea can be funded out of someone's current budget, it will have to be presented to your organization's leadership team.

Q.   **Is that what my champion will do?**

A.   Probably not. Your champion is backing not just your idea but you as well since you will have to execute it if it is approved. That means you will be introduced to the leadership team to present your business analytic project proposal.

Q.   **No sweat. I got As in every MBA course I ever took that required a team project and presentation.**

A.   Forget everything you learned about making good class presentation. Your leadership team is a totally different audience than what you have in a classroom.

Q.   **Why?**

A.   In an academic presentation, your focus is to convince your professor that you know what you are doing via a literature survey, appropriate hypotheses, and correct methodology to test your hypotheses, and that you have drawn the "correct" conclusions.

Q.   **What is wrong with that?**

A.   Your leadership team is not interested in nor has the time to listen to how you arrived at your recommendations. You are employed by them as the expert and if they did not trust your expertise, you would not be standing in front of them. If you are lucky, you will have at most 30 minutes to "sell" by detailing *what* results they can expect, not *how* you are going to get those results. Oh, and by the way, you will be expected to have the answer to any questions they may have.

Q.   **How should I plan my presentation to a leadership team?**

A.   Each member of a leadership team has different responsibilities and priorities, so you must organize your presentation to engage every member during each stage of your presentation:

- *Stage 1:* Connect with your audience by clearly stating the business issue that the presentation will address.

- *Stage 2:* Direct and hold their attention by identifying what is in it for each key member in the room.

- *Stage 3:* Create understanding and memory by emphasizing the benefits of implementing the project.

- *Stage 4:* Drive your audience to action by stating the actions that each key member of the audience must commit to in order to achieve the projected benefits.

Q.   **What happens if I do not get my project approved?**

A.   For the first time, don't be surprised; there may be many good reasons why it was not approved. If it happens again and again, that is probably a sign for a not-so-promising career.

Building a Project Team

Q.   **If my project is approved, what can I expect next?**

A.   Since your champion had the clout to get you in front of the leadership team, he or she will probably be tasked to make it "happen." And, since he had enough confidence in you to get you in front of the leadership team, there is a good chance he will consult with you and put a project team together with you as the project manager.

Q. **What if that doesn't happen?**

A. You know more about the whole project than anyone else, so it is a safe bet that you will be on the team. If he selects someone else as project manager, he will have his reasons, and your best bet is to support the project manager fully and learn from him or her.

Q. **Who else is likely to be on the project team?**

A. Typically, business analytics project teams will have representatives from

- all areas that will be impacted by the project and

- the area in which the project will be implemented, and

- trainers to prepare employees for changes that may occur.

Q. **Will the project manager tell all these people what to do?**

A. If the project is such that you know what the end product will be and you know how to do it, then, yes, the project manager will be a group leader who is expected to take charge—leading discussions, delegating work, and making decisions.

Q. **What kind of a project would that be?**

A. One that is like ones done before—for example, building a new restaurant for a fast-food chain.

Q. **What if the project involves something that has not been done before?**

A. That will be most often the case. A business analytics project usually involves figuring out how to do something that has not been done before. You don't know everything you need to know, so if you act as a group leader, you will limit the results to what you know.

Q. **How can anything get done if there is no leader?**

A. The team, together, figures out what to do, decides how to do it, and works to get it done. We normally refer to that process as "brainstorming."

Q. **What can I do to get the brainstorming started?**

A. Brainstorming requires the elimination of groupthink. All team members must be able to express their ideas freely—the more the better and without the fear of being judged. The presence of a designated leader undermines brainstorming.

Q. **Can you really have teams without someone in charge?**

A. We have had them for years. They are the basis for the successes we have seen in companies that rely on their ability to capitalize on scientific discoveries and basic and applied research. Examples of such companies include Amazon, Alphabet (Google), Samsung, Roche, Johnson & Johnson, and Merck.

Q.   **Why haven't I heard of this before?**

A.   You have, but it was probably called "matrix management." Creation of a new product or service requires input from many different parts of the organization: engineering, marketing, information systems, finance, and so on. Teams were formed with representatives from each pertinent group and were coordinated by a project manager.

Q.   **Isn't "project manager" just another name for "leader"?**

A.   A project manager does not have the authority to evaluate team members. Team members still belong to their functional area and receive their performance review from their functional manager, who might or might not seek input from the project manager.

Q.   **When my project gets approved and I am charged to "make it happen," then I would become what you call a "project manager"?**

A.   Exactly. Your team will have members from different parts of the organization. You need their varying talents, but you do not know enough about their areas of expertise to tell them what to do. So, you get out of the way and let them brainstorm with other team members as to what should be done to get your project done.

Q.   **Do I get to pick who is on my team?**

A.   Since they come from different parts of the organization, they will probably be assigned to your team by their bosses.

Q.   **Would a boss release one of their top performers to work on a project that someone else will get credit for?**

A.   If your project got approved by the leadership team, it was because you did make it clear what was in it for each of them. Thus, it is in everyone's best interest to put the right person on the team.

Q.   **Can I ask for someone if I know I need them?**

A.   If you happen to know people who you feel could make a particular contribution to the team, you should ask your champion to negotiate such an assignment.

Q.   **OK, that makes sense. Now that there is a team, what do I do?**

A.   You must make sure that each team member has a clear understanding of the project's mission, its deliverables, and schedule. You must also deal with difficult team members, and keep your champion informed of your progress and aware of any issues that must be communicated to the leadership team. You also, of course, contribute your expertise to the brainstorming sessions, making sure that you act as a team member, not as someone invested with authority.

Achieving Team Performance

Q.   **I have not been a project manager before. What can you tell me that might help me to be successful?**

A.   You will have team members from several different parts of the organization, many of whom may not know each other. Any time you deal with a new team, you can expect some growing pains, or stages, to occur: Forming, Storming, Norming, Performing and Adjourning (Bruce Tuckman, 1965).

Q. **What happens in the "Forming" stage?**

A. This is the "polite" stage. You've seen this, everybody just sort of mills around, smiling and nodding at each other. If you know someone else, you'll probably go talk to them just so you aren't standing by yourself. There may be jostling for position, to figure out who is the most important person in the room. Some people are nervous, others are excited, and nobody really knows how to act. At the end of this stage, though, everybody is a member of the group.

Q. **Yeah, that's always a lot of fun. What's actually going on?**

A. There are some very common themes in the Forming stage:

- Identifying the tasks that need to be done

- Decisions on what information is needed

- Hesitation to participate, because nobody knows what the wrong thing to say might be

- Everyone will be watching to see how the others behave, and what problems there are

- A lot of the discussion will be peripheral to the actual project

- Suspicion, fear, and anxiety are common

- Very little actual work on the project happens

Q. **Is there any way to avoid this stage?**

A. Avoid it—no. We are talking about human nature here, not some corporate mandate that you are following. There are things that need to happen, and if everyone knows those things, they may happen that much faster.

Q. **What things?**

A. These things:

- Get everyone to agree on the purpose of the team

- They are hokey, but team exercises to build trust and relationships have their purpose

- Make sure the group norms and processes that develop are the right ones

- Learn about each other and what each can contribute (roles)

- Right from the start, share responsibility

Q. **Is it really that easy?**

A. None of that is easy, except it is very easy to fall back into groupthink, where one person takes over and everybody else agrees because it is easier. Convincing a group of people that a team is better than a group is easy, and a necessary first step, but actually creating a team mindset is hard.

Q.   **Storming doesn't sound any easier than Forming. Do we attack the problem in this stage?**

A.   Not yet, unfortunately. "Storming" refers to the interactions that often occur next. Some team members can become hostile, others simply overzealous, but the result is members trying to dominate the setting.

Q.   **That doesn't sound like a team is forming.**

A.   It isn't, and some groups get stuck at this stage. If your team doesn't move past this stage, you end up in a situation where everyone hates being in the group except whoever "won" the domination competition. Members will stop participating or do as little as they can while letting the "leader" make all the decisions and take all the credit.

Q.   **What should we expect to see in this stage?**

A.   As before, there are characteristics to group behavior in this stage, including the following:

- Infighting, defensiveness, competition
- Establishment of unachievable goals
- Disunity, increased tension, jealousy
- Resistance to group task demands
- Polarization of group members
- Sharp fluctuations of relationships and feelings
- Establishment of pecking orders
- Minimal work accomplished

Q.   **Yeah, I think I've been in that group a time or two. Is there anything you can do to get past all that as quickly as possible?**

A.   It is difficult. Once again, it helps if every team member understands that this is a perfectly normal stage in forming a team and is willing to work to do better. Here are some things a project manager can do that help:

- Civility (just being polite really helps)
- Encourage all opinions and viewpoints (listen)
- Redefine roles and responsibilities (sharing leadership)
- Clear up expectations (no one feels overwhelmed when everyone shares the load)
- Clarification of decision-making (shared and transparent)

Q.   **Is "Norming" (they are really reaching with these rhymes) where we finally get to work?**

A.   Some work gets done in the Norming stage, but it is mostly about getting the team members comfortable with one another. This is done in the setting of working on the problem, but, interestingly, finishing the project isn't the real focus.

Q. **Do you have a list of what to expect for the Norming stage?**

A. Of course.

- Conflict is avoided as the members begin to work harmoniously

- Discussions, both personal and project-related

- Team cohesiveness develops, with common goals established

- Team boundaries established

- Moderate work accomplished (finally!)

Q. **Sounds kind of touchy-feely. Is this step really necessary?**

A. None of these steps are necessary so much as they simply occur naturally. As a team moves past the contentious Storming stage, it is natural to talk to each other, tell stories, begin to feel more like a team and less like strangers. Humans are social creatures, so once the early roughness wears away, social interactions will simply happen. We're not saying your team members will become your best friends, merely that you will become more comfortable with them, which will allow the work to begin to progress.

Q. **What do we have to do during this step?**

A. You don't have to do anything, but here are things you will see happening, and can encourage to happen:

- Identifying strengths and weaknesses of the team

- Clear understanding of expectations and consequences

- Development of trust between group members

- Accepting, rather than fighting, differences

- Strategic plan of action develops

- Social interaction

Q. **I guess "Performing" is where the work gets done?**

A. Think of the first three steps as preseason practice. You must go through all that if you want to be a successful team. Once you have built the team (and have a pretty good idea of what the team is capable of), you get the work done.

Q. **What should we expect at this stage?**

A. I don't know; that will depend on the project the team has been assigned. Team members do tend to change somewhat once all the team building has been completed. They learn about themselves (from seeing how they affect the other team members) and perhaps learn to do a better a job interacting with others (interpersonal skills). Mostly, though, you work together to get the job done.

Q.   **You said there was a fifth stage for projects, Adjourning. What does that mean?**

A.   A project, by its nature, is temporary. When the project has been completed, the group breaks up and the members move on to new teams to tackle new projects. You might see some of your old team members, but you might not (it depends in part on the size of your company).

Q.   **Do we have a group hug?**

A.   I doubt it. It is polite, if nothing else, to acknowledge the people you have been working with for the past however-many weeks. Instead of rushing away to the next project, stop for a minute and

- review what the team accomplished,

- create the take-aways that have resulted from the team's work, and

- celebrate the successful completion of the project and acknowledge contributions and support provided by each team member.

Q.   **I guess common courtesy is never wasted, is it?**

A.   Sadly, it is becoming less common, but it always is a good idea, especially in the business world, to maintain contacts. Taking the time to formally adjourn the team will not only leave everyone feeling better but will help you know what to carry forward to the next team you are assigned to.

Q.   **Everything you say makes sense, but, now that I must use them for real, I am nervous. How do I deal with that?**

A.   Everyone gets butterflies at the start of a new project. You can read about what to do all you want, but until you have successfully managed a few projects from conceptualization to successful implementation, those butterflies will not go away. Leadership is something that must be developed over time. It is not something that you can read about and then go out and do. I would approach your project's champion to be your mentor. It is very comforting to have someone you trust to listen to you and provide counsel when you need it—and we will all need it, sooner or later.

Laying the Groundwork for Implementation

Q.   **Don't I just turn the project over to the user for implementation?**

A.   Eventually, you will. Suppose, though, that someone came by your office and told you they had a better way for you to do your job. They drop a folder on your desk and walk out. What do you do?

Q.   **I'd ignore them and get back to work.**

A.   If you want your project to be useful, you have to do something else, then.

Q.   **So, I would be looking for buy-in from the user. Who do I have to talk to?**

A.   Everyone who will even remotely be impacted by your project has to be briefed on what is going to change and why. You can do so by first seeking input and feedback from those who are within the user organization and hence are within the "sphere of influence" of what your project will impact.

Q.   **Do they need anything else?**

A.   Yes, they should also be allowed to provide input and express their concerns.

Q.   **I ask the user for input?**

A.   This is where you must let go of your idea and accept that it can be improved by other people's ideas (you might find that very hard to do). After that, you repeat the whole process in areas outside your immediate sphere with those who are affected by the idea.

Q.   **Once we have consensus, are we ready to go?**

A.   Not quite. In the process of building consensus, people will raise concerns about your idea. Some concerns will be imaginary (although you can't tell people that) and others will be very real. Regardless, you must address all concerns, accepting changes as needed to deal with the concerns.

Q.   **So, I must let other people play with my toys. What happens next?**

A.   Implementation has two aspects, immediate and long term.

Q.   **What are the problems with immediate implementation?**

A.   You are doing something new. Trainers must be trained so that the users will learn the right way of doing things and the "whys" of why it is important to do them that way. The most important thing is to reward good behavior, rather than punish it.

Q.   **Why would I punish good behavior?**

A.   I hope you wouldn't, intentionally, but suppose one person "catches on" to the new process sooner than the rest. It would be natural to ask that person to train the others, giving them more work to do. That is only one example, but you must be careful to reward excellent results, thus encouraging others to deliver the same level of excellence.

Q.   **Let's assume I can do that. How is long-term implementation different?**

A.   There is a tendency in humans to have performance drop off over time. The New & Exciting becomes the standard, and people will be tempted to accommodate exemptions, not realizing that exemptions may undermine the purpose of the project.

Q.   **Can you give me an example of what you mean?**

A.   Sure. At Burger King we had a project to optimize worker schedules. The goal was to minimize labor costs while maintaining service and quality standards. We trained all restaurant managers to use it, but once implemented, they often requested and were granted the ability to change those schedules. This re-introduced the costs that were saved as a result of optimization.

Q.   **How do you prevent actions like that from occurring?**

A.   Reward those who don't ask for exemptions. It needs to be done systematically, not as a bandage when you notice a problem has developed. Again, be proactive.

Q.   **If I do all this, will my projects work?**

A.   Not always. It is mostly a question of whether you are willing to make it work. If so, this is an outline of what you must do to get your ideas accepted and implemented.

Q.   **Where did all this come from?**

A.   A lifetime of experience.

Q.   **Since I don't have an extra lifetime, can you summarize this for me?**

A.   Sure, like this:

- Look for opportunities to apply business analytics; don't wait to be assigned to do so.
- Obtain evidence that your idea is likely to work.
- Find a champion who will push your idea.
- Obtain consensus.
- Find and address concerns (especially unspoken ones).
- Prepare the people who will make your idea work.
- Ensure that trainers are effectively trained and understand the reasons for adhering to the new process.
- Ensure that training results in performance.
- As the world changes, change your processes with it.
- Establish recognition and rewards based on performance.

Q.   **Thanks for sharing. You have given me much knowledge that I feel ready to put to use.**

A.   Our best wishes. As you pursue your professional journey, may God grant you the SERENITY to accept the things you cannot change, COURAGE to change the things you can, and WISDOM to know the difference.

ACTIVE LEARNING: LESSON 7

INFORMS—Franz Edelman Competitions

Finalists by Year 2010–2018: Titles and Video Links

2010

- INDEVAL Develops a New Operating and Settlement System Using Operations Research

  - The S.D. INDEVAL Institución para el Depósito de Valores, S.A. de C.V (INDEVAL), Mexico's Central Securities Depository and Securities Settlement System, implemented a new operating system to achieve best international practices, using operations research techniques. Best practices include high capacity and reliability, real-time settlement, Delivery versus Payment (DvP), secure data storage and communications (based on the ISO15022), and operational transparency. This paper presents the problem definition, a linear programming model and a system simulation, along with a major business process modeling devised for the new system. The novel application of operations research techniques has produced several benefits including: (i) analysis and testing of the DvP settlement mechanism that processes transactions quickly and efficiently, with optimal use of available cash and securities balances, (ii) a secure, reliable and automatic clearing and settlement engine, that operates continuously and efficiently handles all transactions that INDEVAL receives from its participants, (iii) an intelligent and customized pre-settlement function that controls the execution of the clearing and settlement process using business rules and parameters. The new system settles securities operations that average over U.S. $250 billion daily, and its successful implementation is a major improvement in Mexico's financial system.

HTTPS://WWW.YOUTUBE.COM/EMBED/VTOUJOAN-DO

Muñoz, D. F., Lascurain, M. D., Romero-Hernandez, O., Solis, F., Santos, L. D. L., Palacios-Brun, A., ... Villaseñor, J. (2011). INDEVAL Develops a New Operating and Settlement System Using Operations Research. *Interfaces*, *41*(1), 8–17. doi: 10.1287/inte.1100.0523

- Delaware River Basin Commission—Breaking the Deadlock: Improving Water Release Policies on the Delaware River Through Operations Research

  - The Delaware River provides half of New York City's drinking water, is a habitat for wild trout and American shad, and has suffered three 100-year floods in the last five years.

All abstracts are Copyright © by INFORMS. Reprinted with permission.

The water releases from three New York City dams on the Delaware's headwaters impact the reliability of the City's water supply, the potential for floods and the quality of the aquatic habitat. This successful project aimed to revise the water release policies to benefit the fishery habitat without increasing the City's drought risk. We describe the O.R. analyses and the politics that led to the October 2007 implementation by the Delaware River Basin Commission of our optimization based "Adaptive Release" framework. In addition to meeting the stated habitat improvement goals, our algorithm conservatively decreases reservoir levels less in dry years than in wet years thereby offering modest increases in flood protection during the hurricane season and is simpler to administer.

HTTPS://WWW.YOUTUBE.COM/EMBED/C-8AW93UDBK

Kolesar, P., & Serio, J. (2011). Breaking the Deadlock: Improving Water-Release Policies on the Delaware River Through Operations Research. *Interfaces, 41*(1), 18–34. doi: 10.1287/inte.1100.0536

- Deutsche Post DHL—Managing Global Brand Investments at DHL

    ○ In this proposal, we introduce the customer-insight-based approach that has been adopted by Deutsche Post DHL (more than 500,000 employees) to improve its global express delivery business. The O.R.-based brand assessment tool has been used in more than 20 of the largest countries in four continents since 2004. It supports local brand managers in allocating marketing resources to activities that grow the global brand in the right direction in their country market. Its application lead to an estimated increase in brand value of U.S. $1.32 billion over 5 years. This corresponds to an ROI of 38% and an internal rate of return of 24%. The implementation of the tool also had major impact on DHL's strategy and organization, beyond financial success.

HTTPS://WWW.YOUTUBE.COM/WATCH?V=CBAVWJNDQEQ

Fischer, M., Giehl, W., & Freundt, T. (2011). Managing Global Brand Investments at DHL. *Interfaces, 41*(1), 35–50. doi: 10.1287/inte.1100.0533

- New Brunswick Dept. of Transportation—Taking the Politics out of Paving: Achieving Transportation Asset Management through O.R.

  ○ The New Brunswick Department of Transportation (NBDoT) maintains over 18,000 kilometers of roads, 2,900 bridges and various ferry crossings and other assets. The organization faced significant challenges in rehabilitating its billions of dollars in infrastructure assets and maintaining a safe and effective transportation system with a very limited budget. Their goal was to develop long-term plans for managing New Brunswick's highway infrastructure that were transparent and defensible, enabling buy-in from decision makers and support from the public. The O.R. component of the framework uses a unique combination of linear programming and heuristic techniques for a goals-based approach. The model incorporates long-term objectives and constraints from an operations-wide view that weighs all options, costs, timings and asset life-cycles to produce optimal treatments plans. Results of the initial analysis offered the substantiation required to secure increased funding which helped address the growing infrastructure deficit, allowed NBDoT to maintain levels of service, and assisted the local road-building industry by stabilizing funding. NBDoT anticipates $72 million (discounted) in annual savings, amounting to $1.4 billion (discounted) over the next 20 years. The solution provides the capability to commit to long term decisions and has removed politics from the decision-making process because the consequences of deviating from the optimized plan can be easily quantified and communicated. Future program development capital budgets will see highway fixtures and ferries added to the model. The Department of Transportation has become a global leader in the field of asset management, and the success has attracted the attention of transportation officials around the world.

SCAN ME

HTTPS://WWW.YOUTUBE.COM/WATCH?V=8HSBIRXEOWO

Feunekes, U., Palmer, S., Feunekes, A., Macnaughton, J., Cunningham, J., & Mathisen, K. (2011). Taking the Politics Out of Paving: Achieving Transportation Asset Management Excellence Through OR. *Interfaces, 41*(1), 51–65. doi: 10.1287/inte.1100.0520

- Inventory Optimization at Procter & Gamble: Achieving Real Benefits Through User Adoption of Inventory Tools

  ○ Over the past ten years, Procter & Gamble has leveraged its cross-functional organization structure with operations research to reduce inventory investment significantly. Savings were achieved in a two-step process. First, spreadsheet-based inventory models locally optimized each stage in the supply chain. Since these were the first inventory tools installed, they achieved significant savings and established P&G's scientific inventory practices. Second, P&G's more-complex supply chains implemented multi-echelon inventory optimization software to minimize inventory cost across the end-to-end supply chain. In 2009, a tightly coordinated planner-led effort, supported by these tools, drove $1.5 Billion in cash savings. While case studies reveal the mathematics employed, of equal importance is the presentation of the planning process that facilitates inventory management and the decision tree that matches a business to the optimal inventory tool depending on the business' requirements. Today, more than 90% of P&G's business units (about $70 billion in revenues) utilize either single-stage (70%) or multi-echelon (30%) inventory management tools. Plans are underway to grow the use of multi-echelon tools to 65% in the next three years.

HTTPS://WWW.YOUTUBE.COM/WATCH?V=8V328ERXP7S

Farasyn, I., Humair, S., Kahn, J. I., Neale, J. J., Rosen, O., Ruark, J., … Willems, S. P. (2011). Inventory Optimization at Procter & Gamble: Achieving Real Benefits Through User Adoption of Inventory Tools. *Interfaces*, *41*(1), 66–78. doi: 10.1287/inte.1100.0546

- Sasol—Innovative Decision Support in a Petrochemical Production Environment

  ○ Declining fossil fuel reserves, stricter clean fuel specifications, fluctuating oil and gas prices, a recessionary world economy and unique developing world issues are some of the challenges facing Sasol, an integrated energy and chemical company based in South Africa. A passion for innovation has made the company a world leader in unique technologies including the application of Operations Research. A perfect example is Sasol's Modeling Operations using Stochastic Simulation (MOSS) methodology. Historically, the petrochemical industry based business decisions on average production limits. This approach ignored any time-based variability, hence requiring the addition of a design margin and more expensive production facilities. Sasol Technology's Operations Research team developed MOSS to address the critical need to include this key factor in decision making. The team uses MOSS models to develop business cases for gas and liquid production facility modifications, to highlight risks and to assist strategic decision making. They also analyze the impact of changing market conditions, product composition, operations efficiency, operating philosophies and schedules. These models have provided an estimated value addition for Sasol of over $230 million since 2000. Although not audited, this is considered a conservative estimate since it does not account for the improvements in energy efficiency, greenhouse gas emissions, general risk reduction and the overall understanding of Sasol's complex and integrated systems. Sasol believes that this work has applications in the wider chemical and fuels industries and represents a major innovative step forward for Operations Research in the Chemical Engineering discipline.

HTTPS://WWW.YOUTUBE.COM/WATCH?V=DK3H_ITKXZO

Meyer, M., Robinson, H., Fisher, M., Merwe, A. V. D., Streicher, G., Rensburg, J. J. V., ... Cawood, E. (2011). Innovative Decision Support in a Petrochemical Production Environment. *Interfaces*, *41*(1), 79–92. doi: 10.1287/inte.1100.0528

2011

- MISO Unlocks Billions in Savings through the Application of O.R. to Energy and Ancillary Services Markets

  - The Midwest Independent Transmission System Operator (MISO) is a nonprofit organization formed through the action of several electric transmission owners. The company operates in 13 states in the Midwest region of the United States and one Canadian province of Manitoba. MISO transformed the electric utility industry leveraging advances in computing capabilities and using O.R. to create and implement complex algorithms and computer models to introduce centralized wholesale energy markets to the Midwest. These new markets increased the efficiency of the existing electric infrastructure (power plants and high-voltage transmission lines), improved the reliability of the grid and reduced the need for future infrastructure investments in the Midwest. As a result of these advances the MISO region realized between $2.1 billion and $3.0 billion in cumulative savings from 2007 through 2010, with an additional estimated value of $6.1 billion to $8.1 billion through 2020.

HTTPS://WWW.YOUTUBE.COM/EMBED/SZ7C-AEO7WC

Carlson, B., Chen, Y., Hong, M., Jones, R., Larson, K., Ma, X., ... Zak, E. (2012). MISO Unlocks Billions in Savings Through the Application of Operations Research for Energy and Ancillary Services Markets. *Interfaces*, *42*(1), 58–73. doi: 10.1287/inte.1110.0601

- CSAV: A Strategic Empty Container Logistics Optimization in a Major Shipping Company

  - Compañía Sud Americana de Vapores (CSAV) is the sixth largest shipping company in the world. CSAV developed a system (ECO), to manage the problem of inventories and imbalances of empty containers, since some regions are net importers of empty containers (e.g. China), while others are net exporters (e.g. Saudi Arabia). A multi-commodity, multi-period model manages the repositioning problem, while an inventory model determines safety stocks required at each location used by the firm to insure high service level despite uncertainties. A hybrid forecasting system was developed to support both the inventory and the network flow model. Major improvements in data gathering, communications in real time, and automation of data handling were needed to feed the models. A collaborative web-based optimization framework allowed agents from different zones to interact in decision making. The use of ECO led to direct savings of $75 million for CSAV, with a reduction in inventory stocks of 50% and an increase in container turnover of 60%.

HTTPS://WWW.YOUTUBE.COM/EMBED/-CDCQ8RSQUO

Epstein, R., Neely, A., Weintraub, A., Valenzuela, F., Hurtado, S., Gonzalez, G., ... Yung, D. (2012). A Strategic Empty Container Logistics Optimization in a Major Shipping Company. *Interfaces, 42*(1), 5–16. doi: 10.1287/inte.1110.0611

- System Dynamics Transforms Fluor Corporation Project and Change Management

  - Fluor Corporation designs and builds many of the world's most complex engineering and construction projects. It has implemented a system dynamics model-based system that has improved project management, transformed change management, and brought large quantified business benefits to the company and its clients. The model is rapidly set up for and tailored to each major project. It is then used to foresee future cost and schedule impacts of project changes and to test ways to avoid the impacts. Since 2005, this system has been used on over 100 Fluor projects. Quantitative business benefits exceed $800M to date for Fluor and its clients. Further, it has transformed the mindset of our managers away from the industry's retrospective view, in which disputes can become the channel for resolving cost responsibility, and replaced it with a proactive approach, in which Fluor works with clients to find, in advance, ways to mitigate impacts and reduce costs a win-win for Fluor and its clients.

HTTPS://WWW.YOUTUBE.COM/EMBED/OEQCRJHHFCM

Godlewski, E., Lee, G., & Cooper, K. (2012). System Dynamics Transforms Fluor Project and Change Management. *Interfaces*, *42*(1), 17–32. doi: 10.1287/inte.1110.0595

- Branch Reconfiguration Practice through Operations Research at Industrial and Commercial Bank of China Limited

  ○ As the largest publicly traded bank in the world measured by market capitalization, deposit volume and profitability, Industrial and Commercial Bank of China Limited (ICBC) has a vast network of over 16,000 branches. To keep a leading position in the competitive China market, a critical strategic problem for ICBC was the reconfiguration of branch locations and service capabilities to match the regional economy and customer distribution, along with quick identification and relocation to new high potential market areas. Partnering with IBM, ICBC customized an OR based branch network optimization system known as Branch Reconfiguration (BR). So far, BR has been implemented in 40 major cities in China. The increase in deposits attributable to BR in a typical major city like Suzhou was US$1.04 billion. Over time it is expected that ICBC will continue to experience additional deposits. The BR project is a successful example of using OR methods to transform the service channels of a large bank with excellent results.

HTTPS://WWW.YOUTUBE.COM/EMBED/ZBARGDGI8NA

Wang, X., Zhang, X., Liu, X., Guo, L., Li, T., Dong, J., ... Zhang, B. (2012). Branch Reconfiguration Practice Through Operations Research in Industrial and Commercial Bank of China. *Interfaces*, *42*(1), 33–44. doi: 10.1287/inte.1110.0614

- Retail Price Optimization at InterContinental Hotels Group (IHG)

  - InterContinental Hotels Group (IHG) is the world's largest hotel group by number of rooms. IHGs Revenue Management platform, PERFORM[SM] with Price Optimization is the first large scale, enterprise implementation of price optimization in the hospitality industry. The Price Optimization module determines optimal room rates based on occupancy, price elasticity and competitive prices. The approach is a major advancement over existing revenue management systems which assume demands by rate segments are independent of each other and of price. The Price Optimization module is currently deployed to 2,077 hotels globally and will eventually be deployed to all IHG properties. A 2.7% increase in revenue has been verified and acknowledged in the IHG 2009 annual review. To date Price Optimization has achieved $145M in incremental revenue for the IHG hotel estate. At full rollout, this capability will generate $300M per year. PERFORM[SM] = IHGs yield management system featuring retail price optimization principles.

HTTPS://WWW.YOUTUBE.COM/EMBED/IVGSI7_FXH4

Koushik, D., Higbie, J. A., & Eister, C. (2012). Retail Price Optimization at InterContinental Hotels Group. *Interfaces, 42*(1), 45–57. doi: 10.1287/inte.1110.0620

- Tax Collections Optimization for New York State

  - The New York State Department of Taxation and Finance (NYS DTF) collects over $1 billion annually in assessed delinquent taxes. A novel solution was developed to address the challenge of optimizing tax collection activities, in the presence of complex dependencies between business needs, resources and legal constraints. The solution is a unique combination of data analytics and optimization based on the unifying framework of constrained Markov Decision Processes (C-MDP). The developed system optimizes the collection actions of agents with respect to maximization of long term returns and generates a customized collections policy that is efficient and adaptive. The system became operational in December 2009, and there has already been an $83M increase in revenue from 2009 to 2010 (8%), using the same set of resources. Given a typical annual increase of 2–4%, the expected benefit of the developed system is approximately $120M to $150M over the next three years, far exceeding the initial target of $99 million.

HTTPS://WWW.YOUTUBE.COM/EMBED/BLSCUN6PQCE

Miller, G., Weatherwax, M., Gardinier, T., Abe, N., Melville, P., Pendus, C., ... Cooley, B. (2012). Tax Collections Optimization for New York State. *Interfaces*, *42*(1), 74–84. doi: 10.1287/inte.1110.0618

2012

▪ Supply Chain-Wide Optimization at TNT Express

○ TNT Express is one of the world's leading express delivery companies. The introduction of operations research (O.R.) at TNT Express during the past seven years has significantly improved decision-making quality and resulted in millions of Euros in cost savings. The Global Optimization Program (GO) initiative has led to the development of an entire suite of optimization solutions and the GO Academy, TNT's Management development program for teaching the optimization principles. The tools and available knowledge allow operating units to analyze performance, identify optimization opportunities and overcome operational challenges. To date, the most significant savings originate from the network routing and scheduling solution (TRANS), the tactical route planning solution for pickups and deliveries (SHORTREC), and the supply chain solution (DELTA Supply Chain). As a result of all these initiatives, O.R. is now an effective part of TNT Express' DNA, and over the period 2008–2011, more than Euro 207 million in savings were realized.

HTTPS://WWW.YOUTUBE.COM/WATCH?V=H55WAN3EW5G

Fleuren, H., Goossens, C., Hendriks, M., Lombard, M.-C., Meuffels, I., & Poppelaars, J. (2013). Supply Chain–Wide Optimization at TNT Express. *Interfaces*, *43*(1), 5–20. doi: 10.1287/inte.1120.0655

- Carlson Rezidor Hotel Group Maximizes Revenue through Improved Demand Management and Price Optimization

  ○ Carlson Rezidor Hotel Group (CRHG) collaborated with JDA Software Group to use operations research to drive higher revenue for its hoteliers and to stay ahead of the competition. This highly innovative revenue optimization project, SNAP, which stands for Stay Night Automated Pricing, started with enterprise demand forecasting across 600 U.S. properties in 2007. It was followed by a large-scale network optimization solution to dynamically optimize stay night rates based on price elasticity of demand, competitor rates, remaining inventory availability, demand forecasts and business rules. Starting from the optimization prototyping results in 2008, Carlson Rezidor Hotel Group consistently measured a 2–4% revenue improvement in compliant hotels over noncompliant ones. To date, compliant hotels increased revenue by more than $16 million annually. After a successful deployment in the Americas, Carlson Rezidor Hotel Group extended the partnership with JDA to roll out SNAP globally. The worldwide revenue from the solution is anticipated to exceed $30 million annually.

HTTPS://WWW.YOUTUBE.COM/EMBED/LPE7WNOFXXG

Pekgün, P., Menich, R. P., Acharya, S., Finch, P. G., Deschamps, F., Mallery, K., ... Fuller, J. (2013). Carlson Rezidor Hotel Group Maximizes Revenue Through Improved Demand Management and Price Optimization. *Interfaces*, *43*(1), 21–36. doi: 10.1287/inte.1120.0660

- Centers for Disease Control and Prevention: Advancing Public Health and Medical Preparedness with Operations Research

  ○ Planning for a catastrophe involving a disease outbreak with the potential for mass casualties is a significant challenge for emergency managers. CDC public health experts teamed with operations researchers to devise sophisticated modeling and computational strategies that address challenges in mass dispensing. The O.R. technology is integrated into a powerful information decision-support suite, RealOpt©, for tactical and strategic operational planning. RealOpt has been used in hundreds of drills and dispensing events. Careful before/after studies conducted in a sample of these events illustrate throughput efficiencies improved by 175% to 1000%, and staffing needs reduced by 32% to 85%. Having been widely distributed, the RealOpt system has a U.S. user base of over 4,000 public health and emergency directors. By dramatically improving mass dispensing capability and efficiency under limited resources and stressed environments, this work has the potential to enable rapid and effective interventions for at-risk populations, and to lessen the subsequent disease cost, care burden, mortality and economic impact.

HTTPS://WWW.YOUTUBE.COM/EMBED/XDIU6TQ3HL4

Lee, E. K., Pietz, F., Benecke, B., Mason, J., & Burel, G. (2013). Advancing Public Health and Medical Preparedness with Operations Research. *Interfaces*, *43*(1), 79–98. doi: 10.1287/inte.2013.0676

- Operations Research in Ship Management: Maximizing Fleet-Wide Revenue Routing at Danaos

  - Danaos Corporation, one of the world's largest containership owners, has a fleet of 60 containerships. Danaos developed the innovative "Operations Research In Ship MAnagement" (ORISMA) toolkit that effectively optimizes ship routing. ORISMA offers a clear answer to the conventional dilemma between least cost and faster voyage by maximizing revenue using all relevant information: financial data, hydrodynamic models, weather conditions and marketing forecasts. Its power comes from looking at the big picture—it considers economic potential even after voyage completion and drives fleet-wide instead of single-vessel performance. Using O.R. and expert knowledge, a full suite of world-class capabilities in scheduling optimization, intelligent voyage planning, and bunkering and chartering were developed. In its first year of implementation ORISMA has resulted in clear bottom-line benefits. This award-winning product, in addition to profit maximization, minimizes carbon emissions, reduces workload and increases customer satisfaction.

HTTPS://WWW.YOUTUBE.COM/EMBED/DCJGCH4KGWK

Varelas, T., Archontaki, S., Dimotikalis, J., Turan, O., Lazakis, I., & Varelas, O. (2013). Optimizing Ship Routing to Maximize Fleet Revenue at Danaos. *Interfaces*, *43*(1), 37–47. doi: 10.1287/inte.1120.0668

- Hewlett-Packard: Transformation of HP's Business Model through Advanced Analytics and Operations Research

  - Hewlett-Packard (HP) is the world's largest provider of information technology infrastructure, software, services and solutions, to individuals and organizations. Advancements in Internet and mobile technology in the past decade, and consumers' desire to shop "anytime, anywhere" have seen worldwide eCommerce grow three-fold from $160 billion to $481 billion in the 2004–2009 period. Several operations research solutions were developed to address a variety of problems that manifest along the eCommerce value chain. Time series forecasting and regression modeling techniques were applied to help identify and quantify the impact of key drivers of online traffic. Bayesian modeling, Markov analysis and Linear Discriminant analysis methods are used to develop a holistic customer targeting engine that doubles purchase conversion rates and increases order sizes up to 30%. Since 2009, the integration of these solutions into the financial and marketing planning and warehouse operations processes has helped deliver $117 million in sales for HPDirect. com, thereby helping HP establish an effective alternate route to market.

HTTPS://WWW.YOUTUBE.COM/WATCH?V=J0QCJ0YW950

Tandon, R., Chakraborty, A., Srinivasan, G., Shroff, M., Abdullah, A., Shamasundar, B., ... Dhore, P. (2013). Hewlett Packard: Delivering Profitable Growth for HPDirect.com Using Operations Research. *Interfaces*, *43*(1), 48–61. doi: 10.1287/inte.1120.0661

- Optimizing Capital Investment Decisions at Intel Corporation

  - Intel spends over $5 billion annually on manufacturing equipment. With increasing lead times from equipment suppliers and increasing difficulty in forecasting market demand, optimizing capital investment decisions is a significant managerial challenge. A "Capital Supply Chain Velocity Program" was developed for ordering, shipping and installing production equipment. At the core of the Velocity Program is a new procurement framework, dual-mode equipment procurement (DMEP), utilizing dual sourcing and option contracts to optimize capital investments. DMEP seamlessly combines statistical forecasting with Monte Carlo simulation and stochastic programming, and includes built-in scenario and sensitivity analysis capabilities to support Intel's strategic, tactical and executional procurement decisions. The Velocity Program and DMEP have resulted in hundreds of millions of dollars in documented cost savings and at least 2 billion dollars in revenue upside for a manufacturing process transition during a period of economic crisis. The framework is now guiding Intel's decisions for manufacturing process transitions.

HTTPS://WWW.YOUTUBE.COM/EMBED/BAMZ2BFHJYQ

Kempf, K. G., Erhun, F., Hertzler, E. F., Rosenberg, T. R., & Peng, C. (2013). Optimizing Capital Investment Decisions at Intel Corporation. *Interfaces, 43*(1), 62–78. doi: 10.1287/inte.1120.0659

2013

- Dutch Delta Commissioners: Economically Efficient Standards to Protect the Netherlands against Flooding

  - In the Netherlands flood protection is a matter of national survival. In 2008, the 2nd Delta Committee recommended that legal flood protection standards be increased at least tenfold to compensate for population and economic growth since 1953, which would have involved dike improvement investments estimated at 11.5 billion euro. Our research group was charged with developing efficient flood protection standards in a more objective way. We used Mixed Integer Nonlinear Programming to demonstrate the efficiency of increasing the legal standards only in three critical regions. Monte Carlo analysis confirmed the robustness of this outcome. Our results were accepted by the State Secretary in 2012 as basis for legislation. Compared to the earlier recommendation, this successful application of Operations Research yields not only a highly significant increase in protection for these regions (where two-thirds of the benefits of proposed improvements are concentrated) but also some 7.8 billion euro in cost savings. Our methods could be used in decision-making for other flood-prone areas worldwide.

HTTPS://WWW.YOUTUBE.COM/EMBED/ZZA_TVJSEUE

Eijgenraam, C., Kind, J., Bak, C., Brekelmans, R., Hertog, D. D., Duits, M., ... Kuijken, W. (2014). Economically Efficient Standards to Protect the Netherlands Against Flooding. *Interfaces, 44*(1), 7–21. doi: 10.1287/inte.2013.0721

- Operations Research Transforms Baosteel's Operations

  - Shanghai Baoshan Iron and Steel Complex (a.k.a. Baosteel) is the China's largest and the world's third largest steel company. Since it was established in 1978, Baosteel has been using state-of-the-art manufacturing facilities, processing technologies, and IT systems. However, until recently, Baosteel had mainly relied on rule and experience based manual planning methods to make production and logistics operations decisions, which resulted in frequent occurrence of tardy orders on the one hand, and high production, inventory, and logistics costs on the other. In 2005, the research team was tasked to develop advanced Operations Research (OR) based planning tools to improve the operational efficiency of the Baosteel's Shanghai plant throughout its entire production process. In the following six years, we developed various novel optimization algorithms and tailored metaheuristics and implemented four decision support systems (DSSs) to replace the manual planning methods at the Shanghai plant. The use of DSSs has brought scientific operations management to Baosteel and transformed the Shanghai plant's production and final product delivery operations. It has not only significantly increased Shanghai plant's productivity and product quality, but also greatly reduced energy and resource consumptions. It is estimated that in the period from 2007 through 2012, the use of the DSSs at the Shanghai plant has generated a total cumulative economic benefit of US $76.81 million. Based on the current usage of the DSSs at the Shanghai plant, it is also estimated that, the DSSs will continue to generate an annual economic benefit of US $19.80 million, which represents a 16.8% improvement of Baosteel's IT and operations management capability. In addition, due to reduced energy consumption, the carbon dioxide emission at Baosteel is decreased by 585,770 tons annually, making a significant impact on the environment. As a key state-owned enterprise (SOE) in China, Baosteel's pioneering experience in adopting OR based planning methods for its operations management has set a great precedence for numerous SOEs in both steel and non-steel industries in China to follow.

HTTPS://WWW.YOUTUBE.COM/EMBED/ASIJHBN_MZA

Tang, L., Meng, Y., Wang, G., Chen, Z.-L., Liu, J., Hu, G., ... Zhang, B. (2014). Operations Research Transforms Baosteel's Operations. *Interfaces*, *44*(1), 22–38. doi: 10.1287/inte.2013.0719

- Optimizing Chevron's Refineries

  - Chevron has developed a software modeling tool that seven company-owned refineries use to select the most profitable raw materials, evaluate product options, optimize refinery processes, and promote efficient capital investments. The tool, now called Petro, is a linear program with distributive recursion mathematics. This application of operations research, along with its complementary and supporting systems and work processes, have been continually improved upon over the past thirty-plus years and are now deeply embedded into the fabric of Chevron's downstream business of supplying products reliably and efficiently to our customers. The value that these efforts bring to Chevron now approaches $1 billion annually. We estimate that the cumulative value to Chevron over the past three decades is approximately $10 billion.

HTTPS://WWW.YOUTUBE.COM/EMBED/TGOP92HIPWG

Kutz, T., Davis, M., Creek, R., Kenaston, N., Stenstrom, C., & Connor, M. (2014). Optimizing Chevron's Refineries. *Interfaces, 44*(1), 39–54. doi: 10.1287/inte.2013.0727

- Dell's Channel Transformation—Leveraging Operations Research to Unleash Potential across the Value Chain

  - Dell pioneered the direct sales model by offering its customers technology solutions through full-system configurability. High internet penetration and efficient e-commerce ecosystems enabled the success of this model in developed economies. Changing market dynamics, technological advancements and Dell's global expansion required that the company cater to diverse customer needs and purchase behaviors.

    Five years ago, Dell launched several strategic initiatives to drive channel transformation by offering fixed configurations through online channels, retailers, distributors and other channel partners. We developed solutions applying Operations Research (OR) and analytics to address key challenges across the value chain and deliver profitable growth in the new channels. These solutions include (i) Configuration Optimizer to reduce product complexity by identifying fixed hardware configurations (FHCs) to build and stock, (ii) Online Conversion Rate Accelerator to refine the online purchase experience leading to higher revenues and satisfaction of FHC customers and (iii) Retail Margin Maximizer to forecast better, mitigate inventory risk and recommend promotions for margin improvement.

    Further, we have developed solutions to optimize return-on-investment (ROI) on marketing spend, to reduce warranty part dispatches and to optimize pricing across channels. Analytics has solved complex business problems and facilitated Dell's growth in the FHC business to $15 billion in the last five years. These OR solutions have delivered a margin impact of more than $140 million through reduction in markdown expenditure, improved online conversion rate, increased ocean shipment and enhanced customer satisfaction since 2010. The success of these transformational initiatives has strengthened our confidence in the application of OR to resolve complex business problems. It has helped in inculcating a culture of data-driven decision making in the organization.

HTTPS://WWW.YOUTUBE.COM/EMBED/TYOZWZZEZHI

Martin, K., Chitalia, P., Pugalenthi, M., Rau, K. R., Maity, S., Kumar, R., ... Subramanian, S. (2014). Dell's Channel Transformation: Leveraging Operations Research to Unleash Potential Across the Value Chain. *Interfaces, 44*(1), 55–69. doi: 10.1287/inte.2013.0729

- Kroger Uses Simulation-Optimization to Improve Pharmacy Inventory Management

  ○ The Kroger Co. (NYSE:KR) is the largest grocery retailer in the United Sates and the fifth largest retailer in the world. Kroger employs more than 339,000 associates serving customers in 2,422 supermarkets and operates 1,950 in-store pharmacies as part of its convenient one-stop shopping strategy. Improving customer service is at the heart of Kroger's Customer 1st business strategy and towards this end Kroger's Operations Research team, in collaboration with faculty from Wright State University, developed an innovative simulation-optimization system for pharmacy inventory management. In pharmacy, traditional standard statistical distributions fall short of providing accurate pharmacy demand profiles. To overcome business resistance to complex "black box" formulas, the simulation-optimization approach uses empirical distributions to model demand, provides end users an intuitive experience, allows "plug-and-play" experimentation, and at the same time delivers optimal or near-optimal results in milliseconds. The system was implemented in October 2011 in all pharmacy stores nationwide, and has reduced out-of-stock prescriptions by 1.5 million per year, ensuring greater patient access to medications when they need it. It has resulted in an increase in revenue of $80 million per year, a reduction in inventory by more than $120 million, and a reduction in labor cost equivalent to $10 million per year. The innovative inventory system instantly won support from Kroger's executives, revealed OR to Kroger, and significantly contributed to the growth of Operations Research in Kroger. It is now being extended to other business lines and has pushed scientific inventory management to become a strategic core competence of Kroger.

HTTPS://WWW.YOUTUBE.COM/EMBED/QYLIJ-GTV9O

Zhang, X., Meiser, D., Liu, Y., Bonner, B., & Lin, L. (2014). Kroger Uses Simulation-Optimization to Improve Pharmacy Inventory Management. *Interfaces, 44*(1), 70–84. doi: 10.1287/inte.2013.0724

- McKesson: A Holistic Supply Chain Management Solution

  ○ McKesson is America's oldest and largest healthcare services company, helping its customers achieve better health. IBM Research developed an innovative scenario modeling and analysis tool (SCSM) for McKesson to optimize its end-to-end pharmaceutical supply chain policies. Through its integrated OR models, SCSM optimizes the distribution network, supply flow, inventory, and transportation policies; quantifies the impacts of changes on financial, operational, and environmental metrics. This solution provided new insights into the supply chain's profitability that have been incorporated into other pricing models. The modeling work spawned a roadmap of projects with quantified opportunities, including a new Air Freight supply chain, and provided new insights that have been critical to McKesson's improved performance as a Pharmaceutical industry leader. As important as the modeling work has been, the new structured data supporting the model has provided a rich basis for additional improvement projects. This model was the first to directly link OR modeling results to a detailed profit and loss statement by product category for the different supply chains used by McKesson. Since this effort began in 2009 McKesson pharmaceutical division has reduced its committed capital by over $1 Billion.

HTTPS://WWW.YOUTUBE.COM/EMBED/LISP0WJOPT4

Katircioglu, Kaan, Robert Gooby, Mary Helander, Youssef Drissi, Pawan Chowdhary, Matt Johnson, and Takashi Yonezawa. "Supply Chain Scenario Modeler: A Holistic Executive Decision Support Solution." *Interfaces* 44, no. 1 (2014): 85–104. https://doi.org/10.1287/inte.2013.0725.

2014

- The U.S. Centers for Disease Control & Prevention (CDC) and Kid Risk, Inc.: Polio Eradicators Use Integrated Analytical Models to Make Better Decision

  - Achieving and maintaining global polio eradication requires that multiple global stakeholders coordinate and cooperate to invest human and financial resources in interventions that prevent virus transmission. Reaching the goal depends on effective tools and interventions, and their optimal use. Poliovirus transmission occurs in a complex global system, with rapidly evolving viruses that readily cross international borders. Complexities associated with managing poliovirus risks come from: (1) the dynamic spread of the three different poliovirus serotypes that must be individually eradicated, (2) the potential detection of only the small fraction of infections that lead to paralysis, and (3) the use of two vaccines with very different risks, costs, and benefits (i.e., oral poliovirus vaccine (OPV) and inactivated poliovirus vaccine (IPV)). The US Centers for Disease Control and Prevention, one of four spearheading partners of the Global Polio Eradication Initiative (GPEI) (along with WHO, UNICEF, and Rotary International), initiated a collaboration with Kid Risk, Inc. to develop and apply integrated analytical models to answer high-stakes policy questions related to managing the risks of polioviruses with full consideration of both human health and economic outcomes. Over the last decade, the collaboration innovatively combined numerous operations research and management science tools, including simulation, decision and risk analysis, system dynamics, game theory, and optimization to help policy makers understand and quantify the implications of their choices. The insights from these integrated modeling efforts prevented cases of paralysis, saved millions of dollars, sharpened the effective use of polio vaccines, led to management and programmatic improvements, and motivated significant national commitments to increase population immunity and global commitments to finance the GPEI to finish the job.

HTTPS://WWW.YOUTUBE.COM/EMBED/_EJNXZQ7GBS

Thompson, K. M., Duintjer Tebbens, R. J., Pallansch, M. A., Wassilak, S. G. F., & Cochi, S. L. (2015). Polio Eradicators Use Integrated Analytical Models to Make Better Decisions. *INFORMS Journal of Applied Analytics, 45*(1) 5–25.

- Alliance for Paired Donation with Boston College, Stanford University and MIT: Kidney Exchange

  - Many end-stage renal disease sufferers who require a kidney transplant to prolong their lives have relatives or associates who have volunteered to donate a kidney to them, but whose kidney is incompatible with their intended recipient. This incompatibility can be sometimes overcome by exchanging kidneys with another incompatible donor pair. Such kidney exchanges have emerged as a standard mode of kidney transplantation in the United States. The Alliance for Paired Donation (APD) developed and implemented an innovative operations research based methodology of non-simultaneous extended altruistic donor (NEAD) chains, which, by allowing a previously binding constraint (of simultaneity) to be relaxed, allowed better optimized matching of potential donors to patients, which greatly increases the number of possible transplants. Since 2006, the APD has saved more than 220 lives through its kidney exchange program, with more than 75% of these achieved through long non-simultaneous chains. The technology and methods pioneered by APD have been adopted by other transplant exchanges, resulting in thousands of lives already saved, with the promise of increasing impact in coming years. The percentage of transplants from non-simultaneous chains has already reached more than 6% of the total number of transplants from live donors (including directed living donors) in the last year. We describe the long-term optimization and market design research that supports this innovation. We also describe how the team of physicians and operations researchers worked to overcome the skepticism and resistance of the medical community to the NEAD innovation.

HTTPS://WWW.YOUTUBE.COM/EMBED/QJDQCI66N1E

Ross Anderson, Itai Ashlagi, David Gamarnik, Michael Rees, Alvin E. Roth, Tayfun Sönmez, M. Utku Ünver (2015) Kidney Exchange and the Alliance for Paired Donation: Operations Research Changes the Way Kidneys Are Transplanted. Interfaces 45(1):26–42.

- The Energy Authority: Hydroelectric Generation and Water Routing Optimizer

  ○ We describe a software application that enables owners of generation output from a virtualized Federal Columbia River Power System to safely operate the system while also shaping the generation to meet their energy and economic needs. The application, known colloquially as The Optimizer, employs modern Operations Research techniques to convert a highly non-linear problem into a linear one so as to create a robust solution for the entire, six-dam system on an hourly basis; over a ten-day time horizon; within seconds to minutes. The tool permits two operators to manage and optimize the entire generation portfolios for nine utilities simultaneously in a very stringent time frame around the clock, and enables planners to ensure that the operation of the river meets all of the requirements for flood control, fish management, electrical reliability, safe dam operation, and recreation under high degrees of uncertainty. As a result, the Optimizer allows utilities to integrate renewable, environmentally friendly wind and solar generation into their resource portfolio with hydro generation and empowers fast decision making and adaptation to rapidly changing conditions.

HTTPS://WWW.YOUTUBE.COM/EMBED/1GXEEPB1PGM

Hu, Z., Putz, J., Sutjandra, Y., Chan, A., Mount, E., & Baker, K. (2015). The Energy Authority Optimizes Water Routing and Hydroelectric Generation on the Columbia River. *Informs Journal on Applied Analytics, 45*(1), 43–57.

- Grady Health System and Georgia Institute of Technology: Transforming E.D. Workflow and Patient Care

  - When we encounter an unexpected critical health problem, a hospital's emergency department (ED) becomes our vital medical resource. Improving an ED's efficiency and timeliness of care, while reducing avoidable readmissions, is fraught with difficulties arising from complexity and uncertainty. In this paper we describe a new ED decision-support system that couples machine learning, simulation, and optimization to address these improvement goals. The system allows healthcare administrators to optimize workflow globally, taking into account the uncertainties of incoming injuries and diseases and associated care, thereby significantly reducing patient length of stay. This is achieved without changing physical layout, focusing instead on process consolidation, operations tracking, and staffing. First implemented at Grady Memorial Hospital in Atlanta, Georgia, the system helped reduce length of stay by roughly 33%. By re-purposing existing resources, the hospital established a care management observation unit that led to a reduction of 28% in ED readmissions. Insights also led to an investment in an alternative-care facility that removed more than 32% of the non-urgent-care cases from the ED. With these improvements the hospital enhanced its financial standing and achieved its target goal of an average ED length of stay close to 7 hours. ED and trauma efficiency improved throughput by over 16.2% and reduced the number of patients who left without being seen by over 30%. The annual realized revenue and savings amount to approximately $190 million (up 72%), a large amount relative to the hospital's $1.5 billion annual economic impact. The underlying model, which is generalizable, has been tested and implemented successfully at seven other EDs and in 2 other hospital units. The system offers various advantages in that it permits a comprehensive analysis of the entire patient flow from registration to discharge, enables the decision-maker to understand complexities and inter-dependencies of individual steps in the process sequence, and ultimately allows the user to perform system optimization.

HTTPS://WWW.YOUTUBE.COM/EMBED/8IGXTNU0FYQ

Eva K. Lee, Hany Y. Atallah, Michael D. Wright, Eleanor T. Post, Calvin Thomas IV, Daniel T. Wu, Leon L. Haley Jr. (2015) Transforming Hospital Emergency Department Workflow and Patient Care. Interfaces 45(1), 58–82.

- NBN Company with Biari: Optimized Fibre Optic Network Design

  - The National Broadband Network is the largest public infrastructure project undertaken in Australia. Through the use of Operations Research is expected to avoid more than $2.2 Billion in unnecessary construction and design costs on the $36 Billion project.

  - NBN Co, the government company building the network, divided the country into more than 4,100 fiber serving area modules (FSAMs), each covering around 2,500 premises. Over the 10-year project, one FSAM will be designed and constructed every day.

  - NBN Co contracted Biarri, an Australian commercial mathematics company, to optimize the design task. Biarri created FOND (Fiber Optic Network Design), a software product based on a network flow Mixed Integer Program engine. This engine minimizes the cost of materials and labor for each FSAM, subject to a variety of constraints, and solves in less than five minutes. To date, over 650 FSAM initial designs have been completed using FOND. This has saved an estimated $375 million in avoided construction cost, with the planning time per FSAM reducing from 145 to 16 days

HTTPS://WWW.YOUTUBE.COM/EMBED/TKNA9_LO0Y8

Ferris, P., Forbes, C., Forbes, J., Forbes, M., & Kennedy, P. (2015). Optimizing Network Designs for the World's Largest Broadband Project. *Interfaces*, 45(1), 83–97. doi: 10.1287/inte.2014.0785

- Twitter with Stanford University: The "Who to Follow" System at Twitter: Strategy, Algorithms & Impact

  ○ The Who-To-Follow system at Twitter is an algorithmic data product that recommends accounts for Twitter users to follow. Building the system involved algorithmic, analytics, operational, and experimental challenges; OR and analytics techniques played a key role. This product has had significant direct impact on Twitter's growth and the quality of user engagement, as well as being a major driver of revenue. Over 1/8 of all new connections on the Twitter network are directly due to this system, and a substantial majority of Twitter's revenue comes from its Promoted Products, for which this system was foundational. To place this contribution into perspective, Twitter is now a publicly traded company with a market cap over $30 Billion, a projected annual revenue close to $1 Billion, and over 240 Million active users.

HTTPS://WWW.YOUTUBE.COM/EMBED/VO2L8WXADOI

Goel, A., Gupta, P., Sirois, J., Wang, D., Sharma, A., & Gurumurthy, S. (2015). The Who-To-Follow System at Twitter: Strategy, Algorithms, and Revenue Impact. *Interfaces, 45*(1), 98–107. doi: 10.1287/inte.2014.0784

2015

- Syngenta: Good Growth Through Advanced Analytics

  ○ Syngenta is committed to bringing greater food security to an increasingly populous world by creating a transformational shift in farm productivity. Syngenta Soybean Research & Development (R&D) is leading Syngenta's overall corporate breeding strategy by developing and implementing a new product development model that is enabling the creation of efficient and effective breeding strategies necessary to compete in the soybean agriculture market. Key to the new strategy is the combination of advanced analytics and plant breeding knowledge to detect opportunities for increasing the genetic gain of crop productivity and the optimization of our breeding processes. Syngenta used discrete event and Monte Carlo simulation models to codify Syngenta Soybean R&D best practices and used stochastic optimization to create the best soybean breeding plans and strategically aligned research efforts. The new analytical tools dramatically change the way project leads are thinking and planning, the results of which will provide more than $287M in cost avoidance for Syngenta Seeds Product Development from 2012–2016 and substantially improve the probability of successfully delivering a portfolio value exceeding $1.5B.

HTTPS://WWW.YOUTUBE.COM/EMBED/YLES6JLTEBW

Byrum, J., Davis, C., Doonan, G., Doubler, T., Foster, D., Luzzi, B., ... Mack, S. (2016). Advanced Analytics for Agricultural Product Development. *INFORMS Journal on Applied Analytics, 46*(1). doi: https://doi.org/10.1287/inte.2015.0823

- Predictive Cloud Computing Efficiently Manages Digital Experiences and Showcases IBM Technology at Professional Golf and Tennis Tournaments

  ○ Due to the growth of the Internet, mobile and other smart technologies, the demand placed on digital platforms supported by enterprise cloud computing capabilities is rapidly growing. To support IBM's leadership in analytics, mobile and cloud technologies, a small team within IBM Global Technology Services (GTS) developed a system using advanced analytics that addresses the dynamic and unpredictable web traffic patterns produced by a digital enterprise workload, while driving greater operational efficiencies across compute and labor resources. Current cloud platforms are reactive, requiring human intervention to scale compute resources to meet demand. To address this shortcoming the GTS team invented the Predictive Cloud Computing (PCC) system that uses multiple advanced analytical techniques to produce models that forecast Internet traffic demands in near real-time, allocating compute resources as needed. In 2014, GTS applied the PCC system across multiple tennis and golf sporting tournaments reducing our cloud computing hours by 50% while driving a reduction in labor by integrating automation. PCC continues to expand, producing 16 additional patent filings since inception strengthening IBM's analytics patent portfolio and overall Brand.

HTTPS://WWW.YOUTUBE.COM/EMBED/XOUUZVDBEYS

Baughman, A. K., Bogdany, R., Harrison, B., O'Connell, B., Pearthree, H., Frankel, B., ... Upton, C. (2016). IBM Predicts Cloud Computing Demand for Sports Tournaments. *Interfaces, 46*(1), 33–48. doi: 10.1287/inte.2015.0820

- End-to-End Business Analytics and Optimization in Ingram Micro's Two-Tier Distribution Business

  - Ingram Micro, the world's largest technology distributor operates in a high-volume low margin environment. The company started its Business Intelligence & Analytics practice in North America (NA) about 6 years ago. Since then the group has built and deployed a scalable highly innovative price optimization engine, imprime™, for NA's $8B spot business, a set of analytics apps, imsmart™ for its internal sales organization and an integrated digital marketing platform, intelligence.ingrammicro.com, to run data-driven marketing campaigns to its customers and end customers. Since 2011, these products and analytical programs have yielded a cumulative benefit of $1.12 Billion of incremental product revenue and $28M of incremental gross profit. These solutions have been effective in driving profitable growth and are scalable. Our next steps are to continue to drive these best practices within the other regions outside NA and continue our sales enablement activities.

HTTPS://WWW.YOUTUBE.COM/EMBED/SVLNGNOOXLY

Mookherjee, R. (R., Mukherjee, J., Martineau, J., Xu, L., Gullo, M., Zhou, K., ... Li, N. (2016). End-to-End Predictive Analytics and Optimization in Ingram Micro's Two-Tier Distribution Business. *Interfaces, 46*(1), 49–73. doi: 10.1287/inte.2015.0834

- An OR-based decision support system for crowd management during the Hajj

  - The Hajj, the great Islamic pilgrimage to Makkah in Saudi Arabia, is known to be the largest annually occurring pedestrian problem in the world. Each year up to 4 million pilgrims approach the holy sites at the region of Makkah to perform their religious duty. This figure is likely to grow substantially over the coming years. The key ritual "stoning-of-the-devil" is known to be particularly crowded. Until 2006, several sad crowd disasters (stampedes) led to thousands of casualties due to overcrowding. In the aftermath of the crowd disaster in 2006, the Ministry of Municipal and Rural Affairs of the Kingdom of Saudi Arabia (MOMRA) launched projects of total $7 billion to prevent crowd disasters in the future. In particular, MOMRA started to develop an OR-based decision support system (ORDSS) for crowd management that employs a range of tools from operations research, analytics, and crowd dynamics. At its heart a scheduling tool and a real-time video tracking system are implemented. While the video tracking systems measures actual infrastructure utilization, the mixed integer programming tool Pilgrim Scheduler accounts for preferred stoning times, infrastructure capacities, and smooth capacity utilization. Further analytics and operations research tools of the ORDSS assign pilgrims to trips and stations of a metro system that transports pilgrims during the Hajj, support the layout planning of the tent city accommodating the pilgrims, analyze and simulate pilgrim flows, and re-schedule pilgrims in case of critical densities. The ORDSS provides solutions to MOMRA that enable uncongested and smooth pilgrim flows as well as extensive real-time reporting. Operations research helped stop the tragic loss of human lives due to stampedes. 2007–2014 no crowd disaster has happened. The algorithms and their successful implementation in the crowd management of the Hajj and the integrative use of operations research will help to better manage mass gatherings all over the world.

HTTPS://WWW.YOUTUBE.COM/EMBED/_MMDS0K1ACI

Haase, K., Abideen, H. Z. A., Al-Bosta, S., Kasper, M., Koch, M., Müller, S., & Helbing, D. (2016). Improving Pilgrim Safety During the Hajj: An Analytical and Operational Research Approach. *Interfaces*, *46*(1), 74–90. doi: 10.1287/inte.2015.0833

- Maximizing U.S. Army's Future Contribution to Global Security using the Capability Portfolio Analysis Tool (CPAT)

  - Recent budget reductions have caused the U.S. Army to face tremendous challenges in managing their portfolio of ground combat systems—placing many important programs at risk. To address these challenges, the Army and a supporting team developed and applied the Capability Portfolio Analysis Tool (CPAT) to optimally invest in ground combat modernization over the next 25–35 years—providing the analytical rigor needed to help senior Army decision makers allocate scarce modernization dollars to protect soldiers and maintain a combat edge. Using a novel four-phase mixed integer linear program, CPAT delivers unparalleled insight into multi-decadal modernization planning and illustrates a cultural shift in the Army's thinking and processes towards informed analytics. Most importantly, CPAT is used to inform critical funding determinations for major at-risk programs and has helped shape decisions to continue modernization of the $10 billion Stryker family of vehicles (originally slated for cancelation) and to reallocate roughly $28 billion by not pursuing the Ground Combat Vehicle new-start program as originally envisioned. Senior Army leaders have called CPAT a "game changer" and enthusiastically endorsed its use. Over 40 studies have been completed using CPAT, applying sound Operations Research methods and allowing Army acquisition executives to base investment decisions on analytically rigorous evaluations of portfolio tradeoffs—optimally prioritizing billions of taxpayer dollars.

HTTPS://WWW.YOUTUBE.COM/EMBED/CUIBKNV5RTK

Davis, S. J., Edwards, S. B., Teper, G. E., Bassett, D. G., Mccarthy, M. J., Johnson, S. C., ... Rice, R. E. (2016). Maximizing the U.S. Army's Future Contribution to Global Security Using the Capability Portfolio Analysis Tool (CPAT). *Interfaces, 46*(1), 91–108. doi: 10.1287/inte.2015.0824

- PNG: Effective Inventory Control for Items with Highly Variable Demand

  ○ LMI developed the PNG inventory control solution to manage items with infrequent demand (isolated spikes in demand) as well as items with frequent, but highly variable demand. Such items account for the majority of stocked hardware at the Defense Logistics Agency (DLA). Forecasting demands for these items—no matter how sophisticated the forecasting method—had led to years of bad outcomes for DLA: excess inventory for some items, backorders for others, and excessive buyer workload. The implementation of PNG (a software package of two inventory solutions, Peak Policy and Next Gen) shifted DLA from trying to forecast individual items to a portfolio or risk management approach to inventory control. PNG presents a three-way tradeoff between customer service, inventory value, and replenishment workload. DLA can then make a single decision that aligns with its objectives—without separate investments in forecasted demands, safety stock, or order quantities. Since DLA implemented PNG in January 2013, the agency has achieved its inventory-related goals for better customer service and reduced buyer workload, with no increase in inventory and recurring savings of nearly $400 million per year—all from buying more of what sells and less of what doesn't.

HTTPS://WWW.YOUTUBE.COM/EMBED/QMGO105AVNK

Bachman, T. C., Williams, P. J., Cheman, K. M., Curtis, J., & Carroll, R. (2016). PNG: Effective Inventory Control for Items with Highly Variable Demand. *Interfaces, 46*(1), 18–32. doi: 10.1287/inte.2015.0829

2016

- UPS On Road Integrated Optimization and Navigation (ORION) Project

    - The UPS Orion project is based on a sophisticated algorithm that automatically plots the course of more than 30,000 UPS drivers every day, which will increase to 55,000 drivers in 2016.

    - Because ORION provides an optimized delivery sequence that meets multiple operational constraints, the drivers are relieved of the complexity of determining how to make their deliveries.

    - Costing $250 million to build and deploy, ORION is expected to save $300–$400 million annually, reduce annual CO_2 emissions by 100,000 metric tons, and decrease yearly fuel consumption by 10 million gallons.

HTTPS://WWW.YOUTUBE.COM/EMBED/VYQIUXB_QUG

Holland, C., Levis, J., Nuggehalli, R., Santilli, B., & Winters, J. (2017). UPS Optimizes Delivery Routes. *Interfaces*, *47*(1) 8–23. doi: 10.1287/inte.2016.0875

- 360i's Digital Nervous System Generate $250MM in Cost Savings and $1B in Revenue Creation for Clients

    - Digital Nervous System is a suite of paid search optimization and management systems for online marketers that rapidly selects keywords and creates campaigns; reverse engineers the Google second-price auction to identify quality score problems before they arise; calculates accurate bids for keywords with sparse data; integrates advanced application programming interfaces into real-time search bids and ad creation; and creates detailed pricing forecasts to produce bids on keywords.

    - The Digital Nervous System has resulted in $250 million in cost savings and $1 billion in revenue generation for the company's paid search clients.

HTTPS://WWW.YOUTUBE.COM/EMBED/AQYLU26XEDM

Geraghty, K., Sonmezer, E., Maron, M., & Ruble, D. (2017). 360i Generates Nearly $1 Billion in Revenue for Internet Paid-Search Clients. *Interfaces*, 47(1), 24–37. doi: 10.1287/inte.2016.0879

- O.R. Transforms Scheduling of Chilean Soccer Leagues and South American World Cup Qualifiers

  - Over the last 11 years, operations research techniques have been applied to schedule professional soccer leagues in Chile. These techniques have yielded a direct economic impact of more than USD 55 million through a combination of increased ticket sales, cost savings, and subscriber growth for Chile's soccer television channel and cost reductions for the teams due to the better travel schedules resulting from an improved ordering of home and away games.

  - These techniques have also been used to schedule the South American 2018 FIFA World Cup qualifiers.

HTTPS://WWW.YOUTUBE.COM/EMBED/JZQT8FBRGSI

Alarcón, F., Durán, G., Guajardo, M., Miranda, J., Muñoz, H., Ramírez, L., ... Zamorano, G. (2017). Operations Research Transforms the Scheduling of Chilean Soccer Leagues and South American World Cup Qualifiers. *Interfaces*, 47(1), 52–69. doi: 10.1287/inte.2016.0861

- Transition State and End State Optimization Used in the BNY Mellon U.S. Tri-Party Repo Infrastructure Reform Program

  - BNY Mellon is a leader in the tri-party repo market with approximately $2.2 trillion serviced globally, which includes $1.3 trillion or 85% of the U.S. tri-party repo market. In response to the 2008 financial crisis, BNY Mellon worked closely with its clients, their investors, and other market participants to meet the recommendations of the U.S. Tri-Party Repo Infrastructure Reform Task Force sponsored by the Federal Reserve Bank of New York.

○ In August 2012, Karen Peetz, BNY Mellon President, spoke before the U.S. Senate Subcommittee on Securities, Insurance, and Investment about the U.S. tri-party repo market and this initiative to practically eliminate intraday credit risk, defined as a 90% reduction. BNY Mellon has exceeded the 90% goal to reduce secured credit extended in the tri-party repo market as $1.44 trillion risk reduction has been achieved, or 97%.

HTTPS://WWW.YOUTUBE.COM/EMBED/J5H3W4-G6UK

Blank, B., Lunceford, E., Morik, J., He, S., Rana, M., Rajendran, P., ... Kompella, P. L. (2017). BNY Mellon Optimization Reduces Intraday Credit Risk by $1.4 Trillion. *Interfaces, 47*(1), 38–51. doi: 10.1287/inte.2017.0887

■ The New York City Police Department's Domain Awareness System

○ The Domain Awareness System (DAS) is a network of sensors, databases, devices, software, and infrastructure that delivers tailored information and analytics to the field and to precinct desktops enabling police officers to make more informed decisions. Originally designed for counterterrorism purposes, the DAS has been modified for general policing and is now deployed across every police precinct in the five boroughs and will shortly be on all 36,000 officers' smartphones and all 2,000 police vehicle tablets. No other police department in the world shares information and delivers analysis to its officers as effectively.

○ Prior to the NYPD's adoption of the DAS, much of the Department's information was only available to officers in the precinct house with permission to access standalone siloed software applications. For example, only the domestic violence specialist had access to the database of domestic violence records, and only when sitting at his or her desk. Officers who responded to a 911 call for domestic violence were dispatched by radio knowing only the address and the nature of the complaint. They were forced to manage each situation, literally making life and death decisions, without any historical context (such as prior complaints). This situation was not limited to domestic violence incidents—as a whole, the NYPD's decision making was hampered by a failure to take full advantage of the information at hand, and the service we provided to the public suffered as a result.

○ The NYPD is now more effectively using its data to inform decisions at all levels of the Department, allowing it to better serve the City of New York

HTTPS://WWW.YOUTUBE.COM/EMBED/DOWU4SMBVL4

Levine, E. S., Tisch, J., Tasso, A., & Joy, M. (2017). The New York City Police Department's Domain Awareness System. *INFORMS Journal on Applied Analytics, 47*(1). doi: https://doi.org/10.1287/ inte.2016.0860

- Bayesian Networks for US Army Electronics Equipment Diagnostic Applications: CECOM Equipment Diagnostic Analysis Tool, Virtual Logistics Assistance Representative

  - Soldiers in Afghanistan are required to operate and maintain complex electronic weapon systems with minimal resources in combat conditions. The inherent logistics challenges of the Combat Outpost (COP) environment make it difficult to provide timely assistance with support personnel.

  - Research on the life cycle of COP equipment problems shows that early misdiagnoses can initiate a chain of events that can create lengthy system outages and put lives in jeopardy. CECOM has developed and implemented the CECOM Equipment Diagnostic Analysis Tool, Virtual Logistics Assistance Representative (CEDAT VLAR) to directly address the onsite needs of soldiers in Afghanistan by mitigating knowledge gaps in the COP environment.

  - This has resulted in tens of millions of dollars in cost savings, increased maintenance efficiency, reductions in troubleshooting time, and No Evidence of Failure (NEOF) component returns have been reduced to zero over the last 18 months.

HTTPS://WWW.YOUTUBE.COM/EMBED/FXUBT4FLDAE

Aebischer, D., Vatterott, J., Grimes, M., Vatterott, A., Jordan, R., Reinoso, C., ... Hepler, A. B. (2017). Bayesian Networks for Combat Equipment Diagnostics. *Interfaces, 47*(1), 85–105. doi: 10.1287/ inte.2016.0883

2017

- Revenue Management Provides Double-digit Revenue Lift for Holiday Retirement

  ○ Revenue Management (RM) is a business discipline leveraging management science and information technology to drive bottom-line profitability. Holiday Retirement, the largest private owner and operator of independent living communities for seniors in the United States with over $1 billion annual revenue, has changed their pricing process completely using advanced revenue management algorithms starting 2011 and achieved a revenue lift of over 10% since they deployed the application in 2014.

HTTPS://WWW.YOUTUBE.COM/EMBED/AD76LGFVQS8

Kuyumcu, A., Yildirim, U., Hyde, A., Shanaberger, S., Hsiao, K., Donahoe, S., ... Maron, M. B. (2018). Revenue Management Delivers Significant Revenue Lift for Holiday Retirement. *Interfaces*, *48*(1), 7–23. doi: 10.1287/inte.2017.0927

- Implementation of platform-based product development at Barco

  ○ We guided the implementation of platform-based product development at Barco, a high-tech screen producing company. Although the concept of platforms is well known in the automotive sector, its implementation is not straightforward. We developed several decision support models to analyze the value of standardization and platforms, the optimal number of platforms to be developed, and when platforms should be renewed over time.

HTTPS://WWW.YOUTUBE.COM/EMBED/2G2AO3SL9C8

Boute, R. N., Broeke, M. M. V. D., & Deneire, K. A. (2018). Barco Implements Platform-Based Product Development in Its Healthcare Division. *Interfaces*, *48*(1), 35–44. doi: 10.1287/inte.2017.0917

- The DICE Simulation Model Unlocks Significant Value for a Large Greenfield Mining Project

  - BHP Billiton's greenfield potash mining project will establish a foundation for its entry into bulk fertilizer commodities. Our clean slate approach fully integrated a broad and complex scope of underground mining, ore processing, and outbound logistics. During the pre-feasibility phase, the project sought higher returns from lower capital expenditures (capex), lower operating expenditures (opex), and higher production capacity. Competitive advantage in these value drivers was derived from innovative advanced modelling. DICE—a Detailed Integrated Capacity Estimate model—was created using discrete event simulation techniques. Using DICE, we worked with the Engineering Services provider, concerned with capex, and the Owner's Operations team, concerned with opex, to perform holistic trade-offs to maximize the project's return on investment. In the pre-feasibility study, this collaborative approach delivered a significant capacity increase with no capex impact, which added more than $100 million to the project's net present value (NPV).

HTTPS://WWW.YOUTUBE.COM/EMBED/DRD3Y6AAJXQ

Bouffard, S. C., Boggis, P., Monk, B., Pereira, M., Quan, K., & Fleming, S. (2018). Discrete-Event Simulation Modeling Unlocks Value for the Jansen Potash Project. *Interfaces*, *48*(1), 45–56. doi: 10.1287/inte.2017.0930

- GE & Norfolk Southern: A Novel Movement Planning Algorithm for Dispatching Trains

  - General Electric (GE) has partnered with Norfolk Southern (NS) railroad to develop and implement a novel movement-planning algorithm to dispatch trains over a rail network. NS currently uses this algorithm to improve its average line of road velocity by over 10% and save over $400 million per year. GE is currently implementing this algorithm at two other railroads and is in talks to implement it at several other railroads in the US and abroad.

HTTPS://WWW.YOUTUBE.COM/EMBED/4MG5HSRQIVM

Bollapragada, S., Markley, R., Morgan, H., Telatar, E., Wills, S., Samuels, M., ... Brantley, J. (2018). A Novel Movement Planner System for Dispatching Trains. *Interfaces*, *48*(1), 57–69. doi: 10.1287/ inte.2017.0931

- The Off-Hours Delivery Project in New York City

  ○ As part of the off-hours delivery (OHD) project, the team designed and implemented incentives to induce receivers to accept deliveries in the off-hours (7PM to 6AM). The ensuing change of the delivery times enable supply chains to switch to the off-hours to benefit from increased productivity and lower costs; while enhancing safety, sustainability, and fostering livability and quality of life. Operations Research and Management Science (OR/MS) played a central role in the design of the incentives and the implementation; leading to its acceptance as official policy of the City of New York and the New York City Department of Transportation (NYCDOT).

HTTPS://WWW.YOUTUBE.COM/EMBED/QVMNXBMFXLQ

Holguín-Veras, J., Hodge, S., Wojtowicz, J., Singh, C., Wang, C., Jaller, M., ... Cruz, B. (2018). The New York City Off-Hour Delivery Program: A Business and Community-Friendly Sustainability Program. *Interfaces*, *48*(1), 70–86. doi: 10.1287/inte.2017.0929

- American Red Cross Uses Analytics-based Methods to Improve Blood Collection Operations

  ○ The American Red Cross, in partnership with researchers from the Georgia Institute of Technology, have developed a blood collection model to increase the amount of whole blood that can be processed into the blood product cryoprecipitate (cryo). Cryo plays a critical role in clotting and controlling hemorrhaging, and is often used in the treatment of massive trauma and major diseases, including metastasized cancers, cardiac diseases, hepatic failures, and organ transplants. After reviewing blood collecting and processing schedules, collection locations, and other factors, the researchers developed a mathematical model and analysis that led to a Decision Support Tool (DST) implemented by the Red Cross Southern Region. The implementation of the DST led to an increase in the number of whole blood units satisfying the tight collection to process completion time constraint for cryo production (capacity expansion). In particular, during the fourth quarter of 2016, the Red Cross Southern Region was able to process about 1000 more units of cryo per month (an increase of 20 percent) at a slightly lower collection cost (cost avoidance), resulting in an approximately 40 percent reduction in the per unit collection cost for cryo. This DST has been presented at the national level at the Red Cross, and plans are in place to extend the implementation of the DST to the 11 other Red Cross cryo processing facilities in the future.

HTTPS://WWW.YOUTUBE.COM/EMBED/SFAT0ANW5LY

Ayer, T., Zhang, C., Zeng, C., White, C. C., Joseph, V. R., Deck, M., ... Ozkaynak, Z. (2018). American Red Cross Uses Analytics-Based Methods to Improve Blood-Collection Operations. *Interfaces, 48*(1), 24–34. doi: 10.1287/inte.2017.0925

2018

- 2018 Edelman Winner: Unlocking the Beachfront: Using Operations Research to Repurpose Wireless Spectrum

  - The Federal Communications Commission (FCC) recently completed the world's first two-sided spectrum auction, reclaiming spectrum from TV broadcasters to meet exploding demand for wireless services. Operations research tools– including optimization, simulation, and SAT-solvers—were essential to both the design and implementation of the auction. The auction was one of the most successful in the FCC's history, repurposing 84 MHz of spectrum and generating revenue of nearly $20 billion, including more than $10 billion in new capital for the broadcast TV industry and over $7 billion to pay down the U.S. deficit.

HTTPS://WWW.YOUTUBE.COM/EMBED/CSG5D7BOZWQ

Kiddoo, J. L., Kwerel, E., Javid, S., Dunford, M., Epstein, G. M., Meisch, C. E., ... Salasznyk, P. (2019). Operations Research Enables Auction to Repurpose Television Spectrum for Next-Generation Wireless Technologies. *INFORMS Journal on Applied Analytics, 49*(1), 7–22. doi: 10.1287/inte.2018.0972

- Natural Gas Pipeline Transmission Optimization for China National Petroleum Corporation

  ○ China National Petroleum Corporation (CNPC) is China's largest oil and natural gas producer and supplier and controls 75 percent of the country's natural gas resources and pipeline network. Over the past five years China's natural gas consumption has nearly doubled and the demand for natural gas is expected to grow at a steady rate. To better serve the increasing demand, CNPC partnered with researchers from the University of California, Berkeley and Tsinghua University (Beijing) to apply innovative operations research in order to develop and implement a new software that optimizes the operation of its natural gas pipeline network. Previously, all annual production and construction planning for CNPC was manually conducted using spreadsheets. However, the increasing size and complexity of China's natural gas pipeline network caused the manual method to result in excess costs and wasted resources. Since the implementation of the new optimization software at the end of 2014, CNPC has realized approximately $530 million in direct savings and extra revenue. Meanwhile, the increased efficiency of the existing pipeline network has postponed the need for new pipelines, leading to an estimated savings of over $18 billion in construction costs.

HTTPS://WWW.YOUTUBE.COM/EMBED/POFE2X4NGIW

Han, J., Xu, Y., Liu, D., Zhao, Y., Zhao, Z., Zhou, S., ... Shen, Z.-J. M. (2019). Operations Research Enables Better Planning of Natural Gas Pipelines. *INFORMS Journal on Applied Analytics, 49*(1), 23–39. doi: 10.1287/inte.2018.0974

- Europcar Integrates Forecast, Simulation and Optimization Techniques in a Capacity and Revenue Management System

  - Europcar, the leading European car rental company, partnered with ACT Operations Research to create Opticar, a complex decision support system. Opticar features forecasts, discrete event simulations and optimization techniques providing an integrated approach to revenue and capacity management. Opticar anticipates future demand for Europcar's vehicles fleet, up to six months in advance, improving capacity management. In addition, Opticar enables Europcar to optimize its approach to revenue management and rental pricing, taking into account competitors' information, the currently available fleet and expected demand for vehicles. Opticar provides a shared mathematical approach used as a starting point for all daily operations to nine Europcar's corporate countries.

HTTPS://WWW.YOUTUBE.COM/EMBED/3IKQMMYNSQG

Guillen, J., Ruiz, P., Dellepiane, U., Maccarrone, L., Maccioni, R., Pinzuti, A., & Procacci, E. (2019). Europcar Integrates Forecasting, Simulation, and Optimization Techniques in a Capacity and Revenue Management System. *INFORMS Journal on Applied Analytics*, 49(1), 40–51. doi: 10.1287/inte.2018.0970

- Analytics Makes Inventory Planning A Lights-Out Activity at Intel Corporation

  - Intel, which employs more than 100,000 people in over 70 countries around the world and has an annual revenue of $60 billion, implemented a fully automated Multi-Echelon Inventory Optimization (MEIO) based inventory target-setting system managing $1 billion daily in finished goods inventory representing over $40B a year in sales. Algorithm-derived inventory targets at Intel are accepted by planners +99.5 percent of the time and have simultaneously driven higher customer service and lower inventory levels resulting in over $1.3B in gross profit since 2014. In addition, customers are delighted: since MEIO was implemented at all of Intel's vendor managed inventory hubs in 2012, customer satisfaction has never been higher, and Intel has landed in the top-10 of Gartner's Supply Chain Top-25 every year. Faculty in the department of Business Analytics and Statistics at the University of Tennessee, Knoxville and the supply chain software company Logility also contributed to this project.

HTTPS://WWW.YOUTUBE.COM/EMBED/GDIESPRIOOK

Manary, M. P., Wieland, B., Willems, S. P., & Kempf, K. G. (2019). Analytics Makes Inventory Planning a Lights-Out Activity at Intel Corporation. *INFORMS Journal on Applied Analytics*, *49*(1), 52–63. doi: 10.1287/inte.2018.0976

- Collaborative Systems Analytics: Establishing Effective Clinical Practice Guidelines for Advancing Congenital Cardiac Care

    ○ The Pediatric Heart Network enlisted researchers with the Georgia Institute of Technology to create clinical practice guidelines (CPG) for pre-, intra-, and post-surgical care of patients with congenital heart defects (CHDs), the most common birth defect, impacting nearly 1 million children and 1.4 million adults in the U.S. Substantial variances in surgical practices to treat patients with CHDs among different healthcare centers were reflected in inconsistent surgical outcomes, some of which resulted in negative consequences for patients. By studying the nine leading U.S. pediatric centers, the researchers identified seven significant factors for influencing surgical outcome, and implemented a CPG that enables patients to be removed from breathing apparatuses earlier, lowered the rate of reintubation, and decreased the time patients need to remain in the intensive care unit. These guidelines also realized a cost savings of 27 percent, which translates to $13,500 per patient.

HTTPS://WWW.YOUTUBE.COM/EMBED/8U_T_M8RSTG

(No citation found)

- Turner Blazes a Trail for Audience Targeting on Television with Operations Research and Advanced Analytics

  ○ Turner has designed and implemented innovative and integrated forecasting and optimization models that power audience targeting solutions disrupting decades-old paradigms and business processes in the media industry, and producing significant sales and advertisement efficiencies for Turner and its clients. Turner is on track to sell 50 percent of its inventory through audience targeting by 2020, representing billions in ad revenue.

HTTPS://WWW.YOUTUBE.COM/EMBED/KJ5AK4-PRWO

Carbajal, J. A., Williams, P., Popescu, A., & Chaar, W. (2019). Turner Blazes a Trail for Audience Targeting on Television with Operations Research and Advanced Analytics. *INFORMS Journal on Applied Analytics*, *49*(1), 64–89. doi: 10.1287/inte.2018.0971

2019

- Louisville MSD and Tetra Tech: Protecting Community Waterways: Applying Analytics, Optimization, and Real Time Control for the Efficient Operation of Sewer Networks.

  ○ With increasingly intense and more frequent rainfall, urban wastewater collection and treatment systems are often overwhelmed by large rainfall events, resulting in a greater risk to water environments and public health by contamination from overflows of untreated sewage and storm water. As a pioneer in real-time control (RTC), Louisville MSD enlisted engineering services firm Tetra Tech to implement Csoft® as part of its Integrated Overflow Abatement Plan efforts. Csoft® is a RTC software solution developed by Tetra Tech to efficiently manage sewer networks in real-time based on rain forecasts and sensor readings. It has been successfully implemented in the U.S., Canada and France. MSD's fully automated RTC system responds to rainfall and actual system conditions by maximizing all available storage, conveyance and treatment capacities. Excess water is diverted and temporarily stored until it can be redirected toward the appropriate treatment plant. The system has saved MSD over $200 million in infrastructure costs, while improving the community waterways.

HTTPS://WWW.YOUTUBE.COM/EMBED/CMAF4JADM8Q

Tao, D. Q., Pleau, M., Akridge, A., Fradet, O., Grondin, F., Laughlin, S., ... Shoemaker, L. (2020). Analytics and Optimization Reduce Sewage Overflows to Protect Community Waterways in Kentucky. *INFORMS Journal on Applied Analytics*, *50*(1), 7–20. doi: 10.1287/inte.2019.1022

- Boston Public Schools: Optimized School Bus Routing Helps School Districts Design Better Policies

  - Half of Boston Public Schools' (BPS) 55,000 students take a yellow school bus to one of 125 schools each day. Planning the 45,000 miles for 646 buses daily was a significant undertaking, requiring 10 people and more than 3,000 hours. BPS held a nationwide months-long challenge to produce more effective results. The winning submission came from nearby MIT, which created a new bus routing algorithm generating a solution that was 20 percent more efficient in about 30 minutes. With MIT's support, BPS implemented the solution, resulting in the largest-ever one-year reduction in buses, leading to nearly $5 million in annual reinvestment back into schools. Developing an automated routing system has made BPS the first school district in the country to accurately map out the transportation implications from various policies. BPS has used this innovative approach in efforts to re-align bell times, estimate costs for changing transportation eligibility, and develop robust strategic plans, paving the way for other school districts to support policy decisions with analytics.

HTTPS://WWW.YOUTUBE.COM/EMBED/NYX9HC5IDKU

Bertsimas, D., Delarue, A., Eger, W., Hanlon, J., & Martin, S. (2020). Bus Routing Optimization Helps Boston Public Schools Design Better Policies. *INFORMS Journal on Applied Analytics*, *50*(1), 37–49. doi: 10.1287/inte.2019.1015

- Analytics and O.R. for IBM's IT Service Deals

  - IBM Services provides information technology services for clients worldwide, designing, building, running, and maintaining critical infrastructure and IT systems. IBM competes for highly complex IT services contracts, often involving complex client engagement and negotiations. To better manage the highly resource-intensive and complex activities related to contract negotiations, IBM Services introduced analytics and operations research tools to transform subjective, time-consuming business judgments into informed decisions based on data-driven insights. This O.R. and analytics-based toolset allows IBM to negotiate with the client, optimally cost and price IT services solutions, and predict the winnability of each deal being negotiated. Since implementing these tools, IBM Services has increased its relative contract win rate, contributing a significant realized revenue increase.

HTTPS://WWW.YOUTUBE.COM/EMBED/01BXTGOU4GQ

Megahed, A., Nakamura, T., Smith, M., Asthana, S., Rose, M., Daczkowska, M., & Gopisetty, S. (2020). Analytics and Operations Research Increases Win Rates for IBM's Information Technology Service Deals. *INFORMS Journal on Applied Analytics*, *50*(1), 50–63. doi: 10.1287/inte.2019.1023

- Microsoft: Prospective Dynamic Fraud Control for Optimal Profitability in e-Commerce

  - Businesses and consumers purchase a diverse portfolio of physical and digital products and services online. The dynamic nature of shopping patterns and the adversarial posture of fraudsters make it challenging to stop fraud without interrupting legitimate customer purchases. In the U.S. alone, retail fraud amounts to tens of billions of dollars lost. Microsoft has tackled this problem by developing an innovative Fraud Detection System based on state-of-the-art AI, operations research, and automation. This new system employs a multi-stage decision-making paradigm that applies progressive machine learning (ML) models at each stage and co-optimizes these models across the decision chain to maximize profitability. Microsoft has thus dramatically reduced its Fraud Loss Rate resulting in $75 million annual savings and improved both its False Positive Rate and the Bank Acceptance Rate of legitimate purchases generating over $1 billion in additional revenue. This innovation is highly portable and Microsoft is working to make it available to its enterprise customers.

HTTPS://WWW.YOUTUBE.COM/EMBED/-JYWUKWT5J8

Nanduri, J., Jia, Y., Oka, A., Beaver, J., & Liu, Y.-W. (2020). Microsoft Uses Machine Learning and Optimization to Reduce E-Commerce Fraud. *INFORMS Journal on Applied Analytics*, 50(1), 64–79. doi: 10.1287/inte.2019.1017

- Spanish Aviation Safety & Security Agency: RIMAS—Safer Skies in Spain

  - The International Civil Aviation Organization dictates that each nation must develop a State Safety Program (SSP) to develop a preventative approach for aviation safety oversight and management on a national level. These programs enable strategic decision-making and resource allocation to support hazard identification, risk evaluation, safety assurance, and safety promotion. The Spanish Aviation Safety & Security Agency (AESA) partnered with the Spanish Royal Academy of Sciences to introduce analytics methodologies to support the SSP process. Their methodology, the Risk Management in Aviation Safety (RIMAS) tool represents the first time advanced analytics techniques have been utilized in a preventative approach to civil aviation, and manages all the objectives of the SSP as well as the various stakeholders, including air carriers, traffic controllers, airport services providers, and various national aviation safety agencies. Since RIMAS was implemented, it has enabled AESA to realize a 25 percent reduction in annual equivalent safety costs, or nearly $230 million in savings.

HTTPS://WWW.YOUTUBE.COM/EMBED/FTJXWC7RHYM

Elvira, V., Bernal, F., Hernandez-Coronado, P., Herraiz, E., Alfaro, C., Gomez, J., & Insua, D. R. (2020). Safer Skies over Spain. *INFORMS Journal on Applied Analytics*, 50(1), 21–36. doi: 10.1287/inte.2019.1018

- Vattenfall: Operations Research Optimizes Offshore Wind Farm Design and Enables a Fossil-Free Future

  ○ As one of Europe's largest producers of electricity Vattenfall is currently expanding its wind energy operations significantly. Operations research (O.R.) techniques are playing a vital role in this, realizing hundreds of millions of dollars in savings. In the design of wind farms, Vattenfall combines O.R. techniques with technical knowledge, commercial insight and system design to achieve estimated savings of $11-$17 million per wind farm, and more than $170 million overall. By focusing on two complex components of offshore wind park design, wind turbine location and routing for offshore electrical cables, Vattenfall is able to maximize its power output, expand its pipeline, and is on track to reach its target of enabling a fossil free living within one generation. In addition to maximizing energy production, these O.R. techniques enabled Vattenfall to minimize immediate costs relating to turbine foundations and cables, as well as life-time costs, such as cable losses.

HTTPS://WWW.YOUTUBE.COM/EMBED/97QU0T12OUO

Fischetti, M., Kristoffersen, J. R., Hjort, T., Monaci, M., & Pisinger, D. (2020). Vattenfall Optimizes Offshore Wind Farm Design. *INFORMS Journal on Applied Analytics*, 50(1), 80–94. doi: 10.1287/inte.2019.1019

HTTPS://PUBSONLINE.INFORMS.ORG/DOI/ABS/10.1287/INTE.2019.1019

APPENDIX B

INFORMS Software Survey Articles

Forecasting

Fildes, R., Schaer, O., and Svetunkov, I. (2018). Software Survey: Forecasting 2018. *ORMS-Today, 45(3)*.

HTTPS://WWW.INFORMS.ORG/ORMS-TODAY/PUBLIC-ARTICLES/JUNE-VOLUME-45-NUMBER-3/SOFTWARE-SURVEY-FORECASTING-2018

Linear Programming

Fourer, R. (2019). Software Survey: Linear Programming—2019 LP survey focuses on linear and related problems, as well as multiple objective optimization and deployment features. *ORMS-Today 46(3)*. doi: 10.1287/orms.2019.03.05

HTTPS://PUBSONLINE.INFORMS.ORG/DO/10.1287/ORMS.2019.03.05/FULL/

Vehicle Routing

Horner, P. (2018). Software Survey: Vehicle Routing—Higher Expectations Drive Transformation, *ORMS-Today, 43(1)*. https://doi.org/10.1287/orms.2018.01.06

HTTPS://PUBSONLINE.INFORMS.ORG/DO/10.1287/ORMS.2018.01.06/FULL/

Decision Theory

Amaoyal, J. (2018). Software Survey: Decision Analysis—Biennial survey demonstrates continuous advancement of vital tools for decision-makers, managers, and analysts. *Analytics Magazine*, November/December 2018. https://doi.org/10.1287/LYTX.2016.06.04

HTTPS://WWW.INFORMS.ORG/ORMS-TODAY/PUBLIC-ARTICLES/OCTOBER-VOLUME-43-NUMBER-5/SOFTWARE-SURVEY

Simulation

Swain, J. J. (2019). Software Survey: Simulation—A half century of simulation product progress ... and limitless possibilities going forward,. *ORMS Today, 44(5)*. https://doi.org/10.1287/orms.2019.05.10

HTTPS://WWW.INFORMS.ORG/ORMS-TODAY/PUBLIC-ARTICLES/OCTOBER-VOLUME-44-NUMBER-5/SIMULATION-SOFTWARE-SURVEY-SIMULATION-NEW-AND-IMPROVED-REALITY-SHOW

Statistical Analysis

Swain, J. (2017). Software Survey: Statistical Analysist—The Joys and Perils of Statistics, *ORMS-Today, 44(1)*.

HTTPS://WWW.INFORMS.ORG/ORMS-TODAY/ORMS-TODAY-CURRENT-ISSUE/STATISTICAL-ANALYSIS-SOFTWARE-SURVEY-THE-JOYS-AND-PERILS-OF-STATISTICS